A Life for Freedom

A LIFE
FOR
FREEDOM

The Mission to End
Racial Injustice
in South Africa

DENIS GOLDBERG

Foreword by Z. Pallo Jordan

UNIVERSITY PRESS OF KENTUCKY

Copyright © 2016 by The University Press of Kentucky

Scholarly publisher for the Commonwealth,
serving Bellarmine University, Berea College, Centre College of Kentucky,
Eastern Kentucky University, The Filson Historical Society, Georgetown
College, Kentucky Historical Society, Kentucky State University, Morehead
State University, Murray State University, Northern Kentucky University,
Transylvania University, University of Kentucky, University of Louisville,
and Western Kentucky University.
All rights reserved.

Editorial and Sales Offices: The University Press of Kentucky
663 South Limestone Street, Lexington, Kentucky 40508-4008
www.kentuckypress.com

Every effort has been made to ascertain the origins of the images. Unless
otherwise noted, photographs are from the author's family collection.

Cataloging-in-Publication data is available from the Library of Congress.

ISBN 978-0-8131-6646-9 (hardcover : alk. paper)
ISBN 978-0-8131-6686-5 (epub)
ISBN 978-0-8131-6685-8 (pdf)

This book is printed on acid-free paper meeting
the requirements of the American National Standard
for Permanence in Paper for Printed Library Materials.

Manufactured in the United States of America.

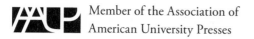 Member of the Association of
American University Presses

Contents

Photographs follow pages 178 and 306

Foreword

As the only white among those convicted and sentenced to life imprisonment in the Rivonia Trial, Denis Goldberg will always have a unique place in that story. These memoirs offer the reader an insight into an important chapter in the history of our struggle from a different viewpoint because the racist dogmas of apartheid dictated that he would be incarcerated apart from his black comrades and colleagues. That segregation denied him both the companionship and the counsel of his fellow accused. His was consequently an exceedingly lonely sojourn. But, true to himself and the cause he had espoused from his youth, he bore it with courage and an immense dignity.

I first met Denis in the Modern Youth Society (MYS) in the 1950s. It was an outgrowth of a body of a similar name on the campus of the University of Cape Town, the Modern World Society. Left-wing students had formed this body to replace the Students Socialist Party (SSP) after the banning of the Communist Party of South Africa (CPSA) under the terms of the Suppression of Communism Act of 1950. Unlike its campus equivalent, MYS was open to all young people.

Its purpose was to try to create a space where white and black youth could interact as equals in an otherwise extremely segregated society. Its core activities were of course political—the society's very existence constituted a political action—but it also sought to attract young people through sporting and other activities. MYS imparted a host of skills to its members and those who came into its milieu. Youth from the black communities, who might otherwise not have been exposed to them, learned techniques such as silkscreen printing, designing banners and posters, and cutting mimeograph stencils, all of which are important organizational skills.

Because its primary purpose was political, MYS held regular programs to train its members as public speakers. At the camps and picnics it organized, in the political debates and discussions that continued late into the night, the articulate and vocal were able to hone their skills while learning from the better-read and more experienced.

Apart from the events unfolding inside South Africa itself in the 1950s, the triumph of the Chinese revolution in 1949, the Korean War, the Battle of Dien Bien Phu in Vietnam, the Suez Crisis, the Twentieth Congress of the Communist Party of the Soviet Union, the independence of Ghana, and the launch of the first earth-orbiting satellite all found space in the animated discussions on international affairs. In the MYS we learned to appreciate that though daily life in South Africa might not seem to confirm it, the oppressed people (and bodies like ourselves) were part of the dominant tide in world history, which was sweeping away the past of colonialism, apartheid, and racism. MYS was able to attract into its ranks comrades from Zimbabwe, Lesotho, Kenya, and Namibia, as well as visiting students from Europe. Through its agency, intricate networks of liberation fighters within the region and beyond were established. Small delegations sent to international festivals helped broaden these to take in Europe and Asia.

By the time I and my peer group arrived in MYS, Denis Goldberg was already considered among the older, more experienced members. With an aptitude for working with his hands, he invariably played the role of instructor, teaching others the skills and techniques we would be called on to use.

In 2009 the president of South Africa awarded him the National Order of Luthuli (in silver) "for his commitment to the struggle against apartheid and service to the people of South Africa." He was awarded the Military Veterans Medal in Platinum Class II by the president in 2012 for his part in the armed struggle for liberation. He has received other honors.

Denis answers some of the questions people often ask, such as: Why did a young white get involved to the point of risking his life for freedom for black South Africans? What happened to his family? How can an armed struggle be justified? Why did black people accept him in that struggle? How did whites respond to his belief in a nonracial society?

He tells of his upbringing and growing awareness of the inhumanity of the racially segregated society he lived in. He describes his growing involvement with organizations of the oppressed population of African, Coloured, and Indian people (to use the slightly polished language of apartheid) to put an end to a society based on "racism by law." It is his personal story rather than a detailed discussion of how and when particular decisions were made, except where he had a direct role in the discussions. He acknowledges errors in policy or their application and he rejoices in what has been achieved. It is a story of passion and the effects of political struggle for freedom on all his family and others. It is a story of love and death and compassion. He believes that revolutions are made for the benefit of all and not only a small elite.

The Sharpeville Massacre and the smaller-scale incident at Langa on 21 March 1960 formed the decisive watershed not only for the struggle for freedom and democracy but also personally for Denis Goldberg and his family. They triggered the decision to constitute a military wing of the liberation movement, which launched Denis Goldberg on the road to Rivonia.

This is a story of commitment and action that led to his spending twenty-two years in prison, and, when he was released, he continued his political activity until and after apartheid was brought to its formal end with the election of Nelson Mandela as the first president of the new democratic Republic of South Africa and guarantees for the equal rights of all its citizens.

His story starts long before he was born.

For close to two centuries the city of Cape Town was the entry point to South Africa of all knowledge, ideas, values, and technologies imported from other parts of the world. South Africa's first Muslim community was established at the Cape of Good Hope. It was through Table Bay, too, that the skill of winemaking first entered our country. Cape Town is also the mother city of South African journalism, where South Africa's first newspapers were published.

It was in this city that two Jewish communists, Sam and Annie Goldberg, from London's East End, settled during the 1920s. Their second son, Denis, was born there in 1933.

Z. Pallo Jordan, National Executive Committee,
African National Congress, 1994–2012;
Minister of Arts and Culture, 2004–2009

Preface

After twenty-two years as a political prisoner and the ensuing twenty-four years, I felt in 2009 that it was time to write about my life in South Africa: in struggle, in prison, in exile, in freedom, and back home in my homeland, South Africa. It has taken me a long time to find my voice, though friends will tell you that once I get talking, it is hard to stop me. I felt that it is "big headed" to write about myself, despite being asked to write down the stories I tell when I am given the least excuse to do so. I have always wanted to speak about the people and places and events and ideas that shaped me and, in a complex interplay, determined my life's trajectory.

I was born in 1933, and that trajectory took me through a happy childhood filled with a deep awareness of the inequalities of the world around me and what that meant for millions of others whose lives were marred by the systematic brutality of inequality, of wars, and of death before they could reach maturity. I was surrounded by my parents' friends and comrades who had a zest for life but who were also serious about changing the world we live in. Happiness could be lighthearted and even frivolous, but the greatest happiness came from service to humankind. Conscience can be such a hard taskmaster!

I lived for eighteen years in Britain (1985–2002) and was active there and in many other countries winning support for our struggle for freedom. This included nine years in the office of the African National Congress until freedom came and we switched off the lights; nine years of creating and directing a charity called Community H.E.A.R.T. in Britain and Community Heart e.V. in Germany to support projects in Southern Africa; and four years as an adviser to South African government ministers. I also traveled extensively in the United States and Canada and have expanded the previously sketchy report of those activities for this edition.

Now, in 2015, I have been retired for over nine years. But perhaps I should say that I am retired from retirement, finding much to do to support social development projects, to write, and to undertake speaking tours to tell my story.

Bertolt Brecht in his poem "To Posterity" says (in a loose translation): "To notice that the trees were blooming in the springtime was a kind of betrayal because we felt that time devoted to beautiful things not directly linked to the struggle was a distraction." And I agree with him that the voice raised too often in anger becomes shrill and the face ugly. Indeed, we worked with artists and especially folk artists as a means of promoting the struggle. Art and culture constituted a "site of struggle," as we later came to say. He ends thus: "We who wanted to make a world where man would be a helper to man did not ourselves have time for kindness. But you who come after, think of us with forbearance."

Well, now I have time for beauty and for sorrow and anger and ugliness too, as well as humor and the insights that artists and musicians bring. I hope that you will come to know why I was so deeply involved in the struggle to put an end to apartheid, and why I am so engaged in community work where I now live, back in my hometown in South Africa. I hope it will lead you to understand how I came to name the South African edition of this book *The Mission,* and why included this phrase in the North American edition's subtitle as well. I had planned to call it "Life! Life Is Wonderful!"—my cry when the judge in the Rivonia Trial sentenced eight of us not to be hanged, but to life imprisonment. Through my opening chapter, "The Mission," I want to honor my murdered comrades Solwandle Looksmart Ngudle and Chris Hani, who did not live to see our freedom, and I took that as the title of my book.

There have been moments that have been turning points in my life. Some were quite dramatic, and others seemed just to happen, slowly and delightfully, sometimes with rather harsh consequences. I suspect that sometimes we make choices not by deeply considered analysis but by drifting along until something definite happens. It is almost like waiting for the moment and then not recognizing until much later that it has come to pass.

I have sometimes been obsessively active, and I had a long period of forced relative inactivity, but I can say without boasting that I have had the

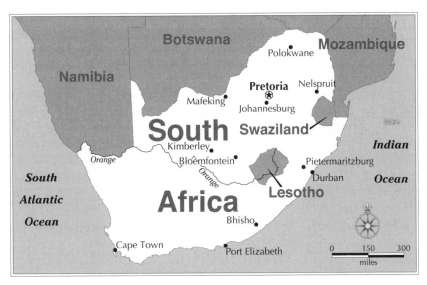

South Africa (Richard Gilbreath, University of Kentucky Cartography Lab)

wonderful fortune to have loved and been loved and that makes me a very lucky man.

My first wife, Esmé, loved me and we worked together as political activists. She brought up our children on her own while I was in prison. She took me back again and loved me some more after I was released from prison and supported me in my political activity until she died and bequeathed me the resources for continuing afterward. We were together for forty-six years, including the twenty-two years of separation. When I was awarded the National Order of Luthuli by our state president for my contribution to the struggle for freedom and commitment to the people of South Africa, I wished that the award could have been given to Esmé, too. Since she had long passed away I asked her cousin Rochelle to accompany me to represent her at the ceremony.

My second wife, Edelgard, brought me love and a whole new circle of friends and intellectual companionship and taught me to speak German. I have loved and been loved since she, too, passed away.

My first name is Denis, spelled with one "n," but many documents and media sources spell my name as Dennis, and I have not changed the spelling where I quote such sources.

I have refrained from detailed discussion of how decisions were made and the debates about major issues unless I was present and took part in them. These memoirs will, I hope, contribute to understanding the complexity of determined action to overthrow a tyrannical regime in moral, political, personal, and family matters.

I have in various places updated this story and added comments about the current situation as of December 2014.

A time line of South African history has been provided as appendix 2.

1

The Mission

Break Down the Walls

The day for sentencing in the Rivonia Trial in Pretoria was 12 June 1964. The prosecution wanted the maximum sentence—and we expected it: death. But in a short statement to the court the judge said the ultimate sentence (implicitly death) would be appropriate in a case of high treason, but as we had been charged under the Sabotage Act, not for treason, he could allow some leniency. His leniency was to impose a sentence of life imprisonment for each of the charges on which we were found guilty. As he spoke, I watched the faces of my comrades light up with the most wonderful smiles of joy and relief. We laughed out loud, overjoyed to live, even though it would mean life behind bars.

My mother was in court and in the commotion could not hear what the judge had said. She called out, "What is it?" and I replied, "Life! Life is wonderful!"

I was thirty-one years old. I would spend all together twenty-two years in prison.

Let me begin my story at a later date, on 26 February 1990, when a remarkably moving ecumenical service was held in Westminster Abbey in London for those who had sacrificed their lives for freedom in Southern Africa. Candles were lit for those who were being remembered; representatives of all the main religions took part, led by Archbishop Trevor Huddleston and the archbishop of Canterbury. The occasion was especially important for me because it was my privilege to speak for Solwandle Looksmart Ngudle, the Cape Town comrade who had played such an important role in my life and without whom any account of my part in the South African struggle would be meaningless.

The religious dignitaries at Westminster Abbey that day spoke first, as the candles were doused. More prayers were followed by beautiful a cappella singing by three South African women whose voices soared to the rafters as the candles were lit again. In the gloom of the Abbey the points of light glowed with the tributes to those who had died. After I had delivered my tribute to Looksmart, one of the exiled preachers present told me that I had been much too solemn. But how could it have been otherwise? Looksmart was dead, and for the first time in my life, aged fifty-seven, I was his "altar boy." I had never seen such a ceremony before. It was inclusive and wonderfully moving.

I first met Looksmart Ngudle in the early 1950s. He was a very handsome young man with an engaging personality and a warm smile. He was born in the Eastern Cape Province and, like so many young Africans, he migrated from the poverty-stricken countryside to the city. He lived in Cape Town in a "native location." He floated from one job to another, as so many did. There was little formal vocational training, and one unskilled job followed another. On weekends he was the shoemaker who repaired the shoes of the young men around him. But he had an unusual attribute: he was literate! He read the newspaper to others around him. Though he appeared to have no interest in politics, all the young men seemed to listen to his opinions.

Archie Sibeko, who came from the same village, slowly won Looksmart's confidence and drew him into political activity. Archie was deeply involved in the liberation politics of the African National Congress (ANC), the South African Congress of Trade Unions (SACTU), and the South African Communist Party (SACP). He said it was easy to be a member of all these organizations. He said there was no conflict between them. When he was involved in the politics of national liberation, then the ANC was the place to be. When he wanted to be involved in the improvement of pay and conditions of working people, then the trade union movement was the right place for that activity. But, he said, when he wanted to understand why there was national oppression, and why working people were paid low wages, and why there was mass unemployment, then he turned to the Communist Party. He said that in the long run the only way to ensure that people of different national groups in South Africa could be free was to follow the program of the Communist Party. He said that national liberation and working-class liberation were all part of "the revolution."

Back in the 1950s we did not talk about the "walls" dividing people of different racial groups in apartheid South Africa. We spoke about "bars" between people because the color bar had many aspects. It barred people from jobs of their choice because of their color. It barred people from living where they chose because of their color. It barred people from mixing socially and it barred them from marrying each other because of their color. It barred people from getting an education because of their color. It barred Africans from moving to the cities from the countryside without passes to get through the color bar of the Urban Areas Act. The penalty for breaking these bars was imprisonment. And breaking the color bar laws as a way of protesting against the laws was made a further crime punished by imprisonment. The bars imprisoned the whole South African society, and breaking down the barriers would set free the political prisoners and the whole society. The jailers and their masters would be free to become human beings.

Looksmart Ngudle became a full-time political activist. He was a natural leader and organizer, and by the end of 1962 he was on the Regional Command of *Umkhonto we Sizwe* (MK), the Spear of the Nation, the underground people's army of which Nelson Mandela was the first commander in chief. But by this time Archie had been forced to leave South Africa, together with Thembisile Martin Hani, after they were convicted of continued involvement in the ANC, which had been declared an illegal organization in 1960. They traveled to the Soviet Union, where they underwent military training. Archie returned to trade union activity in exile, taking the name Zola Zembe. Martin, using the nom de guerre "Chris," became in time one of the outstanding commanders of MK and a leading member of the National Executive Committee of the ANC and the Communist Party Central Committee.

I had joined the Western Cape Province Regional Command of MK as a technical officer. I organized a training school that met three times a week for some months. It was successful and led us to organize a training camp at Mamre, some thirty miles from Cape Town, during the Christmas and New Year holiday period at the end of 1962. I was the camp commander, and the recruits named me "Comrade Commandant." Looksmart was the field commander and was a tower of strength, working well with our nearly thirty recruits.

We taught politics because we wanted a military force of committed young comrades who were not simply soldiers but members of a people's revolutionary army who could act on their own if necessary, explaining to others their own political and military understanding of why and how we should fight. We insisted that we should not lie to our own people about our successes and failures. We had to win support on the basis of trust. Our army would be a people's army that helped our people. It must not become their oppressor.

We taught practical things, too, such as how to write leaflets and type them for reproduction on old stencil copiers (mimeograph machines). There were no such things as photocopiers in those days. The fundamentals of electric circuits were important, so that explosives could be set off from a distance—and we needed to teach about telephones. In addition, we taught first aid for looking after wounded comrades. Implicit in that teaching was the understanding that war always results in casualties. Some of us would be wounded and some would die in action.

We knew we might face arrest and interrogation—and probably torture. We read aloud for everyone to hear and discuss Jean-Paul Sartre's short story "The Wall." That story is set in Spain during the Civil War, which erupted in 1936 and ended in 1939, when the elected democratic government was overthrown by fascist army forces backed by Nazi Germany and fascist Italy. We wanted our young soldiers to understand that even if we had to reinvent the ways we worked in our specific conditions, we were part of a long, ongoing, worldwide struggle against oppression.

General Franco led the fascist mutiny of the Spanish army. The Wall was the place where they executed by firing squad loyalist activists defending their elected social democratic government. In Sartre's story a captured loyalist is tortured as his fascist interrogators try to extract from him where his close comrade is hiding. For days he resists their interrogation and torture. He is threatened with execution at the Wall. Exhausted, he loses touch with reality. They offer him his life in exchange for the information: "Tell us where he is! Tell us and there will be no Wall, for you." He fantasizes about tricking his tormentors. Able to hold out no longer, the prisoner gives them the misleading information that would trick his tormentors into leaving him alone. He knows that his comrade intends to leave their secret hiding place in a crypt in a cemetery. Alas! The country people with whom his comrade plans to stay are sick and he cannot go to them. Desperate for somewhere to hide from the fascists, he returns to the cemetery, even though he knows that his captured comrade may break under torture and give away their secret place. There he is captured.

Hearing gunshots from the Wall, the first prisoner asks who has been executed. The interrogators turn the last screw when they thank him for delivering up his comrade. The walls of his sanity break down from grief into madness. Sartre, of course, was again creating a situation in which extreme moral choices have to be made. Each of us has to make hard choices in times of crisis.

This was a powerfully imaginative "true" story of what we could all be facing when we dreamed of carrying out the heroic armed struggle advocated by Che Guevara. We read from his book *Guerilla Warfare,* published in 1961, because the victory of the Cuban revolution inspired us. We also read about and discussed the struggle of the Algerian Front de Libération Nationale (FLN) against the French colonial occupation of Algeria. We wanted our young comrades to be mentally prepared for what we would have to face. We wanted them to understand that, though armed struggle was necessary to defeat the apartheid state, war is not a romantic escapade.

After fifty years of peaceful struggle, it was not easy to add the element of armed struggle to the overall strategy for liberation. We now leaned in the opposite direction, stressing the importance of armed struggle. Our movement sent recruits out of the country as fast as it could for military training. Some of our leaders seemed to be in the grip of a vision of a people's army transforming the struggle as our returning soldiers crossed the border in force to quickly destroy the apartheid state.

Our MK Regional Command in Cape Town thought that it was important to keep our political structures alive. We kept people back for that reason, but we found that they were ordered through other channels to leave. We were not refusing to supply recruits for training; we simply wanted to try to ensure that we could train our own military units and keep our underground army rooted in the mass movement. All the literature we could find stressed the importance of the mass movement. We wanted to encourage the young recruits to want to take up arms, yet we wanted to be realistic about the prospects for victory.

Many of our best people were ordered to leave. But Looksmart in particular led units of five or six men who sabotaged telephone and telegraph lines and cables in simple ways without using explosives. The events were not spectacular, but they did lead to communications blackouts over widespread areas. They did draw in many police officers from all the neighboring towns to patrol a large area around Cape Town. We were beginning to do what guerrilla forces must do: stretch the state's security forces to the limit. Most important, Looksmart was developing his command skills, and his men were becoming adept at working together in military ways.

By 1963 the apartheid regime had to respond to sporadic waves of explosions and other forms of sabotage in various parts of South Africa. The Ninety-Day Detention Law was introduced. It gave the police the power to hold prisoners for repeated periods of detention until they had answered questions to the satisfaction of the head of the police. That was clearly a licence to torture prisoners, who could be denied all access to lawyers, family, and friends. Another law, the Sabotage Act, made sabotage an action for which the courts could impose the death penalty.

My political and military comrades felt strongly that I would be arrested as soon as the Ninety-Day Detention Law came into force in May 1963. So I left Cape Town to go underground and joined the High Command in Johannesburg. The walls were closing in. Six weeks later we were arrested at our hideout in Rivonia, near Johannesburg. We were no longer just parts of an imprisoned society; we could sense the wall at our backs. We faced the possibility of being executed when we were convicted in a court of law, but we were not even certain that we would be brought before a court.

The politics of the time, however, dictated that the regime hold a show trial that became known as the Rivonia Trial, and Nelson Mandela was the number one accused. Our interrogators were careful to ensure that we could be put on trial in an unmarked physical condition. Over the following years attitudes changed: many activists were tortured to death; others were maimed beyond recovery.

A contingent of more than twenty recruits had been sent abroad from Cape Town by Looksmart. He understood there was danger because so many people knew where he lived. He planned to move as soon as that group had left. The comrades he had sent out of the country by bus were captured near the Botswana border, nearly 1,250 miles from Cape Town. They looked like an innocuous funeral party, but the police became suspicious. They were interrogated and one comrade thought he could trick his interrogators. He told them where Looksmart had been hiding because he "knew" that he was to move immediately after they had left Cape Town. Alas, Looksmart had fallen ill and was too weak to move. He could not go to live with a family in a tiny shelter in a squatter settlement. He was captured. The Wall was there before him—and all around him.

My interrogators told me that Looksmart had hanged himself while under interrogation. I accused my tormentors of murdering him. They denied all responsibility. They said other officers had handled him and they were willing to hand me over to them. Floating in the air from their significant nods and tone of voice was the unspoken thought that they would kill me, too.

During our trial Looksmart's death was referred to. One young man, who had been at the training camp in Mamre, was a witness for the prosecution. He told of the stories we had read and the discussions that had taken place. He mentioned "The Wall" and alleged that the Comrade Commandant (he meant me) had said it was better to commit suicide than to give information to the police. Therefore, said the prosecutor, the Comrade Commandant was responsible for Looksmart Ngudle's death. Tyrants murder at will and blame those who resist their tyranny. And officials like the prosecutor seek favors in exchange for their fawning services to the oppressors, becoming oppressors themselves.

Twenty-two years later, in 1985, when I was released from prison, I went to the ANC headquarters in exile in Lusaka, Zambia. I was outside the walls of the prison in Pretoria, but South Africa was still an imprisoned society. I was free but not yet free of the mission to tear down those walls. I had to see the ANC president, Oliver Tambo, and members of the National Executive Committee to see how I could fit into the work of our movement after being so long away.

In Lusaka I met two young MK soldiers who had been at the Mamre training camp. They greeted me with a military salute and "Comrade Commandant." Several of the Mamre men had gone into exile and had taken part in the armed struggle. Pallo Jordan, a Cape Town comrade and a member of the National Executive Committee of the ANC, told me that they had a good reputation for loyalty and hard work in MK and in political positions too. I rejoiced, but we did not know how many of them had been killed at the Wall.

When Nelson Mandela was released from prison in 1990, we could see that the walls of apartheid were coming down. Yet at least another

10,000 to 12,000 were murdered by the old regime before he was elected the first president of the new South Africa.

Chris Hani was murdered by members of a right-wing political party. He had been elected to the National Executive Committee of the ANC with the highest number of votes cast by the delegates to the first free conference in 1991. He was general secretary of the South African Communist Party, and he would surely have been a minister in the first democratically elected government. There can be little doubt that is why he was murdered.

His assassins miscalculated. His murder stirred such anger among the masses that it forced the apartheid regime to implement the transfer of power to an interim government. This was in terms of a signed undertaking with the ANC to arrange for elections in which all adult South Africans would be able to vote to elect a new government. Chris Hani's murder forced them to set the date of the elections in April 1994. The result was a clear-cut victory for the ANC and its allies, the South African Congress of Trade Unions and the South African Communist Party.

Archie Sibeko suffered a stroke before the first free elections. He had worked under very difficult conditions for twenty-seven years in exile. He exhausted himself, and his body rebelled. He said the economic barriers still have to come down and the liberation of the working class still has to be achieved. Nearly half the people have neither jobs nor land from which to make a living—and there is still the oppression that comes with such poverty. But now the political conditions exist for those problems to be addressed.

Some of the young recruits at the Mamre camp became generals in the new South African National Defence Force. The color bar in all its aspects is now in the past, but the friction and mistrust between white and black officers must be overcome because the walls in their heads have not been completely destroyed.

As a commander I wish to report:

Mission accomplished.

We were ordered to "Break down the Walls."

We report: walls broken down.

We report: there are more walls to be broken down.

We report: there will always be walls to be broken down.

We report: people will build again, and again, and again . . .

Several years after the Westminster Abbey ceremony, in 2007, Looksmart's

8

remains were traced by a special unit in the National Prosecutions Authority to a cemetery in Mamelodi in Tshwane (Pretoria). The remains were exhumed by international experts at a ceremony attended by ANC leaders, including the executive mayor of Tshwane, Dr. Gwen Ramagopa. Because I had worked so closely with Looksmart, I was asked to speak at the ceremony. I sat with Looksmart's relatives at the modest meal that was served afterward. After some months, when DNA tests were done, his remains and those of four Western Cape MK soldiers that had been separately exhumed were handed to their respective families in beautiful coffins. I spoke again at this moving ceremony in Cape Town, where I met Looksmart's father and his son, who was a very little boy at the time of his father's murder. He had worked very hard to get his father's remains found so that they could be properly interred and the family achieve closure at last, after forty-five years.

2

Respect for All

Childhood in Cape Town, 1933–1949

"Mum, please hold my book. Help me learn the lines of a poem."

"What's it called?" she asked.

"'Hiawatha.'"

"Oh, then just say it," she said, her hands deep in soapy washing-up water.

"But, Mum, you've got to hold the book to see if I'm saying it right."

"Oh, just say it."

"Straightway into the forest strode Hiawatha . . . um . . . um . . ."

And then Mum recited the whole passage by heart, correcting me and starting the section as I should have:

Forth into the forest straightway
All alone walked Hiawatha
Proudly, with his bow and arrows;
And the birds sang round him, o'er him,
"Do not shoot us, Hiawatha!"
Sang the robin . . .

"I can't remember it, and you know it all!" I wailed.

She explained that when she was a young woman, just after the end of the First World War, she and her friends would walk hand in hand reciting poetry. They would look for nicely bound editions to give each other. "The Song of Hiawatha," by Henry Longfellow, was one of her favorite poems. It spoke of natural man, the noble savage, courageous and beautiful, and at one with nature. By then, Mum was already politically engaged and going to Socialist Sunday School in Hackney, London. Another of her favorite poems was the mildly erotic *Rubáiyát of Omar Khayyám,* translated from Persian by the anthropologist Edward FitzGerald. Sometimes there would be radio broadcasts of these long poems, and she would recite them along with the reader, almost word-perfect, with a few "um ums" thrown in, but keeping up the pace and the rhythm.

In those post–First World War years it was thought to be daring to read such verse, and even more so to recite it. But Mum and her friends saw themselves as liberated women. They refused to tie down their bosoms, preferring to wear loose-fitting bodices.

My Family

From her photographs, I'd say Mum was a good-looking woman, though I don't remember her as pretty. As I grew up I was aware that she had aches and pains, especially in her lower back. She said it was from crouching over a sewing machine in a clothing factory where the light was bad and the treadle was heavy. She also developed a stomach ulcer and needed to be careful of what she ate, but she still made most of her own clothes and was very good at it.

She did this to save money. There was never much to go around, though I do not remember ever being really hungry. There was usually bread and jam or, if no jam, then bread and drippings: tasty fat from a roast with little bits of onion in it. Nowadays we'd say it was very unhealthy. Perhaps that's why I have high cholesterol and clogged-up coronary arteries.

My mother seemed quite unhappy during my childhood. It wasn't only her ill health or money problems: as politically active communists, she and Dad shared the same interests, but the spark in their marriage had died. I know they made love sometimes, but her lips developed into a thin, compressed line, and he had wandering feet and a roving eye. Yet, like so many women then, and even now, economic necessity kept her tied to the marriage.

After Sunday breakfast—eggs, bacon, and bread fried until it was crisp in the bacon fat—Dad would go out and later reappear, saying he wanted us all to go on a picnic. But Mum would retort, justifiably, that it was absurd: he should have spoken earlier. She had the chicken in the oven, the weekly washing was soaking, and she simply could not leave it. He would counter that she was always obstructive. After a time I realized this was a game he played: he really wanted to go out on his own. He would return much later in the day looking quite content and relaxed, and I sensed that it was more than his eyes that were roving. Later I came to recognize the feeling myself. Actually, I am convinced that I have a half-sister, the daughter of a comrade with whom he had an affair.

Both Mum and Dad were born in London (he in 1898, which made him a year older), the children of Lithuanian Jews who emigrated to England during the second half of the nineteenth century. Jewish families left the Baltic States and eastern Europe during that period to escape the anti-Jewish pogroms. Many Lithuanian Jews settled in South Africa, among them founders of the South African Communist Party. They came together with miners from England who brought their class consciousness and organizing ability with them when they were recruited to work in the gold mines that sprang up from 1886 on the Witwatersrand, today's Johannesburg.

Dad came from a large family of brothers and one sister. My paternal Grandpa Morris and Granny Annie also emigrated to South Africa, though from London, not directly from Lithuania. My cousin Betty—her mum and mine were sisters—told me that our maternal grandmother, Rachel Fineberg, was a very intelligent woman. But Betty would read the newspapers to Granny because—though she stared at the pages—she was never able to master reading English.

My paternal Grandpa had a scrap yard for reclaimed building materials. I believe he had been a rag-and-bone man in the East End of London, where he pushed a handcart. I heard he was also a window mender, pushing a barrow selling panes of glass, crying "mendjawinders" (mend your windows) and fitting them.

Dad went to sea as a merchant seaman during the First World War. He did not want to be a soldier fighting for imperialist Britain, but he also did not want to go to prison as a conscientious objector. So he became a sailor. Did he know that the ships in which he sailed carried military materials for the armed forces in which he would not serve? I once asked him about this contradiction. He replied that he knew, but he had to make a choice. That was the choice he made.

In 1917, in New York, he heard about the Russian Revolution. The triple-decker headlines "Revolution—Revolution—Revolution" proclaimed the Bolshevik victory. It was, he said, the most moving day of his life. To some extent I can understand his feeling. As a merchant seaman he saw the world. He liked Australia and he liked the militant trade unions of the working-class movement he found there. He and my mum went to Sydney in the 1920s. He loved it; Mum barely tolerated it. They went back to London. She joined him in Australia again. When she became pregnant with my brother, Allan, she insisted on having him "at home" in England, so they went back again to London, where he was born in December 1927.

Later, my father insisted they leave, and they settled in Cape Town. I think he felt constrained by having to be a father and husband when what he wanted was to travel and be free. He did settle down but found it hard to love his son. Then I came along, and I gather he fell in love with me. I was open-faced and happy—knowing then, as I know now, that the sun will shine tomorrow, even if today is cloudy and cold. That made it even more difficult for my brother, who spent his life trying to win his father's love. Dad used that to manipulate him in many hurtful ways.

Dad's brother, my uncle Barney, told me that Grandpa Morris used to beat Dad because Dad had rickety legs and was slow in getting about. I have to say that I cannot remember Dad ever beating Allan or me. I do not even remember being seriously spanked on the bottom with a bare hand, which was then a standard means of chastising children. But I do think Dad emotionally abused Allan. That turned normal sibling rivalry into my brother's enmity. When Allan was forty-nine and I was forty-three, he told me that he hated me because, as a three-year-old, I teased him. When he retaliated, I would run to Dad for protection. That, he said, made him feel even more rejected.

I have a mental picture of my brother, a sturdy boy aged about nine, standing with legs astride, hurling my Tigger onto the roof of our house. Oh, the tears that fell until the stuffed toy tiger that comforted me when I slept was back in my arms again.

Later I admired Allan. He was so capable and taught me many things, such as how to make a crystal radio and a small electric motor. I learned to be quite good with my hands because my big brother showed me how.

It is sad what parents unconsciously do to their children. Both Mum and Dad read extensively, and Dad would have said he was careful not to abuse his sons. But, as modern parents who believed in the science of everything, they were sometimes unable to see the unfairness of their actions. And yet, for the most part, I sailed through my childhood feeling loved and protected. Even by my brother. When I was three years old my thumb got caught in a door that the wind slammed shut, and Allan carried me on his back to Dr. Resnikov, who bandaged it. And when I was nearly seven years old and had a minor operation at the famous Groote Schuur Hospital near our house in Observatory and was too woozy after the anesthetic to walk home, my brother gave me a piggy-back.

Dr. Resnikov was a German Jewish immigrant who had fled Nazi Germany. Highly trained, he had to repeat his final years of medical studies in South Africa to show that he was competent. At that time South Africa had its share of militant groups of Nazi sympathizers and anti-Semites. Even as a child I experienced them. Living across the road from us in Cavendish Square behind the Woodstock police station was Sergeant Jordaan, an Afrikaner. His son, who was a few years older than I, would strut about wearing his father's uniform cap and his leather straps with a revolver holster attached, throwing "Heil Hitler" salutes with his arm stiffly extended in front of him. Catching sight of me, he would shout, "I'll get you, Jew boy!" On the way to school every morning I had to pass Oswald's Butchery. Mr. Oswald sometimes came running out to threaten me with his sharp knives and meat cleaver, shouting that he hated Jews and he would "get me." Mum and Dad's advice, intended to reassure me, was to walk on the other side of the street and ignore the "poor deluded madman."

School Days

My sixth birthday, on 11 April 1939, was my first day at Observatory Boys Junior School. Going to that school was a marvelous gift. A typical urban school for white children, with a sandstone plinth and brick walls, the school looked like so many schools and public libraries funded by the Carnegie Foundation throughout the English-speaking world. I really loved going there—which had a lot to do with my first teacher, Miss Cook, to whom I'll refer again later. My family was not at all religious, which meant that I went to school on Jewish holy days, much to the puzzlement of teachers and classmates. Some teachers wanted to send me home on these holidays, but I would simply say my mother had insisted I go to school. When I was about twelve, I asked her to let me go to the beach with my cousins on one such holiday, but she explained that if I stayed away from school on religious grounds, then I would have to go to the synagogue to worship. It would show a lack of integrity to take a religious holiday and misuse it for pleasure. Such logic was impeccable and, since I liked school so much, I happily accepted my mother's ruling.[1]

Dad had had only six years at school, but he read widely and knew much about many things. So when I struggled with homework, even though he did not know the details of an awkward topic, he would ask me questions that led me to the correct answer. Mum also had a knack of explaining things simply. When I was little she would patiently answer my incessant "Why?" and "Yes, but why?" as I tried to understand the thoughts that underlay her explanations. Mostly she told me a bit more than I could understand, leaving some things for me to think about. It was great having two parents who knew so much and enjoyed teaching me whatever I wanted to know.

At the same time I enjoyed being with my friends—at school and after class, when we would walk on the mountain above Observatory, or play cricket in the street, or football, or find a field where we could pretend to be Springbok rugby players. Formal sport was great fun. At nine years old we started playing rugby when the school switched from football. Though it was never stated openly, the switch was made for racist reasons: football (soccer) was played by schools in Woodstock and Salt River, suburbs where many of the inhabitants were people who had "passed for white," whereas rugby was played by posher schools in suburbs where the families were clearly white. Class and color were always closely related, especially in Cape Town, where there were more Coloured people than in other parts of the country.

Apartheid is usually portrayed simply as a white-black conflict. It was much more complicated than that, and we have the evil legacy today of the multiple layers of discrimination. In the Western Cape there is still the inherited attitude among many Coloured people with aspirations to being white and privileged not to be tied to the Africans and the unprivileged. We have a long history in the Western Cape, where first segregation and then apartheid created a hierarchy of oppression of the nonwhite people: Coloureds as the most privileged, Indians less so, and African people unprivileged, in this descending scale. It was a deliberate political policy of the racists to keep groups divided from each other. Later, the various African groups—Xhosa, Zulu, Sesotho, and so on—were segregated in the townships. And in the barracks on the mines there was a policy of tribal segregation. This was applied quite consciously by government and big business. Coloured people were permitted to vote in general elections but not to sit in Parliament until they were disenfranchised in the 1950s. The Afrikaner Nationalist Government elected in 1948 had a small majority of seats, and the votes of Coloured people threatened their supremacy in various constituencies. The disenfranchisement was of course part of the white-supremacist program of the apartheid government.

The divisions between white and Coloured during my childhood were governed by strongly observed social custom and practice rather than by laws. Then the Group Areas Act, based on race, was introduced in the 1950s, in addition to the previous Native Urban Areas Act of 1927, which compelled "native" people to live in separate "locations," generally called townships in later apartheid terminology.

Social separation could be found in a single street. In Observatory, for instance, Rochester Road is about a mile long and runs from Main Road to Lower Main Road, where my school was. At the top end of the road the families were clearly white. Some way down, in the language of the time, there were the "three-eighths" (Coloured) people, followed by some homes with the "halvies" and the "five-eighths," followed by the homes of people who were undoubtedly Coloured. These differences were obvious to all, and the gradations were quite strictly followed by the socially disadvantaged as well as the advantaged. The attempt to pass for white or to "play white" was serious in terms of both income and social status. A few streets along and nearer the city, the suburbs became more clearly Coloured, as only a few whites lived there.

One of my classmates lived on the corner of our street and Main Road. Sometimes, at night, his father would come and sit whispering with my dad. I once asked what he had come for. Dad said he had come to speak to him because he had to have somebody to speak to. "But why?" I asked. Had I not realized that he was Coloured and was passing for white? I understood, on the one hand, that he came to Dad because Dad was a communist and therefore antiracist. But on the other hand, "Oh, so that is why he comes under cover of darkness"—because associating with a communist might draw attention to him.

Another school friend came from a large family. His brothers were of different hues. Some were white, some were dark, and some looked a bit Coloured. "Auntie" Daisy, who always had cocoa for her children and their many friends on a cold winter's evening, used huge amounts of face powder. None of this seemed to affect the enjoyment we had as young people together. I think Auntie Daisy's husband had disappeared as a discretionary action because he was very dark-skinned and that would have been embarrassing for a family who had moved up the social scale. The anxieties of people in such families must have been excruciating, especially in terms of providing protection for one's friends from representatives of the state.

I had a few run-ins at high school with authoritarian teachers. Our mathematics master seemed to think he could beat a grasp of algebra into a dull boy with the flat of his large blackboard compass applied to the calf muscle. He really lost it one day, working himself into a rage at the stupidity of a less than bright pupil. I shouted at him to stop beating the boy. He stopped and turned to threaten me with a beating. He calmed down but I wish he hadn't, because my dad would certainly have gone after him for assault. In such ways, early in life, I learned that tyranny was not to be tolerated and that one must stand up against injustice.

I learned to read from the headlines in the *Cape Argus,* the evening newspaper, while sitting on Dad's lap as a five- and six-year-old. That contributed to my early interest in politics. I read voraciously as a child. My school did not have a library, but there was a cupboard in each classroom with about the same number of books as there were children in the class. We took one book home each week. That was not enough for me, and I borrowed more from the public library. And from quite an early age, I can remember Dad, when he had a few shillings to spare, taking me to Foyle's Bookshop in the heart of Cape Town. There he would turn me loose to choose something that interested me. That was the start of a lifelong habit of reading.

I read about Africans protesting about the pass laws and burning their documents and going to prison for it. I read about poverty and how it was somehow connected to race in South Africa. These were topics that the weekly *Guardian* wrote about. At first I didn't understand why that newspaper was the "workers' paper" when there were no jobs advertised in it. Later I understood that the *Guardian* was a different kind of newspaper and always wrote about matters from the workers' point of view. When there was a strike, the *Cape Argus* and the *Cape Times* always condemned the strikers, but the *Guardian* praised them because the strikers would make the world a better place. And when workers went on strike, my parents and their comrades would take them hot soup and sandwiches to help them man their picket lines. It did not matter whether the workers were white or black; they were workers! So I soon learned that my parents were different and ours was a home where people of all races came to visit. Sometimes there were meetings, but often the people came as visitors to share our evening meal. Somehow there was always a little bit extra in the pot. "Family hold back" (FHB) was the rule, and guests had to be served first. If I eyed the last potato too greedily, it would be offered to a visitor and I would get bread and gravy or bread and drippings to fill up on. Everyone had to be served and respected.

There were times when there was a bit of luxury. Sometimes Mum brought home a small tin of golden syrup imported from England by the large stores, despite the lack of shipping space during the war. Trade must continue, I realized as a child. But golden syrup's refined sweetness on toast was indeed something special. The shop assistants would keep such niceties for their favored customers, and my mum was one: not just because she was a regular customer but because she was one of those women who supported shop workers when they were on the picket line during a strike and needed feeding and solidarity.

On May Day I would sit on the front mudguard of Dad's truck as he led the parade of workers through the city with a band playing revolutionary songs on the platform and a crowd of all races marching behind with their flags and banners flying. In this sense my life was quite different from that of my schoolmates. Some of them would mock me and my parents about our friends and visitors, but I was quite tough—both physically and emotionally—so I could handle it. Besides, I played sports and was one of the guys. With my school friends—Donald, Roy, Neville, and others—I would watch rugby on Saturday afternoons at the famous Newlands rugby ground, then walk home along the pathway next to the railway line passing an imaginary ball with swinging arms, jinking with the hips or "selling a dummy" (pretending to pass the ball to send an opponent running the wrong way), and sidestepping onto the opposite foot to break the line. The tries we scored in our wild imaginations were always match winners.

Cape Town winters are cold, and fingertips and nose would feel the bite of the winter air late in the afternoon when it was already getting dark. At the Rondebosch fountain, originally a drinking trough for horses, we stopped at a fruit shop to buy Granny Smith apples and continue our walk home, munching away with the juice running down our chins. I suppose it was a brisk two-mile walk. It saved money to walk: we knew it was good for us—and it was fun.

Maybe my parents' attitudes influenced my becoming the fullback, the last line of defense in the rugby team. In later years, when size mattered, forwards of the opposing team would come tearing down on me, and I simply had to take the hammering of their weight and force as they piled onto me. The sheer physical exhilaration of the game was a joy. In the winter, playing in the cold, sleeting rain when my gear was soaked through and covered in mud, it was exciting as my body warmed up and I felt I was steaming like a horse. It was pure delight to be young and strong, ready for anything!

We played by the rules. Cheating was frowned on, and there was a sort of code of honor that required us to admit to an infringement of the rules even if the referee had not seen it. A hard, proper tackle was okay. The idea of deliberately injuring an opponent to take him out of the game seemed to creep in through the coaches only when I was at university, many years later. Clever play within the rules, such as a change of pace or selling a dummy, was a legitimate use of athletic skills. But tripping up an opponent was not okay. We played to win, but not by cheating.

I played sport in a team at a white school. By playing rugby, we rubbed shoulders with the elite schools and established a distance between our school and the football-playing schools. But outside this little white island, we children were constantly faced with everyday racism. Among the key moments in my life, I remember an episode when I was nine and a bunch of us were walking home from school together. Outside the greengrocer's we saw a man running to catch a train. Somebody said he was faster than Tinkie (Heyns), our gym teacher. "No, he can't be. Tinkie is the champion [Western Province half-mile champion]. Nobody can be faster than him," somebody else insisted. Our voices rose and a third one said, "But the man is Coloured, so he can't ever race against Tinkie!" How dare white South Africans say today that everything was kept secret. *We* knew what was happening—when we were nine years old!

The history book in my fourth year at school, *Our Country,* said South Africa was a democracy, which meant that all adults could vote in elections for Parliament. But I knew that only whites and Coloureds could vote. "Natives" were not allowed to vote. When I asked my parents about this, they said that, of course, the history book was wrong. Perhaps most children would not have asked anyway, but these things were discussed in my home all the time.

In that same year, 1943, I saw a man sitting on the pavement eating his lunch. He had a small French loaf that he opened down its length and poured a tin of sardines into. He pressed it closed to save the olive oil and feasted on it. He was eating my favorite sardines, King Oscar, imported from Norway. (King Oscar was the golden king with a huge moustache in the picture on the label.) Why could I not have lunch like that instead of having to sit at a table with my elbows by my side and my mouth closed while I chewed? Then a white man appeared, shouting at the man with his sandwich: "Filthy black, you make the street dirty with your food!" The man drew himself up and said, "Don't call me a black! I am a respectable Native person!"[2] The courage that must have taken. The sheer dignity of the man. I see him still, sitting down again, rather quickly, after his tormentor had scurried away.

That year was full of turning points for South Africans in the Second World War. It started with the defeat of the Nazis by the Red Army at Stalingrad. We had large war maps on our dining room walls. Every night we listened to the BBC World Service, and would stick in pins with different-colored heads to show where the battle lines were. We also had maps of Hitler's North African campaign showing the Allied victory at El Alamein in Egypt and the defeat of Field Marshal Rommel's Afrika Korps in Tunisia after the United States landed an army there. Our living room was very small, but there was room for the Pacific Theater as well. I certainly learned a lot of geography. I can remember discussions at home about how wrong were the right-wing Indian nationalists who thought that by supporting the Japanese against the British during the Second World War they would set themselves free from British rule. What they ignored, the grownups argued, was that they would find themselves subjugated to a hungrier and more vicious imperialism: Japanese militarism.

In South Africa we were hardly touched by the war. But I remember some things that we children did, largely because our parents wanted us to do them. I helped address envelopes for appeals for the Medical Aid for Russia Fund (its president, Bishop Lavis, thanked me for my hard work). More notable was the fact that the fund's patron in chief was the conservative prime minister, Field Marshal Jan Smuts. My Uncle Barney was heavily involved in the same fund. How respectable it was to be of the left during the anti-Nazi war years, when the Soviet Union was the "Glorious

Ally." That changed very quickly when the imperialist nature of the Second World War emerged in the form of the Cold War.

Dad frequently spoke on public platforms about current political issues. He held his audiences well and explained political matters in simple language. I think that came from his being a trade union shop steward when he was a sailor, when he learned to speak about complicated things in ways his fellow workers could understand and accept. He was the education secretary in the Woodstock Branch of the Communist Party, and years later my older ANC comrades in the liberation movement told me that they had learned their politics from my dad. And how pleased I was when Moses Kotane, general secretary of the Communist Party, personally thanked me for writing election cards and envelopes, and for stuffing envelopes for his party's candidates in municipal elections.

Gradually, during the war Dad built up a cartage contracting business, and when he was out driving one of his trucks late at night I would answer the phone and take messages for him: "Five three double six seven, Quick Service Transport." Dad owned an early 1930s Diamond T truck and a newer one with an all-steel cab—and, most beautiful of all, a 1933 International with flared front mudguards that made it look like it was flying. Dad hauled materials for military construction for the many training camps and coastal defense batteries that were built. He often came home furious about other truckers who fiddled with their petrol ration coupons so that they could sell them on the black market at exorbitant prices. Then there were those who would drive their trucks with tires showing canvas so that they could get a chit from an army base commander for new tires "for essential war work." They would use the new tires for a few days and then sell them at an enormous profit. Dad also railed against the building contractors who were paid on a "cost plus" basis: the more they spent, the greater their profit as a fixed percentage of the total cost. They would put themselves on the payroll of each construction project they had been awarded, taking both a wage and a profit on each job. "How can they weaken our war effort?" Dad would cry. "Don't they understand that we have to defeat the Nazis and the Japanese if we are to survive at all?" He simply would not be a crook.

Dad was a small businessman, with no special training. In the 1930s he ran a gas station on the main road in Woodstock, almost directly opposite the police station. There was a lift for raising cars and trucks for servicing. It was a source of amazement to me to watch the shiny steel column of the "high jolly jack" (hydraulic jack) emerge from the floor and lift the heavy vehicles. I always wanted to see what the mechanics were doing, and I would dart around them as they wielded their grease guns. Of course, the floor was covered in grease and often I slipped and fell—and had to be washed in gasoline to get the muck off. It was a somewhat messy way to ensure that in later years I was able to do my own maintenance and repairs.

In the mid-1930s Dad, his brothers Joe and Barney, and my grandfather each owned a bus. They competed with the many other owners of individual buses and the tramway company, whose trams had the right of way on their tracks. The situation was chaotic and dangerous, as drivers inevitably raced to get to waiting passengers first. Eventually the authorities and the tramway company agreed that the latter would set up a bus company with a monopoly on the service. A condition was that they would have to buy out the existing bus owners, paying reasonable compensation for their buses. Dad's driver accidentally stalled his bus on the tram tracks and a tram driver simply smashed into it, destroying it. No compensation for Dad. He was sure that the tram drivers were instructed to use their right of way to destroy the buses. Twenty years later Dad was still amazed that the government official who had to issue the licences to the new bus company suddenly became very rich. The official, according to my dad, claimed he won his money at the races. Nodding his head, Dad said that the promoters of the new bus company were also the owners of the racehorses and won their bets thanks to insider knowledge.

Observing current transport conflicts, I can say indeed that we've seen it all before. It has little to do with race but with greed and capital accumulation. And I'm fascinated to see that today's bus and taxi drivers are as susceptible to brutality in the interests of their vehicle owners as they were then.

In the end, after years of hard work, Dad ended up better off than he had ever been. Though there were shortages, my family could rejoice: we had five hundred pounds in the bank! We moved to a better area of Observatory, Dalston Road, and we had a rented house with a refrigerator. No need now to rely on Icy, the ice man, for a once-a-week block of ice.

But the transport business was in bad shape. The two Diamond T trucks were worn out, and the twelve-year-old International truck with its beautiful flared front mudguards was held together with baling wire. Dad could no longer drive: the constant jarring vibration and heavy steering had damaged his spine. Often he wore a great big belladonna plaster covering most of his back just to keep going. But he insisted it was all worth it. We had won the war.

Life was not all politics and social theory. There was time for enjoying the pleasures offered by Cape Town's mild climate, including great opportunities to swim, climb mountains, and play sports. And we played cards, like rummy and *klawerjas* (jack of clubs). Though Dad was never a great chess player, he enjoyed the game and it was fun to learn how to play it with him. We learned because he believed that such intellectual exercises were an important part of our development. By the time I was thirteen he could no longer beat me, but playing with him was a pleasant way of being together. In my first year at high school I beat the school captain at chess with a sneaky back-row checkmate when he was about to defeat me. That was in the final of school chess competition, and so I was a champion. The next year I was up against Ralph Wright, a friend to whom I had taught the game. The night before the championship final I defeated him. But that was the last time: in the final he wiped me off the board and I was never again able to beat him.

Mum was a stickler for doing things properly and for fulfilling one's duties in the home. Two sayings summed up her attitude: "If a job is worth doing, it must be done properly"; and "If you start a task, then you must finish it." At times, of course, I resented both sayings, especially when it seemed utterly important to go out to play ball or idle away an afternoon in the sun with friends. But Mum would insist I finish some chore, such as washing the dishes or sweeping my room. So now I find it hard to tolerate slap-dash attitudes in younger people and government officials who claim rights but neglect their duties. I must add another saying that permeated my upbringing: "Workers are entitled to a fair day's pay for a fair day's work." That lives with me still.

In 1949, my final year at school, there seemed to be the possibility of going to university to study civil engineering. From the age of about thirteen I had become convinced that I wanted to build roads and bridges, dams and pipelines, for people. I had read books about the modern wonders of the world and I wanted to make even greater modern wonders. Then I read books like *Microbe Hunters,* a best seller by Paul de Kruif, and other books about medical science. I discovered that the Panama Canal could not have been built without medical doctors being able to control tropical diseases; that railways had often cost, as it was said, a life for each tie that had been laid. Doctors could also do heroic things, and that is what I decided to do. Then I thought about it some more. Dad would, I knew, find it difficult to keep me at university for four years of engineering studies. Six years of medical studies, then a year of internship, would have been too much for him to finance. I returned to my first love. Even then there was doubt about my being able to go to university. So I wrote the Railways' apprenticeship examination. My classmate Kenny Vinello, we heard, came in first and I came in second in the country. Kenny became an apprentice, and another classmate and I went to university as full-time students and another two were part-time students. It was a miracle!

Miss Cook, Where Are You?

Starting school on the day I turned six was the best birthday present ever. Even though I was the *pikkie* (Xhosa *piccannin,* infant), the little one in our family, I wanted to be a big boy and go to school with my brother, Allan. That first day Mum and Dad were very serious. They told me that I should not get upset if other children or teachers called me *Kaffirboetie* ("Nigger lover" is the easiest awful translation), Commie, or Jewboy. Of course, I knew we were different because none of the people who lived around us had black and Coloured friends who visited them and had dinner in their homes. Nor did other kids sit on the front of their dad's truck leading the May Day parade through Cape Town with flags flying while the band on the back played songs for the people of all colors marching behind.

I could not understand my parents' anxiety. Mum and Dad both took me to school that first day. They made it special and they said they wanted me always to do the best I could. They did not expect me to be the best in my class, I just had to really try hard.

Miss Cook was my first teacher and, oh dear, I thought she was *so* beautiful. She was young and slim and she wore a lovely perfume, and everything she said or did was just right. I thought this was my secret but, many years later, when Mum visited me in prison, she told me she was quite jealous at first because every day I would come home from school and talk about Miss Cook this and Miss Cook that, Miss Cook said this or that or the other. I think I inherited strong genes from my dad.

Miss Cook was distraught one day after the morning break. She asked if any of us had seen the gold wristwatch her parents had given her when she qualified as a teacher. She had left it in the drawer of her table and now it was gone. As one, the thirty six-year-old boys in the class cried out, "Nolan took it, Miss Cook." She asked how we knew that. "Because we saw him, Miss Cook," we chorused. How? She cross-examined us, insisting that we be sure before we blamed him. She knew we could not have seen him take the watch because we were all outside in the school playground during the break.

Nolan had a harelip and cleft palate, and in 1939 plastic surgery was not very good. Nolan had a vivid scar across his upper lip and he spoke funny. His clothes were always dirty, and he did not wear shoes. Because he was different, he was a lonely boy. I suppose we found him strange and he found us unfriendly. Now we were saying he was guilty.

O Nolan, apologies for what we did to you.

Miss Cook was very insistent that we think carefully and questioned some of us one by one. She held me by her side while she sat in her chair. It was embarrassing to be so close to her, but nice, too. When I said we had seen Nolan put her watch in the refuse bin, she said that it was not enough to see Nolan at the bin. We all knew he looked every day for sandwiches that other children had thrown away. The janitor had looked through the bin and the watch was not there. And so it went on, round and round, until Miss Cook made us see that we were blaming Nolan for taking the watch because he was different.

Miss Cook gave me a lesson in bigotry and intolerance that I have never forgotten. Often in prison I thought about her. I wanted to thank her for reinforcing the attitudes of my parents. After all, if Miss Cook could say that what my mother thought was correct, then my mum had to be okay, too!

Dear Miss Cook, the secret is out! You sent me to prison for twenty-two years.

3

University

I was a fresh-faced sixteen-year-old when I started my studies in 1950 at the University of Cape Town. In the long summer holiday between school and university I worked on a fruit farm some eighty-five miles from Cape Town, near the town of Ceres. The hard physical work in the hot sun made me fit and strong—and, for the first time right up front, I witnessed the conditions of farmworkers, and the profits of the white farmers.

Dick Hitchcock, the farmer who took me on, had been an accountant with one of the big corporations and rose to the rank of captain in the South African Air Force during World War II. He served in North Africa and Italy and, upon being demobilized, was given a small grant that, with an investment from his brother-in-law, was sufficient to buy a derelict fruit farm. The export market had collapsed during the war, and these new owners set about rehabilitating the farm. Modern insecticide sprays cleared the orchard of the destructive codling moths and other pests more quickly than on the farms of the older farmers who stuck to the traditional arsenic sprays.

In addition, my farmer and his partner paid their laborers wages that were minutely better than the going rate in those years of unemployment, so they had the pick of the workers, who worked much harder. They also drew the enmity of the other farmers, and the old Boer-Brit, Afrikaans-English antagonisms resurfaced. Our farmers picked the fruit more carefully as it matured instead of stripping it, regardless of size, in one day.

Larger fruit gained a higher price, so their profits were higher. This also lengthened the growing time for each variety, so that more fruit was harvested from each tree. On their small investment they made profits of £13,000 in their first year, and by the time I went to work on the farm, the season had yielded a profit of more than £30,000. Dick had great organizational and entrepreneurial skills. As a newcomer to fruit farming, he quickly learned all he could from books and experts. Yet the rewards were exorbitant in relation to what the farmworkers were being paid. Well-off people in Britain were paying one pound for a single pear, when a worker would have been paid in shillings for a whole day's work.

I marveled at the dexterity of the women fruit packers, who wrapped each pear in a square of colored tissue paper with a few deft movements of their fingers and placed each one nestled in straw in a wooden box so that there would not be any bruising during the journey to the railway station, or during the loading onto and unloading off a train, or on the fourteen-day sea journey to Britain, or on the train journeys to London and elsewhere. All in all, it was an astonishingly complex set of activities, and special refrigerated ships were built for this trade.

I tried to wrap fruit, but my fingers never did learn to fold the paper so that it looked neat and clean. My wrappers were crumpled. If I'd had to earn my living this way, I would have starved. What I could do was make up the wooden boxes from the *shooks,* or planks and cleats, precut at a sawmill and transported to the farm, where on a simple jig they would be assembled and nailed together. One smart blow of the hammer, and the nails would be driven straight in. I discovered that even such handwork—always described as "unskilled"—needed training and experience before one could work fast enough to satisfy the farmer. What I could do was fill in the reams of forms to go with each consignment of fruit. So I learned about scientific farming and the organization of work. And I learned about the need to get up early to refill the fuel tanks of the engines driving the water pumps and how tired one gets. Even the loudest alarm clock would not waken my sixteen-year-old self in the morning. Farmers get surprisingly angry when you neglect your duty.

My cousin Gerry and I worked together and were able to borrow the pickup truck to go swimming and visiting other people because we were friends of the family of the white farmer. It was a great holiday and learning experience. Simultaneously, all that I had heard from my family and read about the exploitation of workers and the role of race in apartheid I saw to be absolutely true. I also discovered that kissing and fondling the farmer's daughter was great fun.

Dick retired after about ten years and went to live in the United States, where one winter he slipped on an icy sidewalk, banged his head, and died from a brain hemorrhage, a relatively young man in his fifties.

Action for Unity

When I started my studies in March 1950 at the University of Cape Town, I was still like a young schoolboy among self-assured young men and women. I felt socially very ill at ease. I played rugby in the under-nineteen D team. That was the lowest one could get, but it gave me the opportunity to kick the hell out of the ball and get rid of my frustrations that way. I did later play for the A team and even for the third senior team, and on occasion for the second team, as I got older and stronger. I was always the smallest, and my bigger teammates protected me as much as they could. I still have a sore shoulder, the result of a vicious deliberate kick and other lesions, but at the time I didn't think of the future, just the exhilaration of competing.

The four-year degree in civil engineering was considered one of the most difficult to get through in the designated time. I managed to do something most unusual, failing applied mathematics, which was usually considered easy, and passing pure math, which was considered to be more difficult. That happened in both my first and second years. The first time it happened I looked again and again at the exam results on the notice board but my name was missing. I felt ill. One of my professors, standing nearby and seeing my distress, casually told me about the possibility, offered only to engineering students, of writing supplementary exams year by year, which I managed. There were fewer than nine of us in a final-year class of thirty out of about two hundred who started who could finish the four-year degree in that time. I was one of them, but, having passed my final exams, I made a design error in a structure in my undergraduate thesis. If it will fall down, so do you. My dream of being a graduate engineer before I was twenty-one was not realized. Not one black student studied engineering at the so-called open University of Cape Town in my time. Black students were discouraged from taking engineering. I believe the first student of color was admitted to the engineering faculty in 1959.

Whatever my initial result, the fact that Dad was able, completely, to finance my studies was something very special for me. It was such a matter of pride for him to have a son at university. Eventually he was able to introduce me to his friends and acquaintances with the words "Meet my son, the engineer." In a contradictory way, he glowed with modesty. My generation was the first in our extended family to get tertiary education, and I have South African cousins who are doctors and business studies graduates. Yet I cannot forget how, every year, I would get a letter from the university saying I could not write my exams until my fees had been paid. The outstanding amount was forty pounds at a time when the total cost of upkeep, books, fees, and so on was about three hundred pounds a year, if one was on a very tight budget, living at home as I did. Dad would give the university three post-dated checks to cover the small outstanding amount, and eventually the dreaded deficits would be met. It always made me conscious of how privileged I was that, because we were white, Dad could have a bank account, while the majority of the people could not because they could not own property and could not earn a wage for which the banks would want to provide a service.

Indeed, access to university, besides being controlled through access to funds, was affected by the severe inequalities in facilities at primary and secondary schools. About half the number of black children could not go to school because there were no places for all of them, and the amount spent on them by the state was about one-tenth of that spent on white children in government schools. Until 1955 the apartheid state took no responsibility for African education other than to pay teachers' salaries. Buildings and maintenance had to be borne by communities and churches. In 1955 the state took control of all schools, introducing a second-rate system of "Bantu education," against which students rose up in 1976.

I knew all about the inequalities, but the pressure of my studies meant I was not active in student politics. I would sometimes attend mass meetings convened by the Students Representative Council when they put up some form of protest about the increasing racial segregation of students at university. It was shaming to see civil engineering students being the main disrupters of such meetings. Their attitude, when we did talk about these things, was crude: "Either whites would rule over blacks or blacks would rule over whites, and so it better be us whites." As government was the biggest source of funds for the work of civil engineers, that's whom they supported. Why black and white skins had social significance was a question they could not answer, nor did they want to understand the inhumanity of our situation and our responsibility for it.

It wasn't easy being always in the minority, often a minority of one, in the groups in which I was involved. My classmates could not see that as engineers, there would be so much more work for us if only we could build for all our people. The prejudices absorbed in their childhood were so deeply ingrained they could not see past them. If I hadn't been a rugby player I would probably have been ostracized completely.

Toward the end of my final year, in August 1953, I met Esmé, who later became my wife. Though she wasn't a student, she was hitchhiking outside the university, as did many students because there was no bus service. We got a lift in the same car. I found her very attractive and the hormones were racing. Later, and totally unconnected to that chance encounter in the car, she came to see my mother. Esmé was the daughter of a Johannesburg political activist, Minnie Bodenstein, a quite famous fund-raiser for the Communist Party, for *Umzebenzi* (*The Worker*), the *Guardian,* and other left-wing publications and causes who worked with Tillie First, mother of Ruth First. I recognized Esmé as the young woman I had met when we shared a lift. She came to see my mother to borrow some blankets because she had just moved to Cape Town.

She said she was a physiotherapist and noticed that I could hardly move my injured right shoulder. She massaged it and it really did help, so I kissed her to say thank you. Esmé was at that time engaged to be married but was going through a bad time with her fiancé. She had become quite ill. I nursed her and gave her moral support. She fell in love with her nurse! We decided to share her blankets for the month of September 1953, before she went off to get married. The romantic *September Song* haunts me still: "The days dwindle down to a precious few"; in the end, she broke off the engagement.

Esmé cooked the most wonderful roast lamb with cloves of garlic nestled in the meat and served with roast potatoes and green peas. Mum would never have used such exotic things as garlic. It was the year I should have graduated but didn't. My mother, till the end of her life, blamed my new girlfriend for distracting me. I graduated later, after we had married and Esmé had given birth to our daughter, Hilary, in January 1955. Our son, David, was born in November 1957.

Esmé was a committee member in the Modern Youth Society, and I accompanied her to meetings and soon became active, too. The MYS was a bit strange because it was a nonracial organization, open to people of all races, when the Congress Alliance was a multiracial group of organizations. That was the language of the time, multiracial. The African National Congress was exclusively for Africans; the Indian Congress was founded in 1924; the Coloured People's Congress was formed in 1953; and the Congress of Democrats was formed in 1952 for whites who allied themselves with the African National Congress, which led the Congress Alliance. There were intense debates and heated arguments about the national question. What constituted a nation, or a national group? When the South African Congress of Trade Unions (SACTU) was formed in 1955, it was also nonracial, but because of the need for workers' unity, SACTU was accepted within the Congress structure. I never had any problem with that structuring of our movement because it seemed to me obvious that all Africans in South Africa were subjected as a group throughout the country to the same denial of political and other rights, social and economic, and therefore had to lead us to freedom for themselves and all our population. In the colonies of the powerful European countries there was no embarrassment about discussing such matters. The League of Nations and the U.N. charters assert the right of self-determination of nations. So we had to deal with these matters.

We argued about a nation being a continuous piece of territory with people who considered themselves a nation because of a common language and a common culture, a single economy, and an accepted political system. In South Africa there were the whites, who came from many countries but considered themselves to be a group with shared interests and all the other characteristics. There were the African people who, even though they came from different tribes in recent times, had, through political organization and the oppression that all experienced under the racist laws, become a group that covered the whole of the territory. They did not, however, accept the political system and were both included in the economy as workers and excluded from the economy as owners of capital, land, and wealth. They were therefore not quite a nation but a national group. The Indians, who had been imported into South Africa as workers, remained a minority and a fairly homogeneous national group; and the Coloured people were always caught between being black African and white—and their politics swung in the wind. The apartheid system treated them as a group. They sometimes accepted this and at other times did not. Our Freedom Charter and our democratic constitution say that South Africa belongs to all who live in it. The issue is how to overcome the historic deprivation of most of the groups and the population, while respecting the rights of all, including the former oppressors. In other words, how do we now transcend the necessary emphasis on national groups during the freedom struggle?

Though the Modern Youth Society general membership was out of keeping with the Congress Movement at the time, we fully supported the Congress Movement. This nonracial youth group was founded by left-wing students at the University of Cape Town who wanted to meet with working-class youth. Since the university did not permit political organizations of nonstudents on the campus, the Modern Youth Society was set up as an off-campus organization. I joined when it was already established.

Our activities were many and designed to draw in young people. We had a meeting just about every Friday night, and eventually we rented our own little hall in a building in Cape Town. We could barely finance it. We had political discussions about apartheid and how to resist it. The Freedom Charter covered an entire wall. We also showed films that raised social issues. We were able to get films from the consulate of the Czechoslovak Republic. The films were often about the resistance to Nazi occupation in World War II. Already then we knew about the need to be able to resist in more active ways than holding a placard or a banner. When the oppression gets too great, you have to fight. We also found films about Africa. We looked for films about people's struggles that would lead to debate and discussion.

One of those who joined us was Andimba Toivo Ja Toivo.

Andimba Toivo ja Toivo, a Friend from Namibia

I met Herman ja Toivo, as he was known in colonial times (now Andimba Toivo ja Toivo), through the Modern Youth Society in 1953. Esmé and I tried to open our home to all our friends to overcome the issues of institutionalized racism that so dominated our lives. Andimba was one of the people who used to visit us in Garfield Road, Claremont, on the edge of Lansdowne in Cape Town. That was on the border between white and Coloured residential areas declared under the Group Areas Act.

He came with friends and we enjoyed each other's company in a political hothouse atmosphere of debate that was possible because Andimba was particularly close to us. Among those who came were Emil Appolus and Jariretundu Kozonguizi. Esmé and I came from families who were not drinkers, but there was always cold milk in tall pilsner glasses with a frosting of water drops on the outside. Our friends found this an inviting luxury. It is sad that such a minor detail sticks in my mind.

There were intense discussions among Andimba, Emil Appolus, and me about the nature of freedom. Was freedom simply the right to be employed by big corporations like Consolidated Diamond Mines or De Beers or Anglo American Corporation? Emil asserted very vigorously that he would be free if he could be a top executive in Anglo American, and for a socialist like me that didn't sound like freedom. It sounded like wanting to be part of the repression and exploitation. The reality of South Africa and Namibia today is that what has been achieved is what Emil was talking about. The economic oppression remains. Globalization, the intensification of the monopolistic trends of powerful multinational and now transnational corporations, makes national economic development even more difficult.

Andimba was a tall, quiet, self-effacing workingman who was a messenger in the Dominion Furnishing Company on Lower Main Road in Observatory. He delivered furniture and went to the factories that supplied the shop. Esmé told me that she once bumped into him outside the service station where she was taking our car. They embraced as they always did and, of course, in the 1950s it was a great shock to white South Africans to see a white woman and a black man embracing. The African workers in the service station also saw it, and our car was thereafter always beautifully cleaned and serviced. That such a minor snippet of memory has stuck in my mind for sixty years highlights the craziness of apartheid South Africa.

I wasn't drawn to Emil Appolus as I was to Andimba. I believed revolutionaries shouldn't get drunk. I had this romantic, puritanical view of what it was to be a revolutionary. I found his concept of freedom inadequate because it would simply change the faces and skin color of the exploiters. I did not yet understand the intensity of the desire for national liberation. I was already looking beyond it because I realized that unless working people were freed from economic exploitation, they would still be oppressed. Now I can express it thus: national oppression was and is the expression of class conflict in the particular context of South African colonial history.

Namibia was not a big issue for us in the Modern Youth Society or for the Congress Alliance in the 1950s and 1960s. South Africa was our issue and Namibia was its colony. How do you cope with that contradiction?

Our issue was clear: How were we to achieve power in South Africa? Namibia's problems would be solved by the seizure of that power. It was a lack of understanding on the part of some of us, though Jack Simons, who taught African studies at the University of Cape Town, and his activist wife, Ray, understood the link: we had to attack imperialism through challenging South Africa's occupation of Namibia and the protection of the interests of DeBeers and Anglo American through Consolidated Diamond Mines and other interests like the copper mines owned by the U.S. Newmont Mining Corporation at Tsumeb in the north of Namibia. This was clearly understood, but we were interested in building opposition to apartheid. It was only later that we began to understand how complete the polarization between the white state and African political aspirations had become. Therefore, the struggle in South-West Africa (now Namibia) became more important as time went on as part of a common struggle against apartheid, particularly as apartheid South Africa used Namibia as a testing ground for various aspects of apartheid legislation.

When we met Andimba, he was looking for a political and ideological home. How do you deal with being an Ovambo and Namibian person being oppressed by South Africa? Is Namibia going to continue to be a province of South Africa? Is it going to become an independent country?

Andimba was one of the founders of the Ovambo People's Congress in Cape Town. I was not directly involved. My memory is that there were considerable differences between those who formed the Ovambo People's Congress and later the Ovamboland People's Organisation and South-West African People's Organisation (SWAPO), on the one hand, and those who formed the South-West African National Union (SWANU), which was essentially a Herero-based organization, on the other. But the differences were not due only to ethnicity. My recollection is that members of SWANU were less progressive because they were more procapitalist. They would be politically allied to the chiefs and the conservatism of a system in which the apartheid system used the chiefs as part of their administrative structure. SWAPO members, on the other hand, were much more revolutionary in their approach. The authority of the Council of Chiefs was a central issue of the conflict. All agreed on national liberation from South African rule, which should have been under United Nations Trusteeship (originally a League of Nations mandate) to bring the trust territory to independence. The issue was the attitude of a future Namibian government to ownership of land and resources and to big business. Namibian workers living in Cape Town were not very supportive of intellectuals who wanted privileges for themselves.[1]

In 1957 the United Nations Special Committee on South-West Africa had called for representations on the situation in that country. The apartheid South African government instructed the administrator of SWA to refuse Chief Hosea Kutako permission to go to New York to represent his people. Andimba asked me to help him send a tape-recorded message to the U.N. committee.

Finding a tape recorder in those days—when they were large, heavy machines—was not as easy as it is now. We had a Dutch friend, a former prisoner of war of the Nazis, who had emigrated to South Africa and had such a tape recorder. "Ike" Eigenstein, a silkscreen artist by profession, worked with us in campaigns against apartheid. He had fallen in love with a woman across the color line, which was a criminal offense under the Immorality Act, so he had personal reasons for opposing apartheid. He and his eventual wife left the country to be able to remain together.

We were not quite sure how to disguise the big open-reel tape. In Ike's living room we started off with my making a fictitious tape-recorded letter to a fictitious person in America. I talked about our fictitious families and told him about the wonderful jazz music I had heard. We recorded the music and then Andimba recorded his statement in the middle of the music.

I do not remember the exact wording, but he said he was making the statement because Chief Hosea Kutako had been refused permission to go to New York, and that this was an outrage and a denial of the rights of the Namibian people under the Trusteeship. Among the thoughts I remember Andimba expressing were that the government of South Africa occupied Namibia illegally, that it denied the rights of the people under the mandate, that it refused them representation, and that it was imposing apartheid policies and laws in Namibia. The people were denied the right to political organization and assembly, and the mandate was supposed to lead them to independence and democracy, but in fact repression was increasing through the arrests of political activists and the denial of political rights. My recollection is that his statement lasted about five minutes and could have been longer and more detailed, but it came from the heart and that made it very powerful.

We then decided that sending the tape as an ordinary package would make it too easy for the apartheid authorities to seize it. Andimba bought a book, *Treasure Island* by Robert Louis Stevenson, and cut a pocket in the inner pages to hide the tape inside. Sent by post to New York, it ended up in the hands of Mburumba Kerina Getzen, who waved it around at the U.N. Special Committee hearings, the book in one hand and the tape in the other. Once the tape was sent off, I was waiting for something to happen. My concern was whether the way the tape was sent to the United Nations could be kept secret. A photograph of Kerina Getzen waving the book and the tape around at the hearing of the U.N. Special Committee appeared in the South African press. That blew our method wide open. But in political terms, what Andimba and his colleagues had done was very valuable because it demonstrated to the entire world the determination of apartheid South Africa to try to hide the reality of its administration of the trust territory as if it were a colony.

Andimba was declared an illegal immigrant and given seventy-two hours to leave Cape Town. He recalls that he left on Saturday, 4 December 1958, after being called in a day or two earlier. He was offered transport money but refused it. The South African Administration of Namibia sent him to Ondangwa in the north of Ovamboland, where he was under the control of a chief who carried out government instructions to harass him.

I was severely criticized, I believe totally unjustifiably, by my older comrade Ray Alexander Simons, a famous activist, for not getting clearance from a higher political authority to help Andimba send the tape recording. My attitude was that if a comrade came to me to ask me to do something, I was not going around behind his back to get clearance. Andimba was a responsible person working with other Namibians in Cape Town, as well as with Ray and her husband, Professor Jack Simons. Why should I have questioned his bona fides? And I would have thought that he had discussed every move with the comrades with whom he was working. I believed that we were trying to overcome apartheid racism so that people would be empowered. I did not feel that I had the right to question a comrade's activities. I felt that sometimes black comrades had a feeling that even committed white activists were themselves infected quite unconsciously with attitudes of racial superiority. I think it would have shocked us to hear this, but there were advantages of education, facilities like cars and telephones, and relative wealth that had to be overcome. That he had not discussed the matter with our comrades Ray and Jack Simons meant that he did not want to be stopped from getting his tape-recorded message to the United Nations.

Ray told me that Andimba had been working with a group who were going to support him in going back to South-West Africa, where he would have a little shop and then undertake underground organization. Ray said that sending the tape destroyed that possibility because now Andimba was being watched so meticulously and his work would be very difficult. As it turned out, the fact that Andimba had been ordered to leave Cape Town and placed under rigid restrictions established his credentials as a leader in Namibia by the very authorities who wanted to silence him. He was able to set up his shop. He withstood the pressures and was able to survive—and even under those conditions assisted in launching the People's Liberation Army of Namibia (PLAN). Indeed, it was a strange twist of history.

In 1968, when I was already in prison, I heard that Andimba was on trial for his activities with SWAPO and PLAN. He was sentenced to twenty years' imprisonment under South Africa's security laws, which had been made retroactively applicable to actions committed before the law was imposed in Namibia. That was a fundamental breach of democratic legal principle and another example of South Africa's abuse of its powers. Even more appalling was the way in which Britain and the United States of America protected apartheid South Africa from criticism and international action intended to terminate its illegal occupation of Namibia. Andimba and I did not meet again for some thirty-five years, when we were reunited in London in early 1985.

When freedom came to Namibia, Andimba, the father of SWAPO, was the secretary general and minister of minerals and energy. He held various ministerial posts thereafter and is now retired.

It was a great pleasure to be present on 27 March 2009 in Pretoria, when Andimba was inducted into the South African National Order of the Companions of O. R. Tambo by President Motlanthe. In a detailed citation the president summarized my comrade's role in the liberation of Namibia. The last sentence read: "Toivo had played a key role in freeing Namibia, and bravely contributing to the freedom that came to South Africa." That I was present on this occasion was purely coincidental because I was awarded the Order of Luthuli at the same ceremony.

Andimba turned ninety years old in August 2014. The Namibian government honored him with a celebration in the Independence Stadium in Windhoek during September. The state president and the prime minister were present among some thousands of guests to acknowledge the "father of the nation." I was happy to be there to see him recognized for his steadfast integrity and belief in freedom and democracy, which enabled him to endure unjust imprisonment and enormous difficulties. In free Namibia one might say that for a time he was out in the cold, but this birthday celebration bathed him in the warm sunshine of acknowledgment.

4

Political Activity, 1953–1964

Esmé was as active as I was, and we enjoyed working together. One of our early activities in the Modern Youth Society was helping to organize non-racial youth camps over the Easter weekends of 1954 and 1957. We felt it important for young people to be able to be together in defiance of the wrongful laws and regulations against such natural solidarity. We felt that people were going to have to defy these laws, and if we could detach whites from supporting the apartheid system we would help the process of liberation from racism. Simultaneously, all of us, of all races active together, were learning how to organize, how to mobilize, and how to get people to stand up against their oppression. I fear that sometimes we better-off whites thought we should be a "ginger group," getting people to stand up for themselves, to bear the brunt of the government's response to protests and defiance of the system. In our defense I have to say that we were trying to realize in practice the growing militancy of the ANC as it shook off its petitioning and sometimes passive response to segregation, now in its intensified apartheid form.

Modern Youth Society

In the Modern Youth Society we would go out selling the weekly *New Age* (originally the *Guardian* newspaper, then under names such as the *People's World, Clarion, Advance,* or whatever the newspaper was called after its various bannings). We would go door-to-door trying to get whites to support the policies of the Congress Movement. They would take one look at us and slam the door in our faces. When the Coloured People's Congress was formed, we would go out with them into Athlone, an area on the Cape Flats declared a Coloured Group Area. We carried on knocking on doors, trying to sell the newspaper and engage in discussion. Many people said they supported General Smuts, whose photograph from the war years was still on their walls next to a photograph of the British king and queen. They still had the vote under Smuts but not under the Afrikaner Nationalist Party, while the response to the Congress Movement was generally quite unfriendly.

So we set about trying to unite people. We also held night classes for working people to become literate—and politically literate: all activities that would raise awareness, consciousness, and solidarity. This was an area of political activity in which George Peake had come along before me. He became a leading trade unionist in the Building Workers' Union. Under apartheid, separate trade unions had to be formed for white and Coloured workers. It was not illegal for black workers to form trade unions, but it was illegal for them to bargain collectively under apartheid labor laws, which also prohibited them from undertaking skilled work. George played a leading role against segregation in his union, insisting on the age-old and valid policy of workers' unity, especially within a single industry.

Together with Ben Turok, Mary Turok, Amy Rietstein (now Thornton), Albie Sachs, and many others, we tried to live out our opposition to apartheid and the increasing racial separation of people. Among the things I was doing then and later was to reproduce leaflets and make posters, the practical things that made the words of other members accessible to the public. Only much later did I write a few pamphlets. One in particular that I remember working on with Esmé compared the Nazi race laws with those of apartheid. We leafleted audiences at the movie *Judgment at Nuremburg*.

During each of the long summer university vacations, I worked for an engineering company in Cape Town. The first time was at the end of 1950, and I earned a pitiful wage; but I did, in the process, learn what it was like to have to get up early and work long hours in a design office. One or two of the older men were helpful in teaching me the details of structural steel construction. Having failed to complete my studies at the first go in 1953, I went to work for the same company. Now, as an almost-graduate engineer, I earned a reasonable wage. When I asked for a Friday afternoon off in April 1954 to get married, they insisted I take a week's paid holiday, even though I had been there only a few months and had no leave due to me. This was fortunate because it enabled Esmé and me to be full-time organizers of our first Modern Youth Society Easter weekend camp for three hundred young people of all races.

This first MYS camp at Easter 1954 was important for Esmé and me. Just married, celebrating our wedding, and spending our honeymoon organizing a political event, we were always excited and very tired. Married lovemaking was free and careless, and Esmé became pregnant immediately. Our daughter, Hilary (always Hilly), was born on 24 January 1955. That made things difficult because I was so often at meetings and Esmé stayed home, very much alone, with our first baby. Then our son, David, was born on 24 November 1957. Like other families, we found time to go to the beach to enjoy the beauty of Cape Town. We were always able to find beaches and places on the mountain where we could picnic with our friends and comrades of all races. It was great to see our kids playing together, eating butter-smeared corn on the cob, the juices running all over their faces. But, in all honesty, I have to say that the burden of looking after the kids fell on Esmé because I was always too busy.

I loved finding the time to read stories at bedtime to try to encourage them to catch my love of books. Again, in the daily rush of making a living, doing politics, being with the family, there was time to decorate the children's bedroom, host nice birthday parties, and take the kids to visit their friends. Sometimes I stayed home with a bunch of six or seven kids, children of our comrades, while Esmé went with the mothers to some political event. I could manage a few hours of interest, but then my mind would wander to "grown-up" things, and I was amazed at how the mothers found the patience to keep their minds and conversations going at the level of their immature children for hours and days and years on end. It upset Esmé that I found it hard to wake up at night when the children cried because they needed their nappies changed or they had colds and could not breathe easily. She said I was not helping enough, but I simply could not wake up.

Besides being active in the MYS, I had also become involved in the local branch of the Congress of Democrats (COD), which was founded in 1952 when the ANC invited whites to become part of the Congress Movement. In Cape Town we coordinated the activities of COD, the ANC, the

South African *Coloured People's Congress* (SACPC), and the South African Congress of Trade Unions (SACTU) through Sunday evening meetings of our Joint Executive Committees, or JEC. Comrades such as Zoli Malindi, Bernard Huna, Reg September, Oscar Mpetha, and others who were in touch with many people through their organizations led the strategic planning of protests in the years of the intensifying apartheid legislation of the 1950s. We did not stop the laws from being passed, but we did build our mass organizations.

The African National Congress

Clearly, the ANC was the leading organization, which led to problems in the Western Cape. Barney Desai and some others felt that Coloured people should lead in the Western Cape because they formed the majority of the population there. Some of us, myself included, argued that the ANC was the leading organization across the country because the deepest exploitation and greatest oppression was of African people; therefore, they should lead. If Barney or others felt that the Coloured People's Congress should be the acknowledged leaders in the Western Cape because of the historical population composition, they would have to win that position by correct policies and hard work among the people. Most of us said political leadership was not a gift from above: it came through activity and policies that won the support of the people. That was our standpoint—and it wasn't always popular.

Fund-raising was another constant problem. Even though we had no paid officials, we had to pay for printing leaflets, hiring halls, and so on. We organized parties, those jolly, defiant events where people of all races could, illegally, entertain themselves together and raise funds at the same time. Gradually we had begun to function more and more carefully—for instance, by not using telephones even when organizing legal events because they might be tapped. Even though what we were doing was not illegal, the Security Police constantly harassed us, and we knew that they were building up their dossiers. They would go to employers and demand that activists be fired. If these were black workers, they could then be ordered to leave the area because, once unemployed, they would lose their right to stay in the city. So we tried to avoid exposing our activists and at least made the Security Police work harder for their information.

National conferences of the COD were held during long Easter weekends in Johannesburg. The train journey was lengthy, about thirty-five hours in each direction. But it was exciting to meet other members and be with comrades from the ANC and the Indian Congress. Every imaginable political topic was raised and discussed heatedly. Some members saw the COD as a socialist organization rather than as one allied to the ANC, which wanted to liberate all nonwhite people and especially Africans from their racial oppression regardless of their social class. It was really very difficult to unite these different tendencies and people and still maintain contact with banned comrades.[1]

The government sometimes acted outside the scope of its own laws. The courts declared that banning orders were invalid because of a legal technicality. The Security Police harassed banned opponents of apartheid, but they could not always get judges to take their side. Progressive lawyers prevented the Security Police from riding roughshod over the hard-won democratic norms of our legal system. One such case, based on a legal technicality, allowed Chief Albert Luthuli, the banned president general of the ANC, to speak at a meeting organized by COD in Cape Town. We would not accept the right of the state to remove elected leaders of our political movements. The apartheid state also deposed him from his post as an elected traditional leader of the Zulu people in the Groutville Native Reserve in Zululand because he was an active opponent of apartheid. Even after he was deposed, his people and we in the Congress Movement always recognized him as "Chief." In 1960 he was awarded the Nobel Peace Prize, the first African to receive any Nobel Prize.

The Congress of the People

In 1953 Professor Z. K. Matthews of Fort Hare University proposed to the ANC National Conference that a "Congress of the People" be organized to express the wishes of all our people in a Freedom Charter. This would point the way to a new constitution that would be democratic and inclusive of all our people in a nonracial political and legal system. The idea was adopted countrywide and organizing committees were set up in many parts of the country. I was invited to join the Cape Town committee, where Athol Thorne, who had great organizing and political skills, was the chairman. He had been banned from political activity, and that required great vigilance on our part not to expose him to the Security Police and get him sent to prison "for furthering the aims and objects" of an illegal organization. Despite such restrictions, we did whatever we needed to do to carry out the campaign for what would be a form of constituent assembly. The campaign for the Congress of the People involved some ten thousand meetings at which people put forward their demands for a democratic, multiracial society. The campaign was a serious challenge to the apartheid government to accept humanitarian values as the basis of our society instead of political domination by naked force.

The organizing committee assigned me to organize in Loyolo location in Simonstown. This was a squatter settlement in an old stone quarry, where people had built their shacks on the benches where the stone had been quarried. It was a terrible place. When it rained, the water cascaded through their homes. Sometimes babies would get washed away. I don't think today we can imagine how these people lived. There was no piped water, no sanitation, yet people found it better to live there than in rural poverty. The apartheid government wanted such settlements closed down, and it forced people to move into big locations, or townships, where pass officials and police could control the population more easily. Even though the conditions in Loyolo were so primitive, people wouldn't move, did not want to move, because they would have to travel long distances and spend more money on bus fares to get to work. In addition, they would have to start all over again to build their shacks. There was also resistance to government control over where they could live. I went to this settlement every weekend to help organize community members, who needed to get ready to elect their delegate to the Congress of the People, and to collect little by little the money needed to cover the delegate's costs.

At that time I was working as an engineering technical assistant on the state-owned South African Railways. I spoke at a meeting one Saturday afternoon. Two Security Policemen were there. On Monday I was fired. I was lucky! They gave me thirty days' notice instead of instant dismissal. It was all done very secretly; nobody would admit that there was political interference except for one official, a personnel clerk, who told me that my file had disappeared, which meant there was something politically very secret involved. He insisted that I should not see him again. And of course I was not to say that he had told me what had happened. People feared for their jobs.

I am sure I was fired because I was organizing for the Congress of the People. We did all we could to make the campaign a success: speaking at meetings and establishing committees in homes and factories to promote the idea of the Congress of the People as a Constituent Assembly and, of course, to challenge the hegemony of the apartheid government.

The people of Loyolo elected a young woman as their delegate. At the last minute her father objected to her going to the Congress of the People, to be held at Kliptown, near Johannesburg. He sent for me to explain why she was not worthy of representing the community. She had had a baby, he said. It was not unusual for an unmarried woman to have a child, and we all knew about her baby. In my youthful enthusiasm I failed at first to understand her father's objections. He was a traditionalist and she was a modern woman in the city. He objected to her not bringing the child home to the family to be looked after. He had only just heard that she had had the child and that it was being cared for by a foster mother who was also the baby's wet nurse. Slowly I grasped that it was that he felt robbed of his grandchild, not that the baby's father was not known to the family. I could not shake him. The people's choice of delegate was overruled and she did not go.

As it turned out, our chosen delegate from Loyolo was saved from a weekend in jail by her father's decision. The Security Police stopped our truckload of delegates from the Western Cape and held them in jail on some transport technicality to prevent them from getting to the Congress.

The Freedom Charter

On 25 and 26 June 1955 some three thousand delegates from all over South Africa gathered at Kliptown. On the second day the apartheid police raided the gathering to cut short this "provocative" event. The Freedom Charter had been adopted, however, and it became our political compass for the next forty years, until apartheid was defeated. It lives on in its influence on the constitution of the new, democratic South Africa, adopted in 1996.

The Freedom Charter was a marvelous document that really captured the voice of the majority of our people. The people actively participated in drawing it up, and that makes it quite unusual: such documents have often been written as manifestos by a small group of political thinkers who set down what they thought the people should have!

The opening words of the Charter are stirring: "*We, the People of South Africa, declare for all our country and the world to know:* that South Africa belongs to all who live in it, black and white, and that no government can justly claim authority unless it is based on the will of all the people." Implicit is the idea that white supremacy was the enemy, not whites as whites.

The ten clauses of the Freedom Charter proclaim what was necessary to create a society that would be inclusive of all our people, thus challenging the exclusivity that existed under apartheid. Line by line, the sections of the Charter define in broad terms the opposite of the inhumanities of apartheid in a quite poetic political statement. In brief, this historic document said, "The People Shall Govern!" All the people, and not just the white minority, must be free to elect their representatives.

That would already begin to change our social, political, and economic reality. It meant that all laws based on race or on national groups would have to be removed from our legal system, so that "All National Groups Shall Have Equal Rights!" Unless all could have equal rights, how would we be equal?

Economic exclusion had to be overcome, and so we had to ensure that "The People Shall Share in the Country's Wealth!" A great deal of controversy arose over this clause. Did it mean nationalization of all factories and mines, for example, or no private property, or other ways to include the excluded majority in the mainstream economy? It was left open for debate without driving away any particular tendency.

The theft of the land by the colonial conquerors was a particular sore point among the African people, who demanded that "The Land Shall Be Shared among Those Who Work It!" Africans were prohibited from owning land and were low-paid agricultural workers or sharecroppers. So this was a crucial demand. But did it mean distributing state-owned land, buying land for redistribution, creating cooperative farms, seizing all the land for collective farms or state farms, or restitution of land? Again, this was left open for future debate and decision.

Black South Africans and Africans in particular were ill-treated by our laws and our legal system, and they demanded that "All Shall Be Equal before the Law!" This and the next clause are logical consequences of equal political, social, and economic rights. Judges and presiding officers often presumed black people to be guilty before they had even heard the evidence because a white policeman had charged them and that was sufficient.

There were also special laws affecting each national group, to the detriment of African people in particular. The pass laws were the most notorious. To achieve this new South Africa our people said, "All Shall Enjoy Equal Human Rights!" to organize, to publish, to meet, to form political parties, and the like.

Equality had to mean that people could earn a living and not be excluded from the economy by laws and regulations, and thus the demand was that "There Shall Be Work and Security!" The economic system deliberately both excluded Africans from the economy and included them in controlled ways to ensure cheap labor in the mines, on farms, in industry, and wherever workers were needed to do menial work. This had to change. Social Security payments for the elderly, infirm, and incapacitated would have to be paid to all and not only to a minority.

Education is a key requirement in a modern society, and therefore "The Doors of Learning and Culture Shall Be Opened!" All our people had to have equal rights to education and not separate educational systems that offered great inequality for the oppressed: without education, the other rights to learn and earn and develop one's talents could not be realized. Languages and culture had to be treated with respect because without that there can be no dignity.

The squalor of urban slums and rural poverty had to be overcome, and so "There Shall Be Houses, Security and Comfort!" The enormous inequalities that compelled millions of people to live in awful conditions would also have to be overcome so that the historically oppressed would not forever live in shantytowns. But also the right not to be arbitrarily raided by the police was demanded. Despite all the harshness of life under apartheid and its denial of dignity, our people said, "There Shall Be Peace and Friendship!" Our people wanted to live in a harmony that was based on mutual respect and dignity, as well as an end to the domination by apartheid South Africa of its neighboring states.

The final words: "Let all people who love their people and their country now say, as we say here: THESE FREEDOMS WE WILL FIGHT FOR, SIDE BY SIDE, THROUGHOUT OUR LIVES, UNTIL WE HAVE WON OUR LIBERTY."[2]

These ideas have been the driving force of my life. How could I take part in organizing the Congress of the People, which produced such a stirring call to realize such a wonderful vision, and then not continue to be involved?

Our Congress Alliance organized thousands of political education classes to explain the meaning of our collective vision for the future. The whole campaign and its follow-up work were exhilarating and created a direct challenge to government. Membership in the ANC increased, and its status as the leading organization of the oppressed was clearly established, even though the Pan Africanist Congress (PAC), under the leadership of Robert Sobukwe, broke away because its members objected to the words "South Africa belongs to all who live in it." They said it belonged to Africans only. It was strange that many essentially white organizations and groups supported the PAC against the ANC, which said that by adopting the Freedom Charter whites had the right to live in this country. I believe it was more likely Cold War anti-communism among liberal whites that led them to this position. The PAC was antagonistic to the Communist Party in part for ideological reasons and in part because communists were seen as whites who Africanists believed would always dominate black people. For both liberals and Africanists the clause that said "the people shall share in the country's wealth" was antagonistic on the one hand to capitalist thinking and on the other hand to the Africanist belief that all those other than Africans—that is, whites, Indians, and Coloured people—were "foreigners" who should not have such rights.

The Treason Trial

At the beginning of December 1955 the apartheid government arrested 156 people, including almost all the leaders of the Congress Alliance organizations, and charged them with high treason. A special prosecutor, Oswald Pirow, was appointed to lead the state's case. Pirow was not only a right-wing Afrikaner nationalist; he had been a pro-Nazi activist in the time of the Third Reich. In a trial that lasted for more than four years, all the accused were eventually found not guilty. The number of accused was reduced in stages as the state could not present cases against some of them. Nelson Mandela really came to the fore at that time. He was the main witness for the defense and explained the policies of the ANC with outstanding clarity and conviction.

Large sums of money were needed to pay the lawyers in the defense team and to sustain the accused and their families for the duration of the trial. Understandably, our fund-raising was itself a highly political activity to mobilize mass support for the Congress Movement. The "Stand by Our Leaders" campaign was an outstanding success. Hundreds of thousands of people attended rallies to show their opposition to the apartheid government, which found the Freedom Charter a revolutionary threat.

I was sadly disappointed by the young, white professionals who had been fellow students at the University of Cape Town, a supposedly liberal institution. They refused to give financial support for the defense of the accused. The lawyers among them said that the accused had to be guilty because the government said so; and since the government also said the accused were communists, my former friends refused to contribute to the costs of a legal team. The usual social-democratic and liberal belief in the assertion that one was "innocent until proven guilty," and the rights of an accused to a proper legal defense by trained lawyers, as well as the duty of lawyers to provide that defense, had no influence on these people, who would have said they were liberal in their political beliefs. They were particularly hostile to any whites who were involved in the struggle for the liberation of black South Africans, saying that all the accused should be hanged. I wonder what they felt when the last of the accused were acquitted. I wonder what they feel now about a leader like Nelson Mandela, who has become an international icon of the struggle for the rights of all human beings, including my former fellow students.

Patrick Duncan, a leading member of the Liberal Party in Cape Town, rather opportunistically tried to woo elements who were once close to the the Non-European Unity Movement (NEUM). This was an organization founded in 1943, mainly by teachers, lawyers, and other professionals who emerged from Trotskyist organizations in South Africa. They insisted that they were the leaders of the oppressed people by virtue of their ten-point program for liberation. There were various splits, and the organization came to an end in 1957. Kenny Hendrickse lived near me in Lansdowne, and he became Patrick Duncan's Kremlinologist for the Liberal Party paper *Contact.* Kenny's opportunism was based on their both being strongly anti-communist, anti-Soviet, anti–Congress of Democrats (the white group in the Congress Alliance), and therefore very anti-ANC. In Kenny's case this was predicated on a Trotskyist view of the South African struggle's being determined by capitalist oppression of the working class, and no place being given to the national struggle.

Another Trotskyist in Cape Town was Kenneth Abrahams. He later married a Namibian woman, Ottilie Schimming, They were the first to distribute a SWAPO news sheet in 1961. They were among the first members of SWAPO and belonged to the political wing of SWAPO in exile. They left SWAPO in 1963 and joined SWANU and then SWAPO-Democrats. They moved even further away from their original beliefs and ended up with views akin to those of Emil Appolus, as Kenny Hendrickse did by joining Patrick Duncan's team.

The Congress Movement

The attitude of some Trotskyists to the Congress Movement was sometimes crudely stated: the Congress Movement always leads the people to defeat, but if one day the movement were successful in overthrowing apartheid, then they would join us. We were not impressed by that attitude.

To protest the Sharpeville Massacre in 1960 (see below, under "We can survive prison"), The Congress Movement called for a countrywide "stay-at-home"—a general strike. The Unity Movement actively opposed the call by the ANC. Boycott was their weapon, yet now they were boycotting the mass movement!

In a 1960 referendum, 52 percent of whites voted yes to South Africa's adopting a new republican constitution. Recently independent African states and India, together with Canada, were strongly opposed to South Africa's racist policies and laws. They refused Prime Minister Hendrik Verwoerd's request for the republic to remain a member of the Commonwealth, which led to its withdrawing in 1961 from the Commonwealth—before it could be expelled.

The ANC-led Congress Alliance had opposed the draft constitution. The issue was not that South Africa would become a republic, but that the basic premise of the new constitution was that there would never be equality between white and black in church and state. Of course, racism was built into the Union of South Africa Act of 1909, the British law that established the status of South Africa in 1910. But this new constitution was a direct rejection of the growing demand for a one-person, one-vote, system of full equality, expressed in the Freedom Charter. This would be a white South African Republic.

The ANC called for a stay-at-home, and the Unity Movement in Cape Town issued leaflets calling on people to go to work. Again they were boycotting the mass movement. We thought this was the most terrible betrayal. Many Unity Movement members also saw the absurdity of campaigning in behalf of the apartheid government and joined the Coloured People's Congress, which was part of the Congress Alliance. This change also signified an ideological shift in the relationship of the Coloured People's Congress and the ANC and Communist Party. The relationship of the Indian

People's Congress and the ANC was also moving to greater cooperation. All these things were going on at the same time.

The South African Communist Party

At the end of 1955 I returned to university to submit new laboratory and design theses and was awarded a B.Sc. degree in civil engineering in December of that year. In 1957, at the invitation of my comrades, I joined the South African Communist Party without any hesitation because it had a fine record of resistance to injustice in South Africa. It seemed to me to embody an understanding of both racial oppression, in the form of national oppression, and its relationship with economic exploitation. This came in a complex set of laws, social practices, and instruments of control of the population—together with apartheid's overarching and awful belief in racial superiority that sanctioned a grossly inhuman system. The newly reorganized party was functioning again, having dissolved itself in 1950 ahead of the coming into force of the Suppression of Communism Act, which made it an illegal organization. I was excited to become part of it because I was sure that our political activity needed to be guided by a coherent analysis of the nature of apartheid as a particular form of capitalist development and intensified oppression.

It was not easy functioning in an illegal Communist Party cell even though the other members, Amy, Albie, Mary, Bubbles, and Sadie, were all white, so that being together did not draw attention. Brian Bunting, our contact with the District Committee in Cape Town, however, was a banned person, and that made things difficult: he was prohibited by his banning order from meeting with any group of people. We would meet in somebody's car and conduct meetings at which we usually had discussions of Marxist theory and about the "mass work" we were doing. At last I found out why the members I was with had opposed without real discussion my proposals for action by the Modern Youth Society or wherever we were active at a particular time. They had previously discussed the issue and adopted a view or had been "instructed" about what their view should be. In later years I was in a cell with Elizabeth Abrahams, a great trade union activist from Paarl, some thirty miles from Cape Town, and Blanche La Guma, who lived in Cape Town. At that point it was even more difficult to meet because we were a group composed of different races, but our political activity continued.

Political texts were illegal, and so preparations for discussion were difficult. Hiding places for books and copies of articles on issues of Marxist theory had to be secure but accessible. The discussions would take place in the dark of night; we had to rely on our memories of the arguments and the conclusions. Sometimes we would meet to discuss a government "Blue Book"—for example, the Report of the Mine Wages Commission, convened after the great strike of 1946. Another was the final report of the Economic and Social Council, whose chairman was Hendrik van Eck. That report provided detailed analyses of the statistics of population, education, wages, and incomes of the various population groups. This report was published in May 1948, shortly before the National Party's victory in the parliamentary election in that year. One of the first actions of the new government was to disband the council because it was too "liberal" in its approach to the need for the removal of race laws if the economy and society were to develop.

As I describe later, in 1961 I joined the underground liberation army allied to the ANC, *Umkhonto we Sizwe* (Spear of the Nation), MK for short, to take part in the armed struggle against apartheid.

We Can Survive Prison: First Experience of Prison, 1960

The ANC had planned a massive anti-pass campaign to take place in 1960, but, in the midst of a heightened political atmosphere, the PAC jumped in ahead. On 21 March 1960, 20,000 people protested the pass laws at Sharpeville and in neighboring townships thirty miles south of Johannesburg. The peaceful demonstration mounted by the Pan Africanist Congress ended in a massacre. Police killed 69 Africans, most of them shot in the back, and a further 180 had bullet wounds. In Langa township in the Cape that same evening, 3 people were killed and 26 wounded when police opened fire. A general strike of African workers ensued. Chief Luthuli, president general of the ANC, called on the people of South Africa to observe 28 March as a day of mourning, which resulted in a massive stay-at-home and protests throughout the country. Whites were in a panic, and the government declared a state of emergency on 30 March, when 30,000 African residents of Langa marched on Parliament, which was then in session. This effectively led to the immediate suspension of the normal workings of legal guarantees against arbitrary action by the police and then to the Unlawful Organisations Act, under which the ANC, PAC, and other groups were banned: they were declared illegal.

Police and military units surrounded the townships in major cities. In Cape Town we had a meeting of our Congress Joint Executive Committees to plan to provide food for the strikers, who were holed up in the various locations (townships) around Cape Town. I returned home from that meeting on 30 March and was arrested at about three in the morning. I was arrested with many others and held in preventive detention for four months. Removing the political leadership was the government's answer to resistance to injustice.

I was taken to Caledon Square Police Station in the heart of the city and was joined by other comrades, among them Bernard Gosschalk, Gerald Goldman, and "Blizz" Storm. When we were taken to the charge office the next morning to be properly booked, the police sergeants shouted, *"Hier kom a klomp wit Afrikas!"* ("A group of white Africans are coming through!"), because we were a defiant bunch who shouted, "Afrika!" (the ANC greeting, given with a clenched fist), at every opportunity. I must admit that the black criminal prisoners who saw us coming looked at us as if we were mad.

The prison in Cape Town was gray and depressing. We slept on the bare floor and had to get used to the arbitrary behavior of the officials, regardless of their rank. On one occasion I was taken to the office of the head of the prison and noticed to my astonishment a black prisoner crouched in front of me under the officer's desk, polishing his shoes. They also put a prisoner who was quite unknown to any of us in our cell. That dampened our conversations because he was without doubt there as an informer.

During that 1960 stint in prison, I saw for the first time the effects of sleep deprivation on a detainee. Johnny Morley-Turner, already in his sixties, appeared at the door of our exercise yard while we were on parade for morning inspection. He was gray under the skin, his clothes stained yellow with urine from the waist downward. He appeared on the point of collapse. I broke ranks and went to support him, embracing him and taking him past my fellow prisoners on parade. The sergeant's jaw hung open and he angrily called to me. I ignored him and got Johnny to the showers, fetched him clean clothes, demanded hot water so that he could shave properly, and washed his clothes for him. He had been forced to stand until delirious from sleep deprivation, and his body functions continued. He seemed ashamed, and I suspect that he had said more than he would otherwise have done.

After graduating in the 1920s from the elite Bishops School in Cape Town, Johnny had gone to Sandhurst Military College in Britain. From there as a young sublieutenant he had been sent to Ireland in the Black and Tans to deal with the uprising by the IRA in its quest for Irish independence. He learned about imperialism and colonialism and, Anglican that he was, he chose to become a Catholic to show his support for the Irish liberation movement. He was shot and wounded by men of the IRA who, upon realizing that they had shot a sympathizer, carried him to safety. He was invalided out and received a lifelong military pension from the British.

Johnny's experience opened his eyes to racial and economic oppression in South Africa. During World War II he insisted on joining the army, even though he was half-blind in one eye, over the age limit, and still had a bullet lodged in his leg from the incident in Ireland. But he used his old-school ties to join the famous Cape Town Dukes regiment. He served in East and North Africa. By this time he had become a member of the Communist Party, as it was the only serious party opposed to racism and exploitation in South Africa. He became a sergeant and led his platoon into action with a red flag at its head. That was the symbol of his total commitment to defeating the Nazis. His platoon wiped out an enemy machine-gun post, and Johnny was "mentioned in dispatches" for his bravery. He trained his African troops, who were supposed to be unarmed auxiliaries, to use firearms. His motive was clear: every bit of firepower was needed against the enemy, and perhaps the men he trained would one day head a revolutionary army to bring freedom in South Africa.

Of course, he was stopped from doing this because white officers hated the thought of armed black soldiers. Johnny later also joined the Springbok Legion, a progressive organization of white soldiers, many of whom were communists. Johnny told me he had persuaded General Dan Pienaar (known as the "soldiers' general") to write the editorial for the first issue of *Fighting Talk*, their journal. Johnny was removed from active soldiering to become a guard in a prisoner-of-war camp where Italian prisoners of war named him "*sergenti sozialista*" because he insisted they sing "Bandiera Rossa" (Red Flag) or the "Internationale" before they could be served their main meal of the day. I talk about him so much because he was an inspirational figure for whom no task was too menial if it would advance the struggle for freedom. He really tried to live his beliefs within the confines of a society that disliked dissent.

My mother was held during these post-Sharpeville detentions in the women's section of the same prison as I, and, because I was insistent about checking up on her health, they brought her to visit me. I think we both tried to outdo the other to say how well we were coping. I should not have worried so much. Sarah Carneson, who was with her, later told me she was a marvelous companion who worked hard to keep up the spirits of the women she was with. Esmé was the one with the greatest burden, attending to both our needs for clean clothes and visits and a bit of pocket money. This became even more difficult for her when we were sent to separate prisons. She visited me in Worcester, eighty miles from Cape Town, twice a week and my mum at Bien Donne, near Franschhoek, also twice a week, some forty miles from Cape Town, on different days. She also had to work to support our children. Esmé managed somehow to be cheerful and to look after all of us. She even found a way of getting news to me through a kiss when I found a small something popped into my mouth. Later, when I was back in my cell, it turned out to be a "newsletter" written in tiny writing with waterproof ink on paper enclosed in a waterproof tip of a condom. My friend and comrade Alf Wannenburgh had done the writing.

This was an especially sad time for Esmé. My brother and his wife told her they would not look after our children if she was also arrested. This led me to break from my brother, who understood the nature of our struggle and yet was too afraid even to look after his niece and nephew if it should become necessary. What hurt even more, Esmé said, was that they said they were prepared to take in our dog. My brother also could not bring himself to visit Mum in prison, which would have given Esmé a bit more time to work and be free of long-distance driving. It was painful to refuse to have any contact with my brother. I simply ignored him and my sister-in-law when they came to take Mum to their home to mind their children when they went out. I suppose I should have told my brother why I rejected him then. Over thirty years later he and his wife wanted to know why, but I refused to discuss such old matters because they were too painful.

Esmé had a small inheritance from her mother and that helped to keep the family going. She was quite ill with a tummy bug when I was arrested, but despite this she worked even harder at her physiotherapy practice to keep the family going. My employers paid my salary for some months until after my release, when I was asked to leave. Because of her visits to my mother and me on four separate days of the week and the long distance she had to drive, her income was severely reduced and her expenses were increased.

Esmé told me that she and Andra Goldman, Gerald's wife, had had an amusing but stressful moment. The list of detainees was published in the press, as the law required. Our two names, however, had been combined to be Denis Goldman (or Gerald Goldberg). They were reluctant to get the matter sorted out because they feared that one of us might disappear. Esmé suggested that they share the one that had been named, but Andra protested that with her luck she would get the half that eats!

All in all, we were a cheerful bunch in our prison. With us was Harry Bloom, a lawyer who represented the South African Non-Racial Olympic Committee (SANROC) in its attempts to get our country expelled from international sport because of its racist policies. He was a good companion and at first had the only book among us, an action thriller, from which he read a few pages aloud each evening to entertain us all. Harry was also a published novelist and was able to spend his days working on the manuscript of a second novel.

There was an amusing situation, too, involving Jack Barnett, a noted architect, and his two staff members, the architects Bernard Gosschalk and Gerald Goldman, who were locked up together. Because Jack had government contracts to design a provincial library and a hospital, the two jailed architects were permitted to bring in their drawing boards and instruments to continue with their work. That kept the practice going and meant Bernard and Gerald could continue to earn their living.

For those who had to service mortgage bonds on their homes, being locked up without an income was a very trying experience. They really feared they would lose their homes if they failed to pay on time every month. I am not sure how it was arranged, but I believe the International Red Cross, through the South African Red Cross, persuaded the government to declare a moratorium on bond payments for those who were being detained under the emergency regulations. That was still a time when the local Red Cross was prepared to stand up to government to do its humanitarian work. The group organized payments of small sums of money to needy families of all races.

We organized political discussions, of which Jack Simons was an outstanding leader. Some others, who shall remain nameless, were less pleasant companions. Everyone in prison has some habit or other that others will find irritating. Living together in a communal cell with a dozen people makes for many tensions. Some took out their frustration at being locked up by turning against their comrades because there was little they could do against their guards.

Not much else happened during that time in detention. We expected to be interrogated, but few were, and it seemed to be more about getting their records straight than seeking information, though some were tortured. We went on a hunger strike to protest being locked up without trial. Bernard fainted one morning upon getting out of bed. Ever since, I have doubted the ease with which characters in the movies pick up wounded companions. My experience is that they are like a dead weight and lack lifting handles!

We were able to pass to our visitors a signed statement about the hunger strike. The report appeared in the press, but unfortunately there was no way the leak could have come from the prison officers, as the letter to the authorities was locked away in the CO's office when it appeared in the daily newspapers. That put an end to contact visits. We spent the time reading, debating political policies and theories, and exercising. I made toys for my kids out of the wood of fruit boxes and coffee tins, and so the four months passed. We were released a few at a time.

When I ask myself if that experience prepared me for my long imprisonment from 1963 onward, I have to answer, "Yes and no." Most of us realized that we could sustain being imprisoned and would continue with our activity against apartheid. But prison after we were sentenced in 1964 was a different kettle of fish: conditions were much harsher and went on for years and years—and the duration of the imprisonment certainly makes a difference, especially when there is no date for it to end, as is the case with a life sentence.

Some of our comrades left the country after the end of the state of emergency because it seemed we were in for much stronger suppression of protest. In the early 1950s people had spoken of South Africa under Afrikaner Nationalist Prime Minister D. F. Malan as a "Malanazi state." Now, ten years later, it was becoming ever truer. Being banned from professional activities meant that these comrades would not be able to earn a living. They felt they had no choice but to go, and some had been harassed enough. I am not too critical of them because I was beginning to feel that people give what they can of themselves at various times in their lives: courage and commitment are fluctuating things.

An example of this was somebody I admired: Sam Kahn, a lawyer, a communist, and a former member of Parliament who was elected by black South Africans in the Western Cape Province to represent them in the whites-only Parliament. I recall his speaking at public meetings, tall, well-built, and impressive, accompanied by Johnson Ngwevela, who was equally impressive and worked as Sam's clerk, interpreter, and political comrade. Sam spoke in English and Johnson in Xhosa with such mutual understanding that the two languages flowed together as in a simultaneous translation, anger and humor being faithfully rendered and points made virtually at the same time.

There were always debates about whether we should accept the token representation of Africans by a white M.P. It was agreed to and I actively participated in the election campaign because members of Parliament had a platform on which to expose the injustices of apartheid. Sam was an outstanding representative who spoke on every possible topic, getting daily headlines during parliamentary sessions on wages, the pass laws, workers' compensation, and race laws such as the Group Areas Act, the Mixed Marriages Act, and the Immorality Act. He always had something pertinent to say. He was expelled from Parliament in 1950 under the Suppression of Communism Act, passed that year. He fled to Swaziland during the state of emergency in 1960 to avoid arrest and from there made his way directly to London and exile.

His wife, Pauline, a medical doctor who had lived in our house when she was a student, left for London to join him when the emergency was over. Esmé and I went to say good-bye to her and their children on board the ship that would take them to Britain. I don't think Pauline was too happy about leaving because she urged me to join her going into exile. She said I would soon be arrested and should leave. She offered to pay for my ticket if I stayed on board. It was a tempting offer, but Esmé and I had discussed this previously and felt it would be wrong to leave when there were probably another three or four years of activity possible before the clampdown became too severe. We felt that we had come so far with our comrades, and, as we'd come through the state of emergency intact, we would stay. We got that estimate right: this was 1960 and I went underground in 1963, three years later.

What did happen to me after the detention was that I lost my job, thanks to the Security Police. At the time I was working for a construction company building the Athlone power station next to the Langa township in Cape Town. A bomb had exploded at my home shortly before the state of emergency was declared. I believe it must have been done with the connivance of the Security Police, who regularly kept an all-night watch outside. The explosion was reported in the press, and a manager in the company I worked for expressed his concern that the workers on the construction site might be less productive because they would think of me, with my political beliefs, as too easygoing. My response was that they would respect me more and therefore be just as productive as before.

Engineering Work

On the day of my release I went to the construction site to see when I could start work again. It pleased me when just about the whole African and Coloured workforce stopped working to welcome me back. If the Security Police had locked me up, then I was their hero.

Our chief engineer told me, however, that I had to see the resident engineer, who on behalf of the owners coordinated all the many contractors and with his staff ensured that the work was of high quality. He had ultimate control over the works. The Security Police toward the end of my four months in detention had written to him to say that I was a security risk: I should not be allowed to work there again because I might blow up the works. The resident engineer informed me of their confidential letter but said he could not show it to me. He then excused himself, leaving the letter on his desk where I could easily read it. The Security Police cleverly established that the letter was "legally privileged" because they had been asked for their professional and official opinion whether I was a security risk. I thought about seeking damages through a court action and discussed it with Jack Simons. He said that if I sued the police, the state lawyers would attack me as a revolutionary. To persuade a judge that I had been prejudiced by the police, I would have to deny my deeply held beliefs about the right of oppressed people to win their freedom, by force if necessary, thus denying my opposition to apartheid and all my political beliefs in a socialist egalitarian society. To kowtow to the apartheid authorities for the sake of damages in the form of money would make me a collaborator with their policies, and even then there was no certainty I would succeed in such an action. I gave up the idea. My employers gave me alternative work for a limited time until I found a new job.

I was fortunate in those hard times after the state of emergency because I was able to find work in my profession. Generally there was greater harassment of political activists by the Security Police. Charles Mokholiso, who lived in the Khayamandi township in Stellenbosch and had worked for many years at a factory nearby, was an example. He was charged in the Treason Trial and found not guilty. His employers showed no loyalty to him, and he was fired. I got him taken on at the construction site where I worked. The charge hand, a Coloured man who told me he was deeply religious and a deacon in his church, went out of his way to get Charles fired for being too old and weak to do the excessively hard work he gave him. I don't think that this was a case of Coloured-black racism because the same man fired a Coloured worker whose hands were covered in blisters from working without gloves smoothing concrete and having to scatter cement on the surface. Instead of finding him alternative work, the charge hand fired him. It was near Christmas, and the worker in desperation came to me for help. I was able to arrange medical care and wages under the Workmen's Compensation Act, but when he returned to work, the charge hand without any compassion gave him the same task of working with cement when there were several other options. Brutality takes many forms.

After I was fired, Jack Barnett introduced me to Basil Kantey, a consulting civil engineer, who gave me a temporary job working in Namibia on the preliminary work for the construction of sixty-two miles of road between Mariental and Assab. It was quite courageous of Basil because his work came mainly from the government and there could have been repercussions.

We would start work at six in the morning or earlier, when it was cool, and continue until eleven, when, because of the light shimmering from the heat, I could not continue with survey work. In those five or six hours we might see two cars, or a truck and a bus. Why build the road? Of course, as an engineer you know that once there is a paved road, there will be more traffic because driving is easier and economic development depends on roads for access. But it was also clear that these roads were being built on the route from South Africa toward the Angola and Botswana borders, and toward the border with Zimbabwe. The apartheid government wanted to be able to move police and military vehicles quickly. It was long-term planning by the apartheid state.

The state was also building the Hardap Dam near Mariental. The attitude of the German contractors toward the contract laborers was outrageous: racism at its worst, paying wages that no one could live on. I went to visit the site, and one of their top engineers complained that the workers did not work hard enough and were stupid. I asked the engineer if he were paid those pitiful wages, would he work? Of course he wouldn't. But, he said, they had signed the contract! Well, they signed the contract because they were ordered to sign it. Interestingly, white South African engineers were better in their labor relations with Ovambo contract workers than the German construction company was.

In the evenings, when I sat in the hotel having a drink, I would be verbally abused by South African commercial travelers. They said they knew (I wonder how) that I had just come out of prison, and they knew my politics, too. They said that I should know I would be among the first to die if the blacks were to rise up.

I designed a short stretch of road that ran through a military base at Cape Town's former Wingfield Airport. Driven there by a naval petty officer, a government engineer and I passed without trouble through cursory security checks. Sitting in a huge aircraft hangar filled with military hardware, we resolved security problems with an army captain. Bends in fences had to be removed. Machine guns cannot shoot around corners, so additional machine-gun and searchlight posts would be required, and that was expensive. Design alterations were agreed on, and the captain handed me a plan showing every detail of the security arrangements. I had to take it home, but fortunately the Security Police did not raid our house that night. It was a relief to stash it away in the office files the next day.

I became the resident engineer when construction started and had interesting security functions. The contractor needed a night watchman to stop military personnel from stealing tools from the encampment. After I arranged this with a naval petty officer, he insisted on showing me the security arrangements, which were a seemingly complex arrangement of keys hidden in various obvious places, though a hard kick would have broken down the door to their gun room. He offered me one of the automatic rifles so that he could show me how it worked. I kept my hands behind my back so that I would not be tempted to leave my fingerprints on the oily surfaces. Was he just being friendly as one white man to another, or was he setting a trap? Later, in 1963, after my arrest at Rivonia, I found out that not even the Security Police had that period of my work in their dossier. Such inefficiency we taxpayers were paying for!

On one occasion I had the opportunity to give the commander of the nearby air force base a lecture on security when he complained that we were inconveniencing his men, who repeatedly opened a security fence that we had to securely close at night. I relished the moment when, as a member of the MK Regional Command, I chastised an air force colonel for his men's lack of discipline.

I was still working for Basil Kantey's firm in 1963 when I disappeared into the underground. I can now reveal that I told him that I might have to appear to leave without warning, but I assured him that my paperwork was up-to-date. Brought to give formal evidence against me in the Rivonia Trial, he simply said I had disappeared one day but did not say that I had done so previously when there was a threat of a police raid and I had to be "unavailable." Cross-examined by Bram Fischer, he gave me such a glowing testimonial that Bram jokingly remarked I should use the trial record as my reference when looking for a job as an engineer.

5

Last Resort

Armed Resistance

After the state of emergency in 1960, when so many of us were locked up for four or five months in detention, there was a widespread feeling that we were moving toward a point where we would have to challenge the armed forces of the apartheid state. We were witnessing an increasing use of armed force—or the threat of it—to suppress resistance to apartheid. Peaceful protests brought increasing use of force by the police. For example, African women in 1953 marched to protest the pass laws being imposed on them. The government used its training aircraft to fly low over the marchers to terrorize them with the noise and knock them off their feet with the wash from their propellers.

Another example was the gathering of twenty thousand women in 1955 who went to the Union Buildings in Pretoria, the seat of government administration, to hand in a petition against the pass laws to Prime Minister J. G. Strijdom. Police dogs were set on the women in their finery, and some were thrown to the ground as the dogs ripped their clothing. The women's response was determinedly defiant, expressed through a song that said, in translation: "Strijdom, you have touched the women; you have struck a rock, you will be crushed." Similarly, when the peasants of Sekhukuniland in the northeastern Transvaal and of Pondoland in the Eastern

Cape organized peaceful resistance over land and the culling of cattle, more and more force was used against them.

In an ironic twist during the 1960 state of emergency, most of the Congress Alliance leaders were detained together, and many were on trial during the Treason Trial, meaning that they were in virtually continuous plenary session for months on end. Not only was there a growing closeness among them, but they also were able to discuss politics and the strategies needed in the months and years ahead to overcome the apartheid state. In many parts of the country there were sporadic outbreaks of sabotage, and there clearly was a need to control the situation. Should the policy of peaceful protest be maintained, or had its usefulness come to an end? Should the Congress Alliance succumb to the popular clamor? There is no doubt that the Gandhian concept of *satyagraha* was deeply entrenched in our movement, and many seasoned leaders, not ready to give up those principles of nonviolence, remained wary of taking up arms. We were influenced by Gandhi, but we were not necessarily in total agreement with him. The British could go home from India, but white South Africans would fight to remain in South Africa. This was recognized in the Freedom Charter, which stated that all citizens had the right to be there as equals. Others said that we had to lead this tendency to ensure that it did not become mindless terrorism but remained under political guidance against the institutions of apartheid and not against individual white politicians or civilians. Armed struggle was a method of struggle that would be added to political mass action, which was fundamental to the politics of the Congress Alliance.

Wherever I could, I argued for armed struggle. I had grown up during the Second World War and had seen how the partisans, operating behind the lines of the Nazi armies, had an enormous influence. There were also now wars of liberation in Cuba and Algeria, and though I could not always accept the idea that every means of struggle was legitimate, there was no doubt in my mind that in apartheid South Africa a principled war of liberation was necessary. I was opposed to acts of terrorism against individuals or arbitrary attacks on civilians; war was to be fought against the police and military forces of the state with the intention of showing that the minority white population would not be able to rule forever in the old way.

In 1961 the ANC called a stay-at-home against the proposed new republican constitution of the apartheid state. South Africa had been forced out of the British Commonwealth when the heads of government of the newly independent states demanded that South Africa end its racist policies or be expelled. Prime Minister Verwoerd withdrew from the Commonwealth before the country could be expelled and called a referendum among the white electorate to declare a republic free from British subservience. A "yes" vote would entrench apartheid because the draft constitution stated that there would be no equality between black and white in church and state. I was asked to go to Worcester, eighty miles from Cape Town, to carry instructions and leaflets to the ANC branch committee. I stopped at Comrade Ayesha Dawood's father's shop, as I did not know where in the township I would find my ANC comrades. Ayesha's brother hid me under sacks in the back of a closed van and drove me to the home of the branch secretary, Comrade Busa. He explained to me that the branch committee had decided not to take part in the stay-at-home. During the previous year's stay-at-home in protest of the Sharpeville Massacre, most of the ANC members had lost their jobs in the textile mills and fruit factories. Coloured people had in general not taken part in the 1960 stay-at-home and were rewarded with the factory posts that had thus opened up. African workers were destitute, and a call to a stay-at-home could not be heeded by the few who had jobs. The antagonism between African and Coloured people was a conscious strategy by the government to divide and rule the various population groups.

Because the protest would not take place, I had to return to Cape Town with the leaflets. On the way back my car faltered, and I was forced to stop at the high point of the Du Toits Kloof mountain pass. With the hood open, I was looking for what was clearly an electrical fault when I became aware of uniformed men around me. I was sure they were after me, but they turned out to be soldiers who were keen to help. They soon found the loose connection and sent me on my way. They would have been shocked to find the illegal strike leaflets in my car, and it would not have helped much being a white in that situation. It was a useful reminder to me about how in South Africa you had, almost daily, to overcome the fear of being caught, whatever your color.

Interestingly, Coloured people in the Western Cape who had heeded the Unity Movement's call to boycott the boycott in 1960 now deserted the Unity Movement. Many joined the Coloured People's Congress to take part in the stay-at-home. Now they felt betrayed by the African workers, who were not sure what support they would get this time. Divide and rule certainly worked for the apartheid state.

On the first day of the strike a comrade told me that some members of the Coloured People's Congress and Congress of Democrats intended to set fire to buses in the Golden Arrow Bus Company garage, which served mainly Coloured and African areas of the city. That would have ensured that workers could not get to work. But our policy was one of nonviolence. What a dilemma that was. I too had long been arguing for the commencement of armed struggle. But undisciplined actions could do enormous harm. Furthermore, I believed that political strikes required workers and the general population of the oppressed to stay at home out of conviction and not because they were caught between the hammer of militancy and the anvil of oppression. Hegemony comes from understanding and persuasion. Being forced to stay away could have turned even more people against us and toward the apartheid regime. I found where the Coloured People's Congress leaders were in hiding and asked them to send out people to stop the bombers from burning the buses. After a long discussion, they did stop them.

Massive force was used by the regime to suppress the general strike, and ultimately, after lengthy deliberation, it was decided that we should take up arms—and thus *Umkhonto we Sizwe,* MK (the Spear of the Nation), was founded by members of the ANC and SACP. Nelson Mandela and Joe Slovo, backed by Walter Sisulu, led the discussions. Though they committed themselves to follow the political policies of the ANC, they agreed that MK would be a separate organization. This was to ensure that not every member of the ANC would be deemed a member of *Umkhonto* because the legal consequences could be severe. Politically it was necessary for members of the ANC to choose whether they wished also to be members of *Umkhonto.*

In the spring of 1961—at a time of year when the usual strong winds have died down and the sun shines between rainstorms—I met one lunchtime with Fred Carneson on a bench in the Company Gardens near the National Gallery. We met there often, sometimes wandering through the gallery before or after our discussions. That day, probably in September, we sat on a bench enjoying the spring sunshine while we fed peanuts to the squirrels and doves. I don't know if any Security Police watchers guessed what we were discussing, but they would surely have liked to: Fred asked me to consider joining the newly established *Umkhonto we Sizwe* as a technical officer on the Western Cape Regional Command. He went through a lengthy explanation while I impatiently said, yes, of course I would join.

He insisted that I think about it for a while. I replied that he knew I had been arguing for at least a year for adding armed actions to our struggle.

I was soon meeting with Fred, Archie Sibeko, and Barney Desai to plot future action. Life was certainly getting more complicated: there were the "aboveground" activities in the Congress of Democrats, with support for the *Guardian* (or whatever the paper was named at the time), "underground" meetings of the Communist Party cell I was in, and now underground MK meetings. In COD I was one of a few older members who could attend branch meetings, because I was not banned from political gatherings under the security laws. I would meet secretly with our branch committee members who were banned and convey decisions to those branch members. After a time I began to feel that we were repeating in COD the style of work that I had resented when I first became politically active—that of being told what to do, when we were supposed to be an open, democratic organization. On the one hand, we did not want to give respect to undemocratic laws that banned our comrades from working toward a democracy and, on the other, we wanted to be open and democratic in our functioning. We also suspected that some of the new members who joined our branch were informers, and we had to protect our banned activists. But some of the new members were obviously genuine in their commitment to what we believed. They became committee members, and I dropped out of the COD branch Executive Committee but remained an ordinary member because, I said, I was too busy in my professional career. I obviously could not say I was too busy developing our illegal armed struggle to remain on the COD Executive Committee.

Then I met Naphtali "Tollie" Bennun, a chemical engineer who ran a leather tanning business in Port Elizabeth and, as an MK member, had devised various simple devices we could use for sabotaging buildings. Two carloads of us drove from Cape Town to Port Elizabeth, some four hundred miles away, to meet with Tollie and Jock Strachan, an artist and explosives expert, for them to show us how to mix unsuspicious ingredients to make high explosives—and chemical devices that would cut through steel beams and columns to bring down power lines and the like—and especially how to make timing devices.

This was at the beginning our activities, and we had agreed that we would avoid actions that smacked of terrorism by way of arbitrary attacks on soft targets. We aimed to go for hard targets only, buildings and installations, especially those that were directly connected with maintaining apartheid. Some of our targets were pass offices and other administration centers dealing with the oppression of Africans; power pylons, whose destruction hurt the economy without injuring people; and telephone lines, the downing of which disrupted communications.

Umkhonto was launched with simultaneous explosions in various centers around the country and the distribution of a manifesto pasted on walls everywhere. Essentially, the manifesto declared that for the oppressed majority there were two choices: submit or fight. We would not submit; therefore, we had no choice but to hit back by all means within our power, in defense of our people, our future, and our freedom. The government, said MK, had interpreted the peacefulness of the people as weakness; the people's nonviolent policies were taken as a green light for government violence against the people, without fear of reprisals. The manifesto asserted that the people would show that they could mobilize the force needed to seize power—but that they were, nevertheless, prepared to negotiate whenever the apartheid government agreed to do so. The statement was issued in the name of the "Command," whose commander in chief was Nelson Mandela.

I had rented a tiny flat in Rosebank in Cape Town as the base for our MK operations. To find one we could afford I had used the leasing agency of my own home, where I insisted, with appropriate nods and suggestive winks, that the agent would not make the mistake of contacting me at home about it. It was, I suggested, our little secret that I was renting the flat for "a friend." With the help of Alf Wannenburgh we prepared the devices in this flat for the sites that had been chosen for the first explosions on 16 December 1961. We took a bit longer than intended to clean up afterward and were late in delivering the devices. Our comrades waited. One device was planted at a pass office, but my timing device failed and it did not go off.

The second device was delivered to George Peake, who placed it at the back door of the prison on Roeland Street, where we had been locked up during the state of emergency in 1960. George was arrested as he placed the device. The police were waiting for him, and it was clear that he had either been careless or been betrayed—and we did not think that George was careless. The police would not let George disarm the bomb by removing the detonator, but luckily for him the sand filter device that I had devised as a timer had a much longer delay than I had planned. Had it worked properly, he would have been blown up. In the event, the detonator went off in the hands of a police explosives expert twenty-four hours later and did no damage. George was sentenced to four years' imprisonment but was allowed to appeal against the severity of the sentence and was, on the day that judgment was to be given in Cape Town, being driven to Botswana to escape when he was again arrested. In this case careful security arrangements had been made with a lead car in which a man we can call Orbri was riding with a walkie-talkie radio link to the car George was in. They drove into a police roadblock, where the police were waiting for George and there was no possibility of his evading capture. No warning was given to George's driver, who was captured with George. I was ill at the time, and Orbri came to see me to tell me about their adventures. I was sure he was trying to find out if I had anything to do with the escape. I gave no indication that I had been involved but listened carefully to his explanation, especially what he had to say about the failed walkie-talkie radios. It appeared that he had "forgotten" to extend the aerial on his transmitter. I was convinced Orbri had betrayed George. There were previous incidents in which he had been involved—and when Orbri was involved, people were arrested. We suspected that Orbri, who was white, had in the course of his new political engagement become involved with a young woman of color and succumbed to Security Police threats to expose his dalliance to his wife. He left the country soon after this incident. We did not have the resources to thoroughly investigate this betrayal. Had we acted harshly against the man, who might have been innocent, not only would we have perpetrated a great injustice, but the real betrayer would have been secure in his position. In practice, nevertheless, Orbri was isolated from further activity.

As part of our MK activities we organized training for our MK recruits on two evenings a week. At a trade union hall in Athlone we studied the history of South Africa, led by Achmat Osman. He was a brilliant teacher who had come over from the Unity Movement to the Coloured People's Congress during the stay-at-home in 1961. Addressing young adults who had little formal schooling, Achmat spoke simply, clearly, and excitingly about what had made the present South Africa. I taught electrical circuitry. Young people with no scientific training or any experience in their homes of the use of electricity were soon able to build simple circuits from pictorial diagrams. I also taught them how to make pamphlets on a duplicator, from writing the leaflet to cutting the stencil on a typewriter and making the copies. In addition, I taught first aid from the Red Cross handbook.

We also did physical training, which was led by Johnny Geduld, a well-known bodybuilder whom we had first met at our Modern Youth Society Easter weekend camp in 1954. That made for a bit of enjoyment, but we could not indulge too much in it because our recruits were all laborers who were very tired by the end of a working day.

On Sundays we had long hikes on Table Mountain, where we did some simple rock climbing, or to Mamre, a small village about thirty miles from Cape Town. All these outings were intended to build a team and to find out who were leaders and who cottoned on quickest to what we were about. Of course, a lot of breath was expended on political discussions and examples of guerrilla wars and liberation wars during World War II behind the German lines, and more recently in Cuba and Algeria.

We were a really disciplined and exciting group of young people, honest and meticulous about being on time and not missing out on any of our training sessions. That in itself showed that we were tapping into an attitude that was deeply rooted. To make certain that there was no hindrance to attendance, we paid for transport, but if we continued too long of an evening and some of the recruits had missed the last bus, I took them home by car. They accounted for every penny and returned what they had not spent. Our Sunday outings and hikes required good boots and money was provided for these, too. They were painstaking in telling each other and me where to go for the best and least expensive boots and returning the money they had saved in this way.

To finance the work, we held a fund-raising party at Cardiff Marney's house in Lansdowne, on the edge of Claremont. He lived near me, but I was in a white Group Area, and only a few streets away was the start of the Coloured Group Area, where Cardiff was compelled to live. We made organizing the party at his house into a disciplined exercise in logistics, planning meticulously what had to be done, who would do it, and at what time: who would set up lights and unload drinks and catering equipment; who would relieve whom on the door or serve food; who would be the bouncers, and how they were to deal with problems. Everything was planned down to who would do the washing up and packing away of whatever was left over, who would sweep and clean the house and grounds, and who would be the floating reserves so that posts would always be manned. The point was to get our recruits thinking and planning and being involved and disciplined. It was wonderful to watch, and we quickly raised the money we needed to cover the costs of the training, mainly political but with an eye to an underground military future.

What I enjoyed most was the tremendous self-discipline and enthusiasm of our recruits. Their hunger for knowledge was enormous. Ronnie Peterson, for instance, had an automotive repair shop, and we took the recruits there to learn about the obvious things one could do to get cars going when they broke down. There were often problems of blocked fuel lines and loose electrical connections, of dirty spark plugs and so on. Looking back, I think there were two important elements in this learning process: the young men were enthusiastic and therefore highly motivated, and we pitched what we were teaching at a level that made it interesting because it was accompanied by hands-on practical work.

This six-weeks-long training program led to the idea of a training camp held at Mamre at Christmastime in December 1962. I was the camp commander, though I was strongly opposed to that. I thought it important that Looksmart Ngudle be the commander and I his technical adviser. He could speak to all our recruits in Xhosa and English, and it was important in a struggle for liberation of oppressed national groups for people to have the self-confidence to lead and to have role models among the oppressed themselves. Our organizing committee—consisting of Achmat Osman, Cardiff Marney, Looksmart Ngudle, and me—decided that I should be the commander, but as always there was a way around decisions: as camp commander I made Looksmart the field commander. Later, during the Rivonia Trial, a witness spoke of me as the Comrade Commandant, and Walter Sisulu was very critical, obviously from an African nationalist point of view. I explained how it came about, but he was not really appeased. I think that what happened was partly a result of the history of divide and rule in the Western Cape; my Coloured comrades on the committee simply resorted to the argument that I was the best technically qualified to be the commander, and I could not convince them that they were evading the political issues.

While we were at the camp, a Christmas fund-raising party was organized by other comrades at our home, and Esmé played hostess. Our comrades stayed on after the party to keep guard, especially as a friend had been at the local police station to report a theft and had heard one of our neighbors complaining to the police, "That man Goldberg in Carbrooke Avenue is away camping and his wife is having a party with 'kaffirs.'" Therefore, our comrades expected trouble. Indeed it came, in the form of whites trying to force their way into the house and our comrades chasing them off. Luckily, they did not catch any of the intruders; I later discovered that our guards had made themselves weapons by taking a pair of garden shears apart to form two machetes. Imagine if there had been a serious attack and somebody had been wounded or killed. I didn't think we were ready for such things. We were also now certain, however, that our neighbors were the eyes and ears of the police.

The camp was an interesting exercise because we had prepared thoroughly for the thirty or so who attended. Menus were made with careful cooking instructions so that any team of four people could cook on open fires for the thirty people there. We made one error. The bread had been bought from a bakery for thirty people for ten days. That's a lot of bread! It was still warm when it was put into plastic bags to keep it fresh. We learned a hard lesson: warm bread in plastic bags goes moldy quite quickly. Cardiff Marney went off to buy more bread at the nearest store. We should have realized that would draw attention to us. Soon an official from the Mamre Mission arrived to tell us that we were camping on trust land without permission. He accepted our apology for the oversight. It was genuine. He became suspicious, however, and a few hours later the Security Police arrived. They took down the names of all at the camp and ordered us to pack up or be arrested. They also said that the young people should report to the police at a later date, after the holidays. One or two did.

The *Sunday Times* of Johannesburg carried a short item saying that the police had uncovered a military-style bivouac and investigations would be made. A top journalist, Stanley Uys, was instructed by his editor to find out more about the camp. He talked to Brian Bunting, editor of *New Age*, and Brian, guessing that I had been involved, asked me to meet with Stanley. I went along with Cardiff Marney and convinced Stanley that he should kill the story. He did—and we heard nothing more about it. Nevertheless, the camp was one of the things with which we were charged in the Rivonia Trial.

The camp showed that our young people were hungry to learn and devise for themselves ways of becoming a disciplined military force. We insisted that we should claim no easy victories; we should not lie to our people. We tried to tell our youth that armed struggle, though necessary, was no easy thing, and that some or many would be wounded or perhaps die in action. We did this indirectly by teaching the elements of first aid so that the sense of physical danger would be there. We insisted on discipline that had to be collectively achieved through the self-discipline that comes from commitment. But we also played games and had a lot of fun. Looksmart was a great leader of men and a great example. Hennie Ferrus from Worcester, a trade union activist and member of the Coloured People's Congress, was also a good comrade to have there. He later died in strange circumstances. I heard that he had been killed in a car accident that some suspected was engineered by government agents, though others dispute this.

"Mamre" among MK comrades has entered the history books as the first training center inside South Africa. Many of these young men were arrested and charged with offenses and afterward went into exile. I knew nothing of these later developments because I was myself imprisoned.

Some months later, Looksmart and I were waiting for Barney Desai to take us to a meeting of the MK Regional Command. Barney was late, and we waited too long in the nighttime shadow of a tree. Police officers spotted us and reported to their station, where our descriptions alerted the Security Police. We went our separate ways home, but the Security Police, knowing that Looksmart had to go home down the highway on his motor scooter, followed him and tried to force him off the road onto the gravel shoulder without actually hitting him with their vehicle. Looksmart told me that it was a very frightening experience. Looksmart himself was eventually killed under the Ninety-Day Detention Law in 1963.

When the Ninety-Day Detention Law came into effect, on 8 May 1963, I was instructed to leave Cape Town. I packed into a large cardboard box all the ingredients we had acquired for making explosive devices and stored it in a Pickfords public storage facility. I gave the rental papers to Fred Carneson, who said he would find somebody to pay for the storage, and, after a time, he would take the stuff out to dispose of it safely. As it happened, he was unable to find such a person because the pressures on us grew stronger. He destroyed the storage contract. During the Rivonia Trial, we tried with Bram Fischer's help to get the box but ran into a problem: Pickfords refused to release the goods without the original documents as proof of ownership. It did not help that I could not remember how I had signed the contract: was it B. Cook, or B. Cooke? I fudged the signature on the letter, but to no avail.

Eventually, Fred was arrested and revealed under torture the existence of this material. The police retrieved the box and it was used in the prosecution against him. He was able to show that he had no knowledge of the contents of the box. He claimed I had said it contained a collection of banned political publications and he had a circumstantial witness, Alan

Brooks, to this. His part in *Umkhonto we Sizwe* could not be proved. Since I was by then already serving four life sentences, there was little they could do to me besides make my life in prison even more uncomfortable. Fred was very fortunate: he was sentenced to five years and nine months for his political activity as a communist, but he was found not guilty on charges of being involved in sabotage, when indeed he was a member of the Western Cape Regional Command of MK.

Fred was, I believe, deeply scarred by the torture he endured under detention. Through sleep deprivation, he was forced to give away information that revealed many of the activities we would have wanted to keep secret. None of us ever blamed him. By the time he was arrested he had functioned underground on his own for a number of years, and sheer exhaustion made him even more vulnerable to pressure and torture during solitary confinement. The awfulness of torture is the self-loathing it induces: we all believed we were superhuman and no one could ever break us, but given enough time, torturers can break almost anyone. Underground activists are told—or should be told—that they should try to hold out for a certain minimum length of time so that their comrades have a chance to escape. It is, nevertheless, necessary to refuse to give evidence against one's comrades in court, where, for political reasons, the state cannot pervert reasonable criminal procedures.[1]

6

Underground in Johannesburg

May–July 1963

After the emergence of MK and also the African Resistance Movement, a group of liberal students and a few others who were opposed to the Congress Movement for ideological reasons, there were more than one hundred sabotage attacks across the country. The government, in response, introduced two savage new security laws, the Ninety-Day Detention Law and the General Laws Amendment Act of 1972, usually known as the Sabotage Act. The latter did away with the previous provision in our criminal law that an accused be considered innocent until proved guilty. Thenceforth, in a case of sabotage, the prosecution needed to show only that the accused might be guilty, leaving the onus of proof of innocence on the accused. Proving innocence is much more difficult, and the state was clearly determined to give the police and the prosecutors the advantage. Upon a guilty finding, a court had now to impose a minimum sentence of five years' imprisonment and could impose the death penalty.

The Ninety-Day Detention Law enabled the Security Police to detain a person for ninety days without bringing him or her before a court of law within forty-eight hours of arrest (as had previously been required), thus overturning the courts' ordering the state to "produce the body," the South African equivalent of habeas corpus. In addition, the prisoner had no right to visits from family, friends, or lawyers, and the period of detention could be repeated indefinitely. The law stated that its purpose was to compel detainees to answer questions to the satisfaction of the police. This was clearly a licence to torture, and it included the probability that confessions and evidence extracted under duress would result in almost automatic conviction because of the virtual impossibility of proving innocence.

The minister of justice and police, the infamous B. J. Vorster, later the president of apartheid South Africa, promised that people could be held in prison to "this side of eternity" by means of repeated periods of detention.

We held a protest near Parliament when the Ninety-Day Detention Law was being passed. The protest centered around a mock gallows with three hanging figures, each with a slogan: "I gave out a leaflet," "I spoke against apartheid," "One person one vote." They illustrated that the draft bill provided for the death penalty, not only for sabotage but also for democratic protests, such as those we depicted. On top of the gallows were two large cardboard vultures, one with the face of Prime Minister Verwoerd, the other of B. J. Vorster, the minister responsible for the new legislation.

The detention law was set to go into effect on 8 May 1963. My contact in the Communist Party, Brian Bunting, and my contact in *Umkhonto*, Fred Carneson, both insisted that I leave the country because it was considered a certainty that I would be arrested immediately. They were sure that even if I did not break under ninety-day detention and probably torture, others would. They argued that I would be tried and sentenced; they thought I would get at least ten years in prison. I could not argue against their assessment of the possibilities and had to decide what to do. I wanted to go underground in Cape Town, but my hometown was difficult because it was about fifty miles long and only a few miles wide. To avoid arrest I would need safe houses all over the place, and I couldn't find enough of them.

The intention was that I would leave the country, get training in sabotage and as an underground activist, and acquire a new identity so that I could later return in a different guise. We had a rule that nobody would leave without clearance from the next highest level of the organization. I would therefore need to pass through Johannesburg to get clearance from our High Command.

For a few days before leaving I stayed in hiding with Reverend Ian Eve, an Anglican priest, and his wife, Shirley, so that I could leave without being trailed by the Security Police, who were often staked out in front of my home. I slipped into our house through a hole in the back fence to say good-bye to Esmé, Hilly, David, and my mum. Both children were asleep when I kissed them, but Hilly half-woke and embraced me.

It wasn't easy to leave everything behind, but by going away I did have a chance of not ending up in prison. I had told Esmé that I was leaving the country but did not tell her by what route. I said I would find a way of getting her to join me in Europe. I disliked not being completely open with her, but, for her safety and mine, it was better that she could honestly say that she did not know where I was going. For the same reason I had not told her that I was involved in MK. During this period I needed our car to get to meetings at night and would say without explanation that I needed it on a certain evening. I did not say whom I was meeting or for what purpose. "What you do not know you cannot talk about." That had to be our joint understanding because Esmé was not always sure about my activities, and it would have been a betrayal to have used the necessary secrecy as a cover for an affair. The stress and the excitement of underground activity certainly created a sexual tension and the opportunities for such relationships. To bolster the fictions, she invented a blonde girlfriend in Camps Bay, which was a long way from where we lived.

It was difficult to go abroad because there was no knowing when we would be together again, yet there was considerable excitement about the adventurousness of it all. Where would I go? Who would I become? All I knew was that I was on the brink of becoming a professional revolutionary.

I left on 7 May 1963 to go by the night train to Johannesburg. Jack Leibowitz, a longtime friend, met me in secret under a tree in a churchyard in Claremont to take me to Bellville by car so that I did not have to board the train at the main railway station in the center of the city. In the same way, as the train was nearing Johannesburg, I got off at Krugersdorp, a town some twenty miles outside Johannesburg. I then took a local commuter train into the city, where I simply disappeared.

A day or two later Joe Slovo met me at the Skyline Hotel in Hillbrow, quite a fashionable place in 1963. Joe asked me to stay to investigate the manufacture of the weapons we would need. Since I had left Cape Town because I could no longer function politically, I immediately agreed to stay. I was relatively unknown in Johannesburg, and we thought I would be able to work effectively. I stayed at the Skyline for a few days. Then I stayed sometimes at Liliesleaf Farm in Rivonia, a northern suburb, and other times at a place in Mountain View, in a small suburb not far from the center of Johannesburg, which belonged to Comrades Leon and Maureen Kreel, who were of the same family as Sadie Forman, the widow of the late journalist Lionel Forman. They were brave, unassuming people who knowingly put themselves in harm's way to help the cause of freedom in South Africa. Maureen's sister Minnie and her husband, Ralph Sepel, cared for Walter Sisulu when he went underground. She would drive him wherever he needed to go and sometimes dodged police roadblocks to keep Walter safe. Maureen and Leon were arrested after it was discovered that Arthur Goldreich and Harold Wolpe had been hidden in their garden cottage after they escaped from detention.

They were able to convince the court that we had imposed ourselves on them and whoever had used the garden cottage had done so without asking them. I am happy that they were acquitted.

Even though I was relatively unknown in Johannesburg, it quickly became clear that things are never simple. For instance, having moved to the Kreels' garden cottage, I had to buy household goods so that I could be self-sufficient. One morning as I emerged from the OK Bazaars, a large department store in Eloff Street, then the busiest shopping street in South Africa, carrying boxes of goods that hid most of me from view, a car swerved to a stop in front of me. My dear friend and old comrade Basil Jaffe, who lived in Cape Town, leaned over from the driver's seat and greeted me by name. He had known me since my childhood and saw through my disguise in a moment. Of course, he knew I had left home because he had lent me the money to pay for the train fare.

Before I had become deeply involved in MK in Johannesburg, I had Sunday lunch at Doney's Restaurant in Hillbrow, quite a swish place with hostesses who led one to a table and took the orders. I settled for a platter of rock lobster tails with salad, beautifully presented on a large silver platter. As the waiter set it down in front of me a family of four, two adults and their young children, stood up to watch this feast arrive. I felt very conspicuous, and that memorably luxurious meal stayed in my mind for all the years of imprisonment and for years thereafter—and even now, more than fifty years later, I can see it still in my mind's eye and savor the flavors that were so deliciously different from the prison food I endured for twenty-two years.

It really was as exciting as I'd imagined it would be. I was a full-time revolutionary. I felt invincible, on the brink of something great. There was a constant rush of adrenalin. In the midst of it all, there was time to buy the materials to set up the antenna for Walter Sisulu's June 26 Freedom Day radio broadcast. Lionel Gay, a Witwatersrand University physics lecturer, had built our radio transmitter, and Walter was to make the first broadcast of the ANC "from somewhere in South Africa." He had been convicted of furthering the aims of the illegal ANC and was out on bail. In the face of continuing arrests under the new laws, there was a need to tell the people that the ANC was still in action and that Walter Sisulu, the secretary general of the ANC, though banned and unable to attend public meetings, was still inside the country and organizing against apartheid.

The speech was inspiring and brave, a defiant call to unity in the face of tremendous oppression by the apartheid state. It spoke of the need to fight state violence with violence and explained that the ANC leadership had gone underground to keep the organization going. It was a call to sacrifice: "We call upon all our people, of whatever shade of opinion. We say: the hour has come for us to stand together. This is the only way to freedom. Nothing short of unity will bring the people their freedom. We warn the government that drastic laws will not stop our struggle for liberation. Throughout the ages men have sacrificed—they have given their lives for their ideals. And we are also determined to surrender our lives for our freedom."

The broadcast also showed that we could use modern technology to reach our people. It created a stir throughout the country and was widely reported.

We had quite a discussion about how the broadcast was to be done. We insisted that Walter make a tape recording of his speech so we could avoid the risk of taking him to the transmitter in a house in Johannesburg. I was to operate the transmitter, and I thought that the speech—written by Walter, Govan Mbeki, Ahmed Kathrada, and others—was much too long. At forty-five minutes, it would give the police too long a time to find the transmitter—and me! During the Second World War, for example, counterespionage units, on all sides, monitored radio frequencies and were able to locate an enemy transmitter within a few minutes. In our case we would have to inform our comrades all over the country about the time and frequency of the broadcast, so it was highly likely that the Security Police would also know about it in advance. Therefore, the speech needed to be much shorter, but as the police were, I hoped, as inexperienced as we were and would not know in advance in what part of the country the transmitter was located, I reckoned a ten-minute speech would be safe. Some of the comrades were unimpressed with my argument, even though it was based on real technical knowledge—they wanted at least double that time. Walter, always reasonable, said that I was the expert and he agreed with me—but could he have fifteen minutes? That was agreed on.

The aluminium poles for the antenna were painted black so that they would not reflect stray light when pulled upright for the duration of the broadcast. Everything was laid out ready at the Parktown home of Fuzzy and Archie Levitan, comrades who had long before dropped out of open political activity, and in their cellar Harold Wolpe had installed his intelligence headquarters with light tables for copying maps. Ruth Finkelstein, a new recruit to our ranks, prepared detailed studies from topographical maps of where state broadcasting facilities, power stations, and distribution substations were located and, of course, the sites of various institutions of apartheid administration, such as pass offices and "Native Administration" offices, which were the obvious signs of apartheid rule.

Ivan Schermbrucker and Cyril Jones, two former Second World War soldiers and good comrades, were my sentries for the night of the broadcast. They were armed with only one pair of walkie-talkie radios and a flashlight to warn me if police were nosing around. Everything went well that night, 26 June, and as soon as the broadcast was done I shut everything down, took down the antenna, and went off to the cinema.

I was much too wound up and needed to be distracted. Because I was underground, I could not seek out friends; I had to stay away from people who knew me. I had to be on my own. I went to the movies. By chance the film was *Square of Violence,* about a Second World War reprisal by the Gestapo who massacred every tenth man in an Italian village in retaliation for the killing of one German soldier. I kept the ticket I had bought and it was still in my pocket at the time of the Rivonia raid. Though the ticket was not of great importance, it did seemingly provide me with an alibi for the evening, though the police luckily did not ask me about the early part of the movie program because I arrived there only at the intermission.

We needed new places to stay for MK and the ANC, and I was asked to find a small farm of a few acres outside Johannesburg. In those days, even a few miles outside the city, the land was mostly rural and undeveloped. I found what we needed on the border between Johannesburg and Krugersdorp. It would enable us to set up the manufacture of explosives and the casings for hand grenades and land mines, camouflaged as a small chicken farm with a house suitable for five or six people. That meant we also needed a new vehicle so that I could move our leaders, such as Walter Sisulu, Govan Mbeki, Raymond Mhlaba, and Wilton Mkwayi. I bought a Volkswagen minibus, which raised a new set of problems that gangsters seem to ignore but I felt we had to overcome. Vehicles have to be licensed. If you are involved in an accident, you do not want the police coming to where you are living underground. Who knows what they might find? The same applies to traffic offenses. I took a room in a boardinghouse and told the landlady that I traveled a lot and would only occasionally be there to sleep. Little did I know that she had an eagle eye and knew exactly when I came and went, and if I had really slept in my bed or merely ruffled the bedding. She was later a witness at our trial.

I got a shock when, trying to find somewhere unobtrusive to get our hand-grenade casings professionally made, I went to a rather dilapidated old foundry, trying to disguise my purpose. The foundry man took one look at my sketch and immediately said he could produce the 210,000 we required within the stipulated six weeks. After a pause, he added that he had produced 15,000 hand grenades a day during the Second World War. Because we were not yet ready and because we were trying to find out if we could produce them ourselves, we did not get around to placing that order.

I also inquired at a wooden-box factory about the planks we would need to make up the 48,000 land mines we wanted to distribute around the country. I needed to give an address for the quotation because the owner implied that he thought I was involved in commercial espionage. He needed to know that I was a genuine buyer. I gave him my false name, Charles Barnard, and the address of Esmé's old school friend Nana Wynberg. Away from my own family, I needed to share normal family life, and I visited Nana and her husband, Dave, a few times, especially for their daughter Rebecca's fifth birthday party. The factory boss later gave the police Nana's address and became a witness in the trial. Nana was also brought to court to give evidence. She was very embarrassed, which I think was as much the prosecutor's intention as was his need to complete a chain of evidence. Walter Sisulu urged me to greet her with a smile to show that her giving that little bit of evidence was not an awful thing to do. She seemed almost to faint with relief and gave a broad smile in return.

We never did make the hand grenades and land mines.

7

Arrest at Liliesleaf

On 11 July 1963 I was sitting in the living room of the Liliesleaf farmhouse reading Robert Jungk's *Brighter Than a Thousand Suns,* the story of the first atomic bomb dropped on Hiroshima in August 1945. My comrades were in the thatched cottage, one of the outbuildings, at a meeting of the *Umkhonto we Sizwe* National High Command and its political advisers when the Security Police arrived and arrested all of us. I could not see what happened to the other comrades, but some jumped out of windows and ran for it, only to be confronted by armed police with attack dogs. It was a dreadful moment. I felt deeply disappointed that we had been stopped in our tracks. Our preparations for intensifying the struggle for freedom were going to come to nothing.

It was a cold winter's day and suddenly it felt much colder.

Liliesleaf Farm was the temporary underground headquarters of *Umkhonto we Sizwe* and had been lent to us by the Communist Party. Arthur Goldreich, with his wife, Hazel, and two young children, Nicholas and Paul, were the apparent owners. Arthur, an artist, a designer of stage sets and of department stores, was an activist in MK who had been sent on a mission to the Soviet Union and China to investigate preparations for increased sabotage and eventual guerrilla warfare. He played with relish the role of a member of the northern suburbs' elite "huntin', shootin', and fishin'" social set.

Nelson Mandela had previously lived in hiding at Liliesleaf. He had been the one who called for the strike in protest against the Declaration of the Republic in 1961. He had left the country without a passport to meet political leaders in Africa to investigate the possibilities of support for an armed struggle against the apartheid regime. Upon his return, he traveled the country in disguise, reporting on his trip to leadership groups of the Congress Movement and the Communist Party. He had been betrayed and arrested at Howick in Natal Province and sentenced to five years in prison in October 1962 for incitement to strike and for leaving the country illegally. His arrest did not lead the police to Liliesleaf Farm.

I was a member of the High Command's Logistics Committee, instructed to investigate and make the weapons and explosives we would need to implement Operation Mayibuye (Operation Come Back Africa) if it was adopted, to advance from sporadic sabotage attacks to a sustained armed uprising. The plan envisaged seven thousand armed guerrilla fighters inside South Africa making ready to receive our returning fighters, who were being trained in the People's Republic of China, the German Democratic Republic, and the Soviet Union. In our Logistics Committee we had discussed the feasibility of this plan. We knew it would be very difficult to implement in a short space of time. For example, how do you provide for the feeding and clothing and general care of seven thousand men? Where would we get the weapons and the ammunition? We were very inexperienced in military matters, whereas the state was really well prepared. But the armed struggle, if unsuccessful at the start, would continue, at least as armed propaganda against apartheid and economic installations, thus mobilizing the people to the prospect of political and worker action against the system. In time we would build our fighting capacity. As was the case in the period after the massacre at Sharpeville, our people were subjected to increasing state violence and wanted protection. Sabotage attacks would inspire our people to renewed mass political action.

There was disagreement on the High Command as to whether Operation Mayibuye had been agreed on or not. Joe Slovo, Govan Mbeki, Raymond Mhlaba, and Wilton Mkwayi insisted that it had been. Rusty Bernstein, Walter Sisulu, and others, including Bram Fischer, wanted further discussion. Joe was insistent and had made arrangements to go abroad to arrange for external support for the operation. He left a short time before we were arrested. Joe Slovo was a cofounder of MK with Nelson Mandela. Rusty was a longtime communist, political writer, and thinker who had among many other activities drafted the Freedom Charter. All these comrades either were on the High Command or were political advis-ers. Even among such close comrades, who had known each other and had worked together for years, arriving at joint decisions was no simple or auto-matic process.

Joe argued in favor because, even though there are no significant for-est areas in South Africa, the Boers had fought the British for four years in a guerrilla struggle in the Second Anglo-Boer War at the turn of the twen-tieth century. Rusty said that for those opposed to the plan that was true, but the Boers had been beaten by a more powerful state, Great Britain, with troops and resources from its worldwide empire. We could expect the powerful Western states to support apartheid South Africa. One could of course argue that the Soviet bloc would be there to support our struggle and thus might neutralize the West. Look at Cuba, for example. Wilton Mkwayi, later, in prison, told Ahmed Kathrada that he and Ray Mhlaba would have beaten him up if he had continued to oppose Operation May-ibuye. They have passed away and I cannot ask them if they would really have sought to resolve such an issue by violence against a comrade, or if the thought was an expression of their frustration at not being able to convince him of the validity of the plan. In the end this argument was not resolved because we were arrested.

In 1963 at Rivonia, before our arrest, the disagreement over sending everyone away for training continued. History—and our common sense—told some of us that an armed liberation struggle was a political struggle that required support from the masses if it was to succeed. Where there is no jungle for the guerrillas to hide in, it is the people who must become their jungle, hiding them, supplying them, and supporting them in every way. In later years we saw that isolated acts of violence did not develop mass support. The Red Army Faction in Germany, the Italian Red Bri-gades, and Che Guevara's guerrilla incursion into Bolivia all failed because of this fundamental inability to win the support of the people.

While there was agreement in MK on the general idea of an armed struggle, how to move forward was less clear. My own view and that of our Logistics Committee was that we would need weapons and explosives, and therefore I would set about making them and training others how to do so. The "militarists," as I thought of them, despite their long political cam-paigning history, or because of it, were impatient and determined to launch an armed uprising. There is a difference between adding a component of armed struggle to a political situation such as the one we confronted and believing that the answer lies in military action alone. I consider myself not a militarist but a political activist for whom armed struggle is a particular kind of political activity.

There was a complicating factor because the leaders who found themselves at Liliesleaf Farm were members of the executive committees of the ANC, SACP, and MK and also had trade union roots. The effect was that viewpoints and decisions made for one of those groups then became decisions of the other groups in the liberation movement. That was why discussions with other members who were not underground—Bram Fischer and Rusty Bernstein, for example—were so important. But the ideas developed a momentum of their own. Ahmed Kathrada, tasked by the Communist Party with ensuring the security of Liliesleaf Farm, was unable to get the others to follow the rules about who might be allowed to visit the farm for discussions. He was adamantly opposed to the grand ideas being advanced.

Many young people fled the country, and the training of fighters abroad continued in the new situation. Ultimately, we had many thousands of trained and armed soldiers based in Angola and Mozambique. Even though they were not able to return in large numbers to wage war, there were some spectacular special operations. More strategically, the presence of these armed forces required the apartheid state to wage war on its neighbors, especially Angola, to stop our MK warriors, together with the People's Liberation Army of Namibia (PLAN), from wresting that country from South Africa's occupation. That in turn would have opened huge lengths of frontier from which to attack and also to use as routes for infiltration.

The same is true of independent Mozambique and the other "frontline states." The effect was to drain the apartheid economy because of the size of the armed forces that had to be maintained. In addition, every young white man had to do military service of two years and then a further part-time total of two years. Soldiers eat but do not produce, and that results in huge inflation. In the end, apartheid South Africa was bankrupted by trying to maintain itself in the face of our multipronged, sustained attacks of political, trade union, international isolation, and military action against the system.

Ultimately, the cost in human lives of young whites killed or maimed in the operational zone in the neighboring countries caused huge demoralization among apartheid supporters. The battles in the streets of South Africa's black townships, in the face of the political uprising of our people, compelled the apartheid state to recognize that it could not continue with its policies. The forms of struggle changed throughout the thirty years after our arrest, and the argument about Operation Mayibuye is of historic interest now. It is a matter of pride for us, the old veterans, that we made the transition from a purely peaceful politics, of pleading and protest, to a politics that included the armed struggle, together with all the forms of internal political campaigning and mass action, as well as international solidarity.

The last meeting of the High Command at Liliesleaf was one too many. It took place there because Rusty Bernstein, who was a longtime activist and represented the Communist Party on the High Command, was subject to a house arrest order. He had to report to the police between twelve and one o'clock every afternoon and be home by six o'clock on weekdays and by one o'clock in the afternoon on Saturdays, Sundays, and holidays. At the previous meeting, held on a Saturday, the members could not agree on another venue. Rusty had to leave or face imprisonment for not being home in time. As a last resort they agreed to meet at Liliesleaf one last time. Walter Sisulu also had a reason for being there. He had a distinctive gap between his front teeth, and his disguise required a denture to be made to change his appearance. Arthur Goldreich arranged for his brother-in-law Reeve Arenstein, a dentist, to meet Walter on that fateful day at Liliesleaf. He took the dental impressions and left.

We had earlier made the decision not to bring people who were not living underground to the place where others were living in hiding. Too many people did not adhere to this decision and knew of or had been to Liliesleaf Farm. The security risks increased. We urgently needed a different place, and the task of buying somewhere new had been given to me because I could as a white person legally buy property. Walter, Govan, Raymond, Wilton, and I had moved to the new dwelling in the Travallyn Agricultural Holdings. It was a quite remote area in the Krugersdorp district, lined with narrow country roads, which served our purposes because there was little passing traffic. We were insistent that no others be brought there. This created a problem of where to meet with those who were aboveground. It was important to maintain contact because it was too easy for those underground to become an isolated clique, out of touch with reality and the others.

Rusty had seen unusual activity at the local police station when he drove by, and so had I when we drove past it in our new minibus, with its pretty blue curtains hiding my important leaders from view as we drove from Krugersdorp to Liliesleaf in Rivonia. What we had seen was a rather shabby-looking van and a few civilians outside the police station and thought nothing of it. In fact, it was the Security Police in a van marked "Laundry," and they were preparing to raid us.

To this day we are not sure how the police found us at Liliesleaf—and even though "we" now control the records and archives of the security forces, nobody has revealed the details. Who knows? It was and is all very strange. What is interesting is that our National Intelligence people, who are our comrades, will not reveal how we were caught. I am sure that the information would all have gone into the files. Intelligence agencies are secretive by nature and do not want to be seen to be leaking information. They want their own operatives to know that the organization can be trusted. Maybe there is an old cop or agent or infiltrator from the old days who is still working there and he remains useful. So they do not want to betray confidential matters and they do not want to put such a person on trial. He was not the real enemy; it was the politicians who gave him his marching orders about whom he should go after and whom to prosecute. Perhaps it was information from agents of another country, given either officially or unofficially, that led them to us.

Nicholas Wolpe, son of Harold Wolpe, who was one of the coconspirators named in our trial, is CEO of the Liliesleaf Trust. With the help of researchers, he has uncovered documents in the British official archives that show that British intelligence had us under surveillance by an agent who lived in a nearby trailer park. We know that foreign agents were active because it is known that Nelson Mandela was betrayed by the United States' Central Intelligence Agency in exchange for one of their South African operatives who had been arrested.

We also have to reckon with other issues, however. All our underground activists had been openly politically active and were well known to the Security Police, and we were still operating partly openly and partly secretly. The transition phase from fully legal to fully underground is difficult to achieve.

There were frequent meetings with people coming to Liliesleaf Farm from various parts of the country. Ahmed Kathrada says dealing with the constant breaches of security was a really serious problem. Bruno Mtolo, from the Durban Regional Command of MK, had stayed there. He became the star state witness, known as Mr. X, in the Rivonia Trial. He told the court that the police drove him around Johannesburg until he found the place for them. That might not be true but, rather, a story used by the police to divert attention from the real source of the information.

Was it inadvertently discovered because Bram Fischer or Joe Slovo frequently came to Liliesleaf and could have been followed there? Could it have been Arthur's brother-in-law, the dentist, whose visit betrayed us? I cannot find a motive, and neither Arthur's sister nor her husband seemed ill-at-ease when I met them later, after my release. I wonder now if sending the money I had borrowed from Basil Jaffe back to him by a circuitous and (I thought) safe route led to my being traced. I don't think so because the cops delighted in letting me know how much they knew about me and my contacts, and he was never mentioned.

The foundry man and the wooden-box maker and the landlady were found by the police because their names were in the notebook I was unable to get rid of when the police entered the house. I rushed for the toilet, but there were policemen everywhere and they grabbed me.

Maybe somebody tipped off the police because I was new in the area and he thought I was behaving suspiciously. That might have led to my being followed. The police certainly did not know who I was when I was arrested, and they were not expecting to find me there. I had been using false names. One of them was Charles Barnard, chosen because I needed a name that fitted a white South African who might be an English or an Afrikaans speaker. The name was picked out of the phone book. Arthur Goldreich, who spoke Afrikaans fluently, telephoned that person pretending to be a government official. Mr. Barnard was asked for his birth certificate because, so went the story, there was a problem with his identity card. ID cards had only recently been introduced, and we were trying to build documentation for me. Mr. Barnard was very embarrassed. Out of the whole of Johannesburg we had managed to pick a man whose birth certificate said "illegitimate" on it! His mother and father were not married, and so he had not applied for an ID card. But this emerged only after our arrest. It did not lead the police to me or to us. Another such person was Don Williams, whose name and address I used when renting a post office box to receive mail.

When I was arrested I said I was Charles Barnard, irrigation engineer. Then I realized that if I retained my anonymity, I might just disappear. Nobody would know who I was, and I would be helpless in the hands of the police; nobody outside would know what had happened to me. So I gave them my real name. They insisted I was Goldreich. I was from Cape Town and these were Johannesburg cops. A Security Policeman who had raided my home in Cape Town a number of times was brought in. I was wearing some kind of disguise, with funny little glasses, and my hair was combed over my head to hide my bald forehead. After what seemed a long time, he asked, "Are you Goldberg?" He asked me the question because he really was uncertain. With great relief I exclaimed: "Yes! Tell them who I am."

Ninety Days' Detention: Three Months in Solitary Confinement

The cold winter's afternoon seemed to become much colder. Walter, Govan, Raymond, Rusty, and I were taken to the Fort, an old prison in the heart of Johannesburg, now a historical monument and the site of our new Constitutional Court. In the courtyard of the prison I looked out over the battlements at the dark evening sky, knowing that it would be a very long time before I would be able to see an open sky again.

Arthur and Hazel Goldreich, Bob Hepple, a lawyer and activist, the farmworkers, and the domestic worker Edith Ngopani were taken to Marshall Square Police Station in Johannesburg. At the Fort we were separated by race. Rusty and I were taken to the white part of the prison and locked up together, but we were then quickly separated. It was a long first night, but I did sleep and found that escape into sleep was a good defense mechanism. A day or two later we were loaded into a truck with separate compartments for black and white prisoners and driven at breakneck speed to Pretoria. The truck's spare wheel was in our little compartment, and it bounced around dangerously. We were lucky not to be injured by it. (Once, during the trial, Rusty and I were again transported in this little front compartment. To avoid being soaked by rain, we were allowed to join our comrades in the back compartment, which was dry. And so apartheid was broken for the duration of the ride.)

Pretoria Central Prison had been built before the end of the nineteenth century—and had not improved with age. It was a rough place to settle into, with a harsh routine of sleeping on thin mats on the floor; eating from chipped enamel bowls and drinking a brew that was called coffee but tasted like the burnt maize and chicory that were its main constituents; using a toilet pot that stank and had to be emptied every morning and evening. The odors of excrement and carbolic disinfectant were the pervasive smells in the prison. Filthy blankets and worn-out mats had to be got used to.

We soon discovered that there were three white political prisoners in our part of the prison, on the floor above us. They were Jock Strachan, Ben Turok, who had weathered the Treason Trial, and Jack Tarshish, a member of *Umkhonto we Sizwe;* each was already serving a political sentence. Jock and Ben had each been sentenced to three years and Jack to twelve years for sabotage activities involving explosives. Jock had been the first of our weapons makers in Port Elizabeth, and Ben had been involved with a bomb that was planted at a post office in Johannesburg. A piece of wrapping paper was found with his fingerprints on it, and, despite his extremely plausible explanation for that, he took the blame for the carelessness of another comrade. His only certain way out was to have named that comrade. Ben held his silence and served his full three years, saving his comrade (Jack Hodgson, who had also been acquitted in the Treason Trial) from prison.

Jack Tarshish had been asked by Govan Mbeki, who chose to bypass the Western Cape MK Regional Command, to transport explosives to Cape Town. Jack had enlisted an old World War II air force friend to fly the dynamite down in his luggage on a passenger plane. The friend got cold feet at the last moment and told the police what was happening. Jack was arrested when receiving a suitcase of dummy explosives prepared by the security police. Because the detonators were ostensibly packed with the dynamite, even though Jack had told his friend they were to be carried separately, the judge said Jack had endangered the plane and all on board and gave him the maximum sentence of twelve years under the Explosives Act. He was fortunate that the specific security laws had not yet been enacted because he would surely have got a heavier sentence, maybe even the death penalty. Jock Strachan had also been convicted under the Explosives Act for making the explosives used by MK in Port Elizabeth.

At night, after the guards had left our section of the prison, I would hear a gentle tapping on the ceiling of my cell. Slowly the sounds began to make sense. Jock, in the cell above me, was tapping out a simple code: 1=a, 2=b . . . 5=e, all the way to 26=z. Rusty, in the cell next to mine, would tap with one finger very lightly, so lightly that I had to have my ear against the wall to hear it. We became very fast and proficient at our tapping, and, crucially, the sense of utter aloneness was lost.

It took some time for the Security Police to start their interrogations.

The prison officers in daily charge of us were very strict about not letting us talk to each other during exercise periods in the courtyard; they were generally as harsh and intimidating as they could be. We learned what all prisoners learn to do: talk to each other when our backs were turned to the guards as we walked up and down in the exercise yard. At weekends the guards, different ones, were much more relaxed, and some were indeed hostile to the kind of pressure we were being subjected to. Some would allow us to talk to each other, thus disobeying their orders to ensure that we not communicate.

My interrogators were the notorious florid and burly Captain "Rooi Rus" Swanepoel and his Sergeant C. J. van Zyl, who looked like a Reformed Church *dominee* in his black suit, white shirt, and tie with its tight little knot at the throat. They started off quite gently, asking me to make a statement about acts of sabotage. I declined. They asked me to sign a statement saying that I declined to make a statement. I declined. They came back and went through the same procedure and then told me what they knew. For example, that a certain Goldberg had flown to Johannesburg on the day I had left home and they wanted to know where I had gone. I did not tell them I had traveled by train under a false name.

In subsequent sessions they became more aggressive. The questions they asked showed that comrades in Cape Town and Johannesburg were talking. The cops knew more and more about the training camp at Mamre. They said someone had given me a pistol. Well, one had been offered to me and I had declined to take it because it was merely the body of the weapon, without any of its inner workings, and I did not trust the person who had offered it. More and more I sweated as they revealed their increasingly detailed knowledge. The pressure that puts on you is enormous, all the more so when your interrogator has his revolver on the table in front of him, aimed at you, as he plays with the trigger, asking questions that make it quite clear that you're going to be convicted under a law that carries the possibility of the death penalty. That possibility becomes all the more real when they state, quite straightforwardly, that they are going to hang you. The reality of the Sabotage Act we had protested against arose very starkly before us.

"One of your people is going to hang you," my interrogators told me.

"One of my people? What does that mean?"

"The prosecutor, Dr. Yutar, is a Jew, and he will see to it that you hang!"

Later, during the trial, I discovered that Yutar really did consider me his personal enemy, seeking to present himself as the loyal apartheid-supporting Jew who served his masters well, probably in the hope of getting a promotion.

I hoped that my underground work in Johannesburg had been adequately concealed and would not be discovered by the police. For example, while in jail, I received some of my own clothes, including a black jacket that had been at Travallyn. From that I knew that Wilton Mkwayi, who was not at Rivonia on the day of the raid, must have gone back to our new place at Travallyn, because only he could have sent the jacket to me. So when the jacket came, I thought: "Oh, that's wonderful. Everything has been cleaned out." I was wrong. There was, in fact, a mass of documentary evidence that turned up in our trial. This included ANC files of correspondence and reports that Wilton had not been able to take away. There were also my documents relating to arms production and the kind of chicken farm we needed to buy as a cover for the weapons production.

During our detention, Bob Hepple, who had a keen legal mind, insisted that there was no way for us around the security legislation. Whatever evidence they found by whatever means, including torture, could and would be used against us. The issue, Bob pointed out with his usual coolness, was that evidence obtained by torture was fundamentally unsafe because people lie to avoid further pain. The advice of our lawyers, long before we were arrested, was that we should give our names and addresses and no more—which was, they insisted, the best way of not incriminating yourself or others.

But this is not so easy to sustain as the pressure grows and you know that they are lying about some things, guessing about others. Was it wrong of me, I wonder, to say that Hilliard "H" Festenstein was never at meetings? Was it wrong to say that Hazel Goldreich was a lovely hostess but had not a clue about politics? I am sorry to have maligned Hazel but, at the time, it seemed a necessary thing to say to protect her.

"H" arrived at Liliesleaf on the evening after we were caught, and he too was arrested, held at a police station for some weeks, and then taken to us in Pretoria Local Prison. He somehow talked his way out of his detention. Though he was the medical doctor on our MK Logistics Committee, there was no evidence of this, and no one betrayed him. I had known him in Cape Town and, looking through their thick dossiers, my interrogators insisted that I had attended meetings of the Congress of Democrats in his flat. I said H was never there because he was doing his internship as a junior doctor and was too exhausted to be involved in anything outside a hospital. It was his wife, Iris, who was the activist. They believed me! She, cleverly, had left Johannesburg for London immediately after H had been arrested, so it was safe for him, and me, to blame her for all and every indication of political activity there might have been found in their flat.

The questions thrown at me by my interrogators told me that they were getting nearer and nearer to what I was withholding—being on the MK Regional Command in Cape Town and the High Command in Johannesburg.

An awful, sickening moment came when they told me it was okay for me to talk about "your comrade" Looksmart Ngudle from Cape Town, because he was dead and I could not do him any harm. Angrily I accused them of murdering him. They denied having anything to do with him at all, but they threatened to hand me over to the people who had interrogated him, and "they will deal with you." The threat of death was clear. Back in my cell, I cut a little piece of black cloth from inside my jacket and put it on my shirt as a sign of mourning for my comrade. At the next interrogation they said: "Has somebody in your family died? You are mourning *Comrade* Looksmart. So," they sneered, "you've got *kaffirs* in your family." And so I had confirmation of the death of Looksmart, the first comrade to be murdered in detention. Being tough was the right thing to do because they then offered me coffee. "What's this about?" I asked. "You're not going to talk to us today, so you might as well just have some coffee." Clearly it was "good cop, bad cop" they were playing. It was not a good time.

Then suddenly they removed me to a remote prison at Vereeniging, some thirty miles southeast of Johannesburg. At the same time they took Bob to a separate prison for interrogation. They felt that we were supporting each other and would be more vulnerable in total isolation. Bob later told us that his father, Alex Hepple, a former MP from the white Labour Party (by then no longer existing), had been to see the minister of justice, B. J. Vorster, later president of apartheid South Africa. Vorster boasted that his Security Police swore their allegiance not to the state but to him as minister, and they would see to it that Bob would be hanged. Vorster had passed this choice piece of information on to the father, who passed it on, putting enormous pressure on his son. Later still, Bob told us that he was negotiating with the police to become a witness for the prosecution in exchange for indemnity from prosecution. Rusty commented: "Bob, if you do that, your friends and comrades will cross the street to avoid greeting you."

Escape

In Vereeniging I discovered that, with brute force and a little ingenuity, I could open my cell. If I did this during the lunch break, when most of the guards went off duty, I could make a run for a copse of trees across the way and then hitchhike to Johannesburg. I managed most of it, including getting the cell door open, pulling myself onto the roof of the single-story building, and finally jumping twenty feet to the ground. I had hoped for at least ten minutes to get clear of the prison, but a criminal prisoner spotted me and raised the alarm. I can still hear the dreadful shriek of the siren and relive the sinking feeling in my stomach as I ran for my life. I had no illusions about the danger of being shot while trying to escape. Later I learned how lucky I'd been to have been stopped by two prison guards and not by the police. The head of the prison told me he'd been instructed by the Security Police to shoot on sight, but he'd ordered his prison staff to arrest me alive.

One prison guard covered me with his rifle while the other kicked my ribs in. It was so disappointing to be caught because in another couple of minutes I would have made it. Instead, I ended up shackled in leg irons, the standard treatment for escaping from prison. With great hostility, an angry sergeant put the irons on, hammering the rivets that fixed them around each ankle so that the metal bit viciously into my ankle. I suppose he was trying to punish me for escaping, but I think he was also angry that I had interrupted his lunchtime siesta. Warrant Officer Perez took over and did the job painlessly. Later, when the Security Police came to take me back to the much more secure Pretoria Central Prison, the same sergeant cut into my leg with a hacksaw while removing the rivets to the leg irons.

Again W. O. Perez came to my rescue. The leg irons were being removed because they were on the inventory of the prison, and the Security Police would not promise to return them. Bureaucracy gave me a bit of comfort! W. O. Perez's action was in keeping with the man's attitudes. He would come to fetch me when the Security Police interrogators descended on the prison and take his time about it. "Your friends are here!" he'd say, and then add: "Take your time. Wake up properly. Wash your face, and when you're ready I'll take you through." A good man.

When I was delivered back to Pretoria Central Prison, I was again put into leg irons. They could be removed with a special key. I discovered that a small piece of wire would also function as this special key, but unfortunately I had no opportunity to take them off and make another run for it. They weighed about ten pounds and stayed on permanently, covered by canvas trousers like a baby's romper; there were buttons down the outside of both legs so that you could take off the trousers to shower without removing the leg irons. That particular discomfort lasted a month, and I had to relearn how to walk without the weight of the leg irons. It was quite a hard time, but I was young and fit, and it was bearable. Now I would find it hard to live through.

Esmé was allowed to visit me. The police wanted to show that I was alive and well because comrades who collected my clothes to be washed found some of them ripped and bloodstained and feared that I had been beaten up. Esmé saw me in the leg irons and was shocked. I tried to be cheerful so as not to weaken her too much. She was so strong, but I felt for her very deeply. After I was detained, she was also arrested under the Ninety-Day Detention Law and interrogated for thirty-eight days. They gave her a bad time. I will never know if she broke down and if they got something from her that led them to finding the post box address I had obtained for her to be able to communicate with me under a different name. I do not know, but it is possible. She said that she convinced them that I had not told her what I was doing in the underground. Indeed I had not. The threat they used was one they made to other wives: they threatened to take our children and put them in separate government orphanages so that we would never see them again.

They also offered me money to turn state witness: 6,000 rand (about $9,500 at that time—worth nearly $75,000 in 2015), to be exact. I said they must be joking. "How much have you earned since you've been here in Johannesburg?" they taunted. "I earn nothing," I said. "You don't expect me to earn money from my movement. What are you talking about?" They said, "Well, we can pay more than your organization"—and they said they would give me a new passport, new documentation, a new life anywhere in the world I liked if I would tell them about all those I had been politically active with, where they lived and everything about them. I made it clear that I would *not* be a state witness. They insisted they had enough evidence to hang me. I didn't care what they would do to me; I would never, ever have dreamed of becoming a state witness.

What I did dream about was how to have a nervous breakdown, so that they would have to take me to a hospital, where it might be easier to escape. But I did not know how to have a nervous breakdown. I didn't know where to start. How do you pretend that you're collapsing? I was a tough little devil and always have been.

In the middle of our exercise yard there was a strange structure open to the skies with showers on one side and a urinal and two toilet seats side by side. At one afternoon exercise I sat down next to a person I had not met. James "Jimmy" Kantor introduced himself very quietly. He said he was not one of us. He said the police had offered him his release if he informed on us. Therefore, he said, I should not tell him anything I did not want the police to know. How I admired such integrity!

He found his detention and the breakdown of his law practice a great strain. His brother-in-law Harold Wolpe was an activist and Jimmy's partner in their law firm. Harold escaped together with Arthur Goldreich, Mosie Moolla, and Abdulhay "Charlie" Jassat from the Marshall Square Police Station. The Indian comrades bribed a young policeman to let them escape. Jimmy had a major breakdown and would sit on a stool hunched over with tears streaming down his face as he tried to deal with his distress. His wife was nearing the end of her pregnancy and Jimmy could not cope. He was released on bail and then, again out of vindictiveness and deliberate misinformation, the Security Police had his bail revoked and he joined us again. Despite all this, Jimmy was as staunch as one could wish. Despite not being an activist and despite his breakdown, he would not betray us. That is courage!

Eventually the ninety days came to an end on 8 October 1963. What would happen? Were we going to be released or rearrested and given another ninety days of detention? Amid a great deal of bustling, Rusty, Walter, Govan, Ray, Elias, Andrew, Jimmy, Bob, and I were brought together in an office near the front of the prison. Captain Swanepoel told us we were released from ninety days' detention. Then, after a moment's pause, he said we were under arrest for offenses under the Sabotage Act, the main security legislation. Once we were back in the exercise yard again, Jimmy Kantor loudly greeted us, much to the annoyance of our prison guard. Jimmy the lawyer preempted the guard's threats of punishment for talking to each other by saying that, since we were awaiting trial, the ninety-day rules no longer applied.

Nevertheless, what lay ahead was a huge challenge. I had no idea how I would arrange for lawyers to defend me. I was lucky: I could trust my comrades to do what was necessary.

8

The Rivonia Trial

Keepers of the law
The judge
is dressed
in red and white
the assessors
in black and white
the prosecutor
in a hostage smile
and I
in the borrowed robes
of my grandmother's wisdom
corn she said
cannot expect justice
from a court
composed of chickens.

—Dikobe Martins (published in the
African Communist in the 1990s)

The day after our ninety-day imprisonment ended, our lawyers—Bram Fischer, with Joel Joffe, Arthur Chaskalson, and George Bizos—arrived at Pretoria Central Prison. The surprise was that Nelson Mandela had joined us. He had been sentenced to five years' imprisonment in 1962 for leaving the country illegally and for organizing a general strike. He was already serving his sentence in Robben Island Prison, yet here he was with us in Pretoria for what became famously known as the Rivonia Trial. I had met him when he had come to Cape Town to tell some of us about the necessity and prospects for armed struggle.

I had previously met Bram but I did not know the other lawyers. They wanted to know what we had been charged with because the police would not tell them. Whatever the charge was, they said, the future was bleak. The media were full of government-sourced stories that we were without doubt guilty of the most dreadful crimes and would surely be executed. At this point we were more interested in finding out about each other than going into detail about legal matters.

I felt immensely relieved that the ninety days were over. I had previously met Elias Motsoaledi and now met Andrew Mlangeni for the first time. These two comrades had not been at Liliesleaf Farm and were arrested in Soweto before being held in Pretoria Local Prison. There, they told me, they had been able to look into our "white" exercise yard and had wondered who the comrade in leg irons could be. Cape Town comrades had told them that I was Comrade Goldberg, and I was certainly pleased to meet them. Joel Joffe revealed in his book about the trial that I said from the beginning that if it would help to protect Nelson and the other top leaders, I would accept responsibility for exceeding my instructions about the weapons manufacture. They looked at me somewhat blankly and did not answer. For my part, the offer was a spontaneous suggestion, made not from bravado but from a duty to protect the leaders. They, on the other hand, would not allow me to take the blame for something we were all involved in. Such wonderful comrades are a rarity, and we had many such rare people.

One point was immediately clear: Bob Hepple was in an invidious position because he had told us he was considering whether to be a state witness, yet he was with us during our opening consultation with our defenders. He withdrew from the consultation. I don't remember thinking very deeply just then about his giving evidence, but I still hoped that he would not do so.

The next day we were taken to court and formally charged as the National High Command of MK with involvement in a conspiracy, that we conspired to overthrow the state by force of arms, of preparing to receive a foreign army of invasion, two other charges relating to buying farms and vehicles, other activities that served the conspiracy, and activities in support of the policies of the banned African National Congress.

Even within the shadow of the gallows—we all expected to be hanged—there were moments of relief and humor. Nelson Mandela, for example, had always been a very snappy dresser, in well-cut, tailor-made suits. Now here he was, appallingly thin with sunken cheeks and wearing prison clothes. Not just clothes, but clothes designed to humiliate African prisoners: short trousers, sandals with no socks, a "houseboy's jacket," and handcuffs and leg irons. Yet he drew the ill-fitting prison clothes around him and made them look elegant. He was still Nelson, tall and strong, concentrating his stare on the judge. I had a small slab of chocolate in my pocket, something prisoners awaiting trial could have. I stood next to Nelson and nudged him to look down at the chocolate in my hands. He nodded ever so slightly. I broke off a piece and put it in his hand. He wiped his handcuffed hands over his face and I could see the little block of chocolate making a sharp bump in his thin cheek. He sucked it until it melted away, then nudged me for more—and so it went until all the chocolate was gone.

Gradually we came to understand the magnitude of the case against us. There was a mass of documentary evidence—and oral evidence, much of it extracted from witnesses under the duress and torture of the Ninety-Day Detention Law. There did not seem to be much hope of our avoiding the gallows. Our defense was a political one, to show why we were prepared to act against the oppression of apartheid and for equal human rights, and also that, though we were considering taking up arms for a full-scale uprising, this tactic had not been agreed on.

How fortunate South Africa has been that people like Nelson Mandela, Walter Sisulu, Govan Mbeki, Ahmed Kathrada, and the rest of us, instead of being martyrs to a cause, have been part of what became a negotiated transition.

How fortunate, too, for South Africa to have had lawyers like Joel Joffe and the rest of our defense team to play such an important role in the support of democratic norms and the transition from oppression to democracy.

Joel Joffe and his wife, Vanetta, were about to leave South Africa to settle in Australia when he was asked to become the attorney in our trial. They felt they had a duty to stay to contribute to upholding the right to a fair trial of prisoners accused of crimes against apartheid. They agreed that Joel should defend us at a time when few other attorneys were prepared to help in the face of a media campaign of vilification designed to maintain the system of white racial supremacy at whatever cost. Courage takes many forms. The Joffes showed how ordinary people can become extraordinary in times of crisis. Joel himself would not speak about himself in this way. He is far too modest for that. He wrote in his book on the trial (*The State vs. Mandela: The Trial That Changed South Africa,* Oxford: Oneworld Publications, 2007) that he told Hilda Bernstein, who asked him to defend us, that according to the media we were very unpopular, and he did not see much prospect for a successful defense. Hilda took him to task, pointing out that among the black majority we were *very* popular indeed. He says he realized how easy it was to slip into the habit of taking what the white-owned and apartheid-aligned media said as being all there was to be said.

The members of our defense team were quite outstanding lawyers and people, led by Bram Fischer, one of the greatest advocates of his time. He was also a remarkably brave man, taking on the defense at the trial when he was himself part of the High Command. He knew throughout the trial that the state could, at any point, reveal his membership and so ruin him personally. Yet he persisted with his public role, concentrating before all else on our defense before the court.

I knew of one typical example: I had left a small delivery van, the farm vehicle, in the garage at the Kreels' home in Mountain View, where I had been living. Found there, it might have incriminated them. Bram at night, on his own, pushed it out of the garage and coasted it down quite a steep hill for as far as he could get it and then abandoned it in a little side street. Clearly there was a conflict: Bram was senior counsel for the defense, and therefore part of the state machinery, while being a valued comrade. He resolved these conflicts in the only way consistent with his belief in freedom: he acted as a revolutionary—and it is in action, ultimately, that these moral conflicts are resolved.

Bram came from an Afrikaner aristocracy but broke with his people to become a political activist. Having literally saved our lives in the Rivonia Trial, he was later himself sentenced to life imprisonment and died of cancer while still a prisoner.

Another veteran of the earlier Treason Trial who joined the defense team at Rivonia was Vernon Berrangé, an acknowledged expert at cross-examination. He had been a World War I pilot, racing car driver, adventurer, and political activist. Berrange came out of retirement to join the team, alongside George Bizos, who had come to South Africa with his father after escaping from fascist Greece in the 1940s. At the time of our trial, Bizos was a relatively junior advocate who combined his passion for freedom with a sharp legal mind and a great insight into the state prosecutor's thinking. This was all joined with great humanity and a wonderful sense of humor. Arthur Chaskalson was also at that point a relatively junior advocate who had a remarkable capacity for fearless logical presentation and argument. All our lawyers had an enormous capacity for detailed analysis and commitment to those they were defending. More than that, they all understood the historical significance of the trial.

During May 2014 I heard from Denis Kuny, another defense advocate who appeared for James Kantor in our trial, that he had long before been asked to drive Nelson Mandela from Johannesburg to Ladysmith in Natal after Nelson had gone underground. His own car was not up to it, and so he borrowed a car from his colleague Arthur Chaskalson. Neither thought of himself as an activist but, when asked in 1961 to help the activist Mandela, both willingly did so. Arthur was later appointed chief justice in the new South Africa!

In particular I believe that all our lawyers showed that ordinary people of integrity can become extraordinary defenders of democratic rights by being prepared to uphold the rights of unpopular political opponents of the regime. George Bizos in his autobiography (*Odyssey to Freedom,* Houghton, S.A.: Random House, 2007) notes that if we had lived in a completely fascist state the lawyers would have been helpless to assist us. But apartheid South Africa needed the support of the major Western powers and thus needed to present a facade of acceptance of democratic norms. And, as Pallo Jordan pointed out in a note to me, South Africa, unlike other colonial regimes, had a democratic system for whites, and that caused stresses and strains when it sought to be totalitarian in relation to the colonized and opponents of the system. I am indeed a lucky fellow.

Adding a note of splendid gentility to consultations in an office in the prison, George Bizos brought packets of Vienna sausages, gherkins, and sweets. That made us feel great, and we were able to proceed like a family gathered together to resolve a few minor problems rather than battling to save our lives. Our attitude from the beginning was that if the apartheid state wanted a show trial, then we would show them! We would show the world that apartheid was an appalling system of racial injustice and a threat to democracy everywhere.

On the day appointed for the start of the trial, our lawyers challenged the validity of the indictment. It was indeed quashed as invalid in law because we were charged as "the High Command," whereas we should have been individually charged as members of a conspiracy called the High Command. Additonally, the prosecution had not given sufficient details to enable our defense team to know who was charged with what activities on behalf of the conspiracy. It seemed to us that the prosecutor had looked for a great headline and had ignored the rules of criminal procedure.

After the indictment had been quashed, we were technically free because there was no charge against us. I had a great moment as we were leaving the court. Prison officers and Security Police tried to herd us down the steep stairs to the cells below. I simply stood there. A rather obese cop tried to shove me down the stairs, and I dug my elbow into his fat gut. His breath exploded out of him and he threatened to charge me with assault. Joel Joffe intervened to tell him to stop assaulting me. The fat cop threatened Joffe. Captain Swanepoel watched this for a moment with narrowed eyes and then put his hand through the mob around me and, touching me on the shoulder, said he was arresting me and the others. We were taken back to the prison and charged individually with a conspiracy under the Sabotage Act.

A new, equally faulty indictment was presented, but Judge Quartus de Wet was by this time fed up with the delays. He ordered the trial to proceed. The prosecutor dropped a bombshell when he smugly announced that Bob Hepple would be a state witness. It was politically devastating, even though we knew it was coming.

In our cell under the court Bob again told me that the case against him was so strong that he had to do anything he could to avoid the death sentence. I understood that, but I also knew that my life was at risk, the more so if Bob was to give evidence. He said in a recent documentary about the trial that it was his plan to be released on bail so that he could leave the country. He said further that he had initially made a very weak statement to the police, which they rejected. He then wrote steadily for forty-eight hours, making a very detailed statement that they accepted as the basis for his becoming a witness for the prosecution. Things turned out differently, however. He did not give evidence in court because Bram went secretly to see Bob and told him that he could not give evidence: keeping his word to the movement was more important than keeping his word to the prosecution. Bram actually made the arrangements for Bob to leave the country.

As an officer of the court and a defense lawyer, Bram should not have contacted a state witness, but he showed again that his loyalty was to liberation rather than the institutions of the oppressive state; there would have been serious consequences if Bob, with the knowledge he had of our operations, had given evidence. Bob sent me a birthday card after he got to Britain. I wrote to Esmé to tell her that I did not want to hear from Bob again. Was I too hard on him? Perhaps so, but I too was then under enormous pressure. Now it is all fifty years in the past, and when we occasionally meet we are able to chat together about those times.

Bram, incidentally, dropped out of the proceedings for a while in the early days of the trial because some of the first witnesses in the trial were workers at Liliesleaf Farm who might have identified him as a frequent visitor. He set about saving our lives and succeeded through the way he conducted the case. The trial was a remarkable experience of fortitude and principle and courage, just as my comrades Nelson, Walter, Govan, Ray, and Mhlaba were remarkable people and great leaders. Similarly, Rusty Bernstein, Ahmed Kathrada, Elias Motsoaledi, and Andrew Mlangeni showed great dignity under nigh intolerable circumstances—courageous, too, and clear thinking.

And there was time for fun. I had some ancient wire-rimmed glasses that had been part of my disguise. They looked like the glasses African pastors typically wore to read from the Bible. Pastors are *mfundisi,* derived from a word meaning "one who teaches."[1] Elias Motsoaledi would put my glasses on the end of his nose and pretend to read until we collapsed amid shrieks of laughter. Walter Sisulu needed new glasses but was not permitted to have an optician fit them. Rusty Bernstein and I, with no equipment but sticky tape and a ballpoint pen, were able to mark the positions of his pupils so that the bifocal lenses could be properly fitted into his new frames. And then Walter would look up and down to find the correct angle for reading or looking into the distance, so I am not sure if we really got it right.

Bram told me that it had been decided that I should try to escape again. There would be people waiting for me to drive me away into hiding. I did not ask who had made the decision—it was sufficient that Bram told me about it. My concern was that, if I went, the police would go for Esmé again. After some days during which he consulted with others, he said I should ask her to go into exile with our children. When I asked her to go, it was at a visit in the prison while surrounded by guards so I could not explain the real reason. She objected to leaving me while I was still on trial. She said that people would see it as a desertion. I simply insisted that I wanted them to be safe. She left early in December 1963, arriving in Britain shortly before Christmas. Our friend Wolfie Kodesh was there, and David leapt into his arms, so there was at least one person he knew in London. Unfortunately, we were so closely guarded I could not escape. Bram and others felt it would be a great political victory if we could escape amid such heavy security, and if anyone among us could, it would be me. Bram also knew that there was a mass of evidence against me, and the death penalty was a real possibility for me.

The prosecution had a very strong case against us: masses of documents and many witnesses. Jimmy Kantor, the brother-in-law and law partner of Harold Wolpe, was acquitted before the defense case began because there was no case against him. We all felt that he was charged so that the prosecutor could take revenge for Harold's involvement in our activities. Jimmy's legal practice was ruined, and he went into exile with his family. He died relatively young, at forty-seven, of a massive heart attack in 1974. Our lawyers also called for Rusty Bernstein's acquittal for lack of evidence. The judge, however, said he had a case to answer.

The great day came: the opening of the defense case. Our defense began with Nelson Mandela's famous Speech from the Dock. He needed to present our political case without the interruptions of questions by the lawyers. Even though he had been the star witness in the Treason Trial, it was decided he should not be subjected to intolerable cross-examination about whom he had met and what discussions he had had when he left the country without a passport.

Delivered in the shadow of the gallows, Nelson Mandela's speech was a masterpiece of legal defence and an immensely courageous political statement. We had all seen the speech and commented on it—and the lawyers had analyzed it from their point of view. Yet it remained Nelson's speech, written in his large, roundhand script. When he came to the final paragraph—where he said he hoped to live to see a South Africa free of racism, where people could live together in harmony, but, if need be, he was prepared to die for this ideal—he spoke in the same tense but measured style of his four-hour-long presentation. His words were a clear challenge to the judge and apartheid South Africa to hang him if they dared to. At that moment I realized he was also challenging them to hang all of us. I felt only pride and perhaps elation at sharing this wonderful moment. Being on trial for your life is not something you choose. You do not go to prison. You get taken! But what a moment in my life that was. I can truly say that we have looked death in face and come through the experience as better, stronger people.

After Mandela, Walter Sisulu, for a very long four days in the witness box, quietly, by force of personality, dominated the proceedings. He set out to explain why we had taken up arms to commit acts of sabotage but had not yet made a decision to embark on full-scale guerrilla warfare. He withstood fierce cross-examination by the prosecutor, Percy Yutar, who seemed to think that he knew more about politics than the secretary general of the African National Congress. Walter was calm and masterly, absolutely overshadowing the pettiness of the prosecutor's ill-informed political questions and arguments. These were based on the typical white South African's belief that whites held the key to civilization and thus had the right to treat all black people as silly children who did not know what was good for them. Only once did Walter lose his cool. Yutar had presented some spurious argument that life for black South Africans was not so bad after all. Walter flashed back, "I wish you could live for just one day as we are forced to do, and you would not make such a remark."

Govan, Rusty, and Ahmed Kathrada (Kathy) all gave evidence about why they had been involved. Kathy was notably humorous. Asked if he knew anybody with the initial K, clearly a reference to himself in one of the documents being used in evidence, he replied Khrushchev, the Soviet leader. This led to a time-wasting but enjoyable exchange between prosecutor and accused. All three of my comrades gave remarkable public lessons in political commitment and rational analysis as the basis for the policies of the Congress Alliance and the South African Communist Party. Yutar opened the way for all this by the nature of his cross-examination.

We had decided that though we were giving evidence, we would not under cross-examination by the prosecutor betray the names of comrades whose liberty would be put at risk. That meant we were not prepared to comply with our oath or affirmation that we would "tell the whole truth and nothing but the truth." The judge told Rusty that he had to answer questions put to him. He declined. The judge said he could imprison him for eight days at a time until he did answer. Then he added, "But that would not change your mind, would it?" The trial went forward.

Raymond Mhlaba did not fare well in the witness box. He had been in the People's Republic of China for military training, and the police and prosecutor were aware of this fact. He had had a large cyst removed from his forehead while he was away. He would not admit where he had been because that would perhaps give the judge an excuse to say we were ready to implement our armed uprising. He became flustered and the prosecutor, knowing that Raymond was not present when certain events took place, insisted that he was present. In democratic court procedure the prosecution is required to make known facts that are to the advantage of the accused. In fact, Raymond was not guilty of many of the things he was charged with because he had been away.

I too gave evidence because I wanted to explain why I had been prepared to give up all the privileges of white racist society to help bring about a just society in which we would one day live in harmony. Our judge from time to time showed that he too was imbued with the typical racist attitude regarding what he believed was his self-evident right. The lawyers were worried that I might antagonize the judge, who indicated that he thought of me as a smart aleck who stirred up "poor but happy blacks" to become "cheeky" revolutionaries, as racists liked to say about the oppressed. The lawyers were worried that the judge might be pushed to hang me because the whites would like that, and black people would not be as upset as they would be if my black comrades were hanged. I knew this was a real possibility, but it was not always uppermost in my mind. What was important was that white and black South Africans should see that there are people of all races who believe in equality.

I was quite respectful of the judge but called him "Sir" rather than "My Lord," and on coming into the witness box, I would nod and greet him with a cheerful "Good morning," to which he felt compelled to reply equally politely.

There was also a legal reason for giving evidence. George Bizos had found a precedent in a judgment involving Nazi supporters during World War II who had investigated the possibility of an uprising against the pro-Allied government in South Africa. Preparation was not an offense, or not a serious offense, unless a decision had been made to go ahead with an armed uprising. My task, I said in evidence, was to investigate as an engineer the possibilities of producing our own weapons "if they should be needed." A decision to go ahead would be influenced by whether we could produce the arms we needed. Therefore, my activity was merely that of a technical adviser to responsible political leaders who needed facts on which to base their decisions. That was my role, and I did not feel it necessary to inform the court that the Logistics Committee of our High Command had decided that, even if Operation Mayibuye was not adopted, weapons would be required for ongoing sabotage and we would make them. I also did not feel it necessary to inform the court that I was a member of the MK Western Cape Regional Command. Nor did I feel it necessary to admit that the camp at Mamre in December 1962 was indeed the first MK training camp inside South Africa. They inferred the nature of the camp, but I would not concede the point. They could not prove these things, and I did not think the judge needed me to confirm their inferences. My conscience has troubled me ever since. But only a little!

For some reason Percy Yutar left my cross-examination to his assistant, thus depriving me of the opportunity to confront the petty little tyrant who the Security Police had said was "one of my people" who was going to hang me. How such little, ambitious people sell themselves to satisfy their ambitions and become the willing servants of tyranny.

I ran into trouble right at the end of the cross-examination when I was asked if I had bought the new place at Travallyn for the ANC or for MK. I had to say it was bought for MK, though it would have been easy to say it was for the ANC—and if I were believed it would let me off one of the hooks, that of not buying a headquarters for MK but "merely" for the ANC. A major issue in the trial, however, was whether we could convince the judge that, though some leaders of the ANC and the SACP were members of the MK High Command, each was a separate organization with overlapping membership but separate functions. This was important, so that every member of the ANC or SACP was not automatically considered a member of MK in terms of the law, and the other way round. Indeed, this division of functions and membership was true because most of us believed that military action is too important to leave to military people alone. Political considerations must determine the strategy and tactics, especially in a war for political liberation.

This issue affected me because I had been the person who had bought the new place. It fitted exactly the type of place described in a document about setting up the weapons manufacturing facility for MK, which was to be disguised as a poultry farm. The document was found among our papers at Travallyn. I did not feel it was necessary to tell the court that I had typewritten the document. Fortunately, there was too little handwriting on it for the experts to identify it as mine. In the face of that document I could not say that the place had been bought for the ANC underground headquarters because that would have tied the ANC into being one with MK. Of course, the little opening that George Bizos had found for me closed with the clang of steel doors. I was merely a part of a much bigger whole, however, and preserving our movement was more important than trying to save myself. I felt pleased with my performance for having been able to say why I had been prepared to risk everything in the cause of justice in our country and not succumb to personal self-interest at the expense of our liberation movement.

Elias Motsoaledi and Andrew Mlangeni each read a statement from the dock rather than go into the witness box. Neither had been at Liliesleaf and they had operated at the level of the Johannesburg Regional Command, and the police did not know that Andrew had been at meetings of the High Command. Their statements were dignified and passionate explanations of why, as patriotic South Africans, they felt they had no choice but to take part in the armed struggle after years of peacefully knocking on the door of apartheid South Africa to be allowed in to share equal rights for all.

There was often time for individual conversations during consultations. Nelson one day took me aside and, with his finger wagging for emphasis, said without preamble that when we taught Marxist theory to our people we had to relate it to the lives of South Africans. He went on to say that speaking of social development in Europe from barbarism through slavery and feudalism to merchant and industrial capitalism had no meaning for our people. We had somehow to relate the theory to fairly egalitarian tribal life, to the pressures of colonial conquest and the leap into industrial capitalism in a very short time. What had taken six hundred years in Britain, for example, took about one hundred years in South Africa. The truth of his observations was self-evident—but why, I asked him, was he telling me? He shrugged without giving a real answer, merely saying that he wanted me to know his thoughts on the matter. I believe he thought he was going to be hanged and I might not be, and he wanted me to carry his message forward.

Nelson always denied being a member of the Communist Party, but from his notes that were presented in the trial he certainly had studied Marxist theory very thoroughly indeed. During his address to the court he said that there were many attractive aspects to the theory, but he implied that as a leader of a national liberation struggle he needed to transcend any one political ideology to build the greatest possible unity. In December

2013, immediately after Nelson passed away, the South African Communist Party announced that he had been a member and a member of the party's Central Committee. I am not convinced that he would have remained a member for very long because he seemed to me to be unlikely to submit to doctrinaire attitudes. On the other hand, he had close political relations with the Communist Party, and, when it came to the founding of MK, he had been in close consultation with some of its leading members. So he had probably attended meetings of the SACP Central Committee. Many of us did not admit to being members of the Communist Party because of the strength of the state's hostility to and hatred of the "Reds," who were among the staunchest opponents of apartheid racism and exploitation.

During another consultation, toward the end of the trial, Raymond Mhlaba spoke to me separately. He said, "Comrade, we have decided after discussions"—I was kept in a separate part of the prison because apartheid racism applied there, too—"that if there are death sentences, we should not appeal." I asked, "Why not?" And he said: "Because we want to get out of the way. We must let them hang us. Our people will be so angry they will rise up and sweep away the apartheid system." I responded: "That's a very interesting theory, but I believe that governments do not hang political leaders until they've got things under solid control. And then they will deal with one and then another and so on and they will be really on the alert to keep control. It's not going to be as easy as you think. And more than that, it has taken thirty years to make you the leader you are, and I don't think we should throw you or the others away. We must use every means to keep you alive. We're going to need you." He thanked me for the compliment.

Two weeks before his death in 2005 we were still joking about that conversation. He said, "Well, you see, comrade, we didn't need to make the choice, did we?"

Bram Fischer said he would insist on appeals if there were death sentences, the reason being that the hysteria in South Africa would die down after a while. Among the media, representing the views of the whites, there was pressure for us to be hanged. Nonetheless, Bram argued, there would be time to organize increased international pressure on the apartheid regime. So, even if we lost the appeal and were executed, the end of the system would be hastened.

The day before sentence was to be passed, the judge had found most of us guilty on all four charges against us. The next twenty-four hours were filled with emotional turmoil, but I did sleep well that night. As Kathy has said, we had all become used to the idea that we would probably be sentenced to death, and I found sleep a great defense against those thoughts.

Recently, while preparing this edition, I was with Andrew Mlangeni, in May 2014. He was not party to the views Raymond had expressed. Andrew recalled that our lawyers thought that he and Elias would be sentenced to perhaps twelve years in prison, and so it came as a shock to him when he and Elias were sentenced to life imprisonment. He said the lawyers thought that Nelson and Walter might be sentenced to death, and I would almost certainly be. I have previously expressed my view that it would suit the state to execute me, the "traitorous white," and not create martyrs of Nelson and Walter. The lawyers felt that the case against Kathy and Raymond was very weak and they should be acquitted.

Had Kathy been acquitted, he would have been tried on other charges to which the evidence and his own explanations had exposed him. Under the Sabotage Act, an accused could not plead double indemnity if evidence given by the accused was to be used in a trial under other legislation. Rusty was acquitted, and I have no doubt that his insistence on seeking bail, as though he were really innocent, helped him, though it was the prosecutor's failures that really let Rusty off the hook. Yutar had become so engrossed in his political confrontation with Rusty that he forgot to put fundamental issues of fact to him. Rusty's declaration that he had not done the things alleged in the indictment had therefore to stand.

On 12 June 1964, the day of sentence, the judge read a very short statement saying that he was not imposing the ultimate sentence (death), which would be appropriate in a case that was tantamount to high treason, but as we were charged under the Sabotage Act, he could allow some leniency: the sentence was life imprisonment on each of the charges on which we were found guilty. As he spoke the faces of my comrades lit up in the most wonderful smiles of relief and joy, and we laughed out loud. I was overjoyed to live, even though it would be life behind bars. I was only thirty-one years old and I did not believe that my life was over.

I suspect that we were fortunate in having the prosecutor we did have. Percy Yutar's personal animosity and his false assumption of moral and intellectual superiority led him into political arguments with some of my comrades in the witness box while he neglected the legal basis of the case against us. Yutar was really out to hang us by political argument in the court of public opinion, and he neglected to provide a thorough basis of legal presentation and argument. He charged us under the Sabotage Act because it gave the prosecution an enormous advantage: it alone in South African law overturned the principle that an accused was innocent until proven guilty. This sabotage legislation provided that, if the prosecution could show that there was a case to answer, the onus was on the accused to prove his or her innocence. That is very difficult to do, even when you are completely innocent.

Yutar the prosecutor, in painting us as desperate people who were mere terrorists, as well as in his antics and craving for dramatic headlines, was probably counterproductive for the state. True, throughout the trial, the mainstream newspapers were extremely hostile to us, but their reports and their frightening headlines may have done more harm than good. Whites would have been shocked into baying for our blood when they read that I, for example, was to make 210,000 hand grenades and 48,000 land mines, but blacks would have rejoiced at the plans we were developing. The mainstream pro-apartheid media spread our propaganda for us. At the same time, Laurence Gandar, editor of the *Rand Daily Mail*, ensured that what we were saying was prominently carried by his paper on a daily basis. In a series of front-page editorial pieces, Gandar asked what was wrong with white South Africans who had instituted and supported policies that turned patriotic, well-educated, serious, and responsible people like Walter Sisulu, Nelson Mandela, and Chief Luthuli, among many others, into determined freedom fighters. On the basis of his analysis, Gandar felt that white South Africans had to recognize that enforcing apartheid laws made the security of whites more problematic rather than making them safer. They needed, he said, to open up society to ensure that black people could lead decent lives so that whites could live in peace without any sense of fear. Gandar did not accept that armed struggle was legitimate, but he was opposed to the style of prosecution that Yutar resorted to: that is, seeking to humiliate the accused and wanting to belittle them with his arrogant white-superiority attitudes.

Gandar's coverage was a remarkable show of editorial independence in the face of white hysteria. His paper was owned by the giant Anglo American Corporation, whose founders said they were liberal in their politics but through their business activities gave their full support to the apartheid state, for that was highly profitable. For his continued opposition, which led to the falling circulation of his paper and therefore falling advertising revenues, Gandar was later fired. Profits triumphed over integrity.

After we were sentenced and before we were taken back to the prison, our lawyers said they had permission to see us the next day to discuss the question of an appeal to a higher court against the convictions and sentences imposed. There was a long delay while the police made sure that they had everything under control, and then we were finally taken back to prison. As we made our way out of the court, the massive crowd of our supporters sang our anthem, *"Nkosi Sikelel' iAfrika,"* and shouted that we would not serve our sentences. A convoy of trucks and cars loaded with police surrounded our truck, and a squad of motorcycle cops led the way, sirens screaming.

At the prison we were again separated and I was taken off to the white section of the prison. Colonel Aucamp, the head of the Prison Security Division, seemed quite pleased at the outcome of the case, though when I remarked that he seemed as pleased as a cat that had licked the cream, he responded quite bitterly that we should have been sentenced to death. He proclaimed that though we had life sentences, we would never leave prison on our own two feet: "You will be carried out feet-first in your coffins." I am happy to confirm that he was wrong.

From the time we were arrested at Liliesleaf, the whole process took eleven months: three months of ninety-day detention, then eight months of trial. We were arrested on 11 July 1963 and sentenced on 12 June 1964.

In my cell I smoked a last few cigarettes, feeling quite calm as I waited to be processed as a convicted prisoner. Prison clothes were issued to me, and all my private clothes and possessions, letters, photographs of my family, and books were taken away. In no time at all I met up with Jock, Ben, and Jack, who were to be my companions as fellow political prisoners for many years. The lawyers, who had said they would see us, were not allowed to visit, and I heard later that my nonwhite comrades had all been flown to Robben Island during the night. I was the only Rivonia Trialist left in Pretoria.

The day after we were sentenced, my mum and dad came to visit me. They had been separated and divorced for years, but they were together to see me because the number of visits was strictly controlled, and at first we were allowed only one visit each six months. Dad, who had worked so hard so that I, his younger son, could have a university education, said he was pleased with me for not flinching in the face of the injustices they had both taught me to understand and to oppose. My mum, who had not allowed herself to show any weakness in public, rather tearfully said that her life was fulfilled through me. She would shortly leave for Britain to join my wife, Esmé, and our children. Dad would stay and be my visitor. So ended my first half-hour visit.

After some days Major Ferdinand Gericke, the commanding officer, told me with what seemed to me to be deeply felt emotion that Molly Fischer, Bram's wife, had died in a car accident. He gave me permission to write a short note of condolence to Bram. The letter was not sent. Bram must have been devastated by her death. They were such a close couple who seemed inseparable in their marriage and in their political commitment.

Bram and Joel came together to see me some weeks later to talk about an appeal against the life sentences imposed on all of us. They said: "We have been to the Island. Your comrades feel there is no point in appealing the sentences. We think there is a risk that the Appeal Court might either increase the sentence or simply remark that, while they were not imposing the death sentence, all of you were fortunate not to have been sentenced to death." That would be an invitation to judges in future trials to impose death sentences. The criterion is "does the sentence cause a sense of shock?" We knew that most whites would have preferred death sentences, and many would have been disappointed that we had been sentenced to life imprisonment. Judges are not immune to the feelings and sentiments of the society of which they are a part.

I said to Bram that the judge by sentencing us all to life imprisonment made no distinction between degrees of guilt of each of us. Bram responded that what the judge had done was to say that the minimum sentence he felt he could impose was life and that there was nothing heavier than that, other than death, which he had decided against. I would not go against the wishes of my comrades and really felt that we were lucky to have escaped with our lives. I have subsequently heard that both Kathy and Raymond turned down the possibility of an appeal against both their convictions and the severity of their sentences because they wished to show solidarity with the rest of us, who would remain for life.

During the trial our lawyers were worried that the prejudices of the prosecutor and the judge might lead the latter to sentence me to death for being the one whom he could sentence to death for stirring up my black comrades. I knew it was, in fact, the other way round: I was there to serve a cause led by such great people.

During the short consultation Bram did not mention Molly, nor did Joel. Bram was thinner and extremely pale. When I expressed my sorrow at her passing and my sympathy for him, Bram simply looked down, became even paler, and did not answer. I was able to reach through the bars of the grill separating us and squeeze his hand. He allowed no more emotional contact than that, screwing up his eyes to stop tears from falling. I did not see Bram again until 1966, after he'd been sentenced to life imprisonment and we ended up as prisoners alongside each other.

Our Rivonia lawyers, each in his own way, continued with their fight against apartheid, and some played significant roles in democratic South Africa. Arthur Chaskalson continued to use the courts to defend democratic principles. He played a leading role in establishing the Legal Resources Centre and became the first president of the new Constitutional Court and then chief justice. George Bizos became a leading civil rights lawyer and is chairman of the governing body of the Legal Resources Centre in Johannesburg. A year or two after the end of our trial, Joel Joffe was forced to leave South Africa by the harassment of the Security Police, who frequently raided his office, seizing confidential documents and statements of those he was defending. He became a successful businessman in Britain and later president of Oxfam. For the latter he was made a life peer, a British lord. He actively supported the liberal press in South Africa in opposition to apartheid. He has always been a kind friend to me.

Vernon Berrange returned to retirement and passed away some years later.

I have written few poems, but here is one I wrote after being sentenced. I called it "Burned out, alone . . ."

Burned out
Alone
I lie
Eat sleep
Body meets calls
All
All within four walls.

Months, years
Pass slowly

When days seem long
Always the same—Nothing done
Nothing achieved
Thoughts focused only on oneself
Behind the walls.

Far off
Carried softly on the night wind
A clock strikes the hour

In the morning
The town rumbles
There
Outside the walls
People live their lives
Factory sirens call their workers
Diesel locomotives shunt
And couplings clatter
Cars hoot and machines drone

Their beat
Even muffled by the walls
Saves me from doubt

But it isn't easy for thoughts to fly
When body and mind are in a stall

But on the rising wind
My thoughts become sharp and focused
take wing
take the right attitude
Fly
Clear
Over the walls
Meet with life
Striving
Joining in
The contradictions

Of life out there
to build anew
and turn my defeat
into victory.

9

Emotional Desert

Prison, 1963–1985

It is not easy to write about prison. When I was freed after twenty-two years I had spent 45 percent of my life inside the walls. Now I have been outside the prison again longer than I was behind the walls. The loss of my freedom represents only about one-quarter of my life, and I do not think every day about it. Yet when I begin to write about it, I find it difficult to sleep. The memories return, and I find it difficult to speak about those times. It was too painful, and sometimes I have nightmares about it.

When I entered prison after being sentenced in the Rivonia Trial, I was still quite optimistic. I reflected on what had happened and, though normal life was over, I believed the apartheid system would soon come to an end. During the trial there was a moment when Bram took me aside to ask what I thought of our situation. I said I thought the system had outlived its usefulness. It had already gone beyond where it could survive. I said that Afrikaner nationalism used apartheid to enable an elite group of white Afrikaners to become big businessmen, owners of big capital. They achieved that goal. Now they were sitting at the top table with Harry Oppenheimer's Anglo American Corporation. Apartheid was going to break down, I said, because white workers were being paid too much to compensate them for controlling black workers on behalf of management.

The cost was that, having achieved its goal, Afrikaner nationalism would become more and more intensely repressive, too much for business to carry, and eventually this would bring it down. The repression would be the seed of its own destruction. Bram understood that I meant the system would collapse not simply because of its internal contradictions but also through the actions of the people, whose resistance and whose demands were the expression of those contradictions. When it collapsed, or became weak, we would be released—unless some stupidity led them to kill us.

The reality of prison soon hit me. After my parents had visited me I was very much alone: no wife, no children, no friendly voices. Prison is a place with bare walls where for many years we slept on mats on the hard floor. There were windows in our cells but without glass. In winter in Pretoria the temperature sometimes falls to zero degrees. We froze! We put on every item of clothing we could find: underpants, pajama pants, work trousers, and when we had it a jersey with a little wool in it, a jacket; and I put whatever I could find on my head to keep it warm while I slept. Later we used empty shampoo bottles filled with hot water, if we could get it, and stuffed the plastic bottle into a sock and used it as a hot water bottle. Our conditions were awful, but always better than they were for black criminal prisoners, who slept ten in a cell intended for one person.

During exercise times we could talk to each other, but mostly we were alone in our single cells. Times for showering or emptying toilet pots were also times to speak a few words to others. The routine was that we were locked up for sixteen to eighteen hours a day and forbidden to talk to each other. We did, nevertheless, whisper under the door to our neighbors on each side of us. When we were working at repairing mail bags, we sat in the courtyard and were not supposed to talk. When it was too cold to be outside, we would be locked alone in our cells. Slowly we worked away at changing that situation, and the authorities gave up trying to force us to be silent. Visiting between cells was never permitted.

We were often ill because there was too little light and too little sunshine. In winter the sun did not shine into our courtyard. Then we stood on a stool to get at least our faces into the warmth. When we sat outside for too long in the cold, it was difficult to move afterward.

My experience of prison was that you lose weight in the first few months, until your body stabilizes, but you do not have much energy. A small scratch takes a long time to heal because you do not get enough vitamins; your eyes are affected by always being indoors and having little change of focus. There is enormous psychological stress from being under constant surveillance: they control when your light goes on, when it goes off, when you sleep, when you wake. Will you get the letters sent to you? Will they send your letters out or say your letter has been posted, though it has been confiscated without your knowledge? Years afterward, when I was released from prison, I got letters that my wife had sent me but that had been withheld. Some of her letters were so covered in chemicals that the ink had smudged.

I missed my wife very much, and the separation was a cruel blow. Dealing with this emotional desert was very trying. I wrote to her in my earliest letters that she should feel free to live her life to the fullest extent she chose, not because I did not love her but because I *did* love her. I did not want her to feel that she had to be so loyal to me that she would end up as a dried-up old stick. After all, I might never be with her again. There were times when I felt a burning and troubling sexual desire, and jealousy raised its head. It took me a long time to overcome my feelings of jealousy and come to terms with the meaning of what I knew was the right attitude to adopt. Thirteen years after being locked away, I woke up one morning free of jealousy. It was a wonderful moment of relief and release. I think it may have been more difficult for her because she was caught between the need to be politically loyal and the wish to be personally faithful while being a woman in her prime, enjoying her womanhood. What conflicts that must have caused her! She was young and attractive and I was imprisoned for life: four counts of life imprisonment. After four years, Esmé was allowed to visit me for the first time. We had five half-hour visits together, with a pane of glass between us so that we could not touch, and a guard supervising each of us, removing all privacy. Then, after another four years, she was allowed to visit again. And then she was refused permission to visit me ever again. We saw each other again after fourteen long years, when I was released. I was never told why they were so malicious but assumed it was part of their wish to break our morale, a wish that stemmed from the same source as the vicious response of the Security Police, who believed that I had betrayed what they thought of as "their white South Africa." So much fruitless pain they caused. Hurting me and my wife would not break our spirit, nor would it stop the inexorable defeat of their unjust system.

At first we were allowed one letter in and one out every six months, and they were supposed to be one side of a folio sheet of paper, or approximately five hundred words. But because there was such a vindictive attitude, letters were often literally cut to that length so that the key words—such as "I love you"—would disappear. Letters were not allowed to contain references to prison conditions or fellow prisoners; we were not allowed to tell our correspondents that their letters had been censored. If a correspondent wrote on both sides of a sheet of paper and words were cut out, you lost the other side as well. Politics or "news" was forbidden. What was there to write about? The number of letters increased over the years, until in the last years of my imprisonment I was allowed to write and receive fifty letters a year. When I was released, letters from my wife that had been withheld were given to me. I had been told they had never arrived. That was inordinately distressing.

Something similar happened with visits. One in six months to start with, when you needed the most reassurance about your family, and over the years the authorities bowed to pressure so that at the end of my time in prison we were allowed up to twenty-five visits a year. The rigid control over what we could talk about was never relaxed. There was no contact allowed. We faced each other through a pane of glass with a guard standing next to the prisoner and another next to the visitor, so that it was almost impossible to create any intimacy.

After eight years my children were allowed to visit me. Then they were allowed to come every second year. At first they came together but later they chose to come in alternate years on their own. They were older and had the confidence to come separately. Hilly always chattered away and made the visits interesting. David had difficulty in finding things to say until he came with his girlfriend Beverley, and, through having a three-way conversation, it was better.

Visits were not easy to deal with. It is quite unnatural to try to talk about everything in half an hour and at the same time to try to rekindle the human contact. It is not possible in such a short time. Your routine as a prisoner is totally disturbed. You can cope with everything when you build a wall around yourself. During visits you are compelled to allow the wall to be penetrated, and to be human you have to break through this emotional barrier.

It had been good to have Dad visit me, but his visits were sometimes very trying, as he tried to tell me things in a kind of roundabout way when what I really needed was for him to chat to me. Ivan Schermbrucker, when he was released, asked his friend Hillary Kuny, the wife of the advocate Denis Kuny, to visit me together with my dad. She was more or less my age, clever, very attractive, and a great conversationalist. She spoke about her studies, her family, and her friends, and her visits became a very pleasant break from the prison routine. She also allowed me to break down the emotional barriers I had constructed, letting me feel human again. Visits were a chance to look through the glass and see myself reflected in the responses of the sympathetic "other." And to work out if I was not a bit crazy or fairly normal.

My mother was allowed to visit me after about ten years. During the visit she told me she was at the end of her resources. I thought she meant at the end of her financial resources. But she lived with my wife and children, so she wasn't going to starve. When she left she wanted to kiss me but contact visits were not allowed. One of the officers, as a special favor, opened a small strip of window about four inches wide, and she climbed up with great difficulty onto the high stool so that we could kiss through the tiny gap. It was such an undignified way of kissing one's mother farewell, but she insisted, and it would have hurt her if I had said no to the indignity. It was, needless to stress, the last time I saw her. What she had meant was that she could not go on living much longer. She died a year later. Esmé told me that Mum had cancer and had asked her doctor to make her comfortable and to let her die. She wanted no heroic measures that would prolong her suffering. David and Hilly and their friends who often stayed in the house with them were sitting around "Granny's" bed because they were so fond of her. She came out of her semicoma and, upon seeing David, spoke to him as if he were me, his father. He was so upset he rushed out of the room to recover his poise.

In prison you hear of the death of a parent, or in others' cases of children, or partners, and there is nothing you can do to comfort those on the outside who remain with the memories and the emptiness. You are robbed of your role as a family member. The sense of inadequacy this evokes is so strong that it seems unbearable. It is the inhuman enemy who has imprisoned us that we should blame, but we had put ourselves in harm's way, which led to imprisonment and separation, even though our motives were good. There's the unresolved contradiction Hilly expressed when I was released. She said I "was and would always be her hero, but you don't have to love your heroes. If he wanted to be so engaged in politics he shouldn't have got married and had children."

Inside, we found ways to support each other. Jeremy Cronin, who was arrested in 1976 on terrorism charges, was devastated when his young wife died while being operated on for a brain tumor. He was withdrawn and silent and became quite pale. After some days I said to him that one response to the death of someone close is to feel angry with oneself for not feeling enough, for being emotionally frozen, unable to feel, unable even to weep. Some time later he read to us some of the most beautiful love poems, which were his way of expressing his feelings, his sense of terrible loss and regret. He was kind enough to tell me that he had felt suicidal because of his inability to feel, and my few words had comforted him and encouraged him. I had similar support from comrades when my mother died, and that enabled me to understand what Jeremy might be experiencing. It was much the same when my father died. I did not ask to attend his funeral. They would have said no, and I did not want to give them the pleasure of denying my request.

Prison was an endless round of pettiness. We had a small, open, chipped enamel bowl to hold drinking water. There was always a layer of dust on the water. I saved up toothpaste tubes that I flattened to make a sheet of aluminium large enough to cover the bowl. My homemade lid was confiscated on the grounds that if the authorities thought I should have water free of dust, then they would issue a lid with the bowl. I made a cloth cover and that too was confiscated. A sheet of writing paper was permitted, however. First thing each morning we would be let out to clean our toilet pots—and why is it that one never accepts the smell of human excrement as a reasonable part of life? It was better to be in a cell on your own, even though it was very lonely, than it was to share a cell with a number of people with their smells. At least one's own excrement is tolerable.

The man in charge of our section of cells was a sergeant—and an unmitigated sadist. He set out to find as many ways as possible to make our life unpleasant. He took away the time for emptying our toilet pots, and for washing and shaving. That now had to be done as part of our precious exercise time, cutting deeply into the half-hour morning and afternoon periods laid down in the regulations. We got that stopped. We showered outside in cold water, even in winter, when it was really cold and no sunshine entered the yard because of the high walls. The sergeant said the shower room would get dirty if we were allowed to use it. Guy de Keller was a young student member of the African Resistance Movement (ARM) sentenced on terrorism charges. His mother, who was no anti-apartheid activist but wanted her son properly looked after, demanded that he be allowed to wash with hot water. So boiling hot water was brought to us in ten-gallon drums. We scooped it into washbasins. Standing in the wind, we would wash with the hot water and then sluice ourselves with clean water to get rid of the soap. It was very pleasant to end the ablutions by sitting in a shallow bowl of warm water to warm one's nether regions. Eventually a senior officer, seeing the absurdity of ablutions in the open air, insisted that we use the shower room.

Mornings started at about six o'clock with a loud bell. During the next hour you dressed, made up your mats and blankets, and stacked them tidily. When your cell-door was flung open, you were required to stand to attention behind the still-locked inner steel grille so that the officials could see that you had not escaped during the night, and a head count was conducted of all the prisoners. Only when the totals for all the sections of the prison were added up and the total agreed with the number of prisoners that should be there were the inner steel grilles opened. Emptying toilet pots followed, faces were washed, and breakfast served. That is too fine a word. Breakfast was brought for many years in chipped enamel bowls. It was always a corn porridge called mielie-meal with a bit of milk—and when it was not too watery it was good and warming. A portion of bread, rather good wholemeal bread baked in the prison kitchens, was provided, and there was a mug of "coffee." This was a mixture of 6 percent coffee for the smell, 75 percent burnt maize, and the rest chicory, dark and bitter. This could be called coffee because it contained the minimum of 6 percent coffee that our food laws required. Sometimes guards would insist that the bread be put in the porridge so that it would be spoiled by being wet. Lunch was usually a stew of mielie rice [corn ground to look like rice], potatoes, a little meat, and some vegetables cooked until they were colorless and tasteless. One day a week we got fish. Our evening meal was brought to us at about three in the afternoon and it was always soup and bread. Properly cooked, the soup—made from dehydrated ingredients ground so fine you could not tell what they were—was edible and warming, and another small portion of bread was provided. I still eat soup as often as I can, but real soup made from fresh ingredients. Sometimes a small portion of butter would appear, and if the bread was still hot from the ovens that made a real treat. The same coffee substitute was provided with an ounce of sugar, sometimes two ounces, a day. Sometimes too there was an ounce of jam. The sweetness was very pleasant. The nutrition was just sufficient, without providing any excess energy.

Food improved a bit when the International Committee of the Red

Cross started to visit us once a year from the late 1960s. They urged the authorities to add peanut butter to the prisoners' diet. It contains many vitamins and trace elements and is high in calories.

Three good meals a day were something I experienced only when I was in hospital. The nurses were pretty and they had nice perfume. They treated me like a patient and not as a prisoner. On the other hand, that made me realize just how grim prison life was. The prison guards hated us because we were white. They came mostly from poorer working-class homes and had these jobs because the apartheid state reserved jobs for whites regardless of their school education and kept black people at a distance. The guards were poorly educated and spoke mostly about their cars or rugby or women. Most of our group of political prisoners had some form of higher education or had the experience of politics and much wider interests. Our guards thought of us as coming from privileged white families and set about using their little bit of power to make our lives as miserable as they could.

It was at this time that we realized that we would be much stronger if we insisted that the officials adhere to their own rules laid down in the official "Rules and Regulations" that were issued to us. We followed the advice of the noted German sociologist Max Weber, who, in writing about rule-bound hierarchic bureaucratic systems of administration, pointed out that higher officers needed to know that their juniors obeyed the rules. We therefore made an important decision that we would treat each guard, sergeant, warrant officer, lieutenant, and all the way up to general as someone who had to be won over to support our demand that he should at least play by the prison's own book of rules. Some were more humane than others, and they had to be drawn to our side of the conflict.

To achieve this we needed to form a committee, which was, of course, strictly forbidden by the authorities, who resisted all forms of organization by prisoners. Nevertheless, you cannot stop political prisoners from creating an elected committee (ours was named "Recce" after the Recreation Committee, allowed by the regulations) to decide on joint action to uphold their rights and privileges. We were accustomed to underground activity in a cellular structure. It was plenary sessions that we could not have. We would decide who was most suited to take up any particular issue, marshaling all the arguments we could find in support of our position. Slowly we compelled the officials to play by their own rules. Higher officers disliked the paperwork involved when their juniors did stupid things. It obviously helped that we had lawyers from outside who would appear for any of us who faced charges for internal prison offenses. The officials came to realize that it would be easier for them to avoid problems and instructed the ordinary guards to treat us with some respect.

We did our own training of young guards. For instance, a new guard would arrive and officiously open and close the steel doors and grilles with loud clangs, which rattled through our brains as if we were inside a steel drum being beaten with a large hammer. After some days the young officer would demand to know why nobody greeted him in the morning. The response was unanimous: behave like a human being with a courteous "good morning," and you will be greeted in return. The guard would answer that he was instructed not to converse with us. When the absurdity of this position dawned on these young guards, most behaved as they should have. Some still relished trying to impose arbitrary punishment, but we resisted that, too.

In time our concealed Recce received formal sanction. Helen Suzman, MP, on one of her prison visits, persuaded the commanding officer to allow us to have board games, such as chess, checkers, and dominoes. We were instructed to elect a recreation committee to ensure fair access of all prisoners to these games. Alan Brooks, who had been sentenced to three years for his activities in the ARM and who behind his rather dry exterior could be very amusing, conducted the election, and, lo and behold, even though it was conducted by show of hands in front of the guards, the election produced a committee, now officially named Recce, with the same membership as the previously clandestine Recce. We allowed members of the committee to have no more than two consecutive terms of office, each term lasting six months, though they could be reelected after a break. We kept Recce quite small; each member represented three or four others, depending on the fluctuating size of the community.

We asked the authorities to allow us to have a record player and to slowly build up a record collection so that we could play music at night for a few hours, which we knew was the custom in Central Prison. I had submitted a letter setting out what equipment would be needed just before Helen Suzman fortuitously visited us. She sat on my prison stool, using my small table to make notes, when I started reading from a copy of the letter. I had my back to the open door and she rather bravely, I thought, wordlessly held out her hand for the letter and popped it into her handbag while shielded from view by my body. After a while everything we needed was delivered to the prison, together with thirty LP records of the great classical symphonies and concertos. What a delight that was. Helen Suzman, alone among MPs, made it her business to try to improve the conditions of political prisoners in whichever prisons they were held. I would get my regular visitor, Hillary Kuny, to give Helen Suzman a potted plant at the end of the year to say thanks for her caring concern. Later we were allowed to buy one record each every two months. At first we old-timers enjoyed concerts of classical music, and as the collection was small, even my untrained ear could hear when Beethoven, for example, had used a sonata as a study for a concerto. Then, as new prisoners joined us, they bought music that fit their individual tastes, so we had more jazz and folk, pop and rock, and—inevitably, because that's who we were—we had hefty arguments about the structure of the evening concerts. We were reasonably tolerant of each other's taste, but the truth of the saying that "taste knows no comrade" is as valid for music as it is for food.

Our daily work was to sew mailbags. That went on for four or five years and felt like a useless way of passing the time. I became quite good at sewing with a large needle, pushed through with a leather and metal palm—and I got used to having the pitch coating the line sticking to my hands. We sat near each other in the exercise yard and, even when not allowed to talk, of course we did. While sewing we organized weekly lectures, making as much use of the intellectual resources among our comrades as we could; these were on such topics as history, engineering, law, physics, and many others. An early example that I remember particularly was a marvelous lecture by Norman Levy, a onetime teacher who had been tried with Bram Fischer and others, on how history is written. Norman based this on a case study of an imaginary prison conflict, and we unfortunately underestimated the guards' ability to understand what he was saying: they thought we were mocking them—and thus ended that session of lectures. As an alternative, we lectured quietly while sewing mailbags, sitting in small clusters. It was not as good as a full plenary, because not all the ideas were discussed by all of us together.

In later years I recall a particularly brilliant paper on African customary law by Raymond Suttner, a lecturer in law at the University of Natal and another by Renfrew Christie, who'd been arrested on terrorism charges, on South African economic history.

Formal studies by distance learning through the University of South Africa (Unisa) were allowed for political prisoners without regard to skin color. These studies were extremely important because they brought an outside stimulus to our lives at a time when we were forbidden access to all news and printed media. I studied for almost the whole of my twenty-two years. First I took a degree in public administration because I really believed that we had to be ready to take power. Then I studied history and geography, then spent seven years studying library science, the only remaining degree for which I could study through Unisa. We found the end-of-year examinations written in the prison to be a great test of our sanity, as we measured ourselves against an external standard.

Informal studies were also very important to us. We constantly discussed the future of our country. We studied to understand apartheid better so we could defeat it more quickly and make the transition to a democratic, nonracial society. I made a study of the major corporations in South Africa. I was allowed to buy three-by-five-inch index cards and eventually had more than three thousand cards filled with information about companies gleaned from magazines we were allowed to read. My interest was the dominance of Anglo American, its relations with the other big mining houses, with Barlows (now Barloworld), an industrial conglomerate, and with other private-sector companies. Anglo American's relations with the Afrikaner finance companies such as Federale Volksbeleggings, Federale Mynbou, Sanlam, and others were important, too, because Anglo American had, for example, given them control in 1964 of General Mining. (Anglo took more than 50 percent of the profits, however.) Why did they do this? Because it was a good political move to placate the apartheid government by satisfying the aspiring Afrikaner bourgeoisie. It was also good business to support apartheid. I was particularly interested in laying the basis for a study of monopoly capital and what effects it had on the economy and on poverty in society, and of the role of low wages in the growth of these companies. Anglo American was involved not only in gold and diamond mining but also in tin, zinc, oil, gas, secondary industry, property, and international construction, and they profited from the low wages supported by apartheid.

Even though I could not get to the official register of companies held at Companies House to analyze ownership and control on a particular date, some researchers were able to make use of my preliminary studies. Duncan Innes was in London working on his doctoral thesis on Anglo American and the book that came out of it, *Anglo American and the Rise of Modern South Africa* (1984). He was able to use my diagrams of the complex holdings and cross-holdings within the Anglo American group. I was delighted when, upon meeting him after my release, he wrote an inscription in my copy of his book, thanking me for my contribution.

I was similarly also very pleased when my daughter, Hilly, visited me and told me that Joe Slovo's wife, Ruth First, who had at one point been editor of the *Guardian,* had used my work in a report to the United Nations on the role of Anglo American in the development of apartheid and its influence throughout the world. I had researched Anglo's holdings in South Africa and all the countries of Southern Africa, Malaysia, and Indonesia, as well as Canada and the United States, Mexico, Brazil, and Chile. It was a worldwide corporation; its holdings matched those of the government in some countries and it was therefore politically very powerful.

Hugh Lewin, a journalist and a leader of the African Resistance Movement, edited a clandestine end-of-year magazine with pieces contributed by those who enjoyed writing. I was the "typesetter and printer," using my neat engineer's handwriting in columns, writing introductory paragraphs and headlines in appropriate font sizes. Only one copy was produced; it was secretly passed around to each of us before being destroyed. We were lucky it was not discovered by the guards, but at Christmastime things were a bit more relaxed.

Besides our lectures, studies, and evenings of recorded music, we used sport as a means of passing the endless hours of imprisonment, even when the only ball we had was made of rags rolled up into an old sock. After a time we were given a tennis ball and played "boob squash" against a wall with our bare hands. I suppose you can say that taking part should have been more important than winning, but we did play hard to win. In winter, when our hands were cold and our skin very dry, the pressure of the ball striking our hands would burst surface blood vessels. As a group we played bucket ball, which was our variation of basketball. Hugh and I enjoyed a game of tennis singles played with wooden beach bats and would rush out on Sunday mornings to have a set before the others were ready. He was younger and fitter, but sometimes I could beat him by wiliness rather than pace.

After the first Christmas, when we managed nothing to match what the regulations termed "entertainment," David Evans, for whom imprisonment inspired poetry writing, got a group of four or five together to prepare a dramatized reading of an excerpt from the verse drama *Murder in the Cathedral* by T. S. Eliot. Soon all the participants knew their lines by heart, and it turned into a dramatic performance by the "Courtyard Players" in the courtyard on Christmas Day. Those of us who could make props and costumes from odds and ends contributed those skills to what was a really enjoyable time at the theater. Then we had a concert. Costa Gazidis, tried along with Bram Fischer, though Bram jumped bail, played a wonderfully rhythmic double bass constructed from a piece of rope, a broomstick, and a wooden tea chest. There were no additional instruments other than a box that served as a drum. Eli Weinberg, sentenced to five years' imprisonment for his membership in the illegal Communist Party, and Hugh had very good voices and led the singing. The Christmas play and concert became an annual affair until we overstepped the mark by making a mock pistol out of cardboard as a prop for a play about gangsters, Harold Pinter's *The Dumb Waiter*. The pistol was so realistic that it could have been used to threaten a prison guard. That was the last curtain for the Courtyard Players—no more drama.

I contributed other things, such as starting the greeting card industry for birthdays and other occasions, cards for many years having not been permitted from outside. Everybody got birthday cards from everybody else. Each made up his own verses, made his own sketch, made it as nice or witty as he wished. Wedding anniversaries were remembered. It was all about building unity.

Christmas inside prison was always a lonely time because it is at that time of year that families want to be together. From the beginning I tried to carve a space in which we could be even more together to compensate for the loneliness. At Christmas we were allowed to buy cookies, dried fruit, and sweets. So each man contributed a few items to a common pool from which we each received gift-wrapped Christmas presents, under the Christmas tree. We knew we had contributed; we knew we might even get back what we had put in. That did not matter because each of us got a Christmas present from under the Christmas tree. It was the giving and receiving that were important.

Of course, we had to have a Christmas tree. At first it was a piece of brown cardboard cut into a classic fir tree shape. A year or two later I found a piece of green string that I fixed to the wall in the fir tree shape year after year. Gradually I found materials to make silver and gold stars from the cigarette packets thrown away by the guards. Eventually the tree had a red star right at the top—that irritated some officers, who tore it off and stamped on it. My feeling: "Gotcha."

Over several years our conditions improved. Jock Strachan's articles in 1965 on prison conditions certainly raised awareness. (See chapter 10.) The commissioner of prisons unexpectedly came to see us. He greeted each in turn with a handshake while he doffed his hat with the other hand. He must have wanted to impress us with such politeness and asked about our conditions. None of my older comrades, speaking in short sentences, said a word to him about the way we were treated, and so I, bearing in mind Miss Cook's assessment of me, spoke up with a direct complaint about the overbearing attitude of the sergeant in charge of our section. Of course the authorities could not allow prisoners to determine who would guard them, but things did improve; when we moved to the new prison—Pretoria Security Prison—specially built for white political prisoners, our vicious Sergeant du Preez, who had tormented us for so many years, disappeared from our lives.

It is possible that these improvements had something to do with President B. J. Vorster's hope of breaking the sanctions that isolated South Africa. His new outward-looking foreign policy saw the way back into the world through Africa, and this required some opening up of society—and the visits of the International Committee of the Red Cross (ICRC) and of Helen Suzman were part of that process. Vorster was probably the first of the hardline Afrikaner nationalists actually to state that white South Africans had to respect the human dignity of black people. Even if he said this with tongue in cheek, it started a process that had consequences that neither his nor successive governments could control.

After five years or so we were moved into a prison built especially for us white political prisoners. The physical conditions were much improved. There were flush toilets and a plank bed with a hard horsehair mattress. There was even hot water and a washbasin in each cell, and a small cupboard with a built-in writing surface. I later saw a newspaper article in which the Prisons Department allowed photographs of our cells to be printed. In addition, there was a carpentry workshop, which I personally enjoyed. Some of my comrades found this kind of work uninteresting and wanted to spend all their time studying, as I had done at first because there was no alternative in the early years. But now I enjoyed working with my hands. An instructor was provided, and I really enjoyed learning how to sharpen the blade of a plane so that when I worked on a piece of wood it sang as the wood was shaved off, and the scent of the wood found its way into my nostrils. I liked the way my whole body was involved in working only with hand tools.

Damaged furniture was brought to our workshop for renovation. Often we made toolboxes to be filled with the tools needed by white prisoners in the main prison who had become qualified artisans—carpenters, plumbers, and so on—during their sentences. There were, nevertheless, some potential ethical problems, such as the rumor that we were to make boxes for ammunition used by the military, and we knew that we would have to refuse to make them. The issue did not arise.

The ICRC delegations were very sympathetic toward us. They pointed out that in Africa and poor countries elsewhere in the world, physical conditions were far worse than ours, but "you do not have to have steak and chips." We would survive as long as we had nutritious food. They said also that they had never experienced anywhere else in the world such harsh attitudes among prison officials to the prisoners as they found in South Africa. They related this to Calvinist beliefs dominant in government circles, where crime was not just a social matter; it was a sin and therefore hateful—and criminals were to be dealt with as sinners. We white political prisoners were the biggest sinners of all because we challenged their white supremacist beliefs from within the system. We were traitors in their eyes. The ICRC visits certainly had a beneficial effect on our treatment and conditions.

Helen Suzman also did much for us, and I cannot fault her sense of justice, though I could not accept her slow reformist political views. But in her concern for individuals, she showed considerable courage and determination—and her exposure of the gratuitous brutality of apartheid outside and inside the prisons played an important role. She tried for a time to help Esmé get permission to visit me. She always wrote to Esmé as "Dear Esmé" until one day she wrote to "Dear Mrs. Goldberg" to say that she could do no more to help and would not correspond with her in future. Esmé, through a mutual friend, discovered that the Security Police had told Mrs. Suzman that Esmé was making bombs for the IRA and was a dangerous person. What is astonishing is that Mrs. Suzman believed them.

I am not religious, but I did ask to see the Jewish chaplain, Rabbi Katz. Given that my mum insisted that if I took off from school for a Jewish religious holiday, I should attend the synagogue, seeing the rabbi was itself a moral issue for me. But I thought it might become necessary to have someone to bear witness if something untoward should happen to me or to others. I did not want him to take messages from me to the outside because that would have endangered him, and it was something he would not have done. He said, "The rules are that I am your spiritual adviser and that's all." But there were some chaplains who, if you were ill and your family did not know, would find a way of letting them know, because that's human. And if a family member was ill, these chaplains would let you know. How would you separate anxiety about your family from your spiritual condition?

Rabbi Katz once apologized to me for not seeing me for over three months because he had taken a tour party to Israel, and he also had his own congregation to deal with. I asked him how things were in Galilee because at the time my daughter was on a kibbutz there. At first he would not answer me. I demanded he tell me if she was at risk. He assured me all was calm at that time. I was quite harsh and said bluntly that either he told me or not, but he could not be my spiritual adviser and ignore my need to know about my family. We had a different relationship after that.

He used to bring parcels at Rosh Hashanah and Passover, and naturally we shared them with everybody. The most I ever had of a parcel was in the early months, when there were Turok, Tarshish, Goldberg, and Strachan, and we were meticulous in sharing the goodies. I got three-quarters of my parcels at that time. Later the whole balance changed. I was one Jew among seven political prisoners in later years. (In the mid-1960s there were as many as twenty-one white political prisoners. The new prison had fifty-two cells, and we wondered whether the authorities were optimistic or pessimistic when they made the political prison so big.)

Perhaps I am being unfair to the rabbi because, though he had this niminy-piminy fear of authority, he could also be quite clever. For example, he was not allowed to give us sweets, but he was able to give us matzos. One year he found a chocolate made to look like matzos. Another time the specialty was fruit juice imported from America. It looked like Passover wine. I was called to the office. "What does it say on this bottle, it's in Hebrew?" I was asked. I replied, "Fruit juice for Passover, nonalcoholic." "How do you know?" the officer demanded. "Because it says so in English on this side." What inner conflicts we make for ourselves—because at the same time there were Jewish soldiers on the border oppressing the Namibians and Angolans, and they were getting the same gifts.

The rabbi did help get my dad into the Jewish old-age home in Sandringham in Johannesburg. And that's a bit ironic, given our attitudes to the organized Jewish community and the Board of Deputies' attitude to us: they believed that, with our activism against the apartheid government, we endangered the whole Jewish community.

Dad looked so well after he moved into the home. But after some weeks he seemed to be weaker, and I felt he would not last very long. Each time he came to visit, his skin seemed thinner and his facial bones seemed to be pressing through his skin so that he looked like his own death mask. After six months there, he died. He had developed pneumonia and had difficulty breathing. At his last visit to me he had started coughing and could not stop. He had been hospitalized. Hillary Kuny came to visit me one Sunday morning. Then at two o'clock on the same day I was told I had a visitor. There had to be a problem. Hillary came to tell me that Dad had died that morning between her phoning him and actually getting to the hospital after seeing me. He was old and tired, but with a mind so alert, so politically acute, it was incredible that he had died. When Hillary knew him, he was an old man with little energy and dependent on others, though trying hard not to be. Hillary's caring for him was generous and warmhearted. I know too that younger people who wanted to know about the history of our liberation struggle and about eras in world history, such as the Cold War, saw him as a living history book—this was a time when it was difficult to get hold of political literature because the government controlled what could be imported. Recently Denis Kuny said he regretted that he had not recorded Dad's history lessons and political analyses.

The day before I was released, I was taken, at my request, to see his grave because I would be leaving the country directly from prison. I was taken under guard to the Jewish cemetery in Johannesburg. Dad had wanted to be cremated, but he was in the hands of the Orthodox Jewish community who ran the retirement home, and Orthodox Jews do not cremate the dead. We found the grave and the guards withdrew to a respectful distance so that I could be alone. I thought, "You old devil, you're still taking up space, making trouble as you did all your life." I thought about it some more and found I was deeply moved and could allow myself to feel the loss I had suppressed while I was inside. There were so many things I had wanted to ask him about, and now I could never ask him anything at all.

I thought back to his burial. Hillary Kuny was very close to Barney Simon of Market Theatre fame, and he wished to read something for me at Dad's graveside. I asked that he read Bertolt Brecht's poem "To Posterity" (or "To Those Who Come After"). In a loose translation it ends:

We who wanted to make a world
where man would no longer be an oppressor to man

a world where man would be kind to man
did not ourselves have time for kindness.
But you who come after,
When you think about us
think of us with forbearance.

I thought it was appropriate to all the years of Dad's life—and it certainly reflects my own life and attitudes. It was then, more than five years after he had died, that I really did grieve and in grieving achieved the closure I had denied myself up till then. At least I thought I had achieved it. Some years later, speeding through the English countryside from one solidarity meeting to the next, I could smell the leather seats of the car and enjoy the sense of speed and found myself talking to my dad, asking him if he would like to drive because he liked cars but seldom had a decent one that ran well. Such depths of memories one has!

Hillary Kuny (now Hamburger) kept a newspaper clipping recording my dad's passing away and sent it to me quite recently. Thirty years after he died, when I read the obituary written by Peta Thornycroft in the defunct *Sunday Express* newspaper, I found myself weeping for my lonely dad and suspect I was really weeping for myself.

Sam will never see his favoured son free of the traitor's brand

Sam Goldberg is dead. But he lives on.

One of the characters in the sell-out play, "Cincinnati," was based on Sam, who died in Johannesburg this week.

Sam was a listed person under the Suppression of Communism Act. This means he was not able to be quoted in life—and the ban on anything he said continues after his death. I cannot tell you what he said to me or anyone about anything at any time.

But Barney Simon, director of Johannesburg's Market Theatre, immortalized Sam by basing one of the characters in "Cincinnati" on him. Barney told me this at Sam's funeral on Thursday. It was a Jewish funeral, which I am sure would have irritated Sam, as it certainly did one of his sons.

But the son who was upset that his father was planted in the traditional way wasn't at the funeral.

He was in Pretoria Central prison where he has already been for 15 years and where he is scheduled to remain for the rest of his life.

Dennis Goldberg was given a life sentence at the sensational Rivonia trial, where he and others like Nelson Mandela were found guilty of trying to overthrow the government.

For 15 years Sam Goldberg, an atheist, visited him whenever he could.

He last saw Dennis, the son he appeared to love so much, three weeks ago. He shouldn't have gone on that visit. He already had the pneumonia which killed him on Sunday.

Mid-way during his chat with his son the shrunken old man started coughing up great gobs of phlegm and was taken back to Johannesburg and admitted to hospital.

It was obvious he was furious at becoming ill. He seemed angry as age and frailty restricted his movements.

As though he resented age standing in the way of his being part of a changing world.

For 11 years, a Johannesburg woman, Hillary Kuny, has been visiting Dennis Goldberg. She was probably closer to Sam than anyone in the world, other than the son he saw for only 90 minutes a month.

"I felt sad that Sam never lived to see Dennis [his son] freed. That must have grieved him," she told me.

More than 20 years ago there was a domestic row which led to an estrangement between Sam and his older son, a son who has asked not to be named because he may be alienated from many people if the connection between him and Dennis Goldberg is made public. This son never saw or spoke to his father again, but he was at the funeral.

Dennis was the favoured son. He went to university to become a brilliant engineer. The older son also qualified professionally, but at his own expense and through UNISA.

The brothers were estranged from each other but the rift started healing about four months ago when they started writing to each other. This week the older Goldberg visited his politically committed brother in Pretoria central. They hadn't met for 18 years.

Earlier this year Sam was admitted to the Jewish old age home.

For many years he remained, despite failing health, in a tatty Berea hotel where the food was frightful. He lived frugally on his old age pension.

"We were so glad when he went to the home. He found the comfort he needed. There was someone to help him get in and out of the bath. They were terribly good to him there," Mrs. Kuny said. For a long time washing his crumpled old body must have been agonizing for Sam. He performed amazing physical contortions getting himself in and out of the hotel bath.

At the old age home, he seemed to enjoy his meals more than he had in years.

Conversation between political prisoners and their visitors is restricted. Certain subjects are taboo, such as politics. It was politics which had absorbed Sam Goldberg throughout his life. His knowledge of history was immense. He read and read. All the librarians in the Johannesburg central library knew him and would keep new books they knew he would want to read aside for him.

Sam went to the library more than anyone else they ever met, bus fare permitting, of course. He knew many of the suburban libraries pretty well too. And the first person he got to know at the old age home was the librarian.

He was a life-long socialist who tried various hare-brained money making ventures.

The day before he died, Hilary Kuny visited the desperately ill old man in hospital. "I knew he was dying because he looked so awful. He was having terrible difficulty breathing. But I felt sure he wanted to live desperately," she said.

"His will to live was so strong, I half-believed he would hold on. When I visited Dennis the next day I told him his father was critically ill, but I also told him I couldn't believe he wouldn't fight back, recover and carry on again. Sam always fought his illnesses with courage—determined, it would seem, to live."

Later that day, after she had learned of his death, the Department of Prisons allowed Mrs. Kuny a special visit to tell the man who has now become her firm friend that his father had died.

She asked for a contact visit for the occasion—normally visitors are not allowed to touch maximum security prisoners, they are separated by a glass screen. But no.

"When Dennis saw me he said: 'So it is all over.' He asked that his father have a cremation with no service," she told me.

"I wanted to just put my arms around him and give him a hug.

But I couldn't so I put my hand to the glass, and he put his hand out to the glass. We nearly touched."

I didn't know Sam Goldberg. I met him only a couple of times.

His daughter-in-law, Esme Goldberg, lives in London, where she went after Dennis was arrested. She is not allowed into South Africa to visit her husband, but her children come occasionally.

Sam, the cantankerous, solitary man, contrary as hell, also did a stint in jail. When he was well into his 60's he failed to notify the police of his change of address, and spent a few days in the Fort. He was let out ahead of his release date because he became ill.

He had a Jewish funeral because it was the only one possible at the time. He had left his body to medical research, but Mrs. Kuny was told the doctors would not be able to use it because it was too old and debilitated. Getting a Jewish body out of a Jewish old age home is very complicated, and arranging private cremation is expensive.

But Dennis Goldberg's other request was carried out. A poem, chosen by him, was read at the grave side by Barney Simon.

Written by Berthold [sic] Brecht it was, all things considered, brutally significant:

"Our forces were slight,
Our goal lay far in the distance
It was clearly visible,
Though I myself was unlikely to reach it.
So passed my time
Which had been given me on earth."

The things I just can't tell you . . .

I am unable, because of the laws of the country, to tell you the following things about Sam Goldberg:

- Where he was born.
- Where he grew up.
- Whether his mum was a duchess or a charwoman.
- Where he was educated.
- Whether he lived his youth in a palace or a hut.
- What he did as a young man, where he was educated.

- Whether he was ashamed or proud of his son in jail.
- Whether he did or did not feel anguish about his son's incarceration.

And many other things about this stoic old man.

He was publicly listed in 1962 and has been silenced for 18 years.

Every sentence of this story has been studied carefully by legal experts. I have had to examine and re-examine—and check again— every single word in this report. To be careful that even indirectly, anything Sam Goldberg said is not quoted.

I can't tell you whether he did or did not want to go to an old age home, whether he did or did not believe his son would one day be freed, whether he did or did not weep occasionally.

There are more gaps than facts in this story. And that's part of my responsibility and yours—unless the law is changed.

But people know people. Fill in your own gaps. They are the emotions, hopes and sorrows of us all.

It's a story that begins in the recorded history of this country, in a series of events that is remembered by everyone who was around to read newspapers in 1964—16 years ago, every year which Dennis Goldberg, for one, remembers.

Those events culminated in the trial that frightened the Government into changing the laws to the degree that I cannot now tell you a whole lot about an old man who died last week.

I tried to get to the Minister of Justice to ask for permission to fill in some innocuous biographical details about Sam Goldberg, but I was unable to contact him.

I have been advised it would have been unusual for such permission to have been given.

During my twenty-two years in prison in Pretoria I had said hello and good-bye to more than forty comrades. They had shorter sentences, had come in and, having served every day of their sentences, been released. (Political prisoners got not even one day off, unlike ordinary criminals, who got remission of one-third or one-half of their sentences.) Every time someone was released, I rejoiced with him, but at the same time it was painful because I wondered if I would really ever get out of there. Sometimes I wondered if I would die in prison. I know this sounds contradictory because I've said I was confident I would not die in prison—apartheid was becoming ever weaker, so surely my imprisonment would have to come to an end. But logic and emotions don't necessarily coincide. Political systems have to be changed by people's action, whereas emotions happen, despite what you think you should feel.

In prison you cannot ask for counseling because you cannot put your mind in the hands of your enemy. You have to be your own therapist. My definition of sanity is being able to bring your emotions into line with what you know, by clear thinking, is objectively right. That is what you do for yourself in the early hours of the morning when you cannot sleep because your thoughts are whirling around inside your head like a dog chasing its own tail. You have to wake yourself up to resolve the inner conflicts because if you don't they will destroy you. At other times you have to talk to someone else during the daytime to try to achieve some equanimity. That I tried unsuccessfully to avoid because it meant burdening someone else, who was also under stress, with my problems. Sometimes I was depressed. Outside you get depressed, so why not inside? And as time goes by it seems that the pit gets deeper and climbing out of it becomes harder. When the mood is very dark, you feel, as you get your fingers over the edge of the pit of depression, that some external event stamps on your fingers and you fall back again. The writer Baruch Hirson and I used to spend lots of time chatting. While he was alive I used to talk to Bram, too. But each of us knew when to leave somebody alone or to offer comfort. These phases came and went over the many years—and sometimes I felt very much alone because of the age difference between me and my younger comrades after those first years when those older than I or about my age had been released. Nelson Mandela was behind bars before us and was released after us, having spent twenty-seven years in prison.

You do not have to like every person you meet. That would be burdensome. Yet to this day there is a special bond between me and my prison comrades. Friendship and shared experience are what bind us. It is phenomenal. And to make even one friend like that in a lifetime makes life worth living. It is not anything like love between a man and a woman, but rather a deep mutual understanding and the great sharing of membership in a movement. We trusted our lives to each other. We had the same political beliefs and a common enemy, and that was a great unifying force. None of us was ashamed of being in prison. Indeed, we were proud of it. This pride nourished us. It gave us strength. We were living symbols of resistance for those outside (and for those with short sentences) who themselves were "imprisoned" by having to live under apartheid.

But it was also true that you did not select who you would be in prison with. You get to know your suffering comrades better than you know your own wife. There is no relief from each other: 365 days a year, twenty-four hours a day, every sneeze, cough, and fart you experience together. Every one of my bad jokes was answered with the response "Oh no! Not again." You have to learn to deal with it. Everyone has habits that you have to tolerate. If possible, you try not to reveal your feelings because that is one way to survive.

Fred Carneson, with whom I had worked in Cape Town on many aspects of our political activity, was broken under torture. We believed before we experienced torture that we could not be broken. When we were, our whole world collapsed. Fred, in a sense, was terribly ashamed. It was painful to see. He came to doubt his own resolve. Sometimes he was overly dogmatic. It was difficult to deal with because all of us were also under strain. We knew he was fragile and we had to be gentle with him, but despite his stature as a leader, he was not elected to Recce until the last period of his imprisonment. He was elected because we felt he had to go out knowing we trusted him and valued him as a comrade. We had to restore his self-confidence. I suspect we should have tried much earlier. In retrospect, life is so full of regrets.

Fred, like all of us, had to deal with the stresses our families had to withstand. We were in the courtyard in midwinter, freezing cold, standing on our stools to get our heads into the sun and sewing mail bags at the same time. Fred was called out. After a time he came back, weeping, cursing, and shouting in terrible distress. We were not supposed to talk to each other, but I jumped down to go to him. He told me that Father Magennis, the Catholic chaplain, had been given permission to tell him that his eight-year-old daughter, Ruthie, had had a breakdown. She was under the care of Dr. Aubrey Zabow, who had been a member of the Congress of Democrats, which meant that we knew she was in sympathetic hands. Fred was outraged by the pressure put on the family. Sarah, his wife, a noted activist, was being constantly harassed and arrested. Ruthie could not handle the pressure. There is terrible anguish when you are in prison and unable to help. I walked and talked with him and let him rage and urged him not to let the Boers have the satisfaction of seeing how deeply hurt he was. I simply felt that being there for him was more important than rules about not talking. I was surprised that no punishment followed my disobedience. It was good that Father Magennis had such a broad interpretation of spiritual need.

In these ways we supported each other. But sometimes we came to blows, and that was over comrades feeling that they weren't trusted. It was clear that they had not learned from their own interrogations that you cannot let slip information about what you don't know. At such moments of conflict someone would intervene and say: "Denis, you were very rude to him and you had better apologize." I would answer: "Okay, I was crude in the way I spoke, but it was right that I spoke out on the issue." Today I would agree: that was only a halfhearted apology. That was always the problem: To what extent can you impose your needs and problems on others? Then I had to bite my tongue in order not to contradict myself immediately.

The problem of secrecy leads to moral problems. How should we deal with traitors? Raymond Thoms's betrayal of our community (see chapter 10) over Jock Strachan's articles on prison conditions resulted in our isolating him from our community for years. It was harsh treatment, but I do not know what else we could have done. I know that Bram Fischer and Ivan Schermbrucker surreptitiously breached the agreement that he was to be isolated. I objected because they were ignoring a majority decision. We could not have enabled the great escape (see chapter 11) with a spy in our midst and not under our control. Standing together enabled us to get news when it was forbidden for sixteen years. We found a way to ask black prisoners who were brought in to clean the administration offices to get us newspapers. They took the newspapers out of the wastebaskets in the offices and put them into our rubbish bin. We paid with tobacco, the normal currency in prison, which we put into our bin for them to find.

All in all we were under these circumstances a very disciplined and civilized group of comrades, and in the end our comradeship, to use that overworked phrase, worked well for us.

I came out of prison a much stronger person than I was when I went in. I was better educated than I was when I worked as an engineer. I read a great deal and studied and yet had nothing to do to satisfy my emotional needs. No entertainment! I grew intellectually because there was endless time for thinking. I learned to cut through great detail to get to the essentials of a topic. I could now explain the complex nature of my country in simple ways.

People often ask me how I remained as I am through all the long years in prison. I can only say that I did not remain unchanged. I became far more introspective, far more aware of my own strengths and weaknesses. That does not mean I can always control them, but I became far more aware of the tensions within myself.

I have to say that many comrades who spent a few days or weeks or even months in prison believe that they know all about prison. They do not, because the length of time has its effects, and as it gets longer the fight against becoming institutionalized becomes more important and harder. It is the resistance to becoming a prisoner in your mind that is the key to survival as a useful member of society. I know that even a short time in prison is heavy going and causes a major disruption in one's life. My purpose is not to denigrate comrades who got "parking ticket" sentences of up to five years but to ask readers to think about what imprisonment means when continued for years and years without definite end.

The sense of powerlessness in the struggle for freedom raging outside the walls of the prison was awful. I felt that my hands were tied. I discussed and debated, but I could not act, because I was cut off from everyday reality.

10

Problems of Imprisonment

To cover twenty-two years of imprisonment in chronological order is too difficult—and I think it would be boring to read about that life within a life in such detail. I have selected some themes that I hope will give some flavor of what prison was like.

The Case for Better Conditions: The Strachan Trial

It took a very long time for prison conditions to improve. A major impetus was a series of articles by Jock Strachan published in the *Rand Daily Mail* after he was released from prison in 1965 at the end of his three-year sentence. He exposed the reality of the treatment of prisoners. Jock, however, had not asked the commissioner of prisons for permission to disclose information about prisons. That was an offense, and his defense had to be that he could prove everything he had written was true.

He said, for example, that it was an everyday occurrence that prisoners were stripped naked in front of other prisoners in contravention of prison rules. On every occasion that he went to or was taken past the place where new prisoners came in, he would see this happen. But being a prisoner, Jock could not be at Reception every day. That each of us confirmed his observation was irrelevant in law. Jock was relying on hearsay and could not "prove" that his whole statement was true.

There was another complication. Jock had sworn to the truth of his statement to the journalist Benjamin Pogrund, but his lawyer, Rowley Arenstein, insisted that he withdraw certain statements because they could not be proved. Jock therefore made a new sworn statement to correct the faulty one but could not persuade Pogrund, the deputy editor of the *Rand Daily Mail*, to destroy his original statement. Benjie, who had been at school with me, wanted it kept as a historical document. Unfortunately, but predictably, the Security Police raided the newspaper's and their lawyers' offices and found both sworn statements. Since they contradicted each other, this constituted statutory perjury, a criminal offense and the grounds for a second charge against Jock.

The court proceedings were interesting, involving three of us in the early stages of our sentences. Dave Evans, Alan Brooks, and I were asked by Jock's lawyers to give evidence in his behalf. It was exciting to go to Durban in November 1965 under guard in a military transport aircraft. We did not see much of the sea, only a tiny glimpse out of a porthole as the plane circled to land. George Bizos, as I have noted, said that South Africa was not a fully fascist state, and that is true. I was writing University of South Africa examinations at the time, and my court appearances took account of when I had to sit for an exam. I was allowed to take my study materials with me to Durban to prepare for the exams.

We were treated very respectfully by the prison authorities and by criminal prisoners in Durban Central Prison. The former ensured that we had very good meals, and the latter supplied us with as much illicit tobacco as we needed. I ate my lunch in the commanding officer's office between morning and afternoon sessions in the witness box. "Do have another piece of fried fish," served with a slice of lemon, he insisted. "Do have a glass of iced milk." I am quite sure he did not want me to tell the court about conditions in his prison. In the end I gave evidence and so did Dave. Not only did I know that everything I said in evidence about the prisons I had been in with Jock was true, but I knew too that I understated the reality. This was especially so about the way that prisoners, and especially black prisoners, were treated. The barbarity and indifference to the humanity of prisoners was beyond anything that you could believe. Jock's lawyers were pleased with my evidence. They felt I had scored well for Jock. They were also very pleased with Dave's evidence.

In the course of giving my evidence I recalled how brave Jock and his wife had been in the 1960 protest over the Sharpeville Massacre. They had stood in the way of armed police who were threatening to shoot black protesters marching from the Berea to the Durban city center. I must admit it was my intention that, when I gave evidence in a courtroom in which there were many comrades, they would see that four life sentences had not intimidated me. The prosecutor, inevitably, spotted this and asserted that I would say anything to discredit the government. I answered to the effect that the truth was enough.

The prison authorities presented around two hundred prison officers to give evidence. Jock, for example, had said that despite the prison regulations requiring that a doctor examine every new prisoner, the doctor did not do so; he simply walked past the prisoners as they stood lined up, often naked, in the open air. The doctor would run a stethoscope over the chest of one or two prisoners, and that was it. The three district surgeons concerned said that was indeed what happened. But prison officials said that every prisoner was properly examined by these doctors. The commanding officer said he personally observed the procedure every day, looking out of his office window while sitting at his desk. An inspection at the prison showed that he could not see the hospital yard from his desk, and only by a tricky maneuver could he do so if he went to a particular window. In his judgment, the magistrate said the doctors must have been mistaken.

One prisoner with us gave evidence against Jock. Raymond Thoms had been sentenced together with Marius Schoon to twelve years' imprisonment for plotting to blow up the Hillbrow Police Station in Johannesburg. They had been lured into a trap by a provocateur who disappeared before the case against them was heard. Thoms said that Jock had conspired in prison with Ben Turok to write misleading articles to expose the government to ridicule. I believe he was promised early release if he gave such evidence.

Before the judgment was delivered, Thoms wrote a note that he slipped into the cell I was sharing with Dave Evans and Alan Brooks after we had returned from Durban. His note said he had betrayed Jock. He said he had "reached the nadir of degradation and despair" and wanted us to inform Jock's lawyers that he had lied to the court. Alan insisted that the note was important and made a copy of it. I hid the original away. Thoms overnight switched sides yet again and told the authorities what he had done. I have never been through a search such as the one each of us and our possessions were subjected to as a result. The copy of the note was found, but not the original. Our comrades wanted all the details of what was happening and why. Ivan Schermbrucker said that all of us had experienced torture and knew how hard it was not to reveal what we knew to the interrogators. Therefore those who were demanding information

146

should show some trust and not blame comrades for the actions of the authorities. I was kept in solitary confinement and I thought back to Miss Cook: Why was I the one to be singled out?

A message was sent to the lawyers, and they came to see Dave, Alan, and me. I had prepared for their visit by removing the note from its very secret place to somewhere more accessible, but I nevertheless went to see the lawyers without the note. I said that it would be taken from me and destroyed. They said the authorities would not dare to do that once they, the lawyers, knew of its existence. They were more trusting than I was. I was taken back to my cell to fetch the note, hoping I would be able to retrieve it unobserved. No such luck. I did hand it to the lawyers and they were delighted, thinking it would really help Jock. But the magistrate said he had not relied on Thoms's evidence at all and dismissed the evidence—and the note. He also dismissed my evidence because he said I was a "gay desperado" who would say anything to discredit the government. Dave's evidence was completely trustworthy he said, but he would not accept it because Dave too was a political prisoner opposed to the government. On the other hand, he said that every official told the truth, and when they contradicted themselves and each other it was because so much was happening that their memory lapses could be overlooked. I know that they lied their heads off.

Jock was sentenced to another four years in prison and was brought back to join us. He was a truly brave man. Despite his being sentenced on technical grounds, his actions did usher in the beginning of a new era throughout all prisons. My dad was very disturbed by the Strachan articles and was given special permission to visit me to find out the truth about our conditions. My comrades were truly impressed with my dad's spirit. "Old Sam is still fighting," they said.

Thoms was not given any time off for his betrayal. He was so frustrated that he bundled matches together, lit them, and stuck the flaming ends into his eyes—hoping, I suppose, that being partly blinded would bring some compassion from the prison authorities. It did not. He served every day of his sentence. In time he regained some sight. Not many months after his release from prison he successfully took his own life.

Memories of Bram Fischer

Bram Fischer was a lawyer highly regarded in mining and business circles, and he is still regarded as one of the greatest liberation lawyers. He was born into an elite Afrikaner family in 1908. I met him in the early 1960s, when I was in Johannesburg on an advanced highways design course. His elder daughter, Ruth, invited me home for Sunday lunch, where I met Bram in a setting of informal prelunch chitchat. It was clear that people simply dropped in, not needing an invitation to visit. Conversation flowed all round the political topics of the time. National and international affairs were intermingled; personalities and gossip seemed to mix frothily over the surface of Sunday at leisure. My own engineering work seemed of interest, but I think out of politeness to a visitor. Bram was clearly the center of it all, while his wife, Molly, was a little off-center as she wandered in and out making sure that the entertainment and lunch flowed as smoothly as the conversation. There could be no mistaking the deference with which Bram's remarks were received, and his unassuming manner was striking. He seemed to twinkle!

The next time we met was at the first legal consultation after we had been charged in October 1963. Bram was leader of our defense team. He was very quiet and still during that first meeting, which, I discovered, was his usual manner. He must have been very worried about us all. But there was more to it than that. He was himself directly involved in our underground activities, and, though he didn't let on at all, he must have been deeply concerned that some of the witnesses arrested at Rivonia might have been in a position to see him and so identify him.

Throughout the trial Bram's manner was striking for his seriousness and determination. He had the ability to concentrate fiercely even in the bleak office set aside in the prison for consultations. That room was surely wired for sound, bugged. His very fair skin seemed thin; one could see the blood close beneath the skin. Sometimes, when he was annoyed, his face would be suffused with a pink blush. But when he was angered, or forced to be silent, Bram's face would be drained of blood, his lips squeezed in a tight, bloodless line. His blue eyes would flash until he hid them behind partly closed lids, or he would tip his head down to hide his feelings. Throughout the time I knew him—then, and later for nine long years in prison—he always hid his emotions, and I understood the stillness as the expression of the depth of his feelings.

He used language beautifully and precisely in both English and Afrikaans. During our trial he hardly ever swore. On one occasion we were chatting together while the other lawyers and my coaccused were busy. He asked me how I felt about our situation. I told him how I saw the politics of the situation. I was convinced that apartheid, for all its seeming strength, was living on borrowed time. He heard me out, and responded, "We'll get the bastards yet, won't we?" The rarity of the curse made it a powerful expression of determination. In retrospect, I realized that he had been asking me how I felt about our position in the trial because such a strong case had been made against us. But that seemed to me in some way irrelevant. Our future was more bound up in the politics of South Africa than in some isolated concept of law and justice or injustice.

Bram throughout the trial generated energy and ideas as he fought to save our lives. He was meticulous in his preparations and once told me that a basic guideline in cross-examination was not to ask a hostile witness a question to which you did not know the answer, because the answer could be turned against you.

The defense strategy was to show that even though there had been much discussion about Operation Mayibuye (the name means Operation Come Back, as in *Mayibuye i'Afrika,* Come back, Africa), no date had been set for starting guerrilla warfare. In that sense, even the investigations we had made into making weapons, land mines, grenades, and detonators were all part of a thorough, responsible study made by serious people. In fact, as I described earlier, there was a dispute about whether Operation Mayibuye had been adopted, but despite that Joe Slovo had already left the country to make arrangements for international support, for weapons supply and military training facilities.

Bram the activist showed enormous courage by appearing in court in the Rivonia Trial. He avoided appearing in court during the first few days of the trial when the farm laborers were called to give evidence. But Patrick Mthembu and Bartholomew Hlapane, both members of the SACP and of *Umkhonto we Sizwe,* knew Bram in both capacities and could have betrayed him, but they did not. It was striking that state witnesses would acknowledge their membership in the ANC and MK but conceal their membership in the Communist Party. I am not sure why. We thought it might be that they wanted to avoid provoking the Security Police, who hated communists as the cause of all their problems. Therefore, when comrades were broken under torture, they retained some sense of self-preservation and covered that association by telling the details of their other activities.

Bram used to arrive at Rivonia looking very dapper in his suit and well-shaped hat, with his briefcase under his arm. I am not sure what Bram thought about the adoption of Operation Mayibuye. He did not say to me during our many discussions in prison that he thought it adventurous or foolhardy. The revolutionary overthrow of brutal regimes was central to many of the discussions in prison, but on Operation Mayibuye I cannot recall his saying yea or nay. But, then, he always had the ability to let you believe whatever you wished to believe, without agreeing or disagreeing. He often listened and said nothing, making noncommittal remarks, while he thought through what you were saying to him, or simply not letting on that he had already made up his mind and was keeping quiet about it. In part it was his way of resolving differences of opinion between comrades, and in part it seemed to be a conscious style of not actively disagreeing with anyone, because disagreement might be offensive. Sometimes that led to difficulties in prison. His prestige was such that two comrades with directly opposite views would state that Bram had agreed with each of them. Knowing him, I figured out that he had not expressed agreement with either. He had simply not disagreed with either of them. Disconcerting!

I experienced such a complication with Bram after he had been convicted and was brought to our prison. Jack Tarshish was a very brave comrade who had a progressive neurological condition called narcolepsy-cataplexy. He would drop off to sleep at the oddest of times. While eating a meal he sometimes ended up with his face in his plate of food. Jack thought he could engineer a release on medical grounds and found ways of bringing on an attack. He would sometimes drag himself to a halt while walking around the exercise yard. His body would go slack and he would start quivering. Even his eyes would grow dull. The guards thought it a joke. But it was very difficult to tell if he was faking or not. After a few seconds, even a self-induced episode would become the real thing. Taken by a sergeant to see Dr. Davies, a physician, Jack told me that he had spoken about a medical release. Dr. Davies told Jack that the prison authorities had instructed him that there would be no medical releases for political prisoners. Jack told Dr. Davies he had to fight that ruling because otherwise Bram, with a life sentence, would never be released. When I remarked that Jack had been silly (I probably said stupid) to say that in front of the sergeant, Jack sneered about the stupidity of the official, who would not understand what was being said. When I insisted that it was an error because the authorities would be reinforced in their belief that he was faking his medical condition as a way of getting released, Jack said that Bram did not think so. Of course, I asked Bram about his response. He said that whatever damage had been done was already done, so there was no point in making an issue of it! But I insisted that Bram ought to make his position clear. He looked at me and said quite gently and sweetly that he was too old to change the habit of a lifetime.

Bram loved music, but like most of the older generation, he could not stand music playing loudly when he was working: thinking, reading, or writing. Classical music he loved. Formal jazz—for example, Dave Brubeck—he thought was good. He liked the complexity of the music and its rhythms. It was also planned and coherent in the way a symphony is—written down, meaning that it had been carefully composed. He thought jam sessions and therefore, by definition, spontaneous music making were self-indulgent and lacking in meaning because they were not composed. But of course they were; they were instantaneous compositions of variations on a theme leading to totally new musical expression. Beethoven's variations on a theme or Bartok's variations for that matter were legitimate because they were planned. But "serious" jazz, which would take a simple pop melody line as the basis for variations of increasing complexity, and a variety of moods and expressions, he thought was fine. I know he found rock music cacophonous. I agreed with him about that, but I found that some rock music had a complexity that made repeated hearing a pleasure because there was always something new in it, unlike most pop music, which did not stand up to repeated hearing. The Beatles and the Rolling Stones were fabulous for their interesting lyrics and the way in which the melody fit the meaning of the songs. The Stones in particular had a large range of sounds and moods that far transcended the "noise" of some other groups who seemed to adopt the same energy levels and sounds but somehow did not match them for sustained development.

Bram loved African rhythms and drum music, but he found jazz drumming decadent, probably because it was American and therefore suspect. But also, I think it was because the limited tonal range of African percussion music seemed to be designed to provide rhythms for dance—and especially ritual dance—and therefore had an internal consistency. In similar fashion, Bram thought the scat singing of Ella Fitzgerald was meaningless, childish noise because it was singing that did not use words to give it meaning. But the making of vocal music by operatic singers who sing sounds that, though they start from the lyrics, are often divorced from any words, was superb, he said. It was easy to agree about the latter, and just as easy to argue heatedly about the former.

Bram never stopped thinking politics. We saw a report somewhere of a Soviet Kirov-class cruiser and its escort vessels sailing through the Malacca Straits under the noses of the assembled heads of Commonwealth governments meeting in Singapore in 1971. The news item reported a frisson of disquiet. Soviet Admiral Gorshkov's blue-water fleet was too much for them. Within a matter of days Bram had the outline of a strategy that would change the balance of power in the Indian Ocean, and therefore the possibilities of liberation for countries on the eastern seaboard of the whole African continent. First Hugh Lewin and then Fred Carneson memorized the final version so that when they were released, Bram's strategy was passed on through the SACP to colleagues in the Soviet Union. Bram's vision was truly international and comprehensive.

As with his attitudes and opinions, Bram seldom allowed himself to show physical or emotional pain. He suppressed physical pain so that he could play sports. Early on, shortly after he was sentenced, we were playing bucket ball. It was played with a tennis ball that had to be thrown into a bucket balanced on a stool balanced on a small table. This supposedly non-contact sport was intensely physical. David Evans once flipped out his arm to send me crashing into a brick wall. The impact seemed to put my elbow through my ribs! Hugh dribbled the ball around Bram in fine style, only to be harried by him. Hugh tucked the ball under his arm like a rugby player and gave Bram a rough handoff. Undeterred, Bram reverted to his provincial rugby-playing days of forty years earlier. He grabbed Hugh's outstretched hand, swung his feet up under Hugh's armpit, and, with a superb maneuver, judo-threw him to the ground. Bram rolled out over his shoulder to stand up. Hugh got up much more slowly as he struggled to get back his breath.

Comrade Bram had a twinkling sense of fun, too. Christmas parties were his specialty. The first time we made our own meal from saved-up tins of spaghetti and meatballs, green peas, canned peaches, Ideal evaporated milk, and the like, his contribution to the fun was to read with great enjoyment the chapter describing the Mad Hatter's tea party from Lewis Carroll's *Alice's Adventures in Wonderland*! He had us in fits of laughter.

In 1974 Bram was frequently ill. He needed a cataract operation. His hip became more uncomfortably sore with what he thought was arthritis, his digestion was bad, and he was beginning to look gaunt and frail. Marius Schoon pressed on me the need for us to urge Bram to insist that the prison doctor refer him to the necessary specialists to find the causes of his various ailments. Together we spoke to Bram, and Marius explained our concern. Bram, as usual, denied the need for such bold measures. His health was not bad, he said. I am sure what disconcerted him the most was that we had seen through his attempts to conceal his bouts of ill health. Finally Bram agreed to do it. I kept a diary of Bram Fischer's medical treatment because it seemed to me that he was not being properly cared for, and I wanted a factual contemporary record on which to base a complaint to the authorities. If there were no response, I hoped that I would be able to get to people outside the prison to use that record as ammunition against the callous attitude of the prisons department.

Bram Fischer—Diary of Medical Treatment, 1974–1975

A facsimile with tiny script was smuggled out, and this has been copied from it. In various places the text has been completed within brackets to make it more understandable.

> What follows about A[bram] F[ischer]'s medical treatment has to be used with great care. (1) Ostensibly there could not be access to his medical file, (2) because there might be simple (!?) medical reasons for what happened—but I doubt it.

12(?) May '74 AF to hospital after ulcer haemorrhaged some days in hospital then in Central Prison hospital for a few days. No op, but transfusion etc.

July '74 Request and with Doctor's recommendation AF has prostatectomy. Surgeon did a section in theatre. Report in file says that it was negative for cancer but showed all signs of being cancerous & therefore sent gland to path lab for thorough histology & path lab report to be sent to prison. This report apparently not on file. Was path lab work done? Was it reported? Was report sent to the prison? Did prison Dr press path lab for report? . . . for histology to be done? Did surgeon or specialist see the histology & surgeon's reports? I added before sending out the notes: In January of 1975 it was established that prostate was the site of primary cancer, i.e. it was missed in July possibly through histology not being done, or done and not reported. i.e. 6 months of delay in treating for cancer of prostate . . .

153

Early Sept 74 saw Dr Brandt—pain in hip acute. AF not examined. Pills to relieve arthritic pain . . . relief—but did aggravate ulcer. Then given physiotherapy. After +/− 2 weeks physio says treatment not helping. Refers him to Dr and suggests need for X ray and orthopod. (This to D[enis] T[heodore] G[oldberg]) don't know what was in his report. But AF not called to see Dr and nothing done. During this period AF asked for a crutch. None available, it was said. We found AF a broom of right length to use as crutch. Then, only then, were proper crutches obtained. AF not sent for X-rays. During Oct Dr Groenewald was in attendance. Sends AF for X-rays. No follow up for 2–3 weeks (I'd say). 5 or 6 days before fall orthopod sees AF at prison at a very rushed consultation. Orders X-rays to be taken (i.e. not given plates until AF tells him they're available). Had made a tape recording of diagnosis before seeing X-ray plates. Don't know if he'd read through file or not.

>*Tues 5 Nov 74* AF sees Dr Groenewald to hear specialist's opinion. Warned of danger of falling—neck of femur very fragile. Talk of replacing head of femur.

Wed 6 Nov AF falls while struggling into shower on crutches.

7 Nov AF asked orderly to get Dr because feared fracture. Orderly says imposs. to get Dr and in his opinion not fractured.

9 Nov Dr Brandt says no fracture. Great pain Tues 12 & Wed 13

Fri 15 Nov AF sees Dr Brandt → X-Rays & done immediately. Radiographer says fracture and sends AF back in wheel chair.

Sat 16 Nov Specialist says fracture and will try to get hosp. bed.

Tues 19 Nov AF to HF Verwoerd Hosp . . .

Wed 4 Dec AF brought back. We find him alone in wheelchair in diningroom at 1 pm. AF confused and unable to speak. By mid-afternoon high temp. Unable to help himself. DTG proposes to CO that he spends the night with AF in cell. This agreed after heavy argument. (At first said I could put him to bed only) . . . all night. Not able to turn him. DG had to pick him up to put him on toilet. Great pain. Not seen by a Dr.

Thur 5 Dec Temp lower in morning. Unable to do simplest things. Still not able to speak. DTG again in cell that night. Wakes up to find AF struggling to lavatory. AF falls and DTG catches him (literally) in mid-air. Not seen by DR though DTG asked CO to get DR.

Fri 6 Dec +/– 10AM, AF to hospital

Heard that cancer of hip found when femur was pinned. Cobalt therapy started.

Acute and constant pain in hip started early in September. (Had arthritic pain there for years, but never so acute or constant.) But no X-rays taken until well into October, and then not followed up for some weeks after physiotherapist had urged referral to surgeon. Why was this not done at once why were X-rays not taken immediately?

Point here is the unnecessary delays which may have been fatal. Esp., as lack of care & increasing debility led to fall & fracture of cancerous femur (& presumably spread of secondaries). Further, it is known that cancer of prostate typically produces bone cancer(s) as secondaries. The extreme weakening of neck of femur in a relatively young man—on 5 Nov could (should?) have alerted GPs (Brandt/Groenewald), specialists, radiographers to possibility of bone cancer & link with prostate cancer, especially IF they had been aware of July report from surgeon & path/histology report if it was done/exists. Were the prison Drs (Brandt/Groenewald) aware of the July report(s)? Was specialist told? Did specialist see X-rays of fracture? Why was possibility of bone cancer missed—even before fracture? It is known that hormone treatment of prostate cancer can induce remission of bone cancer secondaries. But prostate cancer not established until January '75, instead of July '74.

Had X-rays been taken early in Sept & cancer been recognised cobalt radiation could have been started 2½ months sooner than end of Nov. And if X-rays followed up at once in mid Oct, 1½ months could have been gained.

Must ask if cancer was known in July and the knowledge concealed? A fantastic thought but it must be asked.

From the diary can be seen the inadequate availability of the Dr when a prisoner needs & requests to see him (Thurs 7 Nov). [This is general and not only in the case of AF.] Unwillingness of orderlies to call out Dr (Fri 8 Nov)

a) it took 13 days for AF to be admitted to hospital after he fractured femur
b) it took 9 days to diagnose fracture
c) It took 4 days after diagnosis to get AF a bed &/or for administrative detail to be fixed
d) When brought back from hospital on 4 Dec AF was in no condition to be removed from hosp. I'm confident that the Drs in charge of the case would not willingly have agreed to him being moved back to prison from hosp. I suggest they were subjected to great admin pressure. (I know they wanted to keep him in hospital, but can only suggest this was so).
e) 4, 5, 6 Dec. NO doctor even looked in to check the condition of a very sick man.

DTG very willingly spent +/– 48 hours continuously with AF to tend his needs. But he is *not* a trained nurse & this was an inadequate way of looking after him.

Hell! Bram was so emaciated that DTG could pick him up & put him on lav or back into bed. Shaved him. It was a joy to be able to do what was needed; terribly sad that it was needed. That's when I did my crying—in December when I realised he had cancer—& he'd soon be gone.

The finality—yes, terrible to bear in this place. BUT confidence in the future & the CERTAINTY that one day (& not too many years hence) we'll be out of prison leaves no room for brooding. We SHALL BE FREE!¹

Bram died of cancer while still a prisoner. He was taken to his brother's house in Bloemfontein, which had been declared a prison. Yes, it was a privilege, but the whole process was terribly lacking in compassion, despite the minister's promise that he could be released to his daughter's home in Johannesburg. Bram was cremated by the prison authorities and they refused to give his ashes to his daughters. I am sure that they feared the ashes would become a shrine for those in the struggle.

The saga of Bram's last days had a sequel for me. After he had been taken away from our prison I asked my dad to send him a telegram of birthday greetings from us all in April 1975. Some weeks later, after he had died, I was called to see a captain in the Prison Service. He was an Irish-man who had served in the British army. He had later joined the Prison Service in seven former British colonies in Africa, moving from one to the other as each became independent. He was ruthless and rather enjoyed having a go at me because I had once complained to the minister of prisons, the notorious Jimmy Kruger, about his behavior. The captain demanded to know how I dared to go "outside of channels" to complain about him. The minister is officially the head of the Prison Service, yet for that sadist that was going outside of channels. Clearly, the captain had been chastised for his conduct. He told me he would "get me" and would break no rules in the process. Now he was going to get me for communicating with a prisoner without permission from the commissioner of prisons. The captain assured me he was serious. They had a recording of the words I had asked my dad to put in the telegram, and the telegram contained those words. The telegram was illegal and had been confiscated and not given to Bram. "What sort of person are you," I demanded, "that you stop a birthday greeting to a man who has been with us for nine years and is now dying?" His response was that he had warned me and now he had me. At last I would be convicted of a prison offense. Of course, I demanded the right to see a lawyer to defend me. Then I gave him a lecture about inhumanity, ending with a peroration about the need for Nuremburg-style trials of officials who had been complicit in the inhumanity of apartheid. It ended with my spinning about and storming out of the room. Oh, damn! I was in prison and the door was locked. Nevertheless, it was a great performance, even if I was the only one to enjoy it. No charge was brought against me, and I like to think that his superiors saw the potential embarrassment that could come from such a charge against me. The Irish British army officer, who had become a prison officer, was posted to another prison, and we saw him only once again for a short time. I wonder if he was just a man who liked to be in uniform or whether that was a cover for another trade. Was he an undercover agent?

Health Care in Prison

Bram Fischer's fate was the result of systematic negligence in the prison medical service. Other prisoners and I experienced the same treatment for a variety of reasons.

Dave Evans and I both had diarrhea that just went on and on, and we could not get treatment. Sergeant du Preez, in charge of the section we convicted political prisoners were in, would not give us enough toilet paper. He enjoyed trying to humiliate us by doling out a few sheets to each prisoner each day. The fact that his storeroom was stacked with cartons of toilet paper and other toiletry articles was of no significance to him. He loved his power over us.

I asked to see the doctor and was taken to see him by Sergeant du Preez. I asked the doctor to prescribe toilet paper for diarrhea. He angrily demanded to know how I dared to waste his time asking for toilet paper. I said that as I had diarrhea and as I could not get enough toilet paper, which was a question of hygiene and as doctors deal with hygiene, he should prescribe toilet paper. The whole point of this was to drop Sergeant du Preez in it. The doctor responded that I would get toilet paper from the sergeant. Carrying through the principle that superiors do not like to be made responsible for the foolishness of their inferiors in rank, I explained that the sergeant refused to give it to me, which was why I was speaking to the doctor. The doctor, playing the disciplinarian role, threatened, "I'm going to take you to the commanding officer." I said, "Please take me to the commanding officer, then I will get toilet paper."

At that point Sergeant du Preez, recognizing that he might be in danger, said that he would make sure that I got toilet paper. Then I asked the doctor for treatment for the diarrhea. He said that I had diarrhea because I ate too much.

At that time we were hungry. Every day and after every meal, we were hungry. I angrily demanded to know if the doctor knew what the prison rations were. He said he did not know. I replied: "Then don't say I eat too much. I'm ill." He ordered me to be put under observation. I was put into an isolation cell. There was nothing in it except for my floor mats and blankets. Officially, I was put under observation as a start to medical treatment. I was a prisoner; therefore, I must be a liar who complained to the doctor about toilet paper. Under observation I would eat nothing other than the rations. (There was nothing else to eat anyway.) Nobody else was allowed to see me except the guard. And I was told that every time I passed a movement I was to call a medical orderly. There was no bell; there was no way of calling the medical orderly except by yelling at the top of my voice. In the guise of medical correctness the doctor had put me into solitary confinement.

The medical orderly was looking after hundreds of prisoners. He was supposed to take my temperature three or four times a day. He was supposed to examine every stool I passed. He was not interested and seldom came to see me. We used to say about the medical orderly who came to dispense medications: "Run, run, as quick as you can, you can't catch me, I'm the medicine man," playing on the nursery rhyme about the gingerbread man. Doctors would prescribe pills three times a day. The medical orderly would give you them twice a day. It did not matter to the orderly. He was giving you tablets. He couldn't be bothered to come three times a day because that did not fit the schedule. We were locked up so early that there was not enough time to give the third dose during the day shift. The orderlies never told the doctors that there was a problem. They did what they liked. If you were busy with the prison commanding officer, or at a visit, for example, when the medical orderly came, you did without your treatment. Their attitude was "Who cares?" The official reports would say the prisoners had been seen and treated by the doctors, and that was sufficient. I cannot begin to imagine what happened to black criminal prisoners, but it must have been terrible. White criminal prisoners at Pretoria Central Prison were treated with even more indifference than we were.

Some of the orderlies were hopped up to the eyes. They were taking drugs. You could see it in their eyes, their pupils dilated to different diameters. Such people were responsible for the medical records for each patient. There was no doctor responsible for that. What that could lead to was shown in the case of Bram Fischer.

During this time my dad was writing to the commissioner of prisons, demanding that I get proper medical treatment. He told me that he had quoted large sections from a medical encyclopedia about the symptoms I had told him about, and he demanded treatment for me.

Inside the prison Dave and I were both demanding that the commanding officer get us a specialist since the prison doctor was refusing to treat us. He told us that he could not give the doctor orders. On at least one occasion I told him that he would have to be responsible for Dave's and my health. After some weeks a specialist came to see us. I am convinced that it was Dad's work from outside that brought the results.

Dr. Bremer seemed pleased that I recognized his name and confirmed that he was the son of a former Nationalist Party minister of health. The father had introduced a vitamin-fortified whole-wheat bread at subsidized prices known as Bremer bread. Dr. Bremer was such a nice man. He was courteous and correct. He behaved as a professional should. In prison, when someone did what was normal, it was so striking that you'd say, "What a nice man." He took a medical history from me, and he examined me thoroughly with instruments he had brought with him. He told me that I was indeed very ill. I nearly wept, not because I was ill but because at last here was a medical practitioner who believed what I was telling him. He was very quietly competent. He told me that it would take time but "we will have you back on your feet." This was a real mess because it took about three months or more from the time Dave and I became ill until our full recovery.

You could get headache tablets when you needed them. Headaches were rife. Medication for heartburn was never thought of as being necessary, and I resorted to buying milk of magnesia toothpaste, which did something toward dealing with acidity. Sometimes I felt that when I broke wind the toothpaste caused me to blow bubbles. Eyesight deteriorated very rapidly, and most of us who wore glasses needed to change them more often than I have ever done outside. There is a lot of stress if you are to retain your integrity and dignity. Many male prisoners suffer from urinary and genital problems. Prostates seem to respond badly to idleness. Bladder infections and other urinary problems are common, and some have kidneys that act up. After a few months these things afflict even young men in their twenties and thirties. Jeremy Cronin, for example, had pains in his kidneys. They were taken seriously and all the tests were done. He was told that they could find nothing medically wrong. David Rabkin, a journalist serving a ten-year sentence, had pains that seemed to be the pains I had heard about from people who had kidney stones. I have heard that passing a kidney stone is very painful indeed. He had been in prison about three months when he staggered into my cell and he said he felt so ill. The pain would afflict him from time to time. He would go pale under his sallow skin and look drawn and sweaty. He got some pain-relieving tablets, and the pain disappeared—until there were further recurrences. I suppose that stress has something to do with this kind of pain.

Medical treatment in prison was not only bad and superficial. What irritated me was the way in which private medicine and public medicine overlapped. Private practitioners working as government officers, district surgeons, and prison doctors would refer us to specialists or surgeons, and they would then be asked to assist at operations and get a fee for it. All the evils of private medicine crept in. The distortions of private practice were quite starkly revealed in dental care. The prison dentist when we were first imprisoned was really terrible, and the equipment in the dentist's room in Pretoria Central Prison was out of date and dilapidated. It was arranged that we were taken under armed guard to an outside dental practice. They weren't bad dentists in my opinion. At least they set out to save teeth, not to pull them.

The dental surgery at Pretoria Central Prison was modernized and reequipped, and a new prison dentist was appointed. He would find every reason for pulling teeth: the gum was receding, or food had got under the tooth, or there were too many holes, or the tooth had been repaired too many times, and so on. I heard him on several occasions behaving with the rudeness that only a prison guard could show to a prisoner. There he was, a professional dentist, behaving in an utterly unprofessional manner. Eventually that dentist was extracted from that situation. The Department of Health had determined that he was extracting a higher number of teeth than was expected. He earned more by pulling teeth than by filling them. The method of payment determined his practice: he pulled out teeth. I had almost no top and bottom back teeth left. Others had similar experiences. Generally, you trust professionals. You couldn't in prison.

Dr. Brandt was with us for over eight years. It was unusual to have such continuity. When we brought the court action against the minister of prisons, the commissioner, and the commanding officer for access to newspapers and news, we had said in papers placed before the court that to be cut off from the world was psychologically damaging. Dr. Brandt said in his written statement that in all his years of visiting the prison he had seen no signs of psychological deviation in us. Other than refusing to say anything at all, he could not have said less than he did. Our response was quite simple: we had not alleged psychological deviation. We had said that cutting us off from the world of our families and friends could only do psychological damage in the long term. Furthermore, the doctor did not state his qualifications, nor did he state what observations he had made. And, therefore, his statement should be dismissed. I think that was his intention.

Some time later, when I went to see him about some problem or other, he was obviously quite apprehensive about what I would say about his affidavit. I said nothing, because he had been under pressure and he had done no damage. It seemed to us that he had gone out of his way not to harm us. He could have cooked up something if he was totally hostile to us, and so I made no reference to his statement to the court, and, after all, it seemed quite nice to have somebody say that after all those years in prison we were not bonkers! Sometimes I said to him that I did not want to see a specialist. I simply wanted him to treat me because I did not want to wait weeks for treatment for a bad cold, for example. He said he believed that our little group should have the best treatment because of who we were. That seemed to explain why he often called in a specialist.

Perhaps his insistence was a reflection of what was happening in private medicine in South Africa. My understanding was that specialists paid referral fees, the polite term for kickbacks, for patients sent to them. At that time diagnostic procedures and surgery generally took place in the Eugene Marais Hospital, owned by a group of doctors, and the surgeon would have shares in the hospital. Dr. Brandt assisted in the operations and was paid a fee for assisting. That was normal, wasn't it? After all, somebody has to assist. He said he was studying to be a surgeon and that made it all legitimate. In the end you no longer knew whether you needed a specialist or an operation, or any treatment at all.

I often wondered to what extent the doctors allowed themselves to be controlled by the state security apparatus. On one occasion they brought in a specialist when I had asked for an eye test so that I could get new glasses. For a prescription for glasses they sent in a specialist: very nice!

"You need glasses? What do you mean, you need glasses?" he asked.

"Well, I'm getting headaches and my glasses need replacing."

"How old are you?"

I told him my age.

"Well, I can prescribe according to your age."

"Are you a doctor?"

"Yes."

"Are you a specialist?"

"Yes."

"Then why don't you behave like one?"

"What do you mean?" he asked, though it sounded more like "How dare you speak to me in this way!" But he had been pacing up and down quite nervously from the beginning of the consultation. He was a big, florid-faced man and sweating. Since it was not a particularly hot day, it struck me that he was uncomfortable about being there. He had probably been warned by one or other security apparatus not to talk to me and not to be friendly toward a political prisoner.

"Why don't you do an eye test?" I asked him.

"There is no equipment here." He was clearly very offended to have his professional standing put in question by a prisoner. To rub it in I said, "I will not take glasses from you without an examination and an eye test." How could a doctor of some standing submit to the tiny bit of pressure put on him? "Why don't you ask the prison authorities to take me to your rooms at a date and time they decide?" I asked him to try to rescue the poor man from his own unprofessional conduct while at the same time telling the authorities that they could preserve their security.

"Oh, is that possible?" he asked.

"Why don't you ask the medical orderly?"

They did take me to his rooms and he prescribed lenses—that were wrong. He reexamined me in his rooms and prescribed the right lenses. He then phoned the optician, who agreed, at his own expense, not the doctor's expense, to make new lenses.

I had a similar experience some years later at the H. F. Verwoerd Hospital, the state hospital that was the teaching hospital for the Pretoria University Medical School.[2] The prisons had apparently stopped using private doctors and hospitals.

I needed a prostate examination and the authorities turned the event into a military operation. I was taken in a convoy of three vehicles by a strange, indirect route to the hospital. The police vehicles and the prison transporter, with its windows covered with steel wire mesh, were all connected to their radio communications centers. The prison officers were all armed except for the one to whom I was handcuffed and who rode in the back of the van with me. I was also in leg irons. On arrival at the hospital I was put into a wheelchair, covered with a blanket, and wheeled in. There were no hospital medical people around. I was there undercover! The hospital had been surrounded by armed men in civilian clothes. They had a guard wearing jeans and a T-shirt at each intersection of the hospital corridors. And they each had a walkie-talkie. I have to criticize them for not being inconspicuous. They stood out because it is unusual to see ordinary guys wearing jeans and T-shirts and sneakers but with walkie-talkies in hand.

I was wheeled on a gurney to the theater, always surrounded by armed guards. My leg irons were left on; one end was clipped to my leg, and the other end to whatever bed I was on. In the theater I was transferred from the gurney to the examination table, and the leg irons were now clipped to both my ankles. They must have thought I was a Superman who would leap up and away while under anesthetic. Crazy!

The professor of urology at Pretoria University Medical School was to examine me. I have forgotten his name, and I think he deserves to be forgotten. He was young and had a reputation for being a brilliant doctor, but he did not have the guts to throw the squad of security people out of his operating theater.

"You are going to take X-rays, aren't you?" I asked.

"Yes," he replied.

"Then don't you think the leg irons should be taken off?"

You are always asked to remove any metal object, false teeth, anything that can concentrate X-rays and do you harm.

"Oh," he said. "Why?"

I explained what I meant.

"Well, I can't tell you that we can take the leg irons off."

"Professor, I think you should stick to medicine and leave security to the prison officials. You have to be a doctor, not a security officer."

By then the catheter was in the back of my hand and I passed out under the anesthetic. The gang of guards had come into the theater, presumably to watch the urology professor sticking something up my pee-pee. They loved it, those guards.

Even more striking was the conduct in the early 1980s of an orthopedic specialist in the same hospital who examined me because when I walked a few times around our quite tiny exercise yard, my right knee or my left ankle would swell up and be very painful. In an examination room, surrounded by armed, uniformed guards, the professor, without looking at me, asked the medical orderly, Major Buys, "Does the prisoner [this or that, or the other]?" So the major looked at me, and I looked at him and said:

"Doctor, I can speak for myself. I am the patient, not the major."

He ignored me and again asked the major . . .

"Professor, I am the patient, speak to me."

"Oh," he said—and he looked very afraid. He looked as though he was shitting himself. The security people must have spoken to him in their usual manner. At least he had a small bit of conflict between his professional stance and the pressures of "security"; the major's silence must have triggered something in the poor man's brain. He asked, "Can I speak to the prisoner directly?"

What sort of a doctor was this? After Steve Biko, a charismatic student leader of the Black Consciousness Movement who had asserted that to be free, one had to have a proud self-awareness that one could be free, had been killed and two doctors signed false death certificates, the statutory Medical and Dental Council ordered that medical personnel were to deal with medical problems and leave security to security personnel. They did not, however, call on the doctors to reject the intervention by Security Police in medical matters. They continued to instill anxiety and fear of their power in the doctors.

The professor now examined me professionally despite the armed men in the examination room and all around the hospital. I had the beginnings of arthritis in my knees and ankles. He prescribed treatment and said he wanted me to return after six weeks for a follow-up examination; and I knew that once he said that in my hearing, I would not be going back at that time. Some security man would think that I might arrange, through my imaginary communicator, for a whole MK unit to be there to rescue me!

After about eight weeks, without warning, I was taken to see the same professor. This time he was sitting behind a table with little in front of him. I could see there were no files, no records, nothing other than a few sheets of blank paper. Looking up at me through his glasses, he asked quite brusquely, "Well, what is it?"

I responded, "You told me to come back for a follow-up consultation. You are treating me."

"Oh, yes," he said, "what was it about?"

"You don't have my folder?"

"No."

"How can you treat me without your case notes?"

"I can," he asserted.

"But you prescribed medication and you wanted me back so that you could assess the progress of the treatment. You don't know who I am, or what the condition was, you don't have the X-rays. What sort of doctor are you, professor?"

I was being as rude and contemptuous as I could be. He cowered.

"Mr. Van der Merwe . . ."

"My name's not Van der Merwe! My name's Goldberg."

"Oh, but your file is in that name."

"How dare you, a medical professional, treat me under a false name!"

"Now tell me your complaint and we will treat you."

"No, you're not going to treat me, not until you have the files. And my name is Goldberg and you will treat me under that name."

He could not get the file "because it is kept in a safe in the medical superintendent's office, and the medical superintendent is away."

The secrecy—they would say security—surrounding us was astonishing. They had given me the name of one of the guards, and in any case Van der Merwe among white Afrikaners is like Jones in Wales or Cohen in New York! By this time I was really fuming. "If I'm brought in here in a state of collapse and can't talk to you, how do you know that I am allergic to penicillin? How do you know? Or that it could be fatal? You don't know where my file is! You don't know under what name it is! How dare you behave like this?" He looked quite shrunken.

My guards were present, of course. The major was also present. I was too angry to care if they were annoyed, but they did not interfere. I think that because I had been in prison so long I had become a kind of institution, and they knew I would complain in every way possible if they tried to block me from doing what I knew to be just.

I calmed myself and said quite simply: "I don't think you behave like a professional, and I think it's disgusting. I'm not going to allow you to treat me." In situations like this one, I was never sure whether to go for the jugular of formal complaint or back off at the last moment. Having angrily, justifiably angrily, accused the man of cowardice and unprofessional behavior, I had the hope that he might acquire the guts to resist the pressures of the security establishment.

Major Buys apologized to the professor. A professor is, after all, a professor to a prison major. He was very sorry about the incident. It would not happen again. He said they would bring the prisoner back when the medical superintendent would be there. Later, in the prison, Major Buys came as near to apologizing to me as he could. He assured me that I would be known at the hospital under my own name. And indeed, when I was taken back to the hospital, my name was written large on my file, as was the warning about my penicillin allergy. The professor treated me well and with courtesy.

It still amazes me that professional people at the highest level of society, people highly respected in the society, can be so overawed and intimidated—to the point that they stop behaving like professionals. That a professor of orthopedics at one of the great Afrikaner nationalist universities behaved in this way was saddening, especially when his status in that society would have protected him from the security establishment. I could find out his name, but it doesn't matter to me. He was just another terrified little shit who would say he was a democrat who did not believe in terrorizing people.

Bram Fischer was the most tragic victim of this disregard for human life in the prison "health-care" system. There was no medical coordination by a medical doctor. Dr. Mueller of the ICRC was adamant that any reasonably competent doctor looking at the reports of blood tests in Bram's file should have identified that there was something wrong, and that Bram probably had cancer. But nobody bothered to read the blood tests. Nobody bothered to check. It could have been treated months before it was. Dr. Mueller told the minister of prisons, Jimmy Kruger, infamous for his remark in Parliament that Steve Biko's death "left him cold," that his doctors should have spotted Bram's illness long before it was diagnosed. He was insistent to the point that the minister forbade the ICRC to bring Dr. Mueller to South Africa again. I admire that kind of courage.

Jack Tarshish's illness showed another aspect of the prison medical services. Besides his long-term chronic nerve condition, he developed a narrowing of a heart valve that was diagnosed by the ICRC doctor. Dr. Davies, a specialist, was called in and insisted that Jack have open-heart surgery immediately to rectify this problem. Clearly, they would not want to face public and international criticism if they did not provide the available treatment and he died. The operation was done, and Jack was brought back to our prison after a few days in the prison hospital. He had to tend the wound himself. When I asked to look at the wound in his chest, it was clear that something was wrong because where the wires holding his breastbone together came through the skin, there was an infection.

After many protests, Jack did get proper care for that, and the wound healed well. But slowly he seemed to be blowing up like a balloon as fluid accumulated in his lower legs, then his thighs, and then his abdomen. The skin on his tummy seemed to be stretched tight and shiny. I knew that edema is a sign of heart failure, and that as the fluids accumulate the strain on the heart increases in a vicious circle. Jack would not try to see a doctor because he said they were trying to kill him. Eventually I took matters into my own hands; it seemed to me that, so near the end of Jack's twelve-year sentence, they would not have done the open-heart surgery if they wanted him to die. There was so much pressure on the regime that the opposite was probably true: they needed him to survive so that they could point to the complete care they gave to political prisoners. I went to see the commanding officer and arranged that Jack's specialist be called, and I would see him first, ostensibly about my own health.

I compiled a list of Jack's symptoms and passed them on to the specialist, Dr. Davies. In the course of the consultation about Jack I remarked that the balance of medications for his narcolepsy-cataplexy was not right. Jack was falling asleep at strange times. Dr. Davies flared up. He told me that the doctors at Weskoppies Psychiatric Hospital, who had observed and treated Jack, had caused the heart valve condition by giving him excessive doses of medications that had that side effect. What to do? Would Dr. Davies really be an expert witness to that? I doubted it, and it seemed more important to save Jack's life. Jack was called to the doctor and whipped off very quickly to hospital, where nearly two gallons of fluid were drained from his abdomen and legs. His health improved rapidly thereafter.

Jack was always one to work every angle he could. He insisted that his health required culturally specific food so that he would be released in good shape. Suddenly it was important to Jack to eat kosher food. It was agreed that he could, at his own expense, order kosher salami and chicken fat and matzos and fresh tomatoes and fresh fruit. I was asked to ensure that he ate properly. I made his breakfast every day, and the mess smelled wonderfully of garlic salami and fried eggs and fried tomato, or matzos fried up in scrambled egg with salami. Yummy.

I think everyone, my comrades included, expected me to tuck in too, and I must say it was very tempting. I did not indulge, however, despite Jack's insistence. I was taking a longer view that when specific favors were granted for medical reasons, one should preserve the future possibility for others. Second, it seemed unfair for me to not share the goodies with our fellow prisoners. Then there was the fact that, though our prison food was not great, it had improved markedly over the years, and because we by then had the privilege of buying a few rand worth of goodies each month, there was no desperate need to eat Jack's salami. Had I been really hungry, my attitude might have been different, and then I would have seen to it that we all shared in a little of the tidbits that good fortune had brought us. I confess my mouth waters even now as I write about this minor dilemma. It did have an effect on Jack, for he really did respond to the food he was eating. A year or two after he was released, and having gone into exile in London, he died from what was publicly stated to be a massive heart attack. Esmé told me that he actually committed suicide because of the clicking of his artificial heart valve that disturbed him even when he was still in prison, and the paranoia that seemed to accompany his nervous condition over many years, which finally brought him to the end of his tether.

Happily, the nature of health care inside did show signs of longer-term improvement, signaled by the appointment of a fully trained nurse, Major Buys, and coinciding with the campaigning by activist doctors in public life, which in turn coincided with the worldwide outcry over the death of Steve Bantu Biko and the continued caring surveillance by the ICRC. Major Buys was one of the very few people to come out of the Biko affair with any dignity. He realized that urgent medical care was needed and tried in vain to persuade the duty doctors to come out late at night to treat a prisoner. He was a competent and caring, fully qualified nurse. He changed the prison medical service in our prison complex from a farce to one that was quite good.

11

The Escape

In June 1978 two new prisoners joined us in the Pretoria Security Prison. They had not long before completed their studies. They were Tim Jenkin, blond, very thin, and wearing glasses, and Stephen Lee, brown hair, innocent face, and more strongly built than his friend. They had both joined the illegal ANC while in Britain and then returned home. They were both sentenced to twelve years in prison for their illegal political activities.

I was astonished when Tim told me shortly after joining us that he wanted to escape. I had already one attempted escape behind me and during my stay in the old Pretoria Local Prison had often thought of escape. In 1964 and 1965 I had been the chairman of our escape committee. At that time we got no further than thinking about it. We believed that our fellow prisoner Raymond Thoms had betrayed us when it appeared that the authorities had got wind of our plans.

Tim and Stephen asked me to find a hiding place for the money they had smuggled into the prison. Both had "bottled" the money, as it is said in prison slang. They had inserted it, in aluminium cigar tubes, up their backsides. Even more surprising was that they told me that their parents had smuggled the money to them while they were in the police holding cells in Cape Town. That was a brave thing to do. I found a safe place for the money. After fifteen years in prison, I had experience with how to make such things disappear until they were needed again.

Tim was very cautious when he approached me. I think he feared that

I might think they were setting a trap for me. I had no such thoughts. He was one of our ANC comrades and came from a well-established family. I have the greatest respect for them for the unwavering support they gave Tim. His father, a well-known anesthetist, showed himself to be an outspokenly brave man. After the murder of Steve Biko in detention, he was one of the leading representatives of a newly formed group, the Medical Association, who initiated a debate on the ethics of the medical profession and sharply criticized the doctors who allowed Steve Biko to die and who covered up for the Security Police by issuing a false death certificate. As a result, the apartheid government, through the statutory Medical and Dental Council, had to investigate the death of Biko.

For Tim it must have been a great moment to see his father sharing his son's viewpoint. His mother and his brother, also a doctor, supported him, too. Usually a white person who stood up against apartheid became an outsider in his family. Few were in the same comfortable position that I was in since my parents had been political activists against apartheid. My parents stood with me during the Rivonia Trial and in all the years of my imprisonment while they were alive.

Tim must have known about me. I have not asked him why he trusted me because I had no doubt that he would have seen me as an old campaigner and of the *Umkhonto we Sizwe* High Command. He knew that I had been sentenced to life imprisonment in the Rivonia Trial. Who could Tim approach if not me? Nevertheless, he was cautious. He was the leader of the duo. Stephen was a nice, friendly young man whom I liked very much, but he left the talking to his friend.

Tim's plan was quite far advanced before I decided I should take part in the escape itself, as against just helping an escape to take place. I needed to be sure of the details of the plan because I did not want to repeat the experience of being recaptured.

The Great Escape

It was an exciting project. As we began to think about the whole group daring to escape together, the project took on the form of "the Great Escape." Our whole group took part in the discussions during 1979 about the escape with Tim and Stephen—and later with Alex Moumbaris when he joined them. We thought we would leave only two prisoners behind. One was John Matthews, whose fifteen-year sentence would end in 1979.

He did not have too much longer to serve and at the age of sixty-five years, even though he kept himself fit, we thought he would not be fit enough for the undertaking. The second was Tony Holiday, in his late thirties, who had been sentenced to six years' imprisonment in 1976 for building an underground political cell in Cape Town. He had already completed nearly half of his sentence and was a relatively "small fish" who would be released in a few years. As was the case with John, an unsuccessful escape could get him another sentence of up to five years for the attempt. Given the time he had left to sit in prison, that seemed a disproportionate risk. In any case, Tony wanted to finish his university studies in philosophy.

Without the willing cooperation and support of all of us, the planning of this enterprise would have been unthinkable. At that time there were only ten of us political prisoners. Besides Tim, Stephen, Tony, and me, there was Alex Moumbaris, of Greek origin, the "Academics" David Rabkin, Jeremy Cronin, and Raymond Suttner, and David Kitson and John Matthews from the "Little Rivonia" trial of 1964. Everyone was fully aware of what everyone else was doing. Everyone helped in his own way to hide things and to divert the guards from knowing what was happening.

As I was the Rivonia man, the lifer, it seemed to me that the authorities watched me more closely than the other prisoners. My escape would be a great success for the ANC, a real slap in the face for apartheid because it would be a worldwide story. It would also, however, have mobilized the apartheid security establishment to the last man. Every one of our internal political structures would be thoroughly investigated. A new wave of arrests and infiltration by apartheid agents would be unleashed. My escape could not really take place without damage to our structures and more people being sacrificed. I had to think about these costs to our movement. Therefore, I initiated contact with our comrades "outside."

I asked them to provide an escape vehicle. We needed a van or a small truck for eight people because we thought there might be only ten minutes between the escape and the alarm being raised, and by then we had to be clean out of the city. Establishing contact with the outside was a slow process. I had to write a letter using a special code, which could take up to three weeks going through the whole prison security system before ending up in the post. It would be recorded and studied in the prison. Then it would go to the security section at prison headquarters, and then to the

National Security apparatus. Thereafter it had to come back step-by-step through the whole system. When the letter was posted, the Security Police intercepted it in the sorting office to ensure that it had in fact been through the whole security process. Only then was it allowed to go on its way to my contact person in London.

Baruch Hirson was my contact. Now I can tell the story because he died in October 1999. Baruch was sentenced in December 1964 to nine years for his involvement in the African Resistance Movement. Even though we came from different political tendencies—he was a Trotskyist in a liberal movement—we established a good friendship. Shortly before his release in 1973 we created an "all-purpose code." He made the truly generous offer to be my contact person. Despite all the differences he had had with the ANC and the South African Communist Party, and despite the conflicts in South Africa between the Communist Party and the Trotskyites, Baruch offered me his help if it should be needed. He was, of course, also offering his help and loyalty to our movement. Now I needed the code and the communications route—and it worked.

Baruch had not spoken a word about all this before his death in 1999. He did not even mention it in his autobiography, *Revolutions in My Life* (Johannesburg: Witwatersrand University Press, 1995), in which he described our time in prison together.

When I asked him for help in 1979, he had already been in London for some years and was naturally still a well-known Trotskyite with anything but a close relationship to my comrades. At this time he made contact for me with our bases in Mozambique—and with no less a person than Joe Slovo, a leading Communist, known in the South African media as the apartheid regime's "most wanted" man. Baruch must have had to swallow a great deal of pride to make this contact, and I honor him for doing it. When both Slovo and Hirson were politically active in Johannesburg over many years, there were strong disagreements between them. All that had to be set aside in the face of my approach. Slovo too must have swallowed his pride to work with Hirson. I later asked Joe about this, and he said that he worked with Baruch without reservation when he knew that I had sent the message.

Then there needed to be time while our ANC and MK comrades considered the matter. That was surely the longest stage of my letter's journey back to me. Many would not have trusted Baruch the "Trot." That too caused delays, until Joe replied. We had made it! Well, the first step of establishing contact had been made. A date for the escape was then set and how an escape vehicle would be used was established.

During the planning of the escape, we reached an unbridgeable rift between Alex Moumbaris and the group we called the "Academics," David Rabkin, Jeremy Cronin, and Raymond Suttner. Alex had joined with Tim and Stephen. The son of Greek parents and the only non–South African in our group, he was, in terms of apartheid propaganda, the classical communist who operated as the agent of foreign forces. He had been sentenced to twelve years in prison in 1973. The regime sent his pregnant wife to France, her homeland. The Academics, who all had advanced degrees and were great theoreticians, were shortly after the Soweto uprising of 1976 sentenced for underground Communist Party activity.

Alex wanted to reduce the size of the escape group to just three: himself, Tim, and Stephen. The Academics felt that I had to be part of the escape party; they insisted that my escape would be important for our liberation movement. The plan as it had evolved needed a hiding place in a closet that was large enough for three people only. If I were to go, Alex would have to remain behind, or we would have to rethink the whole plan. Alex aggressively refused to remain behind or even to consider alternative plans.

Alex had strong personal reasons for wanting to escape. We all had them! But egoism shouldn't be allowed to triumph in prison. Personal wishes and duties must be brought into agreement, even if not complete harmony. Tim could not stay behind because he was the leader of the attempt. Stephen was also there from the beginning. I therefore had no place in the team. For the success of an escape, absolute unity is necessary, and it could not be achieved.

Throughout the preparations I had assumed the task of chatting to the night guard, Sergeant Vermeulen, for as long as possible during his rounds of the cells. That kept him from his boring task of staying awake all night when there was nothing to hold his attention. Just about every evening we would talk about his favorite rugby team, Northern Transvaal, the Blue Bulls. As a Capetonian who thought that only the Western Province team was worth watching, that bored me to tears, and I had long before lost interest in players I knew nothing about. Still, I used this conversational duty to gradually extract answers to our questions about the security arrangements in and around the prison.

As a construction engineer I knew something about technical matters and, after a time, the guards would call on me when something was broken or not functioning properly. There were often short circuits in the prison electrical system, which had been badly installed. Lightbulbs would burn out, and the safety switches would trip. Since lighting is an important security matter, we would use these opportunities to call Vermeulen to attend to the lights or switches that had tripped out. I would keep him busy as long as I could to give Tim and Alex time to test Tim's keys in one door after another over many months. Vermeulen would come to my cell every night for his chat.

I am an active type. Everybody in the prison was aware that I was there. Tim, on the other hand, could move silently through the prison as if he were not there. He sat so quietly in his cell that he was hardly noticed. He was so exact in his movements and so self-disciplined that he seldom bumped up against prison regulations, even when he was breaking them! His calm and quiet manner was such a valuable asset for illegal activity. I am sure that he showed the same calm and quiet when he was setting off his "leaflet bombs" in Cape Town before his arrest. They were thick packets of leaflets that, with the help of a small explosive charge and a timed detonator, would fly into the air in a crowded place. The explosion drew attention to the leaflets, which would spread quite widely among passersby. The extensive spread of the leaflets made it impossible for the police to gather them all up. Tim told me he would sometimes join the crowd to watch the effect of the explosion and to observe how well it spread the leaflets. He made modifications to the design on the basis of these observations. A real cool one was our Tim!

If I wished to escape with the others, I had to consider certain matters. If Tim, for example, was not standing at attention at his grille but still lying in bed like the cloth dummy when he did escape, the guards would not suspect anything was wrong. But if I was the one not ready at attention, there would be immediate concern, and they would have entered my cell at once. If I had been apparently lying asleep in bed when Vermeulen came by for his chat, even he would have been suspicious.

If I had been walking in the prison neighborhood in the evening as Tim, Stephen, and Alex did when they escaped, I am sure that some prison official or policeman who had seen me would have recognized me immediately. After I had spent more than fifteen years in that prison, even the most junior official knew the notorious Rivonia-man by face and figure. Because of these thoughts and Alex's refusal to accept my role, I had to think about whether my participation would strengthen or weaken the escape attempt. In Alex's mind, but also Tim's and Stephen's, the breakout had become a three-man escape and not a clearing out of the prison. In their minds they had separated themselves from the Academics and the rest of us.

I also had to think about the effects of another failed attempt on the conditions of my imprisonment. They would become much harsher, and I wasn't getting any fitter or stronger as the years rolled by. There was the possibility that the rest of my life would be spent in prison, though I thought it would not be much longer than five to ten years until we were released. In fact, as it happened, it was five and a half years for me, and just over ten years for Nelson Mandela.

I learned very early in life that leadership requires that one accept responsibility for one's companions. During my imprisonment I was always aware that I belonged to the High Command of our liberation army. I felt that I had to try to conduct myself as a commander. Now I saw myself as having responsibility for all those who would remain behind.

During our preparations, building activity began outside the prison. A new guard post was being built at the entrance. Tim, Stephen, and Alex in particular found this unsettling. They thought that all their careful preparations and planning would come to nothing. They wanted to push ahead more quickly. Alex was the most affected by this.

Other changes also affected Vermeulen's duties. After more than ten years of night duty, he was transferred to the daytime shift. I persuaded him to get this reversed when he complained bitterly to me and wanted to resign from the Prison Service. That would have set back the escape quite considerably because we needed him to be on night duty. He was a single father with a sixteen-year-old daughter who needed his supervision when she came home from school in the afternoons because, he told me, she liked to "enjoy herself with young men," instead of studying for her final school examinations. Vermeulen's eyesight was also affected by his long-standing diabetes. He could no longer fill out forms and do the administrative work demanded of him on the day shift. He needed to get back onto night duty. I explained to him how he could do this by threatening to resign and take an early pension. The prisons were extremely short-staffed, and his superiors would put him back on night duty rather than lose him. It worked, and he was very grateful to me for my advice.

Because of the changes to the building, Tim, Stephen, and Alex wanted me to write a letter to move the date of the escape forward. I said we had to think about how long it would take for the slow communications to achieve this. It would have taken up to three months, and that was about how much time we had left until our prearranged date. Alex attacked me for this, calling me a liar who wanted to defeat their escape plan. This was very hurtful.

The conflict between Alex and the Academics also intensified so much that it could not be overcome. Tim kept out of such political disputes. He was interested in the technical matters and preferred to avoid confrontation. He wished to get on with the job rather than wait until every detail of the political line had been worked out. I felt much the same way because, when you've worked it all out and have started to implement your policy, once everything changes, you have to start the discussions all over again. My dialectical comrades failed to understand dialectics!

All these things made it clear that the team that Tim, Stephen, and Alex had created could successfully escape. Since Alex was opposed to my participation, and my presence would cause disunity in the team, there was finally no possibility of my joining the escape. I could not ignore Alex's view that I would be a burden. I think his position came from personality conflicts rather than anything objective. I felt that I was too well known and that I was not fit enough for any long walk to safety in a foreign country. During this time I had sometimes been taken out of the prison to see medical doctors or to an optician, and I noticed the difficulties I had outside. The noise was disturbing. Perhaps I would find it difficult to cross the busy street outside the prison. I could not handle money any more. I cannot say if this was fear or a sudden realization of my physical weaknesses. In any case, none of this mattered to the three escapers who were now determined to escape as soon as possible and not wait for assistance from outside.

I discussed this with Dave Kitson, who was sentenced in 1964, some months after the Rivonia Trial, as a member of the new *Umkhonto* High Command. He had a twenty-year sentence and was fifty-nine years old at the time we were planning the escape. He too saw the problem of age and physical weakness. We concluded that we would no longer insist on escaping and would have to say no.

It is difficult in prison to discuss problems fully because there is no possibility of a plenary session at which everyone could fully express his opinions and finally reach a decision. Dave remained as the last of us on the escape committee. We thought that his advice could help the younger men. We thought that because Alex's aggressive behavior caused so much discord in our community, Dave could be the go-between and calm things down. The three soon demanded to know, however, if he would join the escape, and he had to say he would not. With that there was no longer an escape committee. Tim, Stephen, and Alex acted alone from then on, though our support never wavered.

We still had a major disagreement, however. The three wanted to attack Vermeulen and tie him up while taking his gun and the keys to his private car. We could have done that during a "great escape," but not when the majority of our comrades had to remain behind in the prison. An attack on the life of one of the prison officers and the theft of a weapon would have had an enormous effect on the thinking of the prison authorities on matters of security. That would have brought great hardship to all who remained behind. My responsibility for all of us led me to insist that the escape plan be designed to avoid such actions. No violence against any guard! Our group insisted on this. Alex wounded me deeply during this period when he accused me of trying to stop their escape.

Tim reached an insoluble problem regarding a key for door number six, as he called it, the door to get past the night guard's office. I was able to help. I had hidden a makeshift key made of three pieces of wire held together with cotton thread. It worked in many locks because it was not made with great precision and could be jiggled around until it was in the right position to turn the lock. It had to be adjusted for every door and it worked on door number six.

What I had not solved was how to open my cell door from the inside, where there was no keyhole. My rickety key was of no use in that situation. Tim found a wonderful way to overcome the difficulty: he used a broomstick to hold the key so that he could lean through the passage window and insert the key into the lock and turn it using the broomstick like a crank handle. It demanded an extraordinary level of physical coordination to poke the stick through the window, find the keyhole and insert the key, and then turn the key twice in the correct direction. Tim had not only excellent hand-eye coordination; he had a natural talent for precision that is probably related to that coordination. He told me that as a fifteen-year-old he used to race electric slot-racing cars. These little cars are not properly balanced and are difficult to keep on the track. He rebuilt the tiny electric motors, turning the rotors on a small precision lathe to balance them. This

Protests and demands,
Johannesburg, circa 1953.

Umkhonto we Sizwe warrior logo.

Mum and Dad at a wedding, 1923.

(Left) Mum, age seventy-six, in 1975.
(Above) Dad, age seventy-seven, in 1975
(photo by Stephen Kuny).

Golden wedding anniversary of my grandparents Morris and Annie Goldberg, circa
1941. Dad and Mum are at the far right, and I am in the front row, fourth from left.

Mum, second from right.

Mum (in spectacles, standing near the window) in a clothing factory, London, circa 1920.

Esmé Bodenstein married me on 9
April 1954.

Esmé reads a statement after life sentences
have been handed down in the Rivonia Trial,
12 June 1964 (courtesy of the *Daily Worker*,
London).

Esmé and our daughter, Hilly, await our sentencing on the night of 11 June 1964
(courtesy of the *Daily Worker*, London).

(Left) Esmé and our children, 1963.

(Above) Allan, Mum, Dad, and me, circa 1939.

A conference of the Federation of South African Women, Port Elizabeth, circa 1961 (Robben Island Collection, Mayibuye Centre, University of the Western Cape). Esmé Goldberg stands at the far right.

Myself at age seven, 1940 (school photograph).

My cousin Selwyn, right, and me, circa 1936.

Dad with Hillary Kuny, March 1978 (photo by Stephen Kuny).

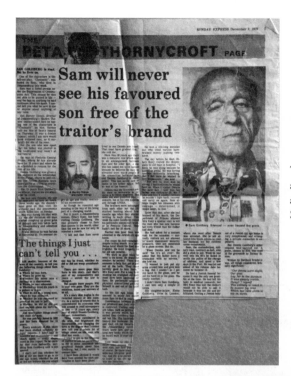

The *Sunday Express* feature article, December 9, 1979, after the death of my father, Sam Goldberg.

(Left) Sam Goldberg's seaman's pay book. *(Above)* Minnie Bodenstein, my mother-in-law, a political activist, circa 1954.

University of Cape Town, Rag (float parade), circa 1953. I am standing at the far right.

At a dance at Bishopsford night club December, 1952. I am second from the left.

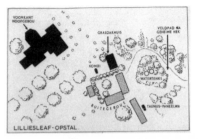

(Above left) Police map of Liliesleaf Farm produced in the Rivonia Trial. *(Above right)* The manor house at Liliesleaf Farm, our underground headquarters.

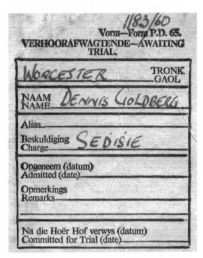

(Left) My prison ID card after my arrest during the state of emergency, 1960. *(Above)* The escapees *(left to right)*: Tim Jenkin, Alex Moumbaris, and Stephen Lee in Dar es Salaam after their escape.

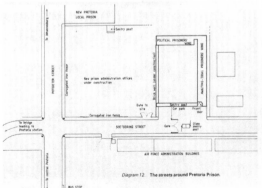

A typical prison key.

The layout of Pretoria Local Prison, from which Tim Jenkin, Alex Moumbaris, and Stephen Lee escaped in 1974.

Solwandle Looksmart Ngudle, who was tortured to death in 1963 (ANC pamphlet).

Delegates to the Congress of the People, 25–26 June 1955 (Robben Island Collection, Mayibuye Centre, University of the Western Cape).

(Above) Chris Martin Hani, who was assassinated in 1993. *(Right above)* Archie Sibeko, a.k.a. Zola Zembe (courtesy of A. Sibeko). *(Right)* Fred Carneson (Robben Island Collection, Mayibuye Centre, University of the Western Cape).

(Above left) Reg September (Robben Island Collection, Mayibuye Centre, University of the Western Cape). *(Above right)* Wilton Mkwayi (Robben Island Collection, Mayibuye Centre, University of the Western Cape).

Communist Party of South Africa Grand Parade, Cape Town, in the 1940s (Robben Island Collection, Mayibuye Centre, University of the Western Cape).

From left: Annie Solinga, James La Guma, Oscar Mpetha, Chief Albert Luthuli, Zoli Malindi, and others, Cape Town, mid-1950s (Robben Island Collection, Mayibuye Centre, University of the Western Cape).

BO LINKS: MANDELA   BO REGS: SISULU
ONDER LINKS: GOLDBERG   ONDER REGS: MBEKI

The accused in the Rivonia Trial, sentenced to life

BO: KATHRADA, BERNSTEIN EN MHLABA
ONDER: KANTOR, MOTSOALEDI EN MLANGENI

imprisonment on 12 June 1964 (police mug shots).

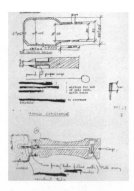

(Left) Andimba (Herman) Toivo ja Toivo (pamphlet). *(Above)* Sketches of explosive devices (police evidence).

Arthur Chaskalson, advocate, later chief justice, with me at the Nelson Mandela Centre of Memory (courtesy of the Nelson Mandela Foundation).

Bram Fischer, the lead advocate in the Rivonia Trial, was later sentenced to life imprisonment and died in prison (Robben Island Collection, Mayibuye Centre, University of the Western Cape).

(Left) George Bizos (Robben Island Collection, Mayibuye Centre, University of the Western Cape).
(Right) Vernon Berrangé (Robben Island Collection, Mayibuye Centre, University of the Western Cape).

(Above) A cell in our prison.
(Right) David Rabkin (Robben Island
Collection, Mayibuye Centre, University
of the Western Cape).

(Above left) Raymond Suttner (Robben Island Collection, Mayibuye Centre, University
of the Western Cape). *(Above right)* Jeremy Cronin (Robben Island Collection, Mayibuye
Centre, University of the Western Cape).

(Left) Hugh Lewin
(courtesy of Hugh
Lewin).

(Right) Renfrew Christie
(courtesy of Renfrew
Christie).

David Kitson was sentenced to twenty years' imprisonment (Robben Island Collection, Mayibuye Centre, University of the Western Cape).

Naphtali "Tollie" Bennun, who researched explosive devices (courtesy of M. Bennun).

Blasted pylons (Robben Island Collection, Mayibuye Centre, University of the Western Cape).

made the cars run faster and made them more controllable. That gave him victory over his friends. Tim always pushed his abilities to the limits. He is a brilliant talent wherever precision is needed.

For the finishing touches to the special key, Tim needed a soldering bolt. We had acquired one for installing our loudspeaker system for the music they played for us. Helen Suzman had bought us our record player, and I had installed it and the loudspeaker system. The record player was kept in the night guard's room, and he played the records for us according to the programs we drew up. I knew that the soldering iron and solder were kept locked up in a drawer of the head of the prison. I was allowed to use it when something went wrong with the system and I needed to repair it.

David Rabkin allowed Tim to break his loudspeaker so that he could get permission for me to repair it. I asked for Tim to be allowed to help me. I stood guard, Tim soldered the key, and then the loudspeaker wires were joined up in seconds.

The trust that David showed Tim cannot be valued too highly. A soldering iron in prison is a dangerous device. I was able to use it because I was seen as a prisoner who could be trusted, a prisoner who had earned respect. In relation to the guards I had adopted the device of "still waters run deep." I worked at showing that I was self-disciplined and could be left alone.

Tim was often not believed when he said later that he had achieved the exact form of the keys by observation alone. It was really so. Observing the bundle of keys the guards carried was enough for me to make even my Heath Robinson or Rube Goldberg ramshackle device. You see the geometry, and then you file the keys until they fit. You also need a technical background. It takes trial and error to make them exactly right. The real difficulty for Tim did not lie in the blade of the key but in the shaft, which had to be the exact size of the keyhole so that it would turn precisely in the lock. Tim made most of the keys out of wood. That was what was special. Naturally, he used tropical hardwood. There was something special about this, too. We thought of a ruler used for drawing lines and needed for our studies. You can bend it this way and that without its breaking. That was what we needed for our key. Wooden keys had another advantage over metal keys. They were very quiet and made no noise when turned in a lock.

We also helped in the search for street clothes. There was a laundry basket of old clothing used as cleaning rags. The clothes were left behind by the *stokkies,* prisoners awaiting trial, who wore their own clothes until they were sentenced or released. What a great moment it was when we found a pair of jeans that were an exact fit, or as they say in prison, *size fit,* for the tall, slender Stephen. Unfortunately, there was nothing to fit the short, stocky Denis (when I was still part of the plan).

Through my initiative, we found shoes for the escape. I had for years had a torn cartilage in my knee. I think I made it much worse when I jumped off the roof when I escaped from Vereeniging Prison. Eventually the prison authorities permitted an operation to remove the cartilage. It took years to heal properly and swelled up whenever I walked too far or ran around the exercise yard to keep fit. At some point physiotherapy was authorized. That was a rare occurrence in prison. The therapist, a real human being, recommended on medical grounds that I have shoes with cushioned soles. That meant buying a pair of Adidas training shoes. What walking comfort! What luxury! I slept with them under my pillow so that I could smell their fresh newness. Suddenly I was nine years old again, dreaming of sporting glory with my first rugby boots under my pillow.

The head of the prison, Captain Schnepel, such a totally unpredictable man, then thought it unfair that I should have exercise shoes and not the rest of *his* men. And so all of us were allowed to buy such shoes. The bright colors were wonderfully cheerful. We turned some of them into smart street shoes using waterproof drawing ink that I had for drawing maps for my geography studies. Years later, in London, Tim told me that bright sports shoes were more the fashion than shiny black "go to church" shoes. One really does get left behind in prison.

Once we had sports shoes, Schnepel thought we should have white T-shirts for exercising so that we did not make our prison uniform shirts too sweaty and thus wear them out with excessive washing. Dave Kitson subscribed to the *Huisgenoot* (*Home Companion*), a family magazine with household tips and short stories. It included full-page photos of film stars that could be ironed onto the T-shirts. He immediately thought of turning the escape shirts into fashion items. I can't remember who got Jackie Bisset! That too was a contribution to the escape. We all felt responsible for not allowing a small oversight to ruin the possibility of success.

Each of us knew the hiding place for the escape clothes and artifacts behind the hot water heater in a locked closet. That key was the work of but a moment for Tim. All of us kept a watchful eye to protect these things, and what a shock we got when we found water running out of the closet. The heater was leaking. We found a temporary hiding place for the clothes on a stairway behind a locked grille. Then the grille was welded closed and we could not easily recover the clothes. Alex, reaching awkwardly around the corner through the grille, felt the sack of clothes fall out of his hand. Now they were out of reach. We fashioned a sort of grappling hook out of very large paper clips and managed to haul the sack back into sight, where we could grab it again. Naturally, all stood around "cleaning" the floor and walls to avoid the grapplers being seen.

Today I can better understand the three men's anxiety over the building renovations than I did at the time. Because of their refusal to wait for the agreed-on escape date, they drove the confrontation between themselves and the rest of us to a breaking point. It became a burning political issue in which they saw themselves as the political activists; we were viewed as the delayers who wanted to stop the escape because we had lost our will to fight. They could think of nothing else. Tim and Alex did not report this conflict when they were debriefed about the escape and did not write about it publicly.

Tim was a loner. He seemed to prefer to be alone with his thoughts. He seldom showed any emotion and shied away from any attempt to express his innermost feelings. We seldom see each other now and I would say that we are friendly but not close.

Shortly before the escape, Alex proposed, in the form of an ultimatum, that I should break the electric lightbulb in my cell to divert the night guard. "It is your duty," he stated, when I said that he was asking too much too crudely. I told him that nobody *had* to help but might be asked to help. We had to find a way to justify calling Vermeulen at the moment it was necessary. We could wait for a coincidental lightning storm, but that was too unpredictable. Alex demanded the short circuit. I would have to cause it in my cell by breaking my lightbulb. But how could I do that without giving the authorities the proof they would love to have that I was part of the escape plot? Torture was always a possibility. Who knows whether he is strong enough to resist blabbing out everything he knows, especially after years of imprisonment? A rough ride in prison thereafter was a certainty. That was of no concern to our Alex!

My study privileges meant a great deal to me. They were a key element in my survival. Everybody took me to be a diligent student. I had been studying for fifteen years already, often for ten hours a day. How do you fill the time without the electric light that goes with the study privilege? Every newcomer to our group in prison found that having so much time to study was a great advantage. They envied me a little. In reality, I would much rather have been free to do many other things!

What upset me most was that Alex demanded of me, with such absolute certainty of his position, that I should make his escape possible. In his mind, I am sure, I was the lifer and therefore of no further value. He could not hear my arguments. I had grown a thick skin during my years in prison, but this was too much.

Some in our group were quite nervous about the escape. Their responses ranged from willing help through guarded participation to reluctant acceptance. For Alex, and for Tim, each was a soldier in the revolution and therefore duty-bound to escape. I found myself in the same position except that I did not see myself escaping.

Alex wanted to escape at all costs. He could think of nothing else. He feared that his life would disintegrate and that his wife and son would turn away from him. He had named his son, Boris, after his Soviet trainer. I do not know if Boris was his real name or a cover name, but it would have made no difference to Alex. Alex believed with absolute certainty that Boris was trying to send him messages. He was so obsessed with this that he wanted to read and examine all our letters for hidden messages. Predictably, Boris made no contact at all.

There were times when Alex was so aggressive and acting without finesse that some of his actions threatened more harm than good. Like a bull in a china shop, he came close to smashing everything on a number of occasions. Of course, he was totally unaware of all this. Sadly, Alex had great unhappiness with his son, who left his parents' home very early in his life.

In the end none of this mattered. Eventually we hit on the obvious solution to the problem: use the trip switches to switch off the lights. Vermeulen would not be suspicious. I called him to reset the switches, kept him talking, and our three got away.

The escape was discovered by Sergeant Badenhorst when he unlocked our cells the next morning. Every day the heavy, steel doors were opened, but we were still locked up behind the steel grille in each cell. Badenhorst had come in through the street door, its lock broken, but had not noticed anything suspicious.

He opened the first door. Stephen Lee was still lying in bed. He opened the second door, and Tim was also still in bed. I was third in line and I was at attention, innocently standing behind my grille. Badenhorst, turning back, saw that the first two had not got up. Suddenly he realized there were dummies in their beds.

I watched him the whole time. He turned chalk white and staggered back against the passage wall. I thought he had fainted or had a heart attack. After a moment he pulled himself upright and called for his superior. From fright his voice came out as a weak little whisper: "Uncle Piet. Uncle Piet." Now he stumbled to the stairs and I could hear him going down. Prison officer Pieterse, in reality a friendly type who seldom lost his nerve, came up the stairs, saw the damage, and then briskly opened all the cells to see if there were others missing. I thought I saw him give me a small smile. Alex, much farther down the passage, had also escaped.

We were told to "carry on as usual" and even got breakfast before the inquiries began. When I was asked about the escape, I naturally knew nothing. I had played my guitar and I had listened to the nightly concert of recorded music. Then I had called Vermeulen because the lights had gone out. Nothing unusual had happened. I did not think it necessary to add that Alex had passed my cell and waved good-bye, the signal for me to give the three escapees time to hide in the closet after they had tripped the light switches before I called Vermeulen.

On the morning after the escape, when the security people descended en masse on our prison, the high officials showed great amazement that I was still there. "Goldberg, you are still here! If anyone had reason to escape, then surely it was you!" One said, "Goldberg, I know why you didn't escape. Communists always hold out and fight to the end. You are one, aren't you?" I held my peace and for once made no comment. Even the prison officers understood that I was the one who had to escape. Only my fellow prisoner Alex could not grasp it.

The Security Police put David Rabkin and Tony Holiday through the wringer. What they thought they would get from them remains a mystery. Many high-ranking security officers came to the prison. Each first made sure that I was indeed still there and seemed to become much calmer when they had seen me.

Perhaps the long-planned and authorized visit of David's father, Gerald Rabkin, from England had something to do with sparing us the worst responses from the authorities. Because of the unusual circumstances, Rabkin senior, now a British businessman, was able to meet General Jan Roux, the second highest officer in the Prison Service. Gerald Rabkin told David that he ended their conversation with this remark: "In business there are gains and losses, and you cannot win every time. I hope that the prisoners remaining behind will not be punished for the escape." Probably because the authorities were always on the lookout to protect themselves against international criticism, our treatment and the interrogations were more moderate than we expected.

The security police arrested Vermeulen and locked him away for some months until they charged him with assisting in the escape. They forced a confession out of him through threats of physical violence. He said that he had been promised a payment of a laughably small amount of two hundred rand. He was found guilty and sentenced to imprisonment. He appealed the conviction and was found not guilty.

During the case against Vermeulen, Stephen, in London, told a British newspaper about the escape and how they had achieved it. Vermeulen's lawyer asked Stephen for a sworn statement that Vermeulen had not been implicated, and Stephen provided it. We prisoners were divided in our opinions about it because that was helping an official of the hated regime. Stephen showed through his action, seen by the whole world, that we, despite anything Vermeulen might have done in his daily life, preserved our sense of humanity and acted honorably. For Vermeulen, the "terrorist" Stephen Lee became, I am sure, a decent person. I support Stephen's action. He was a person who hated injustice and fought against it. He fought against the injustice of apartheid as he would against any injustice.

A ruling was made after the escape that we should remain locked up on Sundays. Previously we had been allowed to use the courtyard to move about and exercise. Now it appeared that this privilege had to be withdrawn because there were not enough guards to supervise us.

I saw this as a hidden punishment and demanded to speak to Brigadier Gericke (he had been promoted) immediately. I had known him since 1963, when he was a captain. I was so insistent in my argument that the weekend staff did not lock us up. Gericke, however, would not allow his Sunday to be disturbed. He came only on Monday morning. He said to me, "You think you can call me whenever you want!" I answered, "It worked. You obviously ordered that we were not to be locked up on Sunday. Thank you. I do know, Brigadier, that you will come only when you wish to." Smiles all round. Honor and ego were satisfied!

In his office he asked me to tell him of the things that were troubling us. I can still see how this huge man took out his very large and very expensive Mont Blanc fountain pen. He noted down our complaints about studies, letters, the way visits were controlled, and, above all, the deteriorating conduct of the guards. He wrote down everything in great detail. I have to say that he dealt with all the issues within a few days, and things did get a bit better.

Tim and Alex managed to cross the border into Swaziland within twenty-four hours and then went farther, into Mozambique. Stephen hid out in Johannesburg and was later smuggled across the border. More than a year later a number of people were arrested, and, because of their involvement with him, they were tried and imprisoned.

Raymond Suttner later told me how severely a prisoner is affected by the terror of a renewed round of interrogation when his constitution has been weakened by long years of imprisonment. After completing his prison sentence with us in Pretoria, Raymond was arrested again and held in preventive detention, in solitary confinement, for a period that had no predetermined length of time. Raymond, who seemed to me to be "Comrade Revolutionary Purity" personified, with no thought for the personal cost involved, came close to a breakdown. In the end he had a little bird for companionship in his cell. It slept on his chest and saved him from insanity, he said. He told me that only when he was in that situation did he really come to understand what "life," a sentence of imprisonment for life, must have meant for me and how difficult it must have been for me to see the others escape and not be able to go with them.[1]

After the first report of the escape, which contained no details of who had fled, many people assumed or hoped that I had to be one of them. That had a deep effect on Esmé because Baruch had become a good friend to her, encouraging her to endure my absence. Marie-José, Alex's wife, often phoned to find out if Esmé had any news about "our men," loading her anxieties onto Esmé, whom she treated as a surrogate grandmother. Her phone calls stopped immediately after Alex was reported to be safe in Mozambique. For Esmé the news that I had not escaped was deeply disappointing. She could not know the complicated reasons for my remaining behind and assumed, with some justification, that once again I had put the needs of others before hers. What hurt the most, she said, was the callous indifference of the younger comrades like Marie-José and those who escaped, who made no effort to comfort her.

Baruch Hirson was deeply disappointed when the escapees arrived in London without me. He was upset that all his efforts, mainly to enable me to escape, had been ignored. Later, after my release from prison, I spoke to him in London about the escape and indicated some of the problems, but not nearly as fully as I have done here. He seemed to understand a little better that there was no real possibility for me to escape, but I think he never really forgave me for letting him down. Of course, I would have loved to arrive in London as the hero who had escaped. It was at the time difficult for me to accept that I had to remain behind. I rejoiced in their success, and, despite my own disappointment I was very proud of my comrades for the roles we had all played in achieving this slap in the face we gave the apartheid regime. Tim's precision, together with his courage, was the secret of the escape. Courage alone, without that precision, would not have been enough.

I could live with my decision and made the best of the rest of my time in prison. My continued presence was a benefit for our whole group. When I was released in 1985, a bit more than five years later, I heard from Rob Adam, who was sentenced in 1982 to ten years' imprisonment for MK activities, that the prison conditions became considerably worse.

The Weather

The weather might not seem to be important in prison. But it is.

After the great escape of Tim, Alex, and Stephen in December 1979, our prison was rebuilt to increase security. Remote-controlled doors, which required a huge key and a massive tommy bar to force them open when the mechanism broke down, were an indication of the seriousness with which the authorities took our incarceration. The whole system of guarding us, whether we were four prisoners or ten, now required a staff of thirty-eight officials, including a captain, a lieutenant, several warrant officers, sergeants, and guards to watch over us. Then there was a system of microphones—bugs—embedded in walls and fittings to enable them to overhear our conversations.

This was not a piece of speculation born of our paranoia. We knew for a fact that they were bugging us. We would plan what we would say to the captain on some matter or other, such as health, food, visits, letters, the conduct of a guard, or the movies we were allowed to see. He would answer our arguments before we had finished. He would even answer the points in the order in which we planned to raise them.

There were times when I would keep back some arguments that I had not spoken aloud and that therefore the captain had not heard through the bugging apparatus. He answered what he had heard. Then I put the reserve arguments to him. The captain would be dumbfounded! He had not had time to prepare his answer. He would look at me with a wry smile, knowing he had been caught out. I would smile sweetly or as innocently as I could manage to avoid embarrassing him further. Sometimes the technique worked and we got what we wanted. Sometimes it failed. But it was one form of amusement!

On one occasion I forgot about the bugging devices. I explained to someone that I often spoke in Afrikaans when I wanted something from the authorities. If speaking "their" language aided the process of communication, that suited me very well. In fact, I spoke Afrikaans well and with enjoyment. The manipulative aspect seemed to me to be a legitimate tactic. It amused me to find the captain insisting on speaking English to me to show that he was resisting the manipulation, and giving up his language rights at that moment. Sometimes, as a long-term prisoner, you just cannot lose.

When we returned to our rebuilt prison after nearly three years in a cell in Beverley Hills, where there were no windows to the outside, I was given a cell with a view. The scene was not very beautiful. Twenty yards away was a blank golden brown brick wall. The ground was concrete from wall to wall. No longer could we bury homemade keys in the garden soil, as Tim had done. But the wind did blow in. I could put my hand out through the bars and feel raindrops and rub the wetness over my face. I could smell the rain.

Pretoria is known for its electric storms. As the electrical charge built up, a massive headache would grow inside my skull until I thought it would burst. My neck muscles would grow tense and I would feel as though I had to vomit. Then the storm would break. The sky grew dark and the lightning flashed. Count the seconds until the thunderclap, and you know how far away the storm is. Five seconds equals one mile, more or less. As the storm moved closer, the thunderclaps would follow the lightning flashes almost instantaneously. Sometimes the flash seemed to be inside my cell. The thunder cracked so loudly I would levitate off the bed if I happened to be lying down. With my heart racing I awaited the next flash. It was like a drug-induced high.

But my headache would disappear in the flash. My neck muscles let go, the blood rushed to my brain, and everything seemed bright again. Sometimes the rain followed as if the lightning had torn the bottom out of the clouds. The rain came down in sheets. There were no individual drops. The smell was sweet and clean—and the oppressive humidity would be gone for a time.

The surge of electric power tripped the electrical system. The weather had struck. The lights went out. Security guards in the lookout posts were pacing up and down. In the words of the "Song of the Peat Bog Soldiers" (*Morsoldaten*) in the Nazi labor camp Börgermoor in Germany near the Dutch border, "Up and down the guards are pacing, No one, no one, can get through." But I developed a habit of shouting for the night-duty guard to come and reset the trip switches for our section of the prison. "Me . . . nee . . . eeer!—Mister!" I would shout to the guard, long and drawn-out to make fun of the call for our attendant to deal with our needs. Up he would come and reset the switches. It was good for security! Security needs lights.

Tim, Alex, and Steve worked out that the way out of the prison was to get past the night guard's office. That meant getting him out of the way. They would trip the switch of the obviously unreliable electrical system and hide in a closet under the stairs. That had a simple key for the expert Tim to copy. I would call Me-e-e-nee-ee-ee-eer. He would come up to our section of the prison. My comrades would walk out past his empty office.

The weather is important in prison.

12

More about Prison

Hangings

After the escape of Tim, Stephen, and Alex, the rest of us bore the consequences. The prison was rebuilt and we political prisoners were held in another prison known as Beverley Hills, gallows' humor for the death cells. It was an awful place where about 150 hangings took place each year. That's two or three hangings every week.

There were some of our brave comrades on death row. On many evenings they sang our freedom songs in the most beautiful harmony while they awaited their executions. I tried to play the melodies on my recorder. Though I am no singer, I could answer them with my recorder. I was reminded of this many years later. After Nelson Mandela's release, there was a "meet the media day" for him and other political prisoners on Robben Island. I saw the Robben Island Prison for the first time. A younger man, James Mange, with Rastafarian dreadlocks, came up and asked if I was Comrade Denis Goldberg. I said I was and he greeted me as the pennywhistle player from Beverley Hills. My musical answer in the deathly nights had told them that I was still alive, and that strengthened them and all had listened to me play. I felt deeply honored. I am not a natural musician and have little talent for music. But in prison I was able to bring music and music notation together, note for note, until I could play a whole song. In those dark nights I discovered for myself how to express emotions in music. You play some notes longer or shorter, higher or lower, sharper or flatter, or louder or softer, and your feelings stream into the sounds you are making. You just have to let it happen. I tried to say farewell to my comrades when we knew we were to be taken away from that prison. We might never see each other again.

Our MK comrades on death row were Simon Moegerane, Jerry Mosololi, Marcus Motaung, and six others. Their singing was quite different from the hymn singing of the other prisoners. It was very disciplined. They sang the most beautiful harmonies for twenty to thirty minutes in the evening, shortly before the eight o'clock bell for lights out. Gradually all the prisoners in the prison learned the songs, too. Their singing was courageous. They sang of their pride in being in the struggle. There were songs from the 1950s and 1960s that I knew quite well, and there were songs that came from our MK camps in Angola and elsewhere. They had new melodies and new thoughts.

One particular song affected me deeply. It was an adaptation of a song from Zimbabwe's Chimurenga War. They sang: "Long live Comrade Ruth First. Long live. We shall never forget you. Long live Comrade Ruth First." And "Long live Comrade Saloojee. Long live. We shall never forget you. Long live Comrade Saloojee." And so on for Solomon Mahlangu, Vuyisile Mini, Wilson Khayinga, Zinakile Mkaba, and others who had been assassinated, killed, or executed by the apartheid regime. Then they would sing of the great leaders who had died, people like Moses Kotane. The singing reflected their sorrow at the human cost of the struggle for freedom. Then the singing would change into a more upbeat mood as they sang in a clipped, optimistic style: "Long live Comrade Joe Slovo. Long live. We shall ever remember. Long live Comra-ade Joe." Long live Comrade Mandela, Sisulu, and others who were in prison—and then the verse I found most moving: "Long live the ANC. Long live. We shall ever remember, long live the ANC." They were men who faced death with courage and optimism about reaching the goals for which they were prepared to die. I know this sounds sentimental, and there will be those who say how childish or blind we all were. Yet, hearing them sing with such control in a variety of moods and shifting stresses, I could not help being moved by their understanding, their commitment, and their courage, which was not the bravado of weak defiance. These were men who knew what they were doing and why they had been doing it.

Each evening they ended with the national anthem, *"Nkosi Sikelel' iAfrika*," and "The Internationale." Sometimes the one and sometimes the other would be the last song. The mixture of national liberation (God, bring back Africa) and of class politics (Arise, ye toilers of the earth) seemed to me to encapsulate the multiple strands within the liberation movement. Nationalism and internationalism and resistance to national oppression as the expression of class oppression in the particular context of South African politics and society—all were there in the songs they sang.

James Mange and some others had their death sentences commuted to life imprisonment, but some were hanged.

During the time in Beverley Hills, it did not matter to me whether the guards approved of my playing freedom songs or whether they would punish me. They did nothing. Just after I was sentenced to life imprisonment in 1964, however, there were three ANC comrades from Port Elizabeth sentenced to death: Vuyisile Mini, Wilson Khayinga, and Zinakile Mkaba. Mini was a noted freedom songwriter and composer. They sang "The Red Flag" and "The Internationale," "*Nkosi Sikelel' iAfrika*," and many other songs throughout the night before they were hanged. My fellow prisoners were terribly afraid of the guards, who had been giving them such a hard time, and they would not join in the singing. They insisted that I too should not sing along because we would all be punished. I submitted to their wishes. I had only just escaped the death penalty myself and was not in the best of shape. Courage is a fluctuating and relative thing, not a permanent quality. Even political prisoners are not always brave. Revolutionaries are not superhuman. They too suffer and weep. I did not sing with them and I regret it to this day. Vuyisile Mini, Wilson Khayinge, and Zinakile Mkaba were executed on 6 November 1964.

In June 1964, after I was sentenced, I had been near the death cells in the old Pretoria Central Prison. Only one white man was executed while we were there in 1964–1965. His special music request program was a strange mixture of hymns and sentimental country-and-western songs. He was allowed to broadcast a message expressing sorrow for his wrongdoing. The prisoners around us were not at all overawed by the execution. He had gone to the gallows like a man should, filled with bravado. There was little comment about just deserts or dignity, only remarks about how brave he was.

Once we heard a woman shrieking in fear as she was taken to the gallows. Guards told us she had to be carried on a stretcher. The white criminal prisoners we were with at Pretoria Central Prison found it amusing to hear her, and they made sickening racist remarks.

Executions were not carried out immediately after sentence had been passed. There was a long procedure of judicial review, and prisoners were kept on death row for many months before the death sentences were confirmed. In the late afternoon the sheriff would inform those who were to die the next morning. The condemned men would start singing hymns. At first the singing would be hesitant, but gradually, as the prison quieted down, the singing would become more full-bodied, and ultimately perhaps three thousand ordinary criminal prisoners were singing hymns together. The singing seemed to me to be a sign of helplessness and hopelessness. Whatever the words of the hymns, the singing had the sound of "I'm going nowhere." The hymns, of course, were about joining God in the life hereafter, but the singing was filled with such despair that it was terrible to live through. It was worse for those who were about to die, but it was awful to hear it and share it week after week.

We stayed out of our exercise yard when the maintenance work on the gallows started. We couldn't handle that. We heard the preparations and the singing all night long until the early morning, when the trapdoors slammed open. We were still in our cells when the executions took place. The nonstop singing would finally end, as though turned off by a switch. The following silence had a feeling of exhaustion, of nothingness, of emotional emptiness. It was dreadful. Slowly we regained our composure, and life went on until the next week and the next . . .

It is a great thing that our constitution now prohibits the imposition of the death penalty, and I cannot believe that there are people who want to reintroduce it. It did not stop crime before, and it will not stop it in the future. All it does is make the state and the officials who carry out the deed—and indeed the whole society—more callous, more indifferent to life itself.

A Case for News

Once we were convicted prisoners, the authorities tried to cut us off from news of the outside world. One official said that if we were safecrackers, they would not give us locks and keys to play with. Since we were political activists, they would not allow us to be informed about political news. Letters were censored and visits closely monitored. One of my visitors was stopped when she tried to tell me that during the popular television series *World at War,* a history of World War II, so many people went to the toilet during commercial breaks that in large cities the water pressure fell. They said you cannot talk about "World War II or any war." In 1976 the United States celebrated the bicentenary of its Declaration of Independence. The censors felt we should not know about that and cut out an item about it in the *Reader's Digest.*

We were allowed to study through the University of South Africa (Unisa). Books we needed for study assignments were provided by the Unisa library. The sergeant in charge of our studies had a middle-school education. He decided whether a book was suitable or not. Many books were withheld and returned to the Unisa Library unread. Colonel Aucamp once told me that I would be allowed to get more books when I had "used up" those I already had.

Bram, through his daughter Ilse, asked Arthur Chaskalson if there was an arguable case to put to a court to win the right of access to news. He replied that there was a very weak case. Bram did not want to embarrass his fellow advocate by asking him to argue a weak case and allowed the matter to drop.

The censorship became ever more absurd, and even the most innocuous magazines were mutilated. Bram had died (this was in the mid-1970s), and I was less squeamish and believed that because the censorship had become so ridiculous, we had nothing to lose by bringing a case against the authorities for access to news. I was studying law and believed that there was an arguable case in administrative law in which Parliament delegates the making of rules and regulations to officials. My fellow prisoners agreed that I should explore the matter. Hillary Kuny at my request found an attorney who was prepared to act for us. I knew the likelihood of winning was small, but an arguable case would so embarrass the ruling party that its intellectuals might press for us to have access to newspapers. There were judges who felt keenly embarrassed by overzealous officials. Only very rarely would a judge in this kind of case order an official with delegated powers to grant what was being demanded. More often the judge would say that, even if an official had made a shocking ruling, the court hoped that he might reconsider the matter and come to a different decision.

Hillary asked the attorney Raymond Tucker, one of the few human rights lawyers at that time, to see me. We sat opposite each other at a table with the commanding officer, Captain Schnepel, sitting between us at the end of the table, his head partially blocking our view of each other. Prison rules permitted this absurd situation. In criminal matters, legal visits were to take place within sight of, but not within hearing of, a state official. In the case of civil matters, the legal consultation was to take place within the sight and hearing of an official. But in this matter the prison authorities were going to be the respondents and should not have been allowed to be present. I instructed our attorney to go to court to get a ruling on this procedural matter. Let us kick off by embarrassing our opponents, I thought. Raymond duly returned with the matter resolved in our favor, but not as a result of a court ruling. A court application would have embarrassed him because he was expected to exhaust administrative avenues before approaching a court. He wrote to the commissioner of prisons, who accepted the claim that we could consult without an official present. Even though I knew that the room in which we met was bugged, I explained the situation for which the court should be asked to provide relief. I had kept records of the censorship because we were not allowed to keep the magazines beyond a few days. Title, volume number, page number, column number, and the position in millimeters from the top of the column to the end of the excision were recorded. It was expressly forbidden for me to give him my notes, and they had to be read aloud while he made his notes. It was a long-winded and tiresome business. He brought a tape recorder to the next visit to speed up the process. The tape recorder was forbidden for future visits.

We agreed he would brief Advocate Sydney Kentridge, and after a few weeks Raymond brought his opinion, which was that we indeed had an arguable case. Now my fellow prisoners were brought in, and we each prepared sworn statements describing who we were and for what we had been sentenced and for what length of time. We asked the court to declare that we be entitled to receive newspapers from outside sources, to receive magazines and journals of our choice, that our letters and visits be censored only to preserve prison security. The legal language and the alternatives were much more detailed. The case number M776/77 was brought in the Supreme Court Transvaal Provincial Division, Pretoria, by Denis Goldberg and Eight Others[1] against the Minister of Prisons, Commissioner of Prisons, and the Officer Commanding Pretoria Prison.

Raymond Tucker acquired two back copies of each of the publications we had chosen as examples of the censorship. One copy he marked up, he said, and the other was cut up according to my recorded details. From my side it was a blind choice because I did not know what had been cut out. In the course of my statement, which was the founding affidavit of our case, I said that in comparison with other prisoners we were treated more harshly, and the deprivation of news of every kind, not only political news, and the effects this had on maintaining meaningful contact with our wives, families, and friends, was a punishment additional to our loss of liberty. Judge David Curlewis heard the case and was extremely hostile to us. In the course of his judgment, dated 5 August 1977, he gave the commissioner of prisons almost unhindered power to treat us in any way he wished. In the course of dismissing our application, Judge Curlewis said: "It is clear to me that a prisoner's punishment is not to be found merely in the fact that he is deprived of his liberty: this seems to be the view of the First Applicant and appears to be the view of certain other people. He is quite wrong. A convicted person sent to prison cannot expect to live in prison as he lived outside prison. A prison is not a hotel from which egress is barred." He did not need to tell us we did not live in a five-star hotel merely lacking the keys to go home. We knew that.

At one point the judge said that the commissioner had said he *prohibits* certain publications, but he did not mean to say that because what he really meant to say in his sworn statement was that he *did not permit* certain magazines. The judge frequently went out of his way to find arguments to support the authorities, even where they had not relied on such intellectual gymnastics. He even said that the treatment of prisoners is to be decided on by the commissioner, though that treatment "cannot be contrary to the [Prisons] Act and Regulations." "In view of the fact that the Regulations themselves give him the right to prescribe rules and conditions," however, "such a qualification is more apparent than real." Our lawyers said that we could not allow that judgment to stand unchallenged because of the wide powers it gave the authorities. Therefore, we had to appeal to the Appellate Division of the Supreme Court, the highest court in the land.

The appeal took many months and was argued in the Appellate Division before five judges on 15 May 1978. Judgment was delivered on 26 September 1978.

I thoroughly enjoyed the whole process because it was intellectually challenging and it brought the outside world into the prison. What is more, we were fighting back.

We quoted from the UNESCO Standard Minimum Rules for the Treatment of Prisoners, which required that prisoners be kept informed about domestic and international news so that they would be familiar with the world when they reentered it upon their release. We found it very difficult to get hold of the full document. (There was no Internet in those days.) The state's lawyers objected to this quotation without the original document. Our lawyers said we would have to accept that we were relying on hearsay and withdraw the assertion. I insisted we not withdraw it, and I made use of the bugging microphones by saying that the state's lawyers knew that what we said was true. If they wished to be dishonest they could be, but in the meantime we would continue to try to get the document we needed. The state's lawyers withdrew their objection.

One of the ways we tried to overcome this difficulty was to ask experts in other countries to send us sworn affidavits about conditions in prisons elsewhere in the world. The Reverend Paul Oestreicher, the director of Amnesty International, sent an affidavit that described the conditions under which political prisoners were held in various countries. They all had access to news. At the end, however, he stated that he could not get permission from the Soviet authorities to enter their country and therefore could not personally ascertain how they treated their political prisoners. He went on to launch a scathing attack on the Soviet Union's treatment of prisoners. My comrades were very upset by this and insisted on ideological grounds that it could not be used. That led to John Hosey's withdrawing from the case. My view was that it would not serve our strategic purpose to use this particular affidavit. The media would have seized on the Cold War tidbit of the attack, based on hearsay about the Soviet Union, forgetting that it was our conditions that our court case was about. It would have been the ultimate red herring. I could imagine newspaper stories urging the authorities to send us to Russia to see if we would like it there! Our purpose was to embarrass the apartheid government, not give them the media escape they needed.

We finally got the original UNESCO Standard Minimum Rules in time to present them to the Appellate Court. As it happened, the South African commissioner of prisons had played a leading role in drawing up this document, and the court would have looked utterly absurd had it objected to our reliance on it.

There was also a startling development: the prison authorities started to broadcast the news bulletins of the government-owned and -controlled South African Broadcasting Corporation. The bulletins were censored, and sometimes we got only the weather report and the rugby or cricket scores. And if our national team, the Springboks, lost to some boycott-busting pirate team, we would get only the weather report!

Acting Chief Justice John Wessels, after careful analysis of the law, concluded that the commissioner did have sole discretion to determine how any prisoner should be treated, but that treatment must not be inconsistent with the law. Then came the passage we had hoped for: "The fact that this court may, on the information placed before it, entertain *grave doubts* [emphasis added] as to the wisdom or reasonableness of the determination made by the Commissioner in regard to the appellants' access to news . . . is a factor which the Commissioner may possibly take into account when his earlier determination comes to be reconsidered."

He said further that "interference by the court in a case such as this on the ground of unreasonableness is only justified if it is gross to so striking a degree as to warrant the inference that the repository power has acted in bad faith and from an ulterior or improper motive." He concluded: "In my opinion, the evidence does not in this case establish by a preponderance of probabilities the requisite degree of unreasonableness warranting the inference contended for on appellants' behalf." It was interesting to see that the judge had "grave doubts" but thought them not to be of "so striking a degree" as to warrant the inference that the degree of bad faith would justify intervention by the Court. In other words, how "grave" must the doubts be to be considered serious enough to warrant intervention by the court?

Acting Chief Justice Wessels specifically said that Judge Curlewis's view of a virtually unfettered power was wrong. It was also quite clear that Justice Wessels politely suggested that the commissioner reconsider the matter and come to a different conclusion, that is, that we have access to news.

Judge Corbett delivered a dissenting judgment that, if followed, would have given us everything we asked for. He relied on a civil rights argument based on the internationally established opinion that basic civil rights can be taken away only by explicit legislation. Therefore, a prisoner has all the rights he had before being imprisoned, except for those taken away by legislation or by necessary implication. For example, if you are to be locked up, by necessary implication you cannot have the keys to your prison. Judge Corbett also found something amiss in the responses of the authorities when they were asked to provide documentation of the commissioner of prisons' instructions regarding censorship. Judge Curlewis in the first hearing had said it was unseemly for counsel on both sides to argue about such a procedural matter. A senior prison officer had given sworn testimony to the existence of the documentation and that, said Judge Curlewis, was sufficient evidence of its existence! Judge Corbett found this very strange and took the opposite view, namely, that there was no such instruction from the commissioner and that the censorship was indeed arbitrary, as was shown by the examples of censorship our side had presented to the court.

John Dugard, a highly regarded academic civil rights lawyer, wrote up the case, which gained considerable publicity. Jane Dugard, his wife, had visited me a few times until she was prohibited because, it was said, she was not a first-degree family member. I believe it was because she was the wife of John Dugard.

Then the Justice Wessels came to see me, together with General Jan Roux, the first deputy commissioner. The general was also chairperson of a branch of the ruling (Afrikaner) National Party. He served on President P. W. Botha's State Security Council. Slapping General Roux familiarly on the thigh, Justice Wessels said that he was sure that "this young man" would see to it that we got the newspapers and magazines of our choice. In his written judgment he said that he had no basis in law for intervening and then intervened in an informal way on our behalf. Even judges, like lovers, can say "no" and mean "yes," or say "perhaps" but mean "definitely." In September 1980 Brigadier Gericke called me in to say we could order newspapers. At my request he repeated the announcement to all of us assembled together. My fellow prisoners showed no excessive gratitude but simply acknowledged the fact. The details were discussed, and it was ruled that we could buy and read all newspapers and magazines available on ordinary bookstalls, and they would not be censored. The SABC's news bulletins were also played uncensored. Hearing them, we came to the conclusion that the news was so slanted even the antenna masts must have leaned to the right.

Between us we ordered all the daily and weekend papers available. I ordered the government-supporting *Beeld* daily and *Rapport* on Sundays. I spoke and read Afrikaans fluently and felt it was important to know what "the enemy" was thinking and doing. David Rabkin ordered the *Weekly Guardian,* which gave us exceptional access to news with its articles from that paper in Britain, the French *Le Monde,* and the *Washington Post* in the United States. I read all the papers voraciously, including all the large and small advertisements and notices.

Thus, after sixteen years, we achieved the last of the ten things I had requested shortly after I was sentenced in 1964. I am glad I had half a law degree. I was even more pleased that there were good lawyers prepared to represent us.

When I asked Raymond Tucker who had paid the costs of the legal action we had brought in two courts, he simply said that the legal fees and expenses had been taken care of. When we were later able to read newspapers as a result of the legal action, it was clear that funds were flowing in from abroad for the legal defense of opponents of apartheid because apartheid government sources regularly attacked the lawyers who had the courage to defend our activists. They ran campaigns vilifying the lawyers, accusing them of racketeering through overcharging, and their hit squads murdered lawyers such as Griffiths and Victoria Mxenge. We knew they had to have done these brutal things, though the proof came much later, after the end of apartheid, through the hearings of the Truth and Reconciliation Commission. I also now know that the funds probably came from the International Defence and Aid Fund.

13

A Negotiated Release, 1985

I had some idea that there were negotiations going on for my release, and I had some sense that somehow my daughter was involved. In 1985 the regime offered all political prisoners, including the Rivonia Trialists, release from prison under the specific condition that they give up the armed struggle. That was an extremely complicated and potentially explosive matter for us.

Going back a bit in time: Hillary Kuny told me she wanted to submit a memorandum to the government calling for my release. I said I could not myself beg for my freedom alone, or that of all my comrades. It was only when writing this chapter of my life in 2009 that I asked Hillary for a copy of her personal memorandum to Minister of Justice Kobie Coetzee and that I found out what she had said about me.

MEMORANDUM BY HILLARY KUNY IN REGARD TO
DENNIS [sic] THEODORE GOLDBERG
23 August 1982

1. I have been requested to set out in this memorandum the basis and the reasons for a plea for clemency which is to be addressed to the HON-OURABLE the MINISTER of JUSTICE in regard to Dennis Theodore Goldberg, who is at present serving a sentence of life imprisonment in the Maximum Security Prison, Pretoria.

2. This memorandum is being presented, not at the request or on the instructions of Mr. Goldberg, but at the request of Mr. Reuben Sive, Member of Parliament for Bezuidenhout, and at my own behest. I submit that I am suitably qualified to advance a plea for clemency on behalf of Mr. Goldberg since I have been visiting him regularly since 1970 and, at present, am his only regular visitor.

3. I am 46 years of age, married to Denis Allister Kuny, an advocate practicing in Johannesburg, and have three children. I am at present engaged on a thesis for my M.A. degree in Clinical Psychology through the University of Witwatersrand.

4. Prior to Mr. Goldberg's incarceration in 1963, I had never known him and, in fact, first met him during 1970 when I was requested by a person who had been imprisoned with Mr. Goldberg and who was released in 1970, to visit him. At that stage Mr. Goldberg only received visits from his elderly father, and had expressed the wish to be visited by other persons, if possible. I was approached because I was considered to be an appropriate person, having regard particularly to the fact that I make contact with people easily and because of my interest in psychology. For a number of years I visited in the company of Mr. Goldberg's elderly father, whom I would convey from Johannesburg to Pretoria for this purpose. From time to time other persons were also permitted to visit Mr. Goldberg, but permission was withdrawn in respect of some of these persons and a number of other persons who have applied for permission to visit have been refused such permission. Mr. Goldberg's father died towards the end of 1979 and his only relative in South Africa is a brother who resides in Cape Town and who has visited Mr. Goldberg on three occasions during the past 19 years.

5. I should at this point say something about Mr. Goldberg himself and his circumstances. He is now 49 years of age. He has been incarcerated since July 1963, when he was detained during the Rivonia Raid. In June 1964, after having been one of the accused in the well-known Rivonia Trial in Pretoria, he was convicted of sabotage and was, together with other accused with whom he was charged, sentenced to life imprisonment. Since that time he has been serving his sentence in one or other of the prisons in Pretoria. He is today the longest serving White political prisoner in South Africa and the only White political prisoner to have been sentenced to life imprisonment.

Mr. Goldberg is a civil engineer by profession, an occupation which he practiced prior to his imprisonment. While in prison he has studied constantly and has obtained a B.A. degree, a degree in Library Sciences and is at present studying for a law degree. You will, of course, be aware of the fact that only in recent years have prisoners been permitted to study for post-graduate degrees.

6. Mr. Goldberg is a man of the highest intellect and has, through his studies and reading during the past 19 years, greatly widened his interests.

7. With this background of a broader education in various fields, Mr. Goldberg is a person who could participate constructively and usefully in the society from which he has, for the past 19 years, been excluded. At the age of 49 he is still young enough to be able to make an adjustment to re-entry into society and to be able to make use of his education, knowledge and skills. I fear, however, that unless he is released from prison in the foreseeable future, his ability to do so will diminish and his very real talents will be lost to society.

8. I appreciate that the offence for which Mr. Goldberg was convicted in 1964 was a very serious one. In making representations for clemency to be exercised on his behalf and, if possible, for his release from prison in the foreseeable future, I do not suggest that such conduct can be condoned or that, should such clemency be exercised, it be seen in that light. Mr. Goldberg has, however, paid the incalculable price of 19 of the most vital and productive years of his life. These years can never be restored to him, but it is submitted that to the extent that the Honourable Minister has the power to do so, he should place a limit on the sentence which Mr. Goldberg is serving and give serious consideration to the question of remission so as to enable him to end the latter years of his life as a useful and productive member of society.

9. During the period that I have visited Mr. Goldberg, his spirits have fluctuated and there have been times when he has maintained some hope that the interminable life sentence which he is undergoing might be converted at some time into a finite sentence. The aspect which he has found the most difficult to come to terms with is the fact that there is no light at the end of the tunnel; that with the previous-stated policy that political prisoners would not be entitled to any remission or parole, it has seemed to him that he is destined to spend the rest of his life in prison. This prospect, as can well be imagined, is tragic and awesome and has led Mr. Goldberg from time to time to a point of despondency

and despair. In the light of the recently-stated change of policy in this regard, he has allowed himself to at least contemplate the possibility that the authorities might be prepared to relax their attitude towards his sentence on personal and humanitarian grounds. In recent years I have noticed a distinct deterioration in his spirits and his resolve to keep going in a situation which has hitherto offered no hope. I believe that unless clemency is exercised on his behalf, Mr. Goldberg may deteriorate and decline to a point beyond redemption.

10. Although this plea is not based upon legal grounds or intended to incorporate legal submissions, I feel it would not be out of place to point to the following:

(a) That Mr. Goldberg was not found by the Court to have been a member of the National High Command of the African National Congress and that he did not participate in the drawing up of Operation Mayibuye or take part in any policy decisions. He was merely a technical adviser. This clearly distinguished him from a number of the other accused who were in more senior positions in the African National Congress and who were sentenced to life imprisonment. In this regard his sentence should be compared with that of Ian David Kitson who was sentenced to a period of 20 years' imprisonment at the end of 1964 in a trial in the Johannesburg Supreme Court, that came to be known as the "Little Rivonia Trial." Kitson was found in that trial to be a member of the National High Command at the time when acts of sabotage were being carried out and that he had participated in such activities after the Rivonia Trial had been held, whereas Mr. Goldberg had not been found to be party to any decision to proceed with armed struggle. Kitson's sentence of 20 years is therefore in stark contrast to the life sentence imposed upon Mr. Goldberg.

(b) In terms of the new Internal Security Act which came into operation on the 2nd July 1982, the maximum penalty in respect of a conviction for sabotage is 20 years' imprisonment, whereas in terms of Section under which Mr. Goldberg was convicted the maximum sentence was the death penalty. The Legislature has therefore, in its wisdom, seen fit to reduce the maximum penalty for acts of sabotage committed after the commencement of the new Act and it would therefore be equitable if recognition and consideration be given to this fact in reviewing the sentence which Mr. Goldberg is at present serving.

11. In conclusion, I would like to say that I have not discussed the contents of this memorandum with Mr. Goldberg nor have I been prompted by him in any way in setting out its contents. I am doing so because I have become a friend of Mr. Goldberg and have acquired respect for him. I am convinced in my own mind that over the years he has mellowed, and that while in prison his outlook has broadened and matured.

During 1980 the kibbutz on which my daughter lived had set up a committee to try to obtain her father's release from prison. They asked Herut Lapid to become involved, as he had set up a committee of the Kibbutz Movement that tried to get Jewish prisoners released from prison in whatever countries they were. Now he tried to speak to Malcolm Rifkind, the British minister of defense. Lapid made use of every imaginable political contact in Britain, using his Jewishness and my Jewish origins, even though I held no religious belief and was not only not a Zionist but an anti-Zionist. This energetic and astute man wanted to get a copy of a letter my daughter, Hilly, had written to Margaret Thatcher to give to President P. W. Botha, who was soon to visit Britain. In the end seven copies of the letter were handed over by British personalities. In the letter Hilly pleaded for her daddy to be allowed to join her on her kibbutz, where she would look after me. Though she was in her late twenties, it was a little daughter's plea that implicitly portrayed me as old and feeble and my life as over. She did not consult me, and if she had I would have opposed such a letter being sent. I have no idea how Mr. Botha reacted to the letter, and as far as I know neither my daughter nor Herut received any reply to it. But the very fact that the prime minister of Britain handed over the letter must have conveyed some implicit message about the treatment of political prisoners to Mr. Botha.

For three years Esmé tried to see Prime Minister Margaret Thatcher, who was the member of Parliament for the East Finchley constituency in London, where she lived. Twice appointments were canceled at the last minute. The third time Mrs. Thatcher really was too busy: she had taken Britain to war against Argentina over the Falkland Islands or, more probably, over potential undersea oil reserves. The question, dear reader, is: Did she go to war simply to justify her not helping gain the freedom of an ANC comrade of Nelson Mandela? Or was it simply that British prime ministers all have the urge to achieve their Churchillian moment of fame as wartime leaders?

Herut had intended to see me in December 1984, but he broke his arm and therefore couldn't fly to South Africa. I subsequently heard from Solly Smith, ANC chief representative in Britain, that he personally passed on the ANC's agreement to the International Defence and Aid Fund, making money available for Herut's efforts to get me out of prison. The Defence and Aid Fund was founded by the Anglican Canon John Collins in the 1950s for the legal defense of anti-apartheid activists. This was a clear indication that the ANC saw Herut's initiative in a positive light.

This was a very difficult time for me. I needed to consult with my Rivonia Trial comrades, but they were far away in Pollsmoor Prison in Cape Town, and I was refused permission to meet with them. I therefore had to gather together and interpret the concealed hints of my organization, the ANC. For example, Bubbles (Colette) Thorne, a dear friend and comrade with whom I organized in the Modern Youth Society, had been to London. On her way home to Cape Town she came to visit me. That she was allowed to visit was surprising because of the difficulties the authorities usually made when somebody asked to visit me. She said that the wish for me to be released was "authentic."[1] Esmé told me afterward that they had spent a long time choosing that word to indicate to me that the highest levels of the ANC approved of the initiatives of my daughter and Herut Lapid. Esmé was herself undecided about it. She put no pressure on me to accept the terms of the release and to give up the armed struggle. Her attitude was that if people wanted to negotiate for my release, she would not try to stop them. But she could not be actively involved in getting only me released and not the others as well. Since the ANC was clearly but quietly backing the negotiation process, then she would go along with it. I am very proud of her for many things and especially for that recognition of the complexity of our situation.

Kathie Satchwell, a lawyer who took political cases, came to London after I was released. She told me that she had been asked by Thabo Mbeki while I was still in prison to tell me in some covert way through one of my younger comrades who was on trial that he was aware of what was happening, and if an offer of release was offered and I accepted it, there would be no criticism from ANC headquarters. Now a High Court judge, Kathie says she passed the message to Roland Hunter, then on trial in Pretoria. We were in separate sections of the prison, and Roland could not pass the message on to me. The story confirms that our leadership was involved behind the scenes in the negotiations for my release.

Letter from Kathie Satchwell, 13 March 2008

Dear Denis,

On one occasion when I was in London in the 1980s—but I cannot give you the exact year or month—all I do know is that it was definitely after the trial of Derek Hanekom and Roland Hunter—I met with Thabo Mbeki at some stage in this visit and he asked if I would be able to safely get a message into Pretoria Central Prison. My answer was in the affirmative because I knew that I had reason to be visiting one or more of the men who were there convicted since there was still room for consultations over possible appeals and I may have been meeting over the litigation for Carl to get married. Thabo asked if I could pass on a message to yourself. My recollection as to the exact wording is now hazy and, of course, has been corrupted by subsequent knowledge. The message was cryptic and I did not ask for details. It was along these lines—"Tell Denis Goldberg that if he receives an offer/if he has to make a decision— there will be no criticism and we will understand."

I must have gone in to the Prison within a couple of weeks. I saw Roland Hunter. The message was passed to him through the glass window—I held up lines of writing—and I am quite sure that Roland would have accurately conveyed whatever it was I had written down.

My subsequent understanding was that there were some negotiations by a man in Israel on your behalf and that these overlapped with or were overtaken by the PW Botha offer and that this led to confusion. I have always assumed it to be so because the message that I was to take was not for the other prisoners to whom the PW Botha offer was also made. But in this I may be wrong because I do not know all the facts.

However, I can quite categorically confirm that I was asked by Thabo—and not by anyone else—to get a message to you and that I was to let you know that the ANC/Movement would understand and not criticise a decision which you would shortly have to take.

I regret that I am so vague over dates and cannot pin down exactly which of my meetings it was with Thabo.
Best wishes
Kathie

Hilly and Bubbles made me aware that release was in the air, and that sharpened my wish to be free. The way the members of the prison staff were treating me gave similar indications that there was some talk of my release. At Christmas in 1984 the chief medical orderly, Major Buys, urged me not to have a prostate operation. He said I was too young for it because I might want to have children when I was outside again. The surgery would remove that possibility. I pressed him to say why he had come up with this information at that particular time. He repeated that I could have the operation outside if I wanted to. He was quite evasive, but it seemed to me that Major Buys was implying that my release was imminent. The thought did cross my mind that an elaborate game of psychological pressure was being played. Major Buys seemed to me to be an unwilling participant in the charade. As I subsequently discovered, the authorities were of course aware that Herut was due to visit me at that time, so my guess was not a wild one.

While guards were searching my cell, they remarked that everything was so tidy that I would find it hard to find a woman to live with me. In answer to my retort that there are no women in the prison, they said that I would soon see. But you also have to fight against being paranoid, against thinking that everything is an elaborate plot against you. There are so many hours in prison for your thoughts to go whirling around and around, like a dog chasing its own tail. You really have to consciously break that vicious cycle of fantasy and despairing belief, otherwise you could destroy yourself.

From the sequence of events, I suspect that what happened was that Chester Crocker, U.S. Assistant Secretary of State for African Affairs, met with Foreign Minister Pik Botha on St. Helena Island in January 1985. According to press reports, Crocker during a three-day meeting demanded that South Africa find negotiated solutions to regional conflicts because that was what the United States and U.S.S.R. were talking about. There was a window of opportunity as the Cold War seemed to be winding down. There was movement over Angola and Namibia. The United States wanted to get Cuba out of Africa, and that required the end of the civil war in Angola. I believe that the U.S. State Department gave South Africa to understand that the price for continued support of the apartheid regime was the release of the political prisoners. The U.S. government was itself under internal pressure from the Congressional Black Caucus to implement the Comprehensive Anti-Apartheid Act. The U.S. government needed something from the South African government to satisfy important congressional factions in the United States itself.

Pik Botha returned to South Africa and within days President P. W. Botha made his announcement that he was prepared to release Nelson Mandela on certain conditions. The main one was that Nelson would have to go to live in the Transkei "homeland" under the protection of his nephew Kaiser Daliwonga Matanzima, an active collaborator with the apartheid regime. The demand for a united South Africa and the total rejection of apartheid made that an impossible condition for Nelson Mandela to accept.

Urged by Helen Suzman in Parliament, P. W. Botha extended the offer of release to other political prisoners sentenced to life imprisonment. It seemed to me they felt they had to get something in return to pacify the white electorate in South Africa. It seemed to be a desperate attitude: "Oh, well, let's see what political capital we can get out of this." Then they slipped in the idea of undertakings by prisoners who would be released.

By then I believed that I was going to be released through the negotiations that predated this offer. That created a conflict in my mind. Did the new situation supersede the old? I suspect that my thinking was shaped by a wish to get out to continue to fight. That was not so good for me because I wanted an unconditional release.

I had not reached the limits of my endurance, though I was very tired of imprisonment. I was finding it heavier to bear and more difficult to bounce back physically and find the will to fight back against the daily encroachments by our prison conditions. Had there been no offer of release, I would not have begged for release. Had they tried to impose utterly humiliating conditions, I would have rejected them. The main condition, put to me in a letter from the government, was that I would not take part in violence for political ends. My acceptance of that condition led to a statement that didn't repudiate my former role in the armed struggle. It was not an apology for having been involved in taking up arms against the state. Nor was I saying that the armed struggle was wrong. I was simply saying that I would not be a soldier anymore—and it took me days and nights to work that out. Part of the process of arriving at my decision was to write the following letter, which was handwritten and submitted fifteen days before my eventual release, on 28 February 1985.

D. T. Goldberg (2/82)
Pretoria Security Prison
13 February 1985

The State President
Mr. P. W. Botha

Dear Sir,

My response to your offer of release is concerned more with where our country is going than with my personal position.

The key element in the growing political crisis in our country is the representation of the black seventy per cent of our people in the central organs of government.

The peaceful solution of political problems requires the creation of the conditions in which normal peaceful politics can be freely and meaningfully practised.

It is clear that any credible moves to resolve key political issues must involve the African National Congress, and its presently imprisoned leadership.

The issue of the involvement of the ANC should not be reduced to a question of "face," of who backs down first. Unless we can by-pass this stance we cannot even begin to resolve the main problem of representation. There must therefore be mutual undertakings, for without them we are no nearer the peaceful resolution of the central issue of our time.

Already I can see a deadlock in the making when there appeared to be a possibility of movement. In the belief that it is necessary to maintain the momentum I suggest that an "undertaking to participate in normal peaceful politics which can be freely and meaningfully practised," should be acceptable to you.

As I see it, your acceptance of this undertaking would signify your acceptance of its terms. The mutual undertaking and acceptance would help to create the required conditions, and would go a long way to achieving a political settlement of our country's political problems.

I call upon you to release the fine people with whom I was tried in the Rivonia Trial and other political prisoners, and to legalise the African National Congress.

With these things achieved there would be a good prospect of attaining a peaceful settlement embodying the guarantees of the Freedom Charter for the rights of individuals, for national groups and for cultural groups in a United Democratic Republic of South Africa.

In what follows I have expanded on the foregoing summary of my approach.

Those of us in prison for political offences involving armed struggle, especially those tried with me in the Rivonia Trial, have a passionate commitment to democracy. That is why we are in prison. We cannot accept a system which provides some form of democracy for the white minority, together with a complete denial of democratic rights to the majority of South Africans.

It was the determination of the White State to close every avenue of development towards a real democracy, by cracking down on peacefully expressed demands and protests that led to the decision to embark on a course of armed struggle. That decision was not lightly taken. It was a choice of last resort made long after there was a widespread demand by black people for protection against the armed might of the state.

Where there is no democracy and no channel for the political demand for democracy it is the duty of democrats to participate in the struggle for democracy.

As a white citizen of South Africa I could see that whites too were becoming less free, despite their enfranchisement.

Freedom is truly indivisible.

The price of freedom for whites is the acknowledgement and implementation of the right of all the people of our country to enjoy the same democratic rights. Failing that, whites will find themselves ever less free as the struggle for a just and democratic South Africa is intensified.

The South Africa we wish to see is one in which our people can live together in peace and friendship; a South Africa in which the creative potential of our marvellously diverse peoples can be liberated for the material and cultural enrichment of us all.

We know that despite their diverse cultural backgrounds, all the people in our country (i.e. the pre-balkanised territory of South Africa) want essentially the same things: to earn a living, to be together in their families, to see their children well fed and educated, to laugh a little. . . . Skin colour, in this fundamental sense, is irrelevant to our hopes and aspirations.

Does it matter that one cultural tradition prescribes stywe pap and tjops for enjoyment, while another specifies putu and the same cut of nyama, or that yet another prescribes yoghurt instead of amasi?[2]

I notice that in your address of 31 January, you did not refer to political rights for blacks, while in your address on the opening of parliament you did so. From memory of newspaper reports you said that possession of property rights did not confer political rights. That could be a very democratic proposition as it correctly excludes a property qualification to the right of franchise.

I suspect, however, that your proposition was profoundly undemocratic in that you were denying to black people the democratic rights which constitute the notion of citizenship.

Mr Heunis (Minister of Constitutional Development) has recently said (again from memory) that your Cabinet constitutional committee has come to the conclusion that the exercise of political rights by what you call "urban blacks" through the euphemistically termed "homelands" is unacceptable to them. "Urban blacks" have no connection with the "homelands." Mr Heunis went on to say that your government accepted this conclusion, but nevertheless insisted that the political links to the "homelands" be retained. (This despite the clear rejection of the whole concept of the "homelands" as pseudo-independent States by black people.)

This is a prescriptive approach. It is not a democratic approach which takes into account the acknowledged standpoint of black people.

This gets to the heart of the matter. In your perpetual quest for cast-iron guarantees for the protection of the position of whites, and especially of Afrikaners, you are defeating your own purposes by denying democratic political rights to blacks.

The ever lengthening delays in the implementation of a truly democratic system in our country (a State which will nevertheless come into being) results in growing frustration and anger. I fear these feelings may lead to the very dangers for whites which you are concerned to avoid.

I fear that if continued any longer the precedents you are setting in the treatment of whole groups of people, of black people in particular, and of individuals, are dangerous. Your precedents will make it more difficult for we who want to build our country for all our people, to prevent some people from invoking your precedents.

It is my firm conviction that the only guarantee you have for the secure future of whites is in a South Africa in which everyone will have full democratic rights backed by the long-held commitment of the African National Congress to uphold those rights.

The ANC has always held that people are of equal worth regardless of the colour of their skins. Precisely for that reason it was, and is, possible for whites to give their wholehearted commitment to the ANC, as I did.

I am convinced that the Freedom Charter, which is written into the constitution of the ANC, provides a solution in principle to the problems of our country. The guarantees it provides for the liberty of individuals, for national groups and cultural groups, are *the* basis for a peaceful South Africa.

The Freedom Charter is insistent that the diversity of cultural and language traditions (which must, and does, include Afrikaans) must be respected and their development encouraged.

We have, as you remarked in your address, vast resources of every kind. You managed, however, to omit the greatest resource: the vast creative energies of our people which can be released only if they are free. Of necessity this requires the freedom to participate in all the central government organs of the State, for then they will have protection against the structural violence of our society and the arbitrary acts of government which drive black people off the land, out of jobs, and into barren lands of gross malnutrition. Their potential is stifled. Poverty-stricken people cannot fulfil the role to which you assign them: that of a market!

It will take generations to realise the full potential of the free people of a truly democratic South Africa. We need to make a start.

By redeploying the human, material, and financial resources at present used to prevent people from developing, we could make a significant start to the building of a new South Africa.

We envisage a South Africa which can meet the material and spiritual needs of our more than 30 million people within the original territory of South Africa.

Let us stop using the armed forces and police, and the civil service, to bolster a way of life which we all know cannot survive. "Adapt or die!" you said. Let us use the resources wasted by these State organs to build anew.

I have told you of our commitment to democracy. You have on occasion asserted your belief in a democratic society. Let us put our beliefs to the test. Let us have a real national convention to draw up a constitution which includes all the people of our country.

The informal toy forum you have proposed is not equal to any serious task. Not the least reason is that the participants in it will be your nominees, not elected delegates of all our people.

Let us call an election of delegates to a constituent assembly, with all adult persons having the right to vote for delegates.

It is clear from recent events, and from commentaries in the Press, both Afrikaans and English, that the credibility of any political moves to solve our problems requires the involvement of the African National Congress, and therefore the release of political prisoners, to participate freely in the political process.

In such circumstances I believe you would not have to fear the continuation of armed struggle. I would willingly participate in a non-violent political process such as I have outlined. (I believe that my comrades in Pollsmoor Prison and on the Island would also participate, but I have been refused permission to consult them on this memorandum.)

I have complete confidence in the political judgment of the people of South Africa, *provided that* their opinions can be freely expressed in a genuinely free and fair election.

Let us do this now before our infrastructure is destroyed; before our economy is damaged; before untold billions are wasted on a futile, Canute-like attempt to stop an irresistible tide. Let us build on what has already been built, not destroy it.

Let us do this now before even more lives are unnecessarily lost.

We surely cannot allow our children to be shot down, nor people to be removed, especially if forcefully removed, nor detainees to die in detention, nor families to be split by the migrant labour system, in the name of policies which you now concede to have been wrong.

Let us make a start.

Let us take a bold leap into the future.

The choice is in your hands. You hold the keys to our prisons. When you have opened the doors and we are free again, the choice will be ours. The fact of the matter is that should anyone, ex-prisoner or not, contravene your laws on violent political action you have the power to impose the sanctions your laws provide.

Our preference has always been for normal peaceful politics. The special circumstances described earlier forced us away from that path. The crux is surely to create the conditions in which normal peaceful politics can be freely and meaningfully practised. We should not allow this to become a question of "face"; of who backs down first. Unless there are mutual undertakings we cannot even begin to address the central political problems to find a peaceful settlement of them.

If we are to maintain the momentum of the process it seems to me that a mutual giving and acceptance of an "undertaking to participate in normal peaceful politics which can be freely and meaningfully practised" should be acceptable to you.

I call upon you, in the interests of our country, in the interest of the great task ahead of us, to release the fine people with whom I was tried in the Rivonia Trial, and other political prisoners, and to legalize the African National Congress.

The great task I refer to is to work towards the political settlement of the problems of our country. We must achieve that political transformation from a system which separates our people and peoples from each other in great strife and growing bitterness, to a system which embodies the guarantees of the Freedom Charter for the rights of all individuals, for all national groups, and for all cultural groups, and in which all our people constitute a United Democratic Republic of South Africa.

Yours faithfully

Signed: D. T. Goldberg

Looking back, I can say that everything I asked for in this letter came about within five years. Well, almost everything. There were then four years of negotiations, murders, and assassinations, mainly by the state, resulting in at least ten thousand to twelve thousand deaths as the hardliners tried to turn the clock back! They failed—but at what an enormous cost in human life and sorrow. The Truth and Reconciliation Commission extracted a large amount of detail about state brutality under apartheid that showed that our allegations had been correct.

The effect of his broken arm was that Herut arrived when P. W. Botha had made his offer of release to Mandela. He told me he had come to fetch me from prison, and he would not leave without me. All his plans had been made before the P. W. Botha offer, and I should not let the new situation interfere with what had been agreed. He was like a bulldozer. Herut said, "Even if I have to cut your throat, I'm taking you out of here, for your daughter's sake on the kibbutz." My wife needed me, and so on. Hillary Kuny was allowed a contact visit with Herut. She made no effort to persuade me to accept the offer of release or to dissuade me. I asked to see Nelson and my other comrades at Pollsmoor Prison in Cape Town, but that was refused. My brother came to see me, and it seemed absurd that now, after all these years, he was concerned about me. Helen Suzman came with Minister of Police Adriaan Vlok to persuade me to accept. Nelson refused the offer of release, but I chose to accept it because I thought the time had come to move things along. It was becoming increasingly clear that we would not be able to defeat apartheid South Africa in military conflict. It was equally clear that apartheid could not defeat the burning desire of our people to be free of apartheid racism. The Cold War was coming to an end because of the weakening of the Soviet economy and of its ability to project its might around the world. The United States also needed a respite from the cost of waging war, either directly or through surrogates like Jonas Savimbi's National Union for the Total Independence of Angola (UNITA). The U.S. Congressional Black Caucus was becoming more vocal and determined to put pressure on its government to act against apartheid.

The United States, France, Germany, and Britain were pressuring South Africa for change. They wanted a regional peace deal in Angola, Mozambique, and southern Africa as a whole. I believed the time to negotiate a peaceful settlement was at hand. Those were the objective factors. In addition, our first MK manifesto in December 1961 had stated that we would be prepared to negotiate a political settlement if the apartheid regime would be prepared to negotiate in good faith.

My subjective opinions appear in my letter to P. W. Botha, which outlined my attitude to political negotiations and conditions. The essential elements of the document I signed were that I personally would not use violence to achieve political ends and that I would not make myself liable to arrest. There were nonviolent methods I could use to take the struggle further. My feelings about getting out were mixed. I'd been there nearly twenty-two years and, of course, I wanted to get out of prison, provided I did not have to repudiate the justice of our struggle.

I felt that I had achieved quite a lot in prison. Whether I liked it or not, I had become a symbol of conscience, of resistance. I dislike the thought of being locked into being a symbol of something, an icon, which makes for rigidity. Living up to the iconography creates the risk of always living in the past. Younger comrades coming into prison told me, "Denis, don't you know that meetings start with people like Samson Ndou, a leader in the Municipal Workers Union and in the United Democratic Front, telling the audience, 'Our struggle is a nonracial struggle. There are people like Bram Fischer and Denis Goldberg, still in prison.'"

Some of my younger comrades said that because I was in prison with four life sentences, I had made it easier for them to break with their privileged white past to take part in the liberation struggle at the risk of their freedom or their lives. "Life" is endless in legal terms; it goes on until you die. That was part of what made it easier for my younger comrades to put their lives on the line, too. Being a symbol is one thing, and I suppose symbols are important, but by nature I am a doer, an activist. I'm not a sitter. I reckoned I'd been a symbol for long enough. I wanted to get out to do things.

I had been arguing this for years with my comrades, long before the offer of release was actually made and long before Herut Lapid came along to convince me that P. W. Botha's offer should be accepted because, he said, my daughter would be heartbroken if I rejected it.

One of the things that made my leaving easier was that my younger, and newer, comrades whom I was leaving behind in the prison accepted the idea that I should go. They said that there was so much to do to carry our struggle forward. Carl Niehaus, who'd been convicted of treason in 1983, smuggled a letter to me from a separate part of the prison. He said he admired me and wished that I had been his father. He thanked me for looking after him and helping him settle into prison and for putting together our Christmas parties. These made that time of year more bearable, when our longing to be with our families was at its strongest.

Why have I written this? Some will say it is a kind of self-justification, and perhaps it is, but my real reason is that I want to tell about a life in difficult times and about difficulties as well as triumphs. It was easier to agree to be part of the armed struggle than it was, at age fifty-two, to say I was now too old to be a soldier.

14

Out of Prison

Life Number 6; Born 28 February 1985 as a Free Person

Once I knew I was being released, I had a problem: I needed to buy clothes. Under guard, I was taken shopping in Pretoria by Hillary, and that was exciting, disturbing, and exhausting. It was lovely sitting in the back of a car looking at the city with her, holding hands. Very new, but as old as the hills! Smelling her perfume was heaven. But after a time in the shop I was so tired. The prison officials were happy for me to stay out longer, but I was quite exhausted from the noise and the kaleidoscope of colors. I asked to go back to the prison, where I had to wait for the paperwork to be done.

My life had consisted of life before prison, and then four terms of life imprisonment; now I was about to be ejected from the unfriendly womb of the prison. By my calculation it had been a long gestation of 7,904 days. I felt some trepidation. It is true that I had been outside the prison walls from time to time, when I had been taken to a hospital or to a medical specialist for treatment, but they were fleeting glances, and now I was exhausted by the short shopping expedition.

On 28 February I was dressed and ready to go. The prison guards insisted I sit with my comrades who were remaining behind, and the conversation became ever more stilted. We had said our good-byes. It was unsettling for them and for me. I had experienced the pleasure of those who had been released and the intense sense of longing to be getting out of there. Lewis Baker, who had been tried in the Bram Fischer trial, in particular had been very tearful when he left us many years before after serving a three-year sentence. That mixture of pleasure and pain is what seems to give life its special flavor, such as sweet and sour, or the bite of strong curry tempered with yogurt. We had been together for years and now suddenly there was no more to say. I asked the guards to take me out of there.

I was going directly from prison to the airport to see my daughter, who lived on a kibbutz in Israel. Even though I had a receipt for myself signed by the authorities saying that I was free again, the commanding officer used his own car to take me to the airport, still guarded by prison officers. We were in a convoy with lead and trail cars packed with police officers. Other plainclothes police had kept a parking place free at the departures terminal. My car pulled in and was surrounded by the plainclothes policemen. There had been a verbal agreement that there would be no press releases until the plane taking me abroad had landed, and they were ensuring that I spoke to no one, and especially the press. I was rushed into a VIP lounge, where I found Hillary with her husband, Denis Kuny, and their son, Neil. The police dealt with my baggage. Hillary and Denis had brought me some money that my dad had saved up for me, and a police officer went off to change it into U.S. dollars. What a sweet normally abnormal moment it was to be with friends for an hour or so while we waited for boarding time, which seemed to be inordinately delayed.

I still did not have my passport. I had insisted that it should be a South African passport. After all is said and done, I was and am a South African, and my actions had been guided by that reality. In 1963 I had obtained a British passport because the Security Police would never have allowed me to get a South African one. It had lapsed and I needed a new passport.

Eventually I was allowed to go aboard, the very last passenger to go up the steps. I was given my new South African passport and found that it was valid for only six months. The security cop who gave it to me said that if I behaved myself they would renew it! In 1985 it was difficult to travel on a South African passport because many countries had restrictions on allowing people to enter their countries with one. Therefore, it would be convenient to have a British passport in the future. I did not get a new South African passport until 1994, when our country became free.

The plane journey was exciting. I'm sure that all 220 tons of that jumbo jet that I'd seen only in the movies but now had me in its entrails took off on my energy alone. I was really spreading my wings. What a feeling of freedom I had. Because Hilly was on a kibbutz, I was flying there to see her and then going on to London.

I was caught in a dilemma. Instead of flying directly to London, I would fly to Israel on an El Al plane, and Hillary Kuny had bought my ticket for me. I wanted to fly on a South African plane, but I feared dirty tricks. On a South African plane with a South African captain, I would still be on South African territory. Who would be on the plane? Would a South African agent rearrest me? Or worse? Would they set up somebody to do me in and proclaim elements in the ANC had dealt with me? It might all sound crazy now, but those were my fears. I was free and I wanted to stay free. It seemed to me the Israelis had more to lose, and I was with Herut Lapid, who represented the kibbutz movement, so I felt I might be safer on an El Al flight. How one tortures oneself when reentering our complex world. I felt I had to tread warily every step of the way. I knew there would be criticism that I was going via Israel, but it seemed to me at the time a useful way of getting where I wanted to go.

The noise in the plane was incredible after the relative calm and silence of our political prisoners' wing in Pretoria, where there were seldom more than ten people at a time and sometimes as few as four. Israelis even when they are among friends speak harshly, and their voices gave me a headache. Maybe it was the shot of cognac that gave me the headache. In prison I once felt tipsy on a little marmalade that I had kept long enough for it to ferment. A real drink was something special.

As the cabin attendants rushed up and down, I asked one of them for some headache tablets, "when you have a moment," I said. In passing she reached into her apron pocket and gave me a little twist of paper with aspirin tablets in it. They were crumpled and powdery. Next time as she flew past getting drinks and settling passengers I asked for some water to take the tablets. "Come!" she said in harsh Israeli English. I meekly followed. Over her shoulder she equally brusquely asked, "Why do you have a headache?" I shrugged and said that it was nothing special, just a headache. "Why? Are you sick?" she demanded. She seemed quite hostile. I suppose she needed to know if I was in need of more serious attention. To allay her fears I answered quite softly that I was not used to crowds and noise. "Why, where have you been?" she asked. By this time we were in a small galley, and she was passing me a glass of water as I replied that I had been in prison. "How long for?" she asked. "Twenty-two years," I replied. She was shocked. Her face froze. She turned her back while grabbing a small, black-handled kitchen knife and started slicing a lemon for drinks, or just for something to do. Her back was rigid, she moved jerkily and I could sense her thinking, "Twenty-two years! Must be something terrible: Rape. Murder. Maybe rape and murder!" Slowly she recovered her composure. She relaxed a bit, turned her head sideways, and asked, "What were you in for?" So I wasn't just imagining her turmoil. "Oh, just conspiracy to overthrow the apartheid government." She threw down the knife and the lemon, spun round and with outstretched arms cried out, "Welcome aboard our aircraft." A steward arrived and insisted I was not to smoke, and she told him to leave me alone.

Her name was Eli, and she was later very attentive when she served the evening meal and drinks. I must say that the meal was something special to behold. Everything served so cleanly and neatly in little dishes on a tray with a napkin. Sure as hell better than anything I'd eaten in twenty-two years! But I had a window seat and I could see the drought-ravaged land of Eastern Africa as we flew northward. I felt ill as I tasted the luxurious foods, finding it difficult to eat while thinking of people starving after the ten-year-long drought as we flew overhead. I am sure most passengers were utterly oblivious to this. To be fair, I have to say that with all the air travel I later undertook, I discovered that airline food is not that great. It was just all so new to me.

When everybody had settled down for the night, stewardess Eli and I talked for hours. How nice to talk—without a prison officer monitoring the conversation—about children and schools and normal human things. How nice to talk to a woman. She invited me to visit her family but she was off somewhere else when I phoned, and her husband said how sorry he was that we could not meet.

I wasn't sure about what would happen between Esmé and me. We had been apart a very long time. We'd been together nine years and then apart for twenty-two years. Could we get together again? Did she want to? Did I want to? It had become ever more difficult to correspond, and we did not write to each other very much in the last few years while I was inside. On arrival at the airport in Tel Aviv, I was rushed off the plane by a steward. Esmé and Hilly were at the foot of the steps. As I reached the bottom of the steps, Esmé smiled at me, and that was that. Older, plumper (she said my little country cottage had turned into a stately mansion), grayer, but the smile was the same. Me, I was older, skinnier, balder, unsure of myself, and far from the robust young man who had gone away and then been taken away all those years ago. Hilly was with her and she embraced me too, but was quite unsure of me, I thought.

Before we could properly embrace, we were bundled into a VW bus and driven off around a corner into the shadows of a large aircraft hanger. My passport had been taken from me, and when I asked what was happening, I was told that they were protecting me from the press, who were awaiting me in the terminal building. My life was still being controlled by others. No consultation with me. They all knew what was best for me! Had Esmé and Hilly not been there, I would have protested very loudly. But they really did mean well, thinking that after all that time in prison I would be incapable of any independent activity. I had been looking forward to telling the world that I was out of prison to continue the struggle against apartheid. That had to wait.

I needed the personal contact and I embraced Esmé in the minibus, wanting to feel her response. She too was quite tentative. Hilly seemed embarrassed by it all.

We were driven through the dark for what seemed like an hour to a house, and as I walked up the steps, a strong light was shined into my eyes, and out of the darkness stepped Arthur Goldreich, whom I'd last seen twenty-two years earlier. He spun me around so that he was in the light. I realized there must have been news cameras, and Arthur always knew about the limelight! He said, "Denis, the last house you were in was my house. And now the first house you will be in is also my house." Knowing a bit about limelight myself, I turned him around so that I was in the light as I replied, "Is it safe this time?"

There was quite a crowd of expatriate South Africans there as Arthur and I chatted away about what had happened in the twenty-two years since we'd last met. At some point I realized that the furry thing that had been pushed near to us must have been a microphone, and everything we were saying was being recorded. Indeed, that was the case, as the next evening I was pulled away from people I was chatting with and more or less compelled to sit in front of a TV set and, hey, there I was talking to Arthur the previous evening. My first experience of television was to watch myself being interviewed. It must have been the tension I was seeking to control that had made me sit extremely still and yet express myself with all the animation produced by my excitement at being out of prison. I spoke then, and on many occasions, of the need to put an end to apartheid, and that it was the people of Israel who could compel their government to break its ties with the apartheid state. I seized the opportunities to raise my battle flag again. I had to show that I and we were not broken by the years of imprisonment.

My new digital watch needed to be adjusted to the current time. I had never seen such a thing, and the instruction book made no sense. Arthur's fifteen-year-old son took the watch from me, touched a few buttons, and hey! Presto! It was set. We had had no clock or watch after the trial for over twenty years, and now there was this new thing without hands to indicate if it was early morning or about teatime or lunchtime, just rapidly changing numbers that needed interpretation.

At the same time I was excited by being with my wife again. How strange it was to lie in bed next to her again. I know that one has fantasies of how one will celebrate, but in my case I have to say the spirit was willing but the flesh was weak. I believe that many men experience erectile problems after long years of imprisonment. Long-term prisoners frequently have prostate problems. The whole thing became a very hit-or-miss affair, and it was disconcerting for Esmé, who thought that I had no interest in her. Even though we knew each other so intimately, it took a long time to overcome those embarrassments and misunderstandings. Still, it was nice to have company and to be able to cuddle and, more especially, to have her hold onto me when the nightmares of the prison experience would have me thrashing about in my bed.

After a few days we went off by road to Hilly's kibbutz, Ma'Ayan Baruch, where her fellow kibbutz members really pulled out all the stops to welcome me. After the emotionally barren years inside, it was overwhelming. I was enfolded in an emotional outpouring of love best expressed by "Hilly's dad's with us and we helped to get him here." It was also special to see the affection and high regard they had for my daughter. A welcoming dinner was held, and I had to speak to them and tell them that it was good to be out of prison so that I could continue the struggle against apartheid. They were a bit wary of that. I was carefully critical of Israel's support for apartheid.

I was interviewed on Israeli television and said that while I was in Israel I would do all I could to persuade Israelis to demand that their government stop their support for apartheid. Through their arms deals they were killing our people. Some members later were upset by the media attention paid to me and my criticism of Israel's support for apartheid. It was not an easy time, but to be meeting the world's media and at last being able to strike back at the apartheid regime was great. In no time at all I felt politically comfortable. I had the Freedom Charter as my policy guideline and found it not difficult to answer questions about our policies with great confidence. It amazed me later to find that I used the same language and phrases as leaders such as Oliver Reginald Tambo, of the ANC, and Alfred Nzo, the ANC'S secretary general, without having had contact with them for more than two decades.

Some days later, as we were about to sleep, Esmé said rather diffidently that if I wished to we might try to live together again. I must have shown that was what I wanted, but before I could say anything she added: "There are conditions! One, I have my way of living, and you can fit in if you want to. Two, I have a circle of friends, and you can join in with them or not, as you wish, but I will not change my life again. Three, you can be involved in politics and I will not stop you, but do not expect me to follow you around like a fifth wheel on a car!" I agreed, of course. I think I would have said yes to anything at that point. It was astonishing, though I should not have been surprised that she was so assertive. Before I disappeared from her daily life, Esmé consulted me about everything we did. She was hopeless at managing finances. Her idea of a bank account was that when the bank bounced a check, then she knew we had no more money. It happened often, until the bank refused to give her an account in Cape Town. Now, here she was being so firm and in control. Of course she had to have become so, but it was both reassuring and disconcerting. Immediately, my firm belief in the full equality of women in relationships was put to the test. I submitted easily, but I was aware of the change in her.

Members of the right-wing U.S. Rabbi Meir Kahane's Zionist movement camped outside the kibbutz gates, demanding my expulsion. Journalists from around the world descended on the kibbutz, and I was doing up to seven long interviews each day. That disturbed some of the kibbutzniks, who felt I should be quiet about Israel's support for apartheid. They expressed their displeasure to Hilly.

My presence and the interviews I was giving gave a boost to the whole idea of "Israelis against Apartheid." How could Israel, the state of Israel, be involved with apartheid South Africa?

In all the time I have been out of prison, and it is now about thirty years, only one journalist has deliberately misrepresented my political attitudes, and that was Tom Segev, an Israeli who was reputed to be the intellectual agenda setter in the Israeli media.

Segev, who wrote for a weekly magazine, *Koteret Rashit,* asked to interview me. He came, he said, because he wanted to know about the ethics of the armed struggle. And I gave him a long interview. After all, it is a very interesting topic for an intellectual discussion.

At the outset I explained, using the words *off the record,* that I would not speak about the Palestine Liberation Organization (PLO) during this interview because I was addressing an Israeli audience about South Africa and apartheid, and no one would give me a hearing if I spoke about the PLO. Those were the conditions of the interview. Now, *off the record* is off the record. He wrote an article of such blatant dishonesty in which he so blended quotations with his own opinions that his views appeared to be mine. His introduction read, "The ANC is the PLO of South Africa. Oliver Tambo is the Yasser Arafat of South Africa. Israel is the Apartheid nation of the Middle East." I had said none of these things.

Because the subject of the interview was the ethics of armed struggle, I had said as a condition of the interview that the examples I would give would be from South Africa and Southern Africa. For example, General Peter Walls of Rhodesia, now Zimbabwe, flew in a civilian passenger plane so that he had civilians covering his military movements. At the last moment the general switched planes. When the plane he had been in was shot down, who was ethically responsible? The general who used unknowing civilians to shield him, or the people who shot the plane down? You can discuss until the cows come home, but the general is not innocent. Segev simply omitted my examples, which were relevant to my discussion, and used examples from the Middle East—Palestine, Lebanon, Israel, and so on—to poison the audience against what I was saying. But more than that, he translated every word related to liberation war, armed struggle, just war, anticolonial war, all such terms, as one Hebrew word, *terrorism.*

How can you discuss ethics if you don't distinguish categories? Worse still, by merging all these different ideas into one, he was saying there is no such thing as ethics. In the political sense he was saying, "The bullets and the bombs and the napalm, and the brutality that comes from the government of the day, are clean, and everything else is terrorism," whether you are talking about Israel, or apartheid South Africa, or any other conflict. His article caused a media uproar. Many journalists who had been in support of Denis Goldberg of the ANC and of the struggle against apartheid now turned around to attack me in the media. I hoped that the controversy would die down, but it mounted day after day.

Peter Allen-Frost, the doyen of Middle East journalists, phoned me after some days. He said that serious journalists were embarrassed by Segev's article because it was such a blatant misrepresentation of everything I would have said. He said that the editor of the magazine, Nahum Barnea, was embarrassed and indicated that if I asked for the right to reply, I would get it. I followed his advice. The editor offered me space for a letter to the editor. I insisted on an article with the same prominence as the original. I wanted a cover story, too. He agreed to an article but not to a cover story. We agreed that I would write the article and that he, the editor, would personally translate it to ensure that it was accurate. He did publish it, and friends told me that it was accurately transcribed.

In the meantime, I had a phone call from a progressive member of the Knesset, Yossi Sarid, who said that he knew that Segev had done a hatchet job. In answer to my question about how he knew this, he said that Segev's article contradicted everything I had said in articles and radio and TV interviews. He implied that Segev was quite notorious for his style of misrepresenting the views of people he interviewed. I still wonder who sent Segev to interview me, or whether he simply knew what his role had to be. I must say that in all the time from my release to the achievement of liberation and beyond, I know of no other journalist, no matter how hostile, who has so misrepresented me. Others have reported my analyses and opinions and then set out to refute them. Their readers have been able to understand me and make an assessment of my views.

A journalist from the London *Evening Standard* arrived directly from Pretoria to interview me. He presented his credentials as no other journalist had done. He laid down his passport, British press card, and other documents. He said he had just had an interview with Pik Botha, the South African foreign minister, who asked him to deliver a message that though I might be obeying the letter of my undertaking, I was not following the spirit of the undertaking: in numerous media interviews I fully justified the armed struggle while demanding the end of apartheid violence against our people throughout Southern Africa. The undertaking was that I would not take part in political violence, but I would not repudiate my role in the armed struggle and the justice of seeking to overthrow a tyrannical regime. That a scheming politician like Pik Botha could see that I had used the situation in my way to fight in another way pleased me greatly. I said that my loyalty was not to the apartheid government but to the people of South Africa, and Mr. Botha was hardly the person to give me lessons in ethics. Having agreed not to advance north of a certain latitude in Angola, apartheid soldiers attacked the Cabinda enclave, far north of that line, on some specious grounds in the hope of strengthening one of the Popular Movement for the Liberation of Angola's foes, Holden Roberto, who was based there. But the political absurdity was also clear to see. Cabinda was an oil producer supplying Gulf Oil, one of the big American corporations that had more pull with the U.S. government than South Africa had! I later saw the article in the *Evening Standard,* and it expressed my views clearly and without distortion.

During all this media frenzy, I was also getting to know my family again. My daughter, Hilly, was proud of me, but she also thought she had to control me to protect me. Really, I had had enough of being controlled! She meant well but, for example, she opened all the letters that streamed in to me. That was like being in prison. She said there was hate mail; not everybody loved me. Hilly said that I was her hero and she loved me, but she also hated me because if I wanted to get involved in politics, then I should not have got married and had children. Children, she said, don't get consulted; things just happen to them, and that is not good enough! She would really have liked everything to be as it was twenty-two years earlier: Mommy, Daddy, and two children aged eight and six, together as we were when I disappeared in 1963 into the underground struggle. But she was thirty years old and no longer a child. She would insist that she knew everything about South African politics, and when I disagreed, she would be very offended. An eight-year-old gets a pat on the bottom and a "yes, darling," and that would be that, but a thirty-year-old is not a child anymore. We did later become a fairly good family again, though I simply could not fit into the pattern she longed for. It took me too long to understand that she had missed the years of breaking away from her dad and, now that I was present, she was able to go through that necessary separation. There were lots of tears.

After about a week I realized that I had to speak to David, who was in London. It was difficult for me to phone by direct dialing because I could not remember such long telephone numbers, and with my new bifocal glasses, I could not look at my notebook and the telephone dial very easily. Hilly put the call through for me. I apologized to David for not coming immediately to London, but I needed to gather my strength. He understood, and then I spoke to Beverley. She told me they had been on a skiing holiday when news of my release reached them, and they had been home for only a few days. Out of the blue I asked if they could come to be with me on the kibbutz. She agreed to come, and when I asked about David, she insisted I ask him myself. He said they already had tickets and needed merely to make their flight reservations. David, I found, would never put pressure on me or anyone. He would wait to be asked and then happily agree to do whatever it was if it was something he wanted to do. He did not often show his deepest feelings, I discovered.

David, a few days after joining us on the kibbutz, asked me, "Why did you do what you did that took you away from us for so long?" I answered the underlying thought when I said that I knew that what I was doing could hurt his mother and sister and him too, but millions of children in our country were forced by the race laws, and especially migrant labor laws, to grow up without their fathers. I said I did not know how to make my children more important than all the other children. I told him I had not run away from him and his sister and his mother, and that I had always loved them. I explained that I had gone off to do something that was important, and what makes us human is that when we see inhumanity, we act to put it right. I looked over at him and saw in my grown-up twenty-eight-year-old son the sad little six-year-old crying his eyes out. We embraced and wept together, until Esmé walked in, and then as men stupidly think we must do, we sat up, wiped away our tears and our snivels, and pretended everything was okay. Indeed it was. Despite his usual unemotional manner, he had needed that question about love and desertion to be answered. That evening he took me aside to ask me my plans. I said I had to take part in putting an end to apartheid. My comrades were still locked up. He said that I had to be involved; otherwise I would be throwing away the twenty-two years I had been locked away behind bars. He then proceeded to give me financial advice and ended by saying that he and his partner, Beverley, would love to see me when I was at home in London, but they would understand if I had to travel a lot.

Later on I heard that when Esmé had telephoned David at his ski resort to tell him I was coming out of prison, he had returned to Beverley and their friends and put his head down and wept. They thought that something must have happened to Esmé, and were astonished that David, who seldom showed his feelings, could feel so deeply. Indeed, while on the kibbutz with me, when he needed to go off, he would without embarrassment simply get up to give me a kiss and then leave. To experience such additional sweetness is more than one can ask for.

One of the lessons I have drawn from my experiences is that freedom struggles have their price, and it is children who seem to pay it. Is it not sad that we have to carry through that struggle against unfeeling rulers so their children will enjoy the fruits of our work?

One of the great pleasures of being free was to see and enjoy the young children on the kibbutz. Most spoke no English, but one or two did. Lee in particular was a very bright three-year-old who, while doing a clever monkeylike maneuver on a jungle gym, greeted me with a brilliant smile, asking, "Do you like it here, Denny?" But I also enjoyed making props for a school play as we would have in prison: a sword cut out of cardboard with the blade wrapped in silver paper and the handle wrapped with the brightly colored wrappers of chocolates made a wonderful jeweled hilt. It was sad that some of the mothers thought then that I was a very gentle person for one who had taken up arms, but later, when Nelson Mandela greeted Yasser Arafat of the PLO, I suddenly became a brutal terrorist in their eyes. Hysteria does not solve political problems.

This blindness to reality shocked me in Israel. Many progressive people who were opposed to apartheid would assert that there was no racism in Israel and that all were treated equally. Naturally, they all knew I am not a Zionist because I spoke about Jewish Israelis and Palestinian Israelis to counter their bland usage of the word *Israeli* to mean only Jewish citizens. There are innumerable laws that make Palestinians aliens in their own land. I was asked to speak about apartheid in South Africa, and it was striking that some in my audience would be very upset because they said I was describing Israeli life and law and segregation and racist ideology implanted in the minds of young people through daily experience, as well as through their school texts, through religious instruction, through the youth movements and so on in their country, when I was really describing our South African experience. I suspect that it was such talk that led Mr. Segev to write the article he did. Like apartheid South Africa, Zionist Israel did not like dissent, even after General Moshe Dayan said that there was not a Jewish settlement that had not been built on a Palestinian settlement that had been wiped off the face of the earth. General Ariel Sharon, equally brutal, later admitted that building settlements beyond the internationally agreed-on borders was in reality military occupation.

As a matter of practical politics, I accept the idea of the two-state solution decided by the U.N. Security Council way back in 1948. That the secular PLO took so long to accept that basis does not alter the international legitimacy of this approach.

This visit to Israel confirmed my opposition to an exclusivist racial, cultural, and religious basis for a state because that could not take forward the development of a society where people would enjoy the real possibility of fulfilling the idea that human beings must have equal rights because all are equally human. Over the years I have read quite extensively about the policies of the Israeli state, which were quite consistent regardless of whether right-wingers or social democrats formed the government. I read serious analyses by Uri Davis, a British-Israeli researcher who studied in detail the legislation and administrative rules that applied specifically to Palestinians and Arabs, and all non-Jewish Israelis, creating a legalized system of racial control and discrimination. Of course, there were many reports in the news media of events that I was aware of. Later I read Benny Morris's *The Birth of the Palestinian Refugee Problem,* which is also a history of the foundation of the state of Israel. Morris, a Zionist, sought to justify the use of Zionism to support the brutality of the conquest. He said that if the purpose was conquest and the expulsion of all non-Jews, then any methods were justified! He therefore documented from their own records the brutality and violence the various forces, such as Irgun and the Palmach, had used to expel Palestinians from their homes and their lands, including such means as rape and murder and the destruction of whole settlements.

My support for the Palestinian people was not an individual position. We in the Congress Alliance backed the solidarity of other peoples struggling for freedom from modern colonial oppression. In the course of my work in the ANC office in London, I wrote and made many speeches. It was an absurdity of our situation that we never seemed to get ahead of our scheduled activities. Speeches were often requested a few hours before they had to be delivered. There was little time for reflection or the development of elegant rhetoric and fine imagery. In a way this led to my personal style of writing simply without idiomatic expressions, as though I were speaking English as a second language, and using my voice intonation and volume to impart emotional effect to keep the ears of my audience open.

The issue of freedom from national oppression of the Palestinian people was ever close to the ideals of the liberation alliance led by the ANC. For me personally, just as being a privileged white South African required me to oppose apartheid as the source of those privileges, being of secular Jewish extraction, I could not be a Zionist because in the name of creating a Jewish homeland it was clear that Israel was an occupying power that stole the land from its inhabitants. I imagine that was why I was asked to make speeches in support of the Palestinian people. The brutality, the rapes, the murders that were perpetrated to drive Palestinians and Arabs off their own lands could not and should not be tolerated. We do not live in the Middle Ages, when such barbarism was the norm. Just as I would not be part of apartheid oppression, I had to avoid being part of the Zionist oppression.

The African National Congress Commemorates *the First Anniversary of the Declaration of the State of Palestine, 15 November 1989*

It is with a sense of great honour, and great pleasure, that we greet the people of Palestine and their leading organisation, the Palestine Liberation Organisation, on this most important occasion.

We look forward to the day when the realisation of the aims and aspirations of the Palestinian people will be achieved through the establishment of the Palestine National State.

We look forward to the day when the world community and the great powers in particular, will come to fulfil their duty in terms of the rights of nations to self-determination; and fulfil their duty in terms of international law, by recognising the Palestinian State under the Security Council Partition Resolution which established the State of Israel.

We in the ANC have no difficulty in understanding the struggles of the Palestinian people for national liberation. We share the same goal: national liberation. We share the same strategy and tactics, the mass mobilization of our people, and the demand for the isolation of the racist regimes by the world community. We share the same kind of growing legitimacy as the world comes to understand the rightness of our cause and the illegitimacy of the racist regimes. The policy and practice of apartheid has rightly been declared a Crime Against Humanity by the United Nations General Assembly. Equally, the General Assembly has declared the Israeli oppression of the Palestinian people to be of the same racist nature as apartheid.

We are also drawn to the Palestinian people by the awareness of the alliance between the Zionist State of Israel and the Apartheid South

African State. The facts of that alliance in the fields of economic cooperation, military supply and technology, nuclear weapons and guided
missiles, military training, diplomacy and counter-liberation intelligence, have been well documented by Abdul Minty [now the South
African governor in the International Atomic Energy Agency], Jane
Hunter [publisher in California of *Israeli Foreign Affairs: An Independent Research Report on Israel's Diplomatic, Military, and Intelligence
Activities Around the World*, from 1986 to 1993] and others.

In South Africa today we see the consequences of years of dedicated struggle by the mass of our people, and of the growing effects of
the international campaigns for sanctions and isolation of the apartheid
regime. We see the De Klerk Regime forced to try to buy time while
trying to maintain itself in being. We have recently seen seven of our
great leaders released from 26 years of imprisonment. We have seen our
people defy the illegitimate apartheid regime's laws to fly the flag of the
ANC and to declare for all our country and the world to know, THE
ANC LIVES! THE ANC LEADS!

Today we bring greetings to the PLO and the Palestinian people, in
the knowledge that
THE PLO LIVES! THE PLO LEADS!
FORWARD TO THE PALESTINIAN STATE

FORWARD TO A UNITED, DEMOCRATIC, NON-RACIAL SOUTH AFRICA!

This was our address to mark the death of the PLO's leader Yasser Arafat:

The late Yasser Arafat's first outstanding contribution was the creation and spreading of the idea of there being a Palestinian Nation.

Among the great features of his life was his versatility as politician,
as agitator, as general, as statesman and his courage in the face of the
enemy's desire to eliminate him. He lived with his people, he escaped
assassination on at least 3 occasions, but he never left his people in the
lurch.

Before the emergence of this understanding of the situation of the
people of Palestine there was the notion of an Arab nation occupying
all the lands from Morocco on the Atlantic Ocean to all the lands of
the Middle East as far as Iraq.

But the situation of the Palestinians was different in that they were subject to the Mandate of the League of Nations after the First World War and the UN after the Second World War. The founding of the State of Israel by UN Security Council resolution 242 in 1947 also called for the existence of a parallel Palestinian state that could not be born for over 30 years because of the opposition of the Pan Arab Movement.

The emergence of the Palestinian Nation began with the founding of Fatah by Yasser Arafat. His historic task was to perform a balancing act between the needs of a powerfully organised Palestinian Liberation Movement and at the same time to maintain the support of the Arab States, governed mainly by feudal Chiefs, Sheiks and Kings, who found the Palestinian Liberation Organisation working amongst the displaced Palestinians living within their state boundaries. This led to the PLO being seen as a threat to their rule at times. The consequence was that the PLO found itself limited in its activities inside those countries. The PLO was sometimes expelled from their countries. For example in "Black September"[1] when the Jordanian monarchy expelled them to Lebanon, and later they were expelled from Lebanon to Tunisia.

At the same time Yasser Arafat brilliantly achieved recognition of the PLO among the people of the powerful western states, to the point where the PLO, of which Arafat's Fatah was the largest and leading organisation, was recognised by the UN as the legitimate representative of the Palestinian People.

There have been long and close ties between the PLO and the ANC as brother-sister liberation movements fighting the same enemies for the freedom of their own peoples and oppressed people everywhere. One of the key elements in this was the role of Israel as a Western imperialist spearhead in support of the oppressive policies of the imperialists. Think of the ties between Israel and apartheid South Africa in the fields of diplomacy, trade and investment, arms supply and military training, and, of course, nuclear weapons technology and rocket delivery systems.

There were also ties between the nationally oppressed people of both countries. This was evident during the First Intifada, from 1987 to 1991, when the strategy and tactics of the PLO, especially the idea of unity in action of all social classes, were adopted from the ANC-led Liberation Movement.

A free Palestinian State has much to do with the oil politics of the Western powers in general and the United States in particular and that country's support for the state of Israel in its policing of the region. Coupled with that was the blind acceptance of Israel's argument that it wanted peace but the Arabs did not. This also implied that there was no separate Palestinian nation, merely an amorphous Arab nation whose elements were emotionally bound to support their Palestinian "family," but not to the point where that would lead to the formation of modern secular democratic states throughout the region. The West and Israel have been able to play on this, while the Zionist enterprise of creating a Jewish national state covering the whole of historical, biblical Palestine, with no Arabs in it, was being pushed ahead.

The expansion of the lands of Israel has been almost continuous, and every successive government of whichever party in that country has taken part in the process. The process has also included the seizure of over 90 percent of the waters of Palestine, both surface water and that from the underground aquifers, to the point that soon all agriculture, the centuries-old source of Palestinians' life itself, will be destroyed.

The clear implication is that this should not be allowed to continue. We have seen that the brutal suppression of the Palestinian people has intensified to an unparalleled intensity.

These are notes on Palestine I made in November 2002. Thirteen years later they are even more valid:

> We in SA know about racial oppression.
>
> We fought it and defeated it because it was unjust.
>
> We fought it to be free to rebuild our country.
>
> The world condemned apartheid, and international anti-apartheid campaigning was an important part of our struggle.
>
> The violence of the apartheid regime, brutal though it was, is overshadowed by the utter brutality of Israel's occupation of Palestine (all of Palestine from which Palestinians and Arabs have been driven out).
>
> The greatest violence is seen in the occupied West Bank and Gaza.
>
> In South Africa we did not see tanks with guns blazing protecting armored bulldozers, though we saw settlements bulldozed to make way for white towns.
>
> Nor did we see armored helicopter gunships "taking out" homes, children, whole families with great precision!

We did not see the destruction by bombing of the whole centers of towns.

We see the similar brutalisation of whole generations of Palestinian Arabs that we saw in South Africa:

The suffering of people prevented from going to a doctor

Of ambulances being stopped

Of pregnant women forced to give birth at checkpoints.

We see the same brutalization of generations of young Israeli soldiers, men and women, called upon to destroy a people and a society.

Whatever the protestations by the Israeli state, its policy has always been to drive all Palestinian and Arab people out of that state.

The boundaries of the state have steadily expanded until but 22 percent of the land is nominally left to the Palestinians.

We know that there are about one million Palestinian Arab citizens of Israel.

They are denied many rights of citizens.

They may not acquire land or property.

Where will their children live when they are adults and raise their own families?

South Africa did the same under the Group Areas Act.

This is land theft on a grand scale. It is accompanied by falsehoods:

"Palestinians abandoned their land and effectively gave it to Israel."

That simply ignores the massacres and deliberate destruction of villages.

Notoriously, General Dayan said that there is not an Israeli village or settlement that is not built on an Arab village.

We add that their names have been deliberately obliterated from maps as they and their people were obliterated.

This theft of land continues.

Palestinians are remarkably generous: they say they will accept the 22 percent of their own land in the West Bank and Gaza as the basis of their independent state based on U.N. resolutions, which are the sole legal justification of the state of Israel.

Yet Israelis settle on the hilltops and then defend the newly stolen land with their enormous military firepower.

Any Palestinians who want their land back, and should have the support of the Israeli courts and the ICJ, are of course "terrorists."

The utter humiliation the Palestinian people, through the domination of their land by illegal settlers who steal and occupy the high ground, is real and inflammatory.

The theft of land has even more serious economic consequences.

In such a water-stressed area, land without water is useless.

Israelis have stolen over 90 percent of the Jordan waters for their economy, destroying the Palestinian Arab economy in the process.

Over 70,000 olive trees, many of them hundreds of years old, have been destroyed by the Israelis.

They say they do this for security reasons: to build apartheid-like razor-wire fences and military roads, but in reality to destroy the Arab economy.

Trees use water.

As an adviser in the Ministry for Water Affairs and Forestry in the new South Africa, we are aware of these equations.

At the same time, Israel, with the help of the Jewish National Fund, supported by Zionists all over the world, has created new plantations and forests, and new lakes, for leisure activities and water sports.

It is easy to forget these facilities have been created on stolen land;

Have been created with stolen water;

Have been created at the expense of the lives of countless Palestinian Arab people.

Israelis claim that they are the elect of God and find a biblical justification for their racism, something like the Afrikaners of apartheid South Africa.

The British did not need such belief. They claimed a pseudo-scientific Darwinian "survival of the fittest" justification for their colonization. Economic power was the means and the rationale for power.

We demand action.

You helped us through anti-apartheid movements to isolate South Africa.

Support the call for economic sanctions on all goods produced in Israel.

We call for an embargo on sporting and cultural contacts.

It is in my view not possible to achieve peace in a theocratic or priest-driven society. Just as I reject the quasi-religious basis of an exclusive Zionist Jewish state, so I reject the quasi-religious basis of Islamic states. One of the reasons for the ultimate lack of success of the secular PLO is that the feudal oil states of the Middle East prefer to have Zionist Israel as their opponent rather than accept a secular Palestinian state. Palestinians are the administrators and a skilled as well as laboring workforce of the Middle East. As foreigners, albeit coreligionists, in the lands they find themselves in, they have virtually no political rights. With the backing of a putative secular Palestinian state, the feudal rulers would find themselves under threat of revolution led by civil society with the support of a probably secular state, demanding a social democratic political system.

Journalists from many countries believed, despite my denials, that I was settling in Israel. From the very beginning of my new life outside prison, I repeatedly stated that it was my wish to join my family in London and work full-time to bring apartheid to an end because that way we could ensure that my imprisoned comrades would also be freed. Yet reports continued to appear saying that I intended to live in Israel.

15

New Activist

London—Lusaka—Dar es Salaam

Eighteen days after my arrival in Israel, Esmé and I left for London. The cabin attendant on our flight was very attentive to both of us, and when the opportunity arose, she asked me if I had said the things that Segev had reported. She was sure, she said, that I had not said them.

About a year later Esmé said that I should have discussed with her what I was going to do instead of just announcing that I had to be a full-time activist in the ANC office in London. We had had some talk about my getting a fellowship from the International Universities Exchange Fund so that I could spend a year writing, but I needed to be fully involved. She and others said that I could be an active member without being a full-time activist, and things were politically and organizationally very messy. I said that I had to be fully engaged, and if things were messy, then I had to try to help make them better. She did concede that she had known I had to be fully engaged in the work of the ANC, and if not I would have been miserable and not worth living with anyway.

Uneventfully we arrived in London in the midst of sleet and rain. When I got to the immigration desk at Heathrow Airport in London with my South African passport valid for six months, the immigration officer asked me how long I would be staying. I must have been quite disoriented because I vaguely said I would be there for perhaps a few years. He looked at me as if I was simpleminded or plain stupid. What was his problem? Esmé came through without delay on her British passport and explained the position. "Oh!" Now I understood what the problem was: my passport was valid for such a short time. I asked the official to contact the Foreign Office, which had promised to help if there were problems. He gave me a few weeks to sort out my papers.

There were comrades to meet me at the airport, and though I had dozens of interviews while in Israel, all fully in line with our policies, one had been delegated to tell me that I was not to speak to the media. I suppose every movement has such authoritarian, arrogant people who make for disunity rather than unity. More offensive was that among the authoritarians were some who had simply fled South Africa without getting permission from their superior in the organization, some who had never previously been in the struggle, and some who knew little about it. From the questions shouted by the journalists waiting for me, it was clear that in London I would face some who were critical of me for being released and others who supported my decision. I already knew that the leaders in Lusaka, Zambia, had not acknowledged their role in the negotiations that led to my release, and if they felt it necessary to keep silent, I would too, even though doing so caused me considerable heartache. I was accurately quoted as saying that maybe I was not as brave and courageous as my Robben Island comrades were, for one has to throw something to the wolves.

Minnie Sepel, accompanied by Hettie September, a longtime comrade who had been married to Reginald September, drove Esmé and me to the ANC office because I had been asked to go directly there to meet Solly Smith, the ANC's chief representative in Britain. I was appalled by the harshness of the gossip that was poured into my ears during the hour-long journey. Hettie's former husband, Reg September, a trade unionist and leader in the Coloured Peoples Congress, had been chief representative, and I quickly found out that the picture painted by Joseph Conrad in his novel *Under Western Eyes,* about the Russian revolutionary underground in Switzerland after 1905, was true and not at all as exaggerated as I had thought. What they told me confirmed what South African exiles and some journalists had already told me: that in exile we were indeed cut across and through and through by personal rivalries and likes and dislikes. It made me more determined to work to overcome these divisions.

Esmé did not want to deal with our comrades, and she went home with Minnie and Hettie. I met Solly Smith and others who were in the office with him: Abdulhay "Charlie" Jassat, Ishmael Coovadia, and Toine Eggenhuizen, a Dutch ex-priest who had been thrown out of South Africa by the authorities. I think that M. D. Naidoo, a full-time member in that office, was there though I am not sure. There may have been others present, but I am not sure because the impressions crowded in so thick and fast that some details are too blurred for me to be sure of them. After some exchange of greetings and quite a lot of reserve on both sides, Solly Smith remarked that he knew all about the negotiations that had led to my release and that he had been indirectly involved in the process.

I told them I wanted to get down to Lusaka to meet the ANC leadership, and they urged me to take my time because there was no hurry. I insisted that I wanted to go as soon as it could be arranged. I needed to know what my future role would be. The next day I got a message that I should be in the office to take a phone call from Thabo Mbeki, who said I should spend time recovering and getting used to being out of prison. Again I insisted that there was work to do and I had been resting for too long. It was agreed that I was to fly to Lusaka on the first available plane six days after arriving in Britain.

Looking around the ANC office, I was amazed that we had such facilities as a telex machine, which enabled us to communicate with Lusaka instantaneously. This was before fax machines, and long before e-mail, of course. I was equally amazed that we could operate so openly while being underground, because after all we were waging an armed struggle inside South Africa and in Southern Africa. Of course, I realized that the British government allowed us to have our office there, and we could be as open as we needed to be. You cannot win public support unless you are open toward it.

I remembered how it was in South Africa in the 1950s and early 1960s. We were very guarded on the phone, and anyway there was no direct dialing, even between cities in the same country. You phoned the operator and waited for hours for your long-distance call to come through. Now the details of my visit were fixed up within a few days.

Joe Slovo was in London when I got there. He took me to a little office, and we chatted for some hours. He told me what I had already realized, that there were people who were upset about my release. He thought that I should spend a couple of years in London finding my feet, speaking about the struggle and our goals. He would welcome me into the military structures again if I wanted that, but perhaps I should work on the political-military structures in London, meeting South Africans from inside the country. I was worried about that because I was quite out of touch with details on the ground. I also said I had a need to talk and I did not want to know too much of a secret nature. I needed to reestablish myself and find my new identity.

After about three-quarters of an hour, I said, "You know, Joe, you've changed." He asked what I meant and I said, "I think you're a nicer person."

"What do you mean, a nicer person? That sounds like a backhanded compliment."

"No, you're able to understand the pain and the difficulty of human decisions."

"Oh," he said, "as a movement we've had to learn that. We had to learn that people are not made of steel, or blocks of wood. We asked too much of our activists and when they cracked, we rejected them. We had to understand what human limits are, and it's been a very painful lesson for the whole movement."

To hear that from someone who seldom had any thoughts about individual personal difficulty back home in South Africa was astonishing. In effect he was saying that exile was very hard for people, and there had to be tolerance for human frailty. I found it interesting that he could say that we should not simply reject people because they are not as pure as we think they ought to be.

Those sentiments matched what I found in prison. I think I acquired a humanity that I had not had before. I no longer questioned people's motives as I once would have. What they contribute to the movement is what matters. And more than that, I learned not to drive people away from our movement because they wouldn't go all the way with us and our fraction of the movement. I tried to build unity; I tried not to create divisions.

A few days later I started going to the ANC office. I read many pamphlets and reports that had been printed in larger numbers than needed and were strewn all over the building. It helped me catch up with history and current positions.

Solly Smith insisted I accompany him to a reception at the Commonwealth Secretariat. When I saw how smartly everyone else was dressed at the reception for some country's freedom day celebration, I felt very uncomfortable wearing the maroon jacket and blue jeans that Hillary had bought me. The trouser legs were rolled up two or three turns to shorten them. Solly added to my discomfort when he said that every ANC representative should have a "diplomatic suit" for such occasions. That he told me this only when I was at the reception did not help, though I did not really mind being taken for the refugee that I was.

During the next days I went shopping for clothes suitable for the tropical climate in Lusaka. I quite enjoyed finding my way around Kentish Town and Camden Town in London, looking for shirts and trousers made of washable cotton. The more formal clothing had to wait.

Minnie and Ralph Sepel gave a wonderful party a few days after I arrived in London so that I could meet many of our exiled comrades. It was lovely to meet people, and getting to know them and the changes in their lives was a great joy. Esmé saw through my politeness when I would ask people about their lives as a means of shielding myself from the repeated questions about how I felt, when I had yet to find my feet in London. It was disturbing to be hero-worshipped by pretty young women who offered themselves to me quite blatantly. Sexual mores had really changed during the youth revolt of the miniskirt and rock-and-roll era. The widespread challenge to authority was something very new to me.

I had to get a British passport to sort out my residence in Britain. It was essential that I not use my South African passport when going to Lusaka. My South African passport would lead Zambia to refuse me entry, even if I came as an ANC member. I went off to the passport office in Petite France near Bond Street, following Esmé's detailed instructions about where to change tube trains because such a large city was very complicated for me.

When I got to the right place I showed my documents to an official who insisted that the certified copy of my birth certificate would not be accepted. I explained that I could not return to Cape Town and I was merely asking for the renewal of the passport that had been issued to me in 1963 but had of course lapsed in the twenty-two years I had been locked up. He was being quite bureaucratic, as I suppose passport officials are supposed to be, until I explained that the British Foreign Office had said it would assist me if I had any problems entering Britain. He thought a moment and then scooped up my papers while remarking that I had to be the South African who had just been released from prison. He disappeared for a few minutes, and upon his return his rubber stamp thumped down on the appropriate forms in a blur of movement and sounds. He carefully explained what I had to do when I said I had to fly at the weekend and still had to get vaccinated for tropical diseases. Having paid the required fee, I found myself in a queue that I guessed would take at least three hours before I would reach the next official. My new friend came out from behind his counter, took my documents, and said I would get a call on a particular telephone on one of the counters ahead of me. Indeed, in just a few minutes I was called to the phone and told to return at three o'clock in the afternoon to get my passport. Such friendliness and such solidarity after the treatment in prison were very welcome changes. Such behavior also spoke of the kind of sympathy many people had for opponents of apartheid.

Thomas Cook's travel clinic provided the injections and vaccinations I needed, and I was off to see O. R. Tambo's wife, Adelaide, who gave me letters and a cake to take to him in Lusaka, which I added to the letters from our office. All the papers were tucked away in a little zipped-up leather document case.

When I got back to Esmé's house, now our house, I felt enormously elated to have navigated my way through this complex city on my own. It was still cold in the early springtime, and my cheeks were flushed when I got home. It seems absurd, but I felt as I had felt as a boy allowed to go into Cape Town all alone some forty years earlier. Everything was new again, and I needed to think ahead every step of the way, literally and figuratively, if I was to manage on my own. Esmé insisted I do everything for myself; otherwise, I would be a social cripple relying on others to care for me. She was absolutely right: when you fall off your bicycle as a kid, you have to get back on immediately to conquer the unknown.

London really is big. I found out because the journey from our home to Gatwick Airport in the south of London took about two hours. I really wanted to be with Esmé, but sorting out my position in the ANC was also very important to me and I was to be away for only ten days. I wandered around the duty-free shops and bought chocolates. Upon boarding the plane, I suddenly realized my document case with the correspondence for O. R. Tambo had disappeared. How unreliable can a courier get? And on my first mission too! I was in a sweat when a flamboyant young woman introduced herself as Janet Love of the ANC and, hearing of my problem, took complete charge of me. She recovered my document case from the duty-free shop, where I had left it, and I settled into what turned out to be one of many flights. Janet must have been a young girl when we were arrested, and here she was a capable young woman who was quite at ease taking command of me and, I am sure, others as well. Later I found out that she was a courageous underground *Umkhonto we Sizwe* activist inside South Africa.

Upon arrival at Lusaka airport, I showed my new British passport and was allowed through customs, but as my ANC comrades had not arranged for me to be allowed in as an ANC member under a special arrangement we had with the government of Zambia, I had to wait hours until everything was arranged. Suddenly the place was filled with soldiers in military greatcoats who had just come off a plane from Angola. In the confusion I was grabbed in a bear hug that stopped me from seeing who it was whose booming voice said, "Denny, so nice to see you." I replied, "Martin [Hani], is it you?" Somebody else leaned down to whisper in my ear that he was now known as Chris. I had not seen him since he had jumped bail together with Archie Sibeko in 1961, after they had appealed a sentence of imprisonment for furthering the aims of the banned ANC. Well over twenty years later his distinctive voice was easy to recognize, and it was wonderful to be greeted so warmly by a younger comrade. I did not yet know that he was one of our top military commanders.

After some hours everything was sorted out and I was taken to stay with Reg September and his wife at the time, Gwen Miller, a British comrade he had married. They made me feel at home in their pleasant flat. She had a small car and drove me to the ANC compound just off Cairo Road, the main street in the city. As I entered, a young man leaning against a wall under the veranda straightened up and greeted me with a military salute: "Comrade Commandant." I did not recognize him, but he had to have been at the Mamre camp. A few steps farther, and another young man greeted me in the same way. This one insisted that I recognize him, and it turned out he was Wilson Nqose, the son of a noted activist in the Blouvlei settlement in Cape Town. Meeting them brought back wonderful memories.

I was taken to see President O. R. Tambo in an office so dark after the glaring sunlight of Lusaka that I could hardly see. He embraced me and welcomed me, and I handed over the cake and letters from his wife and the letters from the ANC office. He said there were members of the National Executive Committee waiting to meet me, and he led me to a room full of sunlight where I met them. Among them were Alfred Nzo, secretary general; T. T. Nkobi, treasurer general; Joe Modise, head of MK; Reg September; and others whom I can only guess at.

There were three comfortable easy chairs in the room. Two were taken by Nzo and Nkobi. I waited for Tambo to sit in the third chair. To my embarrassment, he insisted that I take the third chair. It sounds absurd that at the commencement of an important interview there was byplay about seating. He said I was the guest of honor and should take the chair. He sat on a small stool at my knee, and yet he clearly dominated the proceedings. He introduced me and asked me to tell them about my release. I did so, saying that the only confusion I had was whether the earlier negotiations, which I understood were known about by senior comrades, had clashed with P. W. Botha's offer of release. By the time of that offer I was sure that I wanted to be released to continue to be part of the struggle against the apartheid regime. They interrogated me very sharply but without hostility, but if I had said something that they were not sure about, they tried to get to the bottom of it. They wanted to know exactly when I had decided something and what had given me a particular impression. Did I really know some particular thing? They asked really sharp questions, getting beneath the surface. It seemed to me then that not all had previously been aware that there had been negotiations sanctioned at the very highest level for my release. The meeting ended after an hour or more when Tambo said that he thought their consensus was that I was welcome back as an activist and that I should work full-time in the ANC.

Joe Modise, head of MK, asked me to rejoin the army, and I said that we would soon be negotiating with the regime, and since I had said I would not take up arms, I thought that I should not. But if the committee thought I should, then of course I would, because my loyalty was to our movement and not to the apartheid regime. They said I should be based in London so that I could again be part of my family. It was decided that I would speak in behalf of the ANC wherever I could because international solidarity with our movement was one of the keys to our liberation. I was asked if I knew ANC's policies, and of course I did because I had been reading newspapers since 1980, and I had read masses of ANC information in our London office in the week that I had been there before leaving for Lusaka. I found that by using the Freedom Charter as my policy guide immediately after my release, I had used the same words and phrases in responding to journalists as our movement did, despite having been away for so long. It was reassuring that we were so principled.

In our compound there were always people sitting or standing, waiting for instructions or for bulk food supplies, or just hanging out. When

O. R. Tambo emerged from his office, instantly all were on their feet and rigidly at attention, like soldiers. It seemed to me that the military-like response made him uncomfortable, for he would stroll over to one or another and greet him or her by name and gossip about parents or uncles and aunts and their hometowns or villages. He had a remarkable aptitude for putting people at ease. It was the strength of his personality and the gentleness with which he expressed his stern commitment to freedom that enabled him to hold the ANC together for thirty years of exile.

Comrades said that he disliked laziness and indifference among those who worked with him, and he could flay people with his tongue when he felt it necessary. Characteristically, he quietly promoted his views as he built a consensus, which made him such a great leader. Bram Fischer had a similar capacity to seldom force a confrontation by not strongly disagreeing with another when it was not essential to take a stand on an issue. After meeting Tambo that day in Lusaka, I felt reassured and comfortable about being back and quite sure that there was a job to do: to get my comrades out of prison and to break down the walls dividing our people in our society, where all were imprisoned by institutionalized racism.

I was not very busy at first, and I walked the few miles from Reg and Gwen's flat to our offices, but after a time our deputy secretary general, Simon Nkokeli, forbade me to walk on my own. He said there were enemy agents who looked for opportunities to kill our people. I was always to ask comrades to drive me wherever I had to go, no matter how awkward that might be. I missed wandering about in the city. It was my first time in an independent African country. Zambia had achieved its independence from Britain in 1964. The streets were very busy, and there was lots of friendly jostling. I felt no fear and saw that liberation, even with poverty, could bring a relaxation of tension. The shops were empty, and even a plastic shopping bag had to be bought from young boys selling them outside the shops. On one occasion toilet soap became available in the department store. Customers were allowed one bar of soap apiece and had an indelible mark put on the backs of their hands to show they had received one.

Gwen took me swimming in the municipal swimming pool, and I found that I was very unfit, but the feel of the water was marvelous. Albie Sachs arrived in Lusaka and took me to meet international aid workers who stood me rounds of drinks in their hotel garden. It was good meeting him after all that time and finding out that he had been in London for many years. He told me that Esmé, with her warm personality, had brought many people to our side in Britain, especially in the Woodcraft Folk youth organization. He was busy at the time working with Tambo on a code of conduct for our members in exile. With a contingent of thousands, there were bound to be those who transgressed commonsense rules, and the conduct expected had to be codified, especially with regard to violence and torture, used by some comrades to enforce discipline.

The days stretched out and I wanted to be home with my family. Esmé was waiting for me, and I had said it would be a ten-day trip. There seemed to be some difficulty. There were few planes on the route, and schoolchildren were flying back to Britain for the opening of a new school term and everything was booked up. For the first time in twenty-two years I phoned Esmé on 9 April to mark our wedding anniversary. I was excited to be speaking to her, but she was quite cold and upset because I was not home. Later she said she had been to a therapist, who asked her why she was angry since she had managed alone for so many years and could continue to do so. But she felt cheated after waiting so long for me to come home.

I could not get away from Lusaka. The leadership was trying to work out how to integrate me into the ANC's work, and ten days later a press conference was organized to present me to the world's media. That event was chaired by Thabo Mbeki, Tambo's right-hand man. Typed copies of my letter to P. W. Botha were prepared by our media liaison section, and it was well received. In retrospect, I think I was too cautious in stating my position. I was somewhat apologetic about being released. I should have had the courage of my convictions and stated loudly and clearly that the time had come to negotiate a settlement. The apartheid regime could not defeat our people, and we could not defeat the military and police forces of the state. The situation was deadlocked, and prolonging the struggle would cost unnecessary lives. Yet one does not act alone. The views and attitudes of others had to be taken into account, and there was not yet a willingness to accept the idea that a negotiated settlement was the logical end to that phase of our struggle. My letter stated it, and it was issued to the world's media by the ANC, and that was sufficient for the time being. In fact, the MK manifesto, issued when we started our armed struggle, invited the apartheid regime to negotiate a settlement.

The ANC leadership really worked hard to enable me to find my feet in "my" organization. I found the whole experience of meeting so many comrades in exile very pleasant and interesting. Many people, however, had no conception of what twenty-two years in prison really meant. I sometimes illustrated it for them by telling them that my children were eight and six years old when I entered prison, and now they were thirty and twenty-eight years old. Or I would say that in my last years in prison we had guards who had not yet been born when I was taken to prison. In other words, a whole generation had grown up, gone through school and training college, and was now working; this gave people some idea of what that length of time means.

I was also astonished by the insensitivity of some people. They knew my story, they knew I had spent twenty-two years in prison, and yet they would sigh about "all those years" that Nelson Mandela was inside. In some perverse way I think they felt cheated that I was strong and not bowed by the years inside. I think they might have felt more comfortable if I had emerged frail and broken. That would have enabled them to feel sympathy. I would remark somewhat drily that many of us had many years inside: "We do know about it, you know." Some would be covered in confusion.

I went into the various ANC offices scattered around Lusaka to find out what we were doing so that I would know what I could tell the world about the ANC and the liberation struggle. There were things I learned just by being there that everyone else took for granted. For example, while sitting with Tom Sebina, our media liaison officer, I heard him speaking French, and others spoke other languages to journalists from around the world. Tom explained to me that we had comrades who had studied in many countries, and we could use their languages and had a much wider understanding of the world as a result.

The Zion Christian Church is a black South African–initiated church. It has an estimated four million members. At the time I was in Lusaka, the one-million-strong annual meeting of the Zion Christian Church of Africa at Moria, in the Northern Transvaal (now named Limpopo) Province, was due to take place during the Easter weekend. The Zion Church was the largest African church independent of the main Christian churches. President P. W. Botha had been invited to attend. Secretary General Nzo asked Tom Sebina and me to write a press release about it. That gave me great pleasure! I simply sat down and the words flowed out of my fingertips. In discussion we refined it. It was a harsh condemnation of Bishop Barnabas Lekganyane, head of the Church of Zion, for issuing the invitation to P. W. Botha. Nzo commented that we had to try to detach Bishop Lekganyane from his connection with the apartheid regime. We had not been able to have direct contact with him, so our open letter to him had to appeal to him to see that change was coming, and he and his congregation should contribute to the pace of change. We could not simply condemn him for inviting Botha lest we drive him further into the arms of the apartheid regime. Somehow we had to be harsh about apartheid but careful not to alienate him further. Here I saw the meaning in practice of the ANC's slogan, "Unity in Action," meaning "draw people to us, do not drive them away."

After Nelson Mandela was released, both he and President F. W. de Klerk were invited to Moria. When Nelson Mandela arrived, he was overwhelmed by the welcome he received. Mr. de Klerk, on the other hand, was ignored by most of the congregants.

When I arrived in Lusaka, the question of opening the ANC to full membership for all South Africans was being hotly debated. Thinking I was still in the early 1960s, I felt the structure of the Congress Alliance should continue. But it was more complicated than that. Inside South Africa, in the conditions of underground illegality, membership in the ANC was still for Africans only. Others sort of floated around as ad hoc helpers when asked to assist. Some could travel to neighboring countries as couriers and activists who took all the risks of membership without actually being members. In exile, under pressures from exiles of all colors and from our host anti-apartheid supporters, the ANC no longer restricted membership to Africans, though there was an understanding that only Africans would be on the National Executive Committee of the ANC. In London, however, there were some who followed what in the 1950s and 1960s was called an Africanist line, and they were unhappy about this. They felt that they had lost influence and that the "purity" of the struggle was being contaminated.

There were two small groups who broke away in the thirty years of exile, a group of four and a group of eight, and this had happened before I arrived in London in 1985. Exclusivist sentiment ran deep. I discussed this with Mark Shope, a trade union activist and ANC member, and his daughter Lyndall in Lusaka, and they were all for opening the membership. They insisted that it was a lack of self-confidence among older comrades that made them fear that even a small number of non-African members, especially those who were white, would automatically dominate the ANC. I thought that was a strong argument, but it was perhaps better to maintain unity when people like me and others would continue our support whether or not the organization opened its membership to all.

With Reg September, with whom I had worked closely for so long, the discussion cut much deeper than it had with Mark, who was from Johannesburg and whom I had met once over a weekend when he stayed in our house in Cape Town with Dan Tloome, who had published the left-wing journal *Liberation,* when they were attending a trade union conference. When I said to Reg that Africanist sentiment still existed, and we should not risk dividing the movement by insisting on white membership, he retorted very strongly that white comrades always thought everything revolved around themselves. But what about the place of Coloured and Indian South Africans, who were discriminated against as nonwhites under apartheid; they too were being kept out of the ANC. How did we prepare our countrymen and countrywomen for the nonracial society envisaged in our Freedom Charter if we did not act nonracially in the leading organization of the struggle? That was the issue, and as the ANC at home was on the crest of a wave of popularity and support, that was the time to open the membership.

He was right in that it was true that white comrades took the facile position that we should continue as we had "always" done and not risk facing the future. Reg also pointed out that in elections held among the exiled membership in Lusaka for members of the ANC's Regional Committee, two white comrades, Jack and Ray Simons, had received the highest number of votes from an overwhelmingly African membership. That showed their readiness for open membership, he said. A few months later the membership was opened to all inside and outside South Africa. And with that it became possible for any member, not only Africans, to be elected to the National Executive Committee.

My departure from Lusaka was delayed even further when Nzo said, "Denis, if you're going to be traveling the world to talk about the ANC, you must go to the Solomon Mahlangu Freedom College (Somafco) because it's an important part of what the ANC in exile has achieved." So I flew to Dar es Salaam with many ANC representatives who were going to a fund-raising conference at our college at Mazimbu in Tanzania. Among the passengers was a Norwegian aid worker, Kjetil Nielsen, who was posted to the ANC settlement in Tanzania. He told me how he had met his wife, Eli, a nurse who had also been posted there. I remarked that the ANC fulfilled many roles, including that of marriage broker! From time to time we still meet.

Upon arrival in Dar, I found that our ANC comrades had not arranged my clearance to enter the country. There was nothing to do but wait at the airport until the paperwork was done. I was not alone, for Eddie Funde, our chief representative in Australia and New Zealand, experienced the same problem. We had arrived in the late afternoon, when all offices were closed and all officials, Tanzanian and ANC, were thinking of things other than comrades sitting in an airport. I was becoming accustomed to things not running so smoothly and settled into one of those red plastic chairs with a seat that is bum-shaped and found in many airports around the world. I think some sadist designed them to numb your bottom, and the longer you sit, the harder they get! We dozed intermittently through the night. At midnight exactly Eddie nudged me and said, "Happy Birthday, Comrade," and I realized it was indeed 11 April 1985 and I had traveled more since I was released on 28 February than I had in my whole previous life, and I had seen a bit of South Africa, Israel, Britain, Zambia, and now Tanzania. What an exciting time in which to be reborn. But what a nice comrade and friend I found in Eddie Funde, who was previously unknown to me. The next day we were at the Palm Beach Hotel, having been cleared to enter the country. We had been given a few shillings as pocket money, which Eddie demanded we put on the table. He ordered drinks for a whole group of us and my comrades toasted me in warm sudsy beer. I am moved all over again when I think of their kindness.

We traveled from Dar es Salaam to the ANC settlement at Mazimbu. As a onetime civil engineer, I was appalled by the state of the seventy-five-mile-long road. It was full of potholes and in some places half washed away by tropical rainstorms. Our bus traveled with its hazard blinkers going all the time to make it more visible. That was a necessary safety practice because people drove very fast and often on the wrong side of the road to avoid the washaways and potholes. How the contractors had got away with building a road with such inadequate drainage was a mystery to me. Was it underfunded, or was there collusion between officials and contractor to do a shoddy job? I had no time to investigate.

That was my first working conference. But Nzo had also said to me that when I got back from Somafco, I should give him my impressions of the place. My immediate thought was, "What can the problems be?"

While I was there I gathered material for a seventy-page report on Mazimbu, the official name of the area allocated to our settlement. I eventually presented the results of my first real assignment since prison to Nzo. I wish my recommendations to deal with the problems at Mazimbu, the Solomon Mahlungu Freedom College, had been followed. The situation there, where the reality and the fear of infiltration resulted in an authoritarian suppression of discussion, could have been eased somewhat. Any dissent and all discontent were seen as enemy agitation, when some of it was due to genuine alienation of young people living a narrow life in our settlement in Tanzania.

The Tanzanian government provided a military guard around our settlement to protect it from apartheid agents and prohibited our exiles from wandering freely in the region.

Paid labor was not permitted, and the ANC was in effect mother and father and provider to all in the settlement of all necessities, from food to clothing and hygiene products, education and health care; it was a moneyless society. Many of the young people who had fled apartheid longed for a more glamorous lifestyle. I am convinced that strong political and social leadership and open discussion of problems would have helped. Things were kept secret when there was no necessity to do so. This is not to say that many of the young people were not disturbed and in need of counseling and advice.

Unmarried young women who became pregnant were treated as naughty and subjected to punishment, whereas the young men who had impregnated them were allowed to continue their normal lives there. The settlement had been built on a sisal farming estate, and the ANC had achieved wonders with the help of the Scandinavian countries and the socialist bloc, led by the Soviet Union. Solid homes architecturally suited to a tropical climate had been built, and a farm and dairy farm established. Our young people were reluctant to do physical work, thinking it was beneath them. The Dutch Anti-Apartheid Movement raised the funds for a well-equipped small hospital. German Lutheran activists raised money to buy cows to provide milk for the children. The slogan was *Ein Kuh für Mazimbu* (a cow for Mazimbu).

There were both primary and secondary schools, and many young people went on to study in other countries.

The problems of the community were social rather than political. Malaria was a problem, and it was necessary to keep grass cut short because water gathered where leaves sprouted from the stalks, and mosquitoes laid their eggs in such tiny drops of water. The coarse grass required slashers, sharpened metal staves, rather than mowers, and with regular maintenance the problem could be controlled. Demoralized young people simply ignored the request to look after their own health and that of the whole community. Malaria is really debilitating, and it perseveres for years unless well treated. At the time a new strain of cerebral malaria had reached our settlements, and it was often fatal, as there was no known cure for it. The problem was compounded by there being no medication that would prevent its occurrence. The readily available older medications used against earlier strains of malaria were not certain in their effects.

Dr. Amo Moroka was marvelous. I arrived there with my feet very sore from sweating so much and shoes that did not fit my feet, swollen in the tropical heat. Oh, for some well-made prison shoes! She treated me, and with the help of Rica Hodgson, a longtime activist member of the Communist Party working at Somafco, had the resident shoemakers make sandals that were custom-made for me. In no time the skin on my feet healed. Amo was very interesting on health issues and the role of pregnancy in lonely girls and young women who found that having a baby gave them something of their own. The young men, she said, simply enjoyed the sexual escapade, but the girls were removed from school and the boys continued as if nothing had happened. The pregnant girls were kept together in a house named after Charlotte Maxeke, who was a great social worker and one of the first to take up the issue of the oppression of women in male-dominated African society. This refuge was disparagingly called "The Charlottes," and that dishonored the great Charlotte Maxeke. But even sadder was the demoralization of the mothers-to-be, who simply sat around with no motivation to do anything for themselves. We who talk easily of a nonsexist society imposed sexist domination over these young women. I raised this with the leadership, who could not see any way of dealing with such matters other than an authoritarian "thou shalt not," which was a useless response to a much deeper problem.

Despite these criticisms of our comrades, I have to acknowledge the sacrifices that many made to establish and run the Solomon Mahlangu Freedom College and what was a small township of about five thousand people. Doctors, nurses, architects, and engineers worked for years for no salary, only for their keep, to see that our refugee children and young activists would be cared for, educated, and trained, so that, it was hoped, they would become leaders in the new South Africa.

A beautiful nursery had been built for the babies so that the mothers could do whatever jobs they were assigned to. The walls and ceilings were clinically white and clean, and the bedclothes equally so. The children in the tropical heat were swaddled tightly in white crocheted blankets. There were no mobiles, no colors, no music, and no conversation, no stimulation at all. It was not that it was nap time; that was how it was all day long. I discovered what I named the "tula-tula" (hush-hush) syndrome. The nursery nurses insisted that was how they had been trained. But is that the way to develop inquiring, interested, alert minds?

Talking now to my friend Deidré, who is both a mother and a doctor, we speculate that the way of caring in the nursery came from the custom of babies being swaddled on their mothers' backs while they were working, traditionally, in the fields. Now the mothers were being liberated from the physical burden of the child, but the child, lying in its crib, was deprived of companionship, of voices, of movement, and of human contact. The nursery nurses needed to be actively involved with the babies and infants to compensate for the disjunction from their mothers.

In our equally beautifully built and equipped kindergarten for the three-year-olds and upward, things were much better: colors and singing and brightness and children who were well fed and well clothed. In the play area there were no swings or merry-go-rounds, slides or climbing structures. I said I would ask the management committee to have some made in our workshops. The nursery staff said that was not acceptable because everything had to be supplied by foreign donors so that they could be sure it would be safe. The negativity among so many people was distressing. Somehow we were sapping the initiative of our people and therefore of our children, who would be part of the first generation of free South Africans.

With no disrespect I have to say that the ANC's First Team was taking on the apartheid enemy at home, and our First Reserve Team was taking on the less glamorous but necessary game of looking after our people and winning international support for our movement. After all, our exiled liberation movement was able with international aid and aiders to achieve what some governments could not do: create and manage a settlement the size of a small town without having state power at its back. Nevertheless, when asked to stay and work there, I felt I needed to be more directly involved in building solidarity by speaking around the world to people and governments and fund-raising for the work of our First Team.

While I was at Mazimbu I took part in a workshop with Eddie Funde and most of our chief representatives based in many countries. The ANC had diplomatic representatives in more countries than the apartheid government did. We discussed fund-raising for another settlement to accommodate even more refugees, including our MK soldiers who had to be withdrawn from Swaziland and Mozambique because of the onslaught by the apartheid military on our people and the governments of the region in a policy of massive destabilization.

The workshop was interesting because it enabled me to meet dozens of comrades working in many countries. But there were also ideological arguments about the nature of the settlement we were developing. The official view was that we were building a Soviet-style state farm. That approach may have been adopted to satisfy Tanzania's President Julius Nyerere, whose concept of Ujamaa villages was based on a similar approach. Since his government had made the land available to us in an extraordinarily generous act of solidarity, we appeared to follow his ideas. Some of us argued for allowing individuals to have small plots of land that they would develop and retain a share of the produce and thus have an incentive to achieve higher levels of production. This approach would also have laid the basis for intensive farming when we returned home to South Africa. I and others argued that our exile community should become more self-sufficient. Indeed, we needed our people to be occupied rather than being idle and disengaged. Like the caregivers in the nursery, our exiles became dependant on international solidarity that provided for all our physical needs in the settlements. There was a determined counterattack by leaders such as Treasurer-General T. T. Nkobi on such "deviant" ideas held by "capitalist roaders." It was said that our policy was to create a state farm. I think that there was also a fear of change, and the leadership would feel threatened if groups with some semblance of economic power were to emerge in the exile community.

I discussed my report with members of the leadership at Somafco, and they said they would study it carefully, but I think the stresses were already too great to make any significant change, which would have required giving more power to the youth so that they would have more responsibility and be motivated to show initiative and leadership.

When I returned to Lusaka, I gave my report to the Secretary General Nzo. He asked me to discuss it with Jack Simons and Billy Modise, who were on the ANC's Education Committee. Jack was more interested in my observations than Billy, the principal of the U.N. School of Administration for Namibia, who was involved in training future civil servants for Namibia and appeared to have little interest in rectifying problems I had identified at Mazimbu. I was not able to follow up on the results of my report, but later I was asked to research the education needs of our exiles. Organizational changes led to a change of plans, and I did not carry out this task.

Jack Simons was already showing signs of age and told me that the trouble was that your mind stays alert but your body won't allow you to do all the things that you know you have still to do.

Jack and Ray Simons and Ray's sister Dora, who had known me since I was a mere twinkle in my pregnant mother's eye, gave a dinner in their home for me to meet people they knew. In response to a question, I went through what I thought was a pretty solid piece of analysis of "colonialism of a special type," one based on the interrelation of class oppression and national oppression, which were inseparable in the South African context. Essentially, the argument was based on a paper by Harold Wolpe and the historian Martin Legassick that gave a theoretical basis for Michael Harmel's 1960s description of colonialism of a special type, in which oppressors and oppressed share the same territory, whereas in classical colonialism the imperial power has its own remote land.

I talked about the way in which capitalism is subsidized by those not actually employed and who live in the reserves, or Bantustans, as they came to be known. This is the most difficult part of the argument to substantiate in practice. Professor Jack had listened intently and pounced on this point of the argument—he had not lost his sharpness, and this was typical of him. He said I had to be able to show how the transfer of funds takes place. Of course, the answer to Jack's problem is that it is a theoretical argument because there is no actual transfer of funds, and it is legitimate for an analysis to have different levels of abstraction. Here it is postulated that a transfer of economic wealth from the population of the reserves to the capitalist class was occurring when what was happening was that the capitalist class was able to reduce the cost of reproduction of the working class by the legal and administrative controls that apartheid used to reduce the living standards and cost of living of the oppressed population, who provide the bulk of the workers in mining, manufacturing, and farming. In this sense capital was and is subsidized by the additional exploitation of the nationally oppressed population through the reduction of the wages needed to sustain them and their families.

Indeed, the Chamber of Mines put forward a "cost of reproduction of the workers" argument in their submission to the Commission of Inquiry into Mine Wages, which had been instituted after the miners' strike in

1946. Interestingly, a worker in 1919 involved in the bucket workers' strike in Johannesburg had said something similar when he told a Commission of Inquiry that the "pass laws make wages small." The point is that a menial worker through his lived experience had captured the essence of the relationship of national and class oppression so many years before the theoreticians found an explanation. The discussion and the questions that followed showed that I had some effect on the views of those who were there at that dinner party in Lusaka.

The fact is that the ending of apartheid allowed government to intervene by establishing national minimum wages for various industries. Enforcing the laws is more difficult, especially in farming and in the rural areas in general.

Before I left for London, Secretary General Alfred Nzo was very insistent that I take a holiday, a solidarity holiday, and I said, "But I've rested all this time." In reality it was not a rest in prison. It was a devastating physical and emotional experience. In Tanzania, about six weeks after coming out of prison, I woke up one morning free of pain for the first time in years. No stiff back, no stiff and sore joints, and I felt really alert. I wondered if I should have had blood tests to determine if we were being doped in prison. But I suspect that it was being removed from the daily stress of imprisonment and being actively engaged in dealing with real issues at Somafco that led to my health being so radically improved. Dr. Mueller of the ICRC had told the authorities that psychosomatic illnesses are real and have to be treated. I can add that freedom is a wonderful treatment for all sorts of aches and pains.

I refused to go on holiday. I said, "I need to be in the world and of the world and working in the world and making the transition to reality." I knew the transition back into the world would be very tiring. I said that after six or nine months, or maybe a year, I would then like to get such a holiday to rest and reflect and then consolidate and move on. We had quite an argument about it. I felt I was coping well and there was no way Comrade Nzo could make me go on holiday at that time.

My ticket to London was eventually booked, and, instead of being away for the intended ten days, I had been away for six weeks.

16

The World Is My Oyster

Life Number 7, 1985–1994

Solidarity

When I returned to London after six weeks, Esmé was not very pleased with me for being away so long. We were both faced with shaping our new life together. We had to get to know each other again, and I had to find my feet in my new home.

After the lonely time in prison, Esmé's house was quite a shock. She had many young people boarding with her. It was how she paid her rent and satisfied her need to be a mother and to have company. For me it was overwhelming. I was accustomed to being with just a few people who generally spoke softly in one-on-one conversations. Now there was a continuous babble as well as the television going at the same time. It was difficult to hear what was being said in a roomful of chattering people. It sounded like a waterfall in my ears and I had to concentrate hard on the person speaking to me to understand anything. I preferred to watch TV on a second set in our bedroom. It had a remote control, so I did not even have to get out of bed to change the channel.

Esmé was the physiotherapist at a ballet school, and six of the young students had been living in her house for some months. They were preparing for their annual concert and used every countertop or edge of the kitchen sink as a barre as they flexed and bent their supple limbs. They would walk ahead of me and suddenly stop to place their hands flat on the floor with their knees locked and their bums in the air, which was disconcerting in an age of miniskirts. Our friend Sadie Forman asked if I thought they were pretty. I said I wasn't sure because I had not yet got around to looking at their faces. Sadie was not amused. Feminism had progressed, and I learned that such remarks were in bad taste. One evening there was much giggling outside our bedroom door and Esmé invited the girls in. I was half dozing when they came in *en pointe* around our bed. They were showing Ez their tutus, which they had altered to make them fit exactly right. I opened my eyes and, seeing their loveliness, asked, "Am I in heaven?" They sweetly pretended to swoon.

There was also a constant stream of young people who had been volunteers on Hilly's kibbutz who, on their way home to the United States, Canada, Australia, or South Africa, spent a few weeks or months in London. The young white South Africans found acceptance in Israel but would be met with hostility in most European countries. They told me they tried to conceal their South African origin to avoid embarrassment. I was not sure about them, wondering if they were innocent passers through or if they were South African agents. I do not know the answer, but some of them certainly learned a great deal of the truth about apartheid South Africa that they had not allowed themselves to see or hear. Ez was a remarkably patient teacher who, because of her informality, was more like a surrogate granny than a mother to them. She seemed to be able to attend to the needs of each of them while doing her daily work as a physiotherapist.

I had to relearn ordinary daily routines. Getting dressed in the morning and keeping time were difficult for me. Now I had to choose what clothes to wear: blue socks or brown, sweater or warm shirt, and so on. Television advertisements were a real distraction but fascinating, too, because a complex story would be told in thirty seconds and the name of the product would be fixed in your mind. There were also very clever cartoons and animated films that I had been starved of for so long.

Making appointments to see people was difficult. Sometimes I could not get to the one I needed to see first. Esmé took me in hand. She said, make the appointments you can and the others will then fall into place. She also insisted that I do everything for myself. Comrades who had come out of prison after much shorter prison terms had taken much too long to adjust because their families pampered them. I confess that she often figuratively pointed me in the right direction and sometimes literally did so to stop my dithering.

She wanted me to have my own bank account as another step toward independence. She dropped me off outside the Abbey National Bank in Golders Green. I could not see the bank. I did not know its logo, and there was no sign saying "Bank." Banks looked like shops and not like the stone fortresses I knew in South Africa. I felt quite foolish when a passerby told me I was at its front door. Inside, the problems multiplied. I found the required application form, but the questions made no sense to me. I understood the English words, but even with my four university degrees I did not know what answers were required. Perhaps I simply froze because I was afraid to appear stupid. I asked a young assistant to help me.

The International Defence and Aid Fund (IDAF) gave me a settling-in grant in two portions of one thousand pounds each (about one hundred pounds for each year of my imprisonment), and that was very significant because I had no personal funds at all. The grant enabled me to make a contribution to the costs of new clothes and household necessities that Esmé paid for, as well as my keep. The fund had kept so many people going and paid for our legal defense with no fanfare at all. In the nature of clandestine work undertaken for good humanitarian reasons, the success of the work has to be the reward that those who did it may hope to receive. Perhaps my few words of gratitude after so many years will have meaning for those who helped us survive until victory.

In London, after all the years of prison, the fruit and sweets and cakes with sweet cream were overwhelming and irresistible. There seemed to be no season for fruit. Everything was available, winter pears and summer grapes, peaches and plums. Granny Smith apples were piled up high, but that had to be a no-no because I knew that there was a fruit boycott to bring pressure to bear against the South African economy. I was feeling quite strange in London, and it would have been lovely to bite into a Granny Smith apple, large, green, and crisp to the bite. The very thought took me back to my childhood and youth. The beautiful grapes on sale at the kiosk next to the Angel tube station in Islington, near the ANC office, were irresistible. There was nothing to say they were the "Product of South Africa." I ate them with huge enjoyment, crushing the green globes and feeling the semisweet juice burst in my mouth. I told Esmé of my mouth-watering delight. She spoke sharply, "We have to boycott South African fruit, you know." I said I had looked very carefully to see where they came from. She insisted they were South African grapes because only the forbidden fruits were available in London at that time of the year. "Did the label say, 'Cape Grapes'?" "Yes." "That's the trade name for the boycott product," she said, as though I should have learned this in my prison cell six thousand miles away. My enjoyment turned a bit sour—but those grapes were the best export quality.

I found living in London quite difficult. I had no experience of living in such a metropolis, where you are never alone. By the end of every day the kaleidoscope of sights and the jumble of the sounds of the big city left me exhausted. I was also not used to the weather. It was dark when I got up and dark again by three in the afternoon in the winter. The cloud-filled sky felt as though it was draped over my shoulders. Getting about on my own was exciting, however. Traveling in the London underground trains was a new experience and very disconcerting. There were always people crowded around you, leaving you no space to be and no air to breathe—and the air was awful. If you got a seat, you sat with your nose in the groin of a standing passenger. It took me two years to get used to living in London.

I had hoped that I would come out of prison into a free South Africa, and that my family would come back to join me in South Africa. What I wanted was to be with my family. I had not thought about exile. For a long time I felt like an exile; friends needed explanations for what seemed implicit to me because I had grown up in South Africa. I had to consciously remain a South African freedom fighter in order to do my work building solidarity. I had to express myself in such a way that my audience could understand a situation or conflict that was beyond their daily experience. For example, in Britain you could live anywhere you chose if you could afford to buy or rent the house of your choice. In South Africa you were forced to live in an area set aside by law for people of your own race. In Britain you could try to get any work for which you were qualified, but in South Africa there was Job Reservation of skilled work for whites only, such as bricklaying or plumbing. I needed always to study an audience to see if they were following what I was saying.

My knowledge of the ANC office was limited to my first quick visits after I had arrived in London from Israel. Now I had to get accustomed to the daily work going on there and try to fit in with it. After the headquarters in Lusaka, the London office was the most important representation in the world. The ANC office was quite familiar. It was dingy, it was dirty, it was like all the left-wing offices I had known all of my childhood while growing up in Cape Town. It was old-fashioned and cramped, on many floors at number 28 Penton Street, in London. There were piles of leaflets and pamphlets that had never been distributed lying around. Wherever I traveled in northern Europe and America and Canada and Greece and Italy, I went into offices that all looked the same. They were dingy, walls painted gray, reached via old-fashioned elevators, and the people looked the same. The Scandinavian countries were different. There everything was clean and tidy, the new, modern equipment funded by national or regional governments.

My negotiated release from prison created difficulties among some of my comrades in exile. It seemed to me that the farther I got from South Africa, the harsher just a few of them were. Even in Lusaka, only a few were aware of the matter. In London, only Solly Smith, the ANC chief representative, was informed, and he later turned out to be an informer for the apartheid regime. Without discussing it with anybody, I made the decision that I would preserve the leadership's silence about its involvement. If quiet negotiations were going on, revealing them could defeat the purpose. Since the leadership chose not to say that it was involved or at least informed, that was a good enough reason to keep quiet. I was a kind of trial balloon for both the ANC and the South African government in terms of how to deal with the issue of political prisoners. So I kept quiet and swallowed hard when people said, "Nelson Mandela rejected P. W. Botha's offer, why couldn't you?" Most of the compatriots I met were marvelous and welcomed me and refused to add to the media hype that sought to sow divisions within our ranks. Comrades who came from South Africa to London at that time went out of their way to literally embrace me. They said they understood exactly what I had done, and they knew I was working in the ANC and speaking all over the world about our struggle. They had heard radio and seen TV interviews with me, and they were pleased that I was back in action. It was not an easy time for me because it was easier to get involved in the armed struggle than to say that I would not in future be involved in it. I did not and never have repudiated the rightness of our decision to take up arms. One makes one's choices and lives with the consequences! That's life! "C'est la vie," or "Kunjalo-ke" in Zulu.

Some years later I toured Canada and received an unexpected affirmation when I met several exiled South Africans. One of them was a young woman, the daughter of Achies Patel, a trade union activist originally from Johannesburg. She had visited "Uncle" Ahmed Kathrada (Kathy) at the Robben Island prison. He gave her a message for me: that circumstances prevented my Rivonia comrades from accepting their release but that they fully understood and supported my decision. Such thoughtful comrades. They had no way of knowing that I would indeed end up at some point in Vancouver but yet felt the need to reassure the exile community and me of their support. It seemed to me as if Kathy had put a message into a bottle and thrown it into the sea, and it washed up on the distant shore I was then standing on.

Now when I reflect in my more philosophical moments on these conflicts in our movement, I come to the conclusion that our exploitative society—apartheid in particular—has damaged all of us. That has affected our behavior and relationships inside our movement. Yet I have to add that, despite all that damage, to this day all of us in the movement have a vision of a better society that we are trying to build together with people who are not angels and some who are deeply scarred by the past. Yet we move forward to achieve that vision. If we do our work properly, the next generation will be less traumatized. And maybe the one after that will be even less traumatized, and we shall get closer to achieving the goal of what society ought to be. This is another way of saying that every society bears the birthmarks of the one from which it emerged.

Why should people who have grown up in an acquisitive society, where status depends on your position and especially your income and whether you are known or not known (are you a celebrity?), whether you can give people orders, be any better than those who have not? But the human capacity to do what is right is enormous. Our vision of what we have to achieve is no mere pipe dream. The potential is inherent in our existing society.

I felt no need to discuss these ideas with Esmé because I knew that she shared this belief, even though she had lost respect for many who were leaders. Yet over and over again I experienced Esmé's influence in Britain. An example of this occurred at a dinner organized by anti-apartheid activists in Sheffield. She had on this occasion accompanied me. Most of the guests were coal miners and their wives who had shortly before ended a yearlong strike. During my after-dinner address there was that wonderful attentive silence I have described. I ended with great praise for Esmé, who had stood by me, and now we were together again. The miners' wives were amazed by her fortitude. They were rightly proud of their role in the miners' strike, coming out of the shadows of traditional working-class women's obscurity to play a leading role. They said they had found it hard to endure one year of struggle, and she had been politically engaged and then been through twenty-two years of my absence. It pleased me greatly that they took her off to one side to hear her story and give her the recognition she deserved.

At home I found her collection of newspaper clippings dating from her arrival in Britain at the end of 1963 while the Rivonia Trial was still going on. She spoke to many audiences and lobbied Parliament. She met important people, calling on them to stop the trial and start negotiating an end to apartheid. But if that could not be achieved, then the death sentence should not be imposed. I also found a photograph of Esmé and Hilly sitting together, waiting for the sentence to be pronounced. Their anxiety is palpable. When I pressed her she told me that the moment the trial was over our comrades found her of no further interest and had little to do with her. She set about earning her living through building up her physiotherapy practice. That enabled her to be available for our children when they needed her, and when my mum joined her after the end of the trial, she was there to be with the children when Esmé was working.

Esmé had her own political and friendship circles. Among them is the still existing Woodcraft Folk, which is an organization that seeks to educate children and youth to self-awareness, peace, and cooperation. It grew out of the radical labor movement in the 1920s. It is a wonderful organization that opens young people to collective action and awareness of social questions. One of the great moments in Woodcraft Folk history was the saving of hundreds of young people from the Nazis in the 1930s and getting them to safety in Britain. They are my kind of people.

This organization of 30,000 people, parents and children, took Esmé and our children under their wing when they arrived in Britain. Esmé made many good friends, and the Folk, as they always called themselves, became ever more connected to antiracism issues and opposed apartheid in every way they could, especially through the boycott of South African fruit. The cooperative retail movement supported the Folk, who in turn demanded that the Co-operative Movement, with its many retail stores, stop selling South African fruit. When I arrived, I was accepted as Esmé's husband and acquired a whole array of new friends. Among them were Peter and Gina Mynors and their two children, Lara and Natasha, who were great family friends. Gina was a social worker and Peter was a fireman and was studying social work. I was able to advise him on his work for his master's degree in social work. It pleased me that the academic work I had done in prison could help someone who had given Esmé so much support.

I spoke at many meetings of the Woodcraft Folk and at their annual conferences. Jess Cawley, another of Esmé's friends, asked me to stand for election as president because some members wanted to overcome the encrusted organizational structures and make room for new ideas. I agreed, provided that I could function as an honorary president rather than executive president. I was elected with a majority of just one vote and did not play an active role. I was able to raise issues such as their use of pseudo–Native American ("Redskin') greetings and doggerel. Having lived under apartheid, I believed that even though they meant well, and the founders in the 1920s intended to honor the "noble savages" who lived in harmony with their natural habitat, these figures of speech represented an undignified way of treating people of color. Slowly others took up the issue, and it was good that it became widely debated. I was happy to step down when the Folk decided to appoint longtime members as honorary life presidents. Esmé and I spent many hours with the Folk and enjoyed our leisure time with them.

I was away from Esmé for many weeks at a time. At the end of 1985 I made a six-week-long tour of Scandinavia. Having made 120 speeches and given over a hundred interviews on television, on radio, and to newspapers, I was both exhilarated and utterly exhausted and needed ten days in bed to recover. That was what my life was like in my first year out of prison: I was away for more than half of it.

Esmé wanted more normality in our life together. Coming home from long speaking tours, I would find she had little to say to me. When I remonstrated, she said that all I could talk about was the struggle, the people and places I had met and seen, and had no time for her and our family. I admit that I was guilty as charged, and I tried to focus more on her when I was home in London. Then I understood the conditions she had imposed when she said we could try to be together again. She was not prepared to invest too much in the relationship unless I could reciprocate more fully. I needed her support and understanding and caring for me because I could not have done the work I did without her backing. She was asked to work with a ghostwriter on her autobiography, and she said that the working title would have to be "He's Gone Off Again." In a very real sense my contribution to liberation was her contribution, too. She not only gave me moral support, fed me, clothed me, and loved me, but she also kept me financially, because the amount of pocket money we were given by the ANC was minute.

Perhaps my commitment at the cost of family life was an unconscious need to justify having been released. Perhaps I felt subconsciously that I had to prove that I had come out of prison to fight back against the apartheid regime. I was away from home more, and I could think of little else than solidarity campaigns and inner-office politics within the ANC and how to rise above the pettiness. That was because of the difficult relationships within the ANC office that I experienced almost from my arrival there. In Britain and other countries ex–South Africans and exiles said that I could achieve more if I did not work in the ANC office. The London office of the ANC was said to be especially bad. Among journalists it had a reputation of holding people back, of manipulation and maneuvering, of playing favorites. I could not see this at the beginning. And in any case if it was true, I would have to work within the office to resolve these conflicts.

In our exile community there were many crosscutting currents and factions, and sometimes we seemed to be our own enemies, and the oppressive apartheid regime was forgotten in the internecine conflicts. There were full-time officials and there were members who were sometimes consulted. But full-time officials have to get on with what has to be done, without time for consultation. Our work was public inside Britain, and it was not so public or had to be secret when it related to Africa and South Africa; these two strands caused many conflicts because it was easier to be silent about everything, and therefore undemocratic, than to decide what could be public and what confidential. Some full-time officials had more direct contact with the top leaders than others and used the "need for secrecy" as a means of exercising power—"leader so-and-so has said,"—and an office committee decision was overturned without discussion, which caused even more frustration.

Each faction among the exiles believed its members alone possessed the truth. There was a small group of people who never had been in prison and had suffered very little but assumed that they should sit in moral judgment of all others. Some of them in their personal relationships betrayed each other in immoral ways. They lied and misled others when they did not like a certain comrade. One such case involving David Kitson, who had done twenty years in prison with me, was discussed. I insisted that we could not exclude or expel a member without a proper indictment, and he had to have the right to defend himself. They said they had done all these things. Years later we found there was no documentation at all. They lied and committed a fraud that caused divisions among our supporters in the British anti-apartheid movement. That did real harm to our movement and to our comrade.

I would not permit others to prescribe to me what I should think. Sometimes people in our office tried. "Why do you think you must try to break me?" I asked. "Experts tried for twenty-two years while I was in prison, and they failed. So do not even try because you will not succeed. But what puzzles me is why you want to break me. We have too much to do; let us get to work." Some had the grace to look embarrassed.

Often the little conflicts were completely unnecessary. My specific role was to speak to as many and as wide a variety of audiences in Britain and internationally about our struggle, and I needed lots of our excellent publicity material. Very often invitations to these speaking engagements would emerge with very short notice, and it became a battle to get the information material from the publicity section. "Why do you come at the last minute? You can have the stuff tomorrow!" "Tomorrow I will be in America or Greece or Italy, or . . ." "You can't have it!" I could not understand why it should be kept looking nice and neat on the shelves when it was intended for audiences to build solidarity with our struggle. Maybe it was hidden jealousy. Yes, I was in the limelight, but it had cost twenty-two years of my life to open up the ears and eyes of people to our struggle. I could not understand their envy when it was to our advantage to use my political credibility for our cause.

Many of our chief representatives in numerous countries did a wonderful job of representing the struggle for freedom in South Africa. Some who spoke in behalf of the ANC, however, made me cringe. There were so many others who could do it better. Perhaps it was because in exile the ANC was mother and father and employer and protector of everybody. Therefore, there was no possibility of firing those who were less capable. All that pettiness was abhorrent, and it affected Esmé and me, too, because only to her could I rail against the personalized internal antagonisms that had no political basis. After many months, Ez said she had wanted to warn me but knew I would have rejected her opinions because I did not want to believe that they could be true. They were true, and I am grateful to her for letting me find out for myself and dealing with and overcoming those obstacles. Like all exile movements, we were not immune to internal quarrels and personal animosities. When I was traveling so much, I had little to do with all that and those conditions.

During the previous twenty years apartheid had become a worldwide issue. From the wave of arrests in the early 1960s, our movement was crushed for nearly a decade. During this time the external ANC was the only overt sign of resistance, together with the growing external pressure on the South African regime. These two elements were possibly the dominant forces against it until 1973, when the strike by African workers in Durban led to the emergence of the modern trade union movement. That and the rebellion of the students in Soweto in 1976 led to an international public outcry. The formation of civic associations and many other groups that became the United Democratic Front (UDF) in 1983 made the internal struggle again very important. In 1985 the UDF had perhaps as many as two million affiliated members, the most solid support coming from the trade unions affiliated with the Congress of South African Trade Unions (COSATU). The UDF signaled its policies when it adopted the Freedom Charter and when it adopted, among others, the eight of us sentenced in the Rivonia Trial as patrons. The distribution of anti-apartheid literature in South Africa and communication through Radio Freedom were important. The works of South African writers, such as the Nobel Prize–winner Nadine Gordimer, were significant. The ANC's transmitters functioned for more than twenty years from bases in Tanzania, Zambia, Angola, Ethiopia, and Madagascar. The broadcasts began with machine-gun fire and a voice-over that said: "This is Radio Freedom, the voice of the African National Congress and its military wing, *Umkhonto we Sizwe.*" Listening to these broadcasts could result in a prison sentence of up to eight years. We had comrades based in Swaziland, Lesotho, Botswana, and other neighboring countries, so there was a coming and going between internal and external forces that laid the groundwork for forward movement together.

Those internal developments strengthened the international support for the struggle against apartheid. Activists in many countries, through words and protests, compelled their governments to publicly take positions against racism and apartheid. In the United States, for example, both major parties had to take into account in the long run the Congressional Black Caucus's policy on apartheid in South Africa, and the question of divestment, because the caucus held the balance of power in Congress.

I traveled in many countries in Europe and Scandinavia, in the United States and Canada, meeting wonderful, caring people from religious organizations, workers, civil servants, academics, and members of socialist, communist, liberal, and conservative parties, some of whom were in my view somewhat reactionary in their own countries' politics but gave strong support to the anti-apartheid movement. The struggle against the immorality of apartheid inhumanity transcended practically all ideological positions.

These developments encouraged us, and I met very capable ANC representatives in various countries who did excellent work. The ANC chief representative in Denmark, Aaron Mnisi (the pseudonym of Themba Kubeka), was a remarkably astute representative who knew the ins and outs of Danish politics, trade unions, and nongovernmental organizations (NGOs). He opened many doors to get me to where I could persuade influential people to support our cause. He had said that every time someone bought a Granny Smith apple he or she was buying a bullet to kill our people. I quoted him often, and his saying became the theme of the documentary *Fruits of Fear,* made for the British Anti-Apartheid Movement to publicize the fruit boycott against apartheid South Africa. It was written and directed by Ngozi Onwurah, a young Nigerian woman, who had recently graduated from film school near London.

I seemed to be always in planes and trains, traveling the world, speaking at meetings, doing radio and television work, working in the London office of the ANC. The United Nations had declared apartheid a crime against humanity on 16 December 1966, and many people in many countries supported that declaration. The U.N. General Assembly had established the U.N. Special Committee against Apartheid in November 1962. The governments of the major powers, such as the United States, the United Kingdom, and France, used their veto power in the U.N. Security Council to protect apartheid South Africa against resolutions calling for action against apartheid. Our task was to press for the imposition of all the sanctions provided for in Chapter 7 of the U.N. Charter against South Africa in that the country posed a threat to international peace and stability. Kader Asmal, a South African who was a professor of international law at Queens College Dublin, and other lawyers wrote influential papers in academic journals and the mass media.

The U.N. Special Committee against Apartheid observed a Day of Solidarity with South African Political Prisoners on 12 October 1987, and I represented the ANC.[1] I wrote and delivered the following speech:

This gathering is truly a solemn event, convened to mark the international Day of Solidarity with South African and Namibian Political Prisoners.

We wish to thank the Special Committee against Apartheid, and especially its Chairman, Major-General Garba, for the work it has done to make known the situation in South Africa and in southern Africa and to mobilize opinion against the apartheid regime.

We wish to honour those already executed by the apartheid regime for their actions to achieve the national liberation of the colonially oppressed mass of the peoples of South Africa and Namibia. That goal, the right to self-determination of peoples enshrined in the United Nations Charter, and their actions, including armed struggle, are politically right and lawful in terms of international law. We would cite an article by Kader Asmal entitled "Reagan Administration betrays the new laws of war," published in *The Legal Front* recently in New York.

Yet those heroic comrades of ours have been executed. Those known to us and those we wish to honour are our comrades Vuyisile Mini, [Wilson] Khayinga and [Zinakile] Mkaba, Solomon Mahlangu, Jerry Mosololi, Simon Moegerane, Marcus Motaung, Benjamin Moloise, Lucky Payi, Sipho Xulu, Mawasi, [Alex] Matsepane, [Moses] Jantjies and [Wellington Mlamli] Mielies, who were executed just a couple of days ago, as we have heard.[2]

We call upon the world to act—and I would stress the word "act"— to put a stop to executions for political and military acts against the illegitimate racist regime and its collaborators. Right now on death row, as far as we can ascertain, there are 30 or 31 of our heroic comrades. I shall not read the full list of names. In prison at this time are some hundreds of political and military activists whose so-called crime has been their opposition to the internationally recognized crime against humanity of apartheid.

Some of our comrades have been imprisoned for a quarter of a century, but even those who have been freshly imprisoned are entitled to our support. The most famous of the political prisoners are, of course, Nelson Mandela, Walter Sisulu, Govan Mbeki, Raymond Mhlaba, Ahmed Kathrada, Andrew Mlangeni and Elias Motsoaledi, all sentenced in the Rivonia Trial in 1964, as well as Wilton Mkwayi, sentenced in December of that year.

We call upon the world to act now to achieve the unconditional release of these comrades of ours—outstanding people not only in the history of South Africa but in the struggles of all peoples throughout history against tyrannical oppression. We call upon the world to act now to achieve the unconditional release of all political prisoners in

South Africa. There are untold thousands of people, mainly young boys and girls, sentenced to terms of imprisonment under laws which make them criminals for their politically motivated actions against the apartheid regime. Their acts are acts of conscience. They, equally with those sentenced in overtly political trials in the racist courts, are prisoners of conscience.

We call upon the world to act now for the release of these comrades of ours. Since the most sustained and widespread uprisings in our history began at the end of 1984 and since the imposition of a state of emergency tantamount to martial law, some 30,000 people have been detained by the police and military forces of the regime. The Detainees' Parents Support Committee has estimated that one-third of them, some 8,000 to 10,000 people, are under 18 years of age. Some are as young as 8 or 10 years of age. They are called "threats to the security of the State."

Torture is the norm in the interrogations [by] security police of the racist regime. A study conducted by experts at the University of Cape Town reveals that 83 percent of those interrogated by the security police had been tortured. Beatings, electric shocks to the genitalia, suffocation, injection of drugs and physical brutality dreamed up in the nightmare minds of the interrogators are the order of the day. And this does not take into account the psychological torture imposed by the system of detention without trial. The former South African ambassador to Britain, Mr. [Denis] Worrall, conceded in a press interview that child torture occurs in South African prisons. He added, disingenuously, that this was against Government policy. He did not say that it was also against the law. He did not explain why it continues, despite being against Government policy. The implication is clear: torture is not only tolerated, it has been encouraged by successive Ministers of Justice and Police Commissioners. How otherwise do they explain the secrecy provisions in the legislation enabling detention for the purposes of interrogation?

It is impossible to know the exact number of those murdered under interrogation in South Africa, which must be taken to include the pseudo-independent pseudo-homelands or Bantustans. Our estimates are that well over 100 of our comrades have been murdered while in police hands since 1963. My comrade Looksmart Ngudle was among the first, in 1963. We have since seen such famous names as Steve Biko, Dr. Neil Aggett, Andries Raditsela, and many others.

We call upon the world to act now to put an end to these tortures. The recent Conference on Children, Repression and the Law in Apartheid South Africa, held at Harare, Zimbabwe, heard direct testimony of the systematic torture of children while in detention. Inevitably, many have died. Almost all survivors require psychotherapy to enable them to overcome the trauma in their young lives. With Archbishop Huddleston, we can say that a regime which wages its war of oppression against children is morally bankrupt. It must be overthrown.

We should ask: Why a war against children? We must answer that the people of South Africa, men and women, have not been cowed, have not been broken, by the repression and the torture. This is a regime that seeks out quite consciously the most vulnerable—the weakest, the children—in its effort to intimidate the adults determined to be free. We call upon the world to act now to put an end to the ceaseless destruction of young lives.

The apartheid regime has also murdered and abducted our comrades in defiance of international law through their actions in neighbouring States. Our comrade Ishmael Ibrahim Ishmael[3] is now on trial, having been brought before the court after being kidnapped in Swaziland. Our comrade Priscilla Njanda was also kidnapped in Swaziland and seems to have disappeared. Nobody knows where she is. Our comrades Paul Dikeledi and Cassius Make were recently brutally murdered in Swaziland by agents of the apartheid regime.

I did not know the works of our comrade [Dumile Feni] that are hung here today. They show far more graphically than any words can describe what prison means. They show the distortions of life; they show a mother and her babies in prison. They show a people in prison but on their feet, not cowed, not broken—their lives distorted, true. Despite all these actions by the apartheid regime, it has not been able to stop the people's movement towards the overthrow of the apartheid system, the movement towards people's power in this the seventy-fifth anniversary year of the founding of the African National Congress of South Africa (ANC). The ANC has named this year, 1987, the Year of Advance to People's Power.

We must always bear in mind that apartheid is very much more than the brutalities practised by the apartheid regime in its desperate attempts to maintain itself in power. Apartheid itself is a denial of human rights and dignity. In their daily lives—we cannot in all conscience call them "ordinary lives"—the majority of the people of South Africa live lives which the philosopher Hobbes would have described as "nasty, brutish and short." Our people live under a virtual military and police occupation. Death squads, euphemistically called vigilantes, are not only tolerated by security police but are actively encouraged by agencies of the Apartheid State.

Apartheid is a system of State terrorism. South Africa is an imprisoned society. Our people, in destroying the apartheid system, will put an end to that State terrorism. They are tearing down the walls of that prison. Our people will be free in a united, democratic, non-racial South Africa.

We call upon the world to act now to help free our comrades literally in prison and the whole of our people from the prison which is apartheid. No—we do not call upon the world: we demand that the world—and especially those Western countries such as the United States of America, Britain, the Federal Republic of Germany, and their allies Israel and others, which actively support the apartheid regime and protect it through diplomatic and other means—act now.

Do not tell us to wait for reforms. Do not tell us to wait for the apartheid cancer in our society to prescribe its own cure. Ernesto [Eduardo] Galeano cites a Guatemalan Foreign Minister saying over 100 years ago that asking the United States to solve the problems of Guatemala was asking a cancer to cure itself. Who shall know better than President Reagan that a cancer must be excised?

Do not tell us to be non-violent. Tell the apartheid regime to stop its violence against our people. Do not tell us that sanctions will harm the oppressed people of South Africa. In the darkness of the suffering caused by the system of apartheid in the daily lives of the people and the suffering caused by the State terrorism employed to maintain the system, it is an impertinence to say: "We will not impose sanctions so that you will not suffer." It is an impertinence for the United States and the United Kingdom to veto Security Council draft resolutions intended to impose mandatory comprehensive sanctions. It is an impertinence to equate the legitimate violence of a people struggling to be free with the State violence of the repressive apartheid State.

We demand of the world to impose mandatory comprehensive sanctions now. Do not tell us that the trifling sanctions that have been enacted are ineffective. You unwillingly enacted them, are lax in applying them and then tell us they do not work. You trifle with the lives of our people.

We demand an end to the apartheid crime against humanity. In relation to Namibia we demand mandatory comprehensive sanctions to enforce compliance with Security Council resolution 435 (1978) and an end to apartheid South Africa's illegal occupation of that country. In relation to apartheid South Africa's continuing aggression against Angola, Mozambique, Zambia, Zimbabwe, Lesotho, Swaziland and Botswana, action is required urgently. We demand of the world the full application of all the provisions of Chapter VII of the United Nations Charter to bring an end to that aggression. Nuclear-armed apartheid South Africa is already at war with its neighbours and is a threat to international peace and security.

We wish also to express our solidarity with the Palestine Liberation Organization (PLO) and with the people of the Sahraoui National Liberation Front, as well as with people everywhere fighting for their freedom from national oppression.

This is a solemn meeting of solidarity with political prisoners in South Africa and Namibia. It should also be a joyful occasion on which we celebrate the triumph of the human spirit, of endurance, of determination to destroy the evil apartheid system. In the words of the prologue to our Freedom Charter, "these freedoms we will fight for, side by side, throughout our lives, until we have won our liberty."

I have not talked about my own experiences. We have heard from our comrade, Dean T. S. Farasani [Farisani], what torture means. It is much more difficult for me to strip aside all the protections one builds up over 7,904 days of imprisonment. But what we know is that we will fight side by side all our lives until we have won. I would only say in closing: *"Amandla Ngawethu: Maatla ke a rona: Jana Shakti!"* Power to the people!

The Anti-Apartheid Movement (AAM) in Britain had achieved a huge response by remaining a single-issue campaign based on the inhumanity of apartheid. It appealed, as did the ANC itself, across class lines to people who simply believed in the equality of all people. Many British people had strong family connections to South Africa because so many had settled there during the colonial era and after both world wars. British investors held the largest share of foreign investment and had the lion's share of trade with South Africa. That the founding segregationist constitution, The Union of South Africa Act, was a law passed by the British Parliament was a matter of conscience for many.

My first public encounter was on 26 June 1985, when I was asked to speak at an AAM rally commemorating our Freedom Day. The podium was on the plinth of Nelson's Column in Trafalgar Square. A large array of speakers, including Neil Kinnock, the leader of the Labour Party, spoke that day, and I was quite overawed by the occasion. I was called to the microphone and simply stood there, savoring the moment. I had not previously been a public speaker, and here I was facing perhaps as many as thirty thousand people. I knew what I would say to describe apartheid and the systematic brutality of the regime. I had, after all, had a long time to prepare myself. Because I don't like demagoguery, I decided when I came out of prison to appeal to people through a simply stated logical argument. Naturally, an appeal to emotions of abhorrence at the brutality of apartheid would play a role, but only as a way to open minds to a logical argument. My reasons were simple. Relying on a crude emotional appeal leaves your audience open to being swayed by an appeal to the opposite emotions. A logical argument prepares your audience to reject appeals to racism and bigotry, to naked prejudice and intolerance. Second, the case against apartheid was so strong that it was irresistible to all people other than simple race supremacists. That is why the journalist Segev shocked me. Under the guise of an invitation to a serious discussion of such important things as freedom and oppression, he used me to propagate his narrow-minded prejudice against the Palestinian people and black South Africans.

There is always a considerable buzz among so large an audience as people around the fringes come and go, but after a while I felt a complete silence with real attention being paid to what I was saying. All my life I had heard speakers shouting into microphones, straining their voices as though every word had equal weight. Reading Shakespeare in prison, I saw how he built up each scene, and successive scenes were built into an act in which the dramatic tension finally reached a climax. Then he started on another line of his drama in a second act and again built to a climax. Then, in the final act, all the threads of the dramatic tale are drawn together. You therefore speak about many details fairly quietly and informatively, carrying your audience to the point you wish to make. You then start again and build up to another reason to condemn apartheid, and another, and end perhaps with a throwaway line explaining what help your audience can give to change the lives of many people. All the years of reading and studying in prison came together, and I was able to hold the attention of an audience. It is a gratifying result of all that work. I say I was not nervous but today, still, after thousands of speeches, I get butterflies in my stomach before making a speech. I have promised myself that when I do not feel their wings fluttering, I will stop because it is insulting to an audience to roll words off your tongue without real interest and feeling for what you are trying to achieve.

I knew that I was riding on the coattails of hundreds of anti-apartheid activists who had worked for many years to create the platform and draw the audiences for us to address. I felt very privileged to meet them and experience their commitment to helping us end apartheid. London activists were constantly aware that they were in the capital city and in touch with government. Indeed, that was their function—to get the British government to actively oppose apartheid and not use its veto in the U.N. Security Council to protect apartheid South Africa. It was clear that the billions of pounds of investments in South Africa were more important to the government than the suffering and the lives of our people.

What did surprise me was that the mainstream press generally ignored the meeting in Trafalgar Square. One paper carried a photograph of Neil Kinnock, together with a thirty-eight-word caption. That was the sole report on a meeting of thirty thousand people. (I really made an effort to count them.) I had not believed Bram when he told me that the British ruling class simply ignored those they did not agree with, and here I was seeing it in action.

Britain was familiar to me through its literature, movies, and radio programs. My parents were born in London and they had talked about it, and South Africa was a British colony. I came and found myself in a world where political issues are not as stark and simple as they are to South Africans involved in the progressive movement. We knew quite simply that racism is apartheid, and apartheid is part of capitalism, is part of imperialism, and this was acknowledged throughout the ANC and the liberation movement. Activists knew from their workplaces who their employers were, and that the capital was British and American, mainly, but also German and French. General Motors, Ford, General Electric, Siemens, and Allgemeine Elektrizitäts-Gesellschaft (AEG) were the big employers, and I learned from my African comrades the lesson that you worked in the trade union movement or the National Liberation Movement, consisting of the ANC and its allies, or, for those who were communists, in the Communist Party, without any problems about how these organizations fit together. They fit together quite naturally, through the lived experience of people. But in Britain and Europe when I came out of prison, we were into the climactic period of the Cold War, and these simple truths got blurred through the way that the media shaped our views for or against the power blocs.

As I was based in London, most of my work was in Britain and Europe. I enjoyed my visits to Scotland and Wales. Both countries had their own anti-apartheid movements affiliated with the U.K. Anti-Apartheid Movement. These national minorities had a good intuitive understanding of the national oppression on which apartheid was based. Because of this, the people I met seemed less constrained than their London colleagues. Scottish trade unions were marvelously militant in our cause. I mention the Fire Brigades Union and local government officials in their various unions in particular. Allan Campbell and Pat Kelly were among my earliest contacts, and I enjoy seeing them whenever possible. How can I mention all of them? Let me fall back on the excuse that it would take too long to mention everyone. Among my greatest pleasures was attending and addressing UNISON annual conferences as a guest of the Scottish regional body of the combined union of local government workers. It was equally great to address the Scottish Trades Union Congress when the late Bill Speirs was its general secretary.

The Scottish AAM had many dedicated members. I must mention Brian Filling, its chairman, whose full-time job was as vice principal of the Glasgow College of Building and Printing, and John Nelson, a community worker who was its secretary. Two totally different personalities, they got through a terrific amount of work. Brian was the coordinator who seemed to know everybody who could get things done. If mobile phones had not been invented, Brian would have grown the one that seemed to be permanently attached to his ear. John was the meticulous detail person, rather shy but always there providing the publicity material and fund-raising through selling anti-apartheid memorabilia.

David and Sheila McGeoch always offered me a place to stay in Glasgow, and their young daughter, Rhona, became a special friend. Iain and Isabel Whyte, both pastors in the Church of Scotland, were quite special. They knew that I was a rationalist but knew that we cared equally about the well-being of ordinary people. Iain hinted to me that he had made a number of trips to apartheid South Africa to give support to the South African Council of Churches. Brian and Lorraine Purdie were marvelous supporters in detail work that helped us fulfill our solidarity functions. There were many others. Professor David Walsh of Glasgow Caledonian University proposed that I be awarded an honorary doctor of laws degree. David Kenvyn was a Welshman, a librarian in London, and a great activist who ended up in Scotland.

The Irish AAM invited Esmé and me to attend their Annual General Meeting in 1985. We stayed with Professor Kader Asmal, the chairman, and his wife, Louise. They made us very welcome, and at various social events we met their closest Irish friends and allies in anti-apartheid circles. As always, I consulted leading people such as Kader to find out what issues were important and should be raised in my address. As was true all those years ago in the Congress of Democrats in the early 1960s, there were people who wanted to push an ultra-left political line, which would turn the anti-apartheid movement into a narrow sectarian socialist group instead of the vibrant organization whose appeal transcended class and ideological positions. Kader kindly wrote a note of appreciation to Solly Smith in London, thanking him for sending someone who did his homework before speaking. Praise for me seemed to bring hostility from some elements in London. We were such a complicated and complex group of people.

I was also sent on a number of occasions to speak to Irish nationalist groups, and there I had to be careful not to fall into the trap of responding to loaded questions, such as "We support your armed struggle, but why don't you support ours?" A simple affirmative answer would have meant going to prison under British terrorism laws. Anyway, their armed actions were very different from ours, in that we tried as a matter of policy to avoid attacking civilians.

My first major speaking tour outside Britain was in November and December 1985 in Scandinavia. I was away for over six weeks. In Sweden I was the guest of the Social Democratic Youth Organization (SSU), going from town to town, a new town every day, on my own in a foreign country, making speeches up to three times a day and giving interviews. Fortunately, Swedish people, certainly the younger ones, speak English, so I felt comfortable. I learned a few words of Swedish and saw that people appreciated the respect for their culture that represented. It reminded me of home, where it was important to at least be able to greet people in their own language if possible, and it was the same for minority groups in Europe. Besides that, I was open to new experiences, and these tours broadened my horizon. It was very effective when I asked in Swedish for donations to the ANC. Then I went to Finland, and from Finland back to Sweden, and from Sweden on to Norway, and Norway to Denmark, completing six weeks of traveling.

In Finland Burye Mattson drove me to smaller towns over ice and snow, and I hoped that his car was reliable because temperatures of 15 degrees Centigrade below freezing would have been unbearable if it had broken down. Matti Viiallainen, the chairperson of the anti-apartheid movement, guided me through Helsinki and I discovered the delight of a sauna. I was introduced to the Parliamentary Anti-Apartheid Committee. Its members represented each of the Conservative, Social Democrat, Liberal, and Communist parties. The minister of economic affairs, a conservative, was to speak on why the government would not impose economic sanctions on South Africa. The committee wanted to know what questions I would ask the minister. I explained that the U.N. General Assembly had declared apartheid a crime against humanity. Why give apartheid support through trade? With them I developed a question-and-answer series. The minister made his predictable speech, and the first member of the Anti-Apartheid Committee said that a person in the gallery, if he were a member, would ask . . . The minister responded as he had to, and the second, third, and fourth all said they asked their questions on my behalf. More fascinating was that the minister answered as if he were reading from the script we had just written. It was a great moment for a nonelected person to make four vicarious interventions in a foreign parliament.

I arrived in Denmark in time to be invited to Yuletide dinners given by a number of organizations. Among these visits was one to the Danish Communist Party headquarters to meet their international department to brief them on the state of our struggle at national and international levels. I then joined them at their *Jultids* luncheon, which had been going on for some time. They were singing songs familiar to me, punching out the rhythm like they were punching out the fascist enemy. When they faltered, I asked why they had stopped singing. They did not know any more songs was the answer. So I started singing some of the songs from the International Brigade that fought on the side of the democratic Loyalists in the Spanish Civil War. I sang in English and despite my poor voice, halfway through the first line they picked up my song in German or Danish or Spanish, and there we were together singing the songs I learned literally at my mother's knee when I was five years old. Such experiences of international solidarity were always wonderfully encouraging.

Highlights from Visits to the United States of America

Late one afternoon shortly after my release from prison in 1985, Alfred Nzo, the secretary general in Lusaka, instructed me to fly to New York to address the U.N. Special Committee against Apartheid in behalf of the ANC in two days' time. A special meeting to commemorate thirty years of the Freedom Charter was being convened.

Early the next morning I was at the U.S. Embassy in Grosvenor Square and found a long queue of people who had arrived even earlier. I presented the telex invitation from the U.N. Special Committee and my visa application carefully and truthfully filled out (particularly the question about communist contacts, answered in the affirmative). The official curtly responded to my request to be informed if there would be any problem because I had to fly that evening if I were to get to the event in time. "Why do you think there might be a problem?" he asked. Then, "Be here at three p.m. and your visa will be waiting." And indeed it was there, permitting multiple entries to that country and bearing no expiration date. I thought that this was some kind of message to apartheid South Africa that the United States would assist the ANC in applying pressure to bring the system to an end.

Back at the ANC office, Ishmael Coovadia asked if I had brought my luggage. No. "Well, it will take you too long to go home, pack, and get to Heathrow." I phoned Esmé. She had been awaiting my call and had packed for me. She told me where to meet her on the Heathrow underground train. What a sweat. I changed into fresh clothes on the train. She really understood that I had no real comprehension of how long every trip takes in a city the size of London.

On the plane I dozed quite a lot, but mostly I wrote the speech I had to deliver. I do not have a copy, but, shortly after arriving and being taken to the ANC office, I sat down to type my speech. What an experience of organized chaos. But going to the U.N. headquarters was also something very special. The U.N. Special Committee against Apartheid had constantly kept the issue of apartheid in the public eye, and its celebration of a day of commemoration of the Freedom Charter was also a sign of its support for the ANC.

Over the years I visited the United States a number of times, speaking to trade union locals where there was positive support for us, to groups of people organized by local anti-apartheid activists in many cities, and in schools and colleges. Vicki Erenstein of the National Lawyers Guild and Charlene Mitchell (who in 1968 had been the first black woman to run for the U.S. presidency) were great activists taking me in hand on alternate days, rushing me from one appointment to another in New York. They were great and had many contacts. Vicki kindly found a Toys"R"Us store where I could buy a swing for my newly born granddaughter, Katie. Esmé was insistent that I find the time for it, and I was pleased I could. Driving in from the airport and seeing the tunnels and bridges and the distant skyline was exciting because I had been inspired by such marvels of construction to become a civil engineer. I also enjoyed being taken by Vicki to a friendly Italian bistro–style eatery, which seemed utterly familiar because of the influence of Hollywood movies.

One trade union visit in particular was memorable. Local 1197 of hospital workers, cleaners, porters, and so on showed me how generous in their support the lowest-paid workers could be. I was also invited to meet Gus Hall, the general secretary of the Communist Party USA (CPUSA), and members of his politburo, which they had recently renamed the Executive Committee to sound more American. But the style of presentation was very much old guard, filled as it was with certainty that the revolution was just around the corner. When I called on them to pay more attention to ending apartheid and to Africa in general, I was told that Central and South America were their real fields of action because of the naked exploitation of those countries and peoples by the United States. Of course that was true, but Africa was also important, and as Southern Africa was the last bastion of indirect colonial rule or control by apartheid South Africa, they should pay more attention to our struggles. I said that there would be a natural support for such an approach because of the importance of African Americans in the political sphere in the United States. I found them quite inflexible and thought the name changes from Central Committee and Politburo to less foreign terms had not changed the way that political issues were expressed: in rigid terms divorced from the feelings of the people they were trying to influence. I was pleased, however, to meet Paul Baran, who with Paul M. Sweezy had written a marvelous set of essays on the structure of U.S. society, providing a solidly researched critique of social and economic conditions and covering such things as the inequalities of education and the mouthing of democratic principles but the negation of these concepts in practice.[4] They were particularly strong on the articulation of the indirectly controlled neocolonies and the U.S. metropole, where finance capital was playing an ever more important role, even to the point of having more or less direct influence over the country's intelligence arms.

They quoted directors of famous universities who made it clear that education was a means of ideological control. Baran and Sweezy's description of the role of the top highly educated 5 to 10 percent of the population, who moved effortlessly from academia to government to corporate structures as if through revolving doors, was enlightening. A further 10 to 20 percent of the population needed to be well educated to implement policies. The rest needed to be educated enough to be able to understand what they were required to do without real thought.

In Chicago I usually stayed with Hymie and Hazel Rochman. He had been politically active in Cape Town, and it was good to have another guide to the complexities of politics in Chicago. Hazel worked at the American Library Association and got me invited to a pleasant brown-bag lunch with the staff members. I told them of our efforts to ship books for young children from Britain to South Africa. To make such a scheme work in Chicago, I would have had to find somebody who would devote a lot of time to that kind of work.

In Chicago I met a very strong anti-apartheid coalition, which on one occasion asked me to sit in on a discussion hosted by Susan Gzesh between a few African Americans and Jewish Americans. They were seeking to strengthen their activism by recovering the cooperation between former activists who had worked together during the civil rights era of the 1960s and 1970s. In short, the problem revolved around some of the African Americans' feeling aggrieved because they had achieved many of their goals of political equality, but their former coactivist Jewish Americans still behaved as though they were part of the superior white group who always knew best what should be done. From the Jewish American side there was a feeling of being neglected and unwanted now that some semblance of equality had been achieved: "You [blacks] don't listen to us anymore." What a lesson in human relationships: the very achievement of the desired goal of equal relationships required an adjustment that the former relatively privileged found very hard to make. The organizers of the event were sincere and showed their genuine desire to move on, but some on both sides could not overcome the hurts that seemed so petty. Both sides shouting at each other prevented them from finding a way forward. All I could do was try to point out what was happening, but I know that I could not shift them from their entrenched positions. I hoped that when tempers had cooled, some progress would be made. I recount this story because I see in South Africa at the time of writing, in 2012, the same scenario being played out in the broader community. In the words of the Pete Seeger song, "When will they ever learn, when will they ever learn?"

Jerry Herman of the American Friends Service Committee (AFSC, a Quaker organization) was in London at the time of my first speech at Trafalgar Square. He said he would like me to come to the United States to speak about the campaign to end apartheid and to talk about my own experience in the liberation movement. This led to my being invited on a memorable tour organized by an ad hoc African Peace Tour Committee, in which Jerry Herman was the lead organizer on behalf of the AFSC's Africa Program. Jackie Wilson of the Washington Office on Africa played a leading role, accompanying me to several meetings. The Red Cross, Fathers of the Maryknoll Order, militant human rights campaigners, and others were involved. By chance we arrived in Los Angeles on my birthday, 11 April 1989. The Fathers of the Maryknoll Order had built a replica of a South African mine-proof armored personnel carrier. It was awesome, huge and threatening and painted in military camouflage. They had driven it up the steps of the South African Consulate and blocked the entrance. The staff had battened down the hatches, so to speak. A crowd including many Beverly Hills High School students had gathered. Their mothers were standing proudly by. Things became threatening when the police arrived because the students were in breach of the laws giving protection to diplomats and their buildings, and they had forced the consulate to close. The students were ordered to disperse. They remained defiant. The police said that if they would sign admissions of guilt for the misdemeanor of obstructing the sidewalk in breach of municipal bylaws, they would not be arrested. If they persisted, they would be charged under federal law and have a serious criminal record. I was asked to address them and thanked them for their principled stand against racism in far-off South Africa. I also thanked them for the wonderful birthday present they were giving me. I then suggested that they had made the point that U.S. support for apartheid was unacceptable, and that they could in good conscience go home. They dispersed.

There were meetings up and down the West Coast, and Muhtadia Rice and a group of Bahá'í believers ensured that I got to every meeting in time. One Sunday morning I was met by a man, suntanned, healthy looking, much older than I, at a Unitarian Church where I discovered I was to give the Sunday lesson from the pulpit. He greeted me and said he knew what I must have been through because he had been through quite a lot as well—"But nothing like what you, Denis, have been through." I asked him to tell me about himself. It was a sincere inquiry, though I also found it a very good way to ward off having to dig into my own feelings and emotions about my own experience. He had been in the Lincoln Battalion of the International Brigade fighting in Spain on the side of the Spanish Republican Loyalists against the fascists. "You fought in Spain! How wonderful to meet you." Together we sang one of the songs of the International Brigade. People around us asked if we knew each other. He replied with one of the nicest remarks that I have ever heard from an older comrade. He said, "We've never met before, but we've known each other all our lives."

Nevertheless, Comrade Goldberg met with doubts because North Americans shivered on hearing the word *comrade*. What, I asked them, should I call someone to whom I entrust my life and who entrusts his or her life to me? "Mister" or "madam" is too formal. Using just a name and no title can be demeaning. "Comrade" is the right word. I knew that they were really asking about communist influence on our movement and our armed struggle. I tackled it head-on. I said that Americans claimed the right to determine the way they governed their country. That's what we call democracy. Our people claim the same democratic right. "But you can't tell us what we can and can't do. We've had enough of oppressors." And most of the audience would acknowledge the validity of this argument.

Jane Hunter was active in Palestinian support. We had met during a tour of Scandinavia on the issue of Palestine and Israel and became very good friends. Later we met from time to time at seminars in London organized by the Council for the Advancement of Arab-British Understanding (CAABU), and privately in various cities around Britain, the Scandinavian countries, and the United States. She edited an informational bulletin, *Israeli Foreign Affairs,* and appeared to have many sources for her articles, which sometimes seemed to me to be based on a deep-seated conspiracy theory of politics. She gave me a very interesting short course on American Israel Political Action Committees (AIPACs) and their powerful influence on U.S. electoral politics through their ability to destroy support for candidates at federal and state levels on the basis of their being for or against Israel's policies, especially in relation to the Palestinians. She said that in California the FBI had been interdicted from interfering with anti-apartheid groups and that the Jewish Defense League, composed of ardent Zionists, was collecting information on such groups and passing it to the FBI.

On one of my tours Jane picked me up in Los Angeles and drove me up to Sacramento, where we spent some very pleasant days together, and I addressed a meeting in the Town Hall. We also drove to San Francisco, where the Bay Area anti-apartheid movement was very strong. I met and addressed the dockworkers who had refused to offload South African ships and been served with a lifetime injunction declaring their action illegal. They gave strong support to the anti-apartheid movement. I was astonished by the readiness of the dockworkers to sacrifice their livelihoods to support a struggle so far away in South Africa. I also saw that their constitutional right to free expression did not extend to interfering with trade (and profits)!

The dockworkers were upset that the film *Cry Freedom,* which was presented as being about the life of Stephen Bantu Biko, the Black Consciousness student leader who had been murdered by the Security Police, turned out to be about a white man, Donald Woods, the editor of the *East London Daily Dispatch* newspaper who took up Biko's call for the ending of apartheid racism. Woods was harassed by the South African Security Police with threats to his life and those of his wife and children. I understood their distress and tried to explain that Hollywood moviemakers are more interested in profits than political veracity. I asked if they could not see the heroism of Steve Biko, who turned a skeptical white establishment editor from apathetic tolerance of apartheid into an active and influential campaigner against the system. I thought we needed to separate the issues: what Biko stood for and seizing the opportunity to spread the word. The resentment over the use of his heroism, his clarity of thought, and his organizing ability for the purpose of turning the white man into the hero was what angered the dockworkers I met. Once again the black man, the hero, was not only dead, but also his greatness was glossed over.

Shortly before the formal ending of apartheid, I went as part of an

ANC study group to meet with David Albright, director of the Institute for Science and International Security, in Alexandria, Virginia, near Washington, D.C. Albright had a masterly grasp of the issues of nuclear military power, nonproliferation treaties and the attempt to keep nuclear weapons out of the hands of smaller states, diplomacy and international relations, and civilian use of nuclear energy and its environmental dangers. I came away with a much more detailed understanding that led to a paper presented to an ANC seminar titled "Nuclear Policy for a New, Democratic South Africa" in February 1994.

The crux of the matter in discussions about the Non-Proliferation Treaty (NPT) was that there were so-called rogue states that wanted to acquire nuclear technology that would enable them to build nuclear weapons of mass destruction. In the United States' view, Israel was not a rogue state, even though it was commonly accepted that it had nuclear weapons and the country refused to sign the NPT. Because Israel had not signed the NPT, the United States said the Israelis were not in breach of the treaty. Of course, this is contrary to the norms of international law, by which all states are bound by majority decisions of the United Nations; such decisions become law, even though it is weak law. In the end it was clear that such niceties were irrelevant because the United States decides who are the rogues and who are the good guys. From the point of view of the rest of the world, the ones who might start a nuclear holocaust were America's allies, and given the nuclear standoff in the Cold War with the Soviet Union, it seemed to some of us that the United States was the biggest rogue state of all.

Students at Dartmouth College in Hanover, New Hampshire, built a shantytown on campus to protest U.S. support of apartheid, demanding that Dartmouth divest from all involvement with South Africa, including selling shares in any U.S. corporations that were invested in South Africa. The college management offered a public seminar on divestment to get the students to stop their protest. I was sent by the ANC as a keynote speaker. I was fortunate that one of the students, Kim Porteus, was detailed to look after me. She told me of the background of their protest and the college's response. The students held their ground very strongly. Kim made sure I was taken to venues to meet people and provided a computer for writing up my address.

There was a second keynote speaker, Ron Dellums, a Democrat in the House of Representatives. He spoke on U.S. policy on apartheid South Africa. He said that successive U.S. governments could not see past their fear that a free South Africa might ally itself to the Soviet Union. Anti-communism, anti-Sovietism, he said, was not a substitute for a policy based on principles of freedom because that precluded taking a correct stand against the injustice of apartheid. Their fear of what might be was what denied freedom to the majority of South Africans. I thought that it was a courageous speech. I presented him with a set of fine enamel jewelry based on the ANC logo and flag: badge and tie pin for him, brooch and earrings for Mrs. Dellums. I had not previously met Dellums and found out that he had long spoken about the inextricable link between peace and justice. He consistently spoke out in Congress to end U.S. support for the racist apartheid regime of South Africa. He and the Congressional Black Caucus eventually succeeded in getting the Comprehensive Anti-Apartheid Act passed in 1986 by the House of Representatives and the Senate, where the Republican Party had a majority. He is quoted as saying that was the high point of his political life. I am pleased to have met him.

I was invited to a working breakfast with the college's Investment Committee. The chairperson was an ex–Price Waterhouse vice president. I took the position that their bad business practice in relation to South African investments was harming the college and its students. I explained that they had lost one-third of the value of their investments because of the depreciation of the rand against the dollar owing to political upheaval. If they persisted in retaining their investments, it would be for political and ideological reasons, and I would advise the students to charge the trustees with failure of their fiduciary duty. There had been such a case (I believed it was in Texas) and the trustees were indeed held to be in the wrong. I said I was surprised that experienced businesspeople would spend so much time defending bad business decisions when there was a simple way out. They should sell their shares in IBM, for example, to voice their protest and make it public. They said IBM would withdraw their grant of computers and software, and that would harm the university and its students. My response was simply that IBM would be reluctant to appear so (indirectly) blatantly racist in their response. And if they did, there were other corporations that would be happy to leap in to take their place at Dartmouth. They were surprised that my criticism was based on business principles rather than an all-out attack based on the clear immorality of their position. I used this argument during my public address in a hall packed with students and the public, having described the nature of apartheid and the need for their support for our struggle inside South Africa. I recall being asked from the floor if I was not afraid of being assassinated by apartheid agents. I agreed that was a real danger, and I had been told by people in the know that I was number twelve on a hit list of thirty activists. I said that international public support was our only protection. They had to ensure that if I was killed they would put such pressure on their government that the political consequences for the apartheid government would make it not worth their while to kill me. The only other protection, I said, was to crawl into a hole and do nothing to end the injustice of apartheid racism by law. That would be to surrender to the injustice!

On one occasion while I was in New York, the ANC's deputy chief representative, Solly Simelane, insisted I fly to Denver to take the place of Chief Representative Neo Numzana, who had disappeared on personal affairs despite being scheduled to speak at the U.S. Peace Corps alumni dinner. I had a prepared speech, which was later published by the Peace Corps. The annual report was presented by a spokesman who marched onstage like a U.S. Marine Corps officer with his crewcut hair and his clicking heels slapping the floor in a military cadence. That led me to make a more personal introduction about our perceptions of the role of the Peace Corps.

My remarks were based on *The Ugly American,* the famous novel by William J. Lederer and Eugene Burdick. I said that the Peace Corps seemed to many of us to have multiple functions. It was not only an internal U.S. ideological tool to convince young Americans of their country's essential "goodness" but also an instrument to make America look good in the eyes of the people of countries in which they were waging wars. It seemed also to be a way of inserting their intelligence agents into numerous countries. I said that was our perception. I was pleasantly surprised that the audience acknowledged that as fair comment. I said, however, that I had met many people during my visits to their country and had to acknowledge that these young Americans had themselves been educated with a better understanding and tolerance for people of other countries and their different cultures, rather than wishing to impose their own culture and values on the people of those countries. Their response to our call for support against apartheid was indeed proof of that. Once again I was compelled to recognize the dangers of simple stereotypes that could drive supporters away from us. I am reminded that many people, young and old, from many sections of society, whom I met in many places, gave us and our struggle for freedom direct and indirect support that in the end helped change the U.S. government's attitude to the ANC and the struggle against apartheid.

I had always admired Harry Belafonte as a singer and actor. Then I got to know him as a political activist who supported the struggle for liberation in South Africa. He was active in pushing through the boycott of South Africa in the fields of arts and culture. I "met" him over the air when Nelson Mandela made his first visit to the United States. A radio journalist in New York, a Mr. Marks, who had interviewed me a number of times on a local Pacifica Radio Station, called me in London and patched me through to Harry, who was on the tarmac awaiting Nelson's arrival. We chatted about the significance of the visit and the marvel that it was actually taking place. I met Harry in the flesh later at the Vanguard Foundation's twenty-first-anniversary celebration in San Francisco. He was the keynote speaker and I sat at his table. He spoke of a "fire in the house," implying that even though the civil rights movement had achieved a great deal, the economic and social situations of many African Americans had worsened, and he was really making a call to concerted action to change things around. I also met Whoopi Goldberg, who spoke, and spoke strongly, about African Americans allowing themselves to be beaten down by their history. At that event I met Joan Baez and had the opportunity to tell her how much her records had entertained us and given us hope in prison.

One of the things that struck me, and it should have been obvious to me, is the huge diversity of opinions held by Americans, despite the massive daily indoctrination with conservative ideas about everything from health care, civil rights, employment, and unemployment to the right to education. Wherever I went there were significant groups of people who rejected the dominant conservatism of both major political parties, Republicans and Democrats. It was exciting to find kindred spirits in so many places.

Much later, in 1994, shortly before our first free elections, the ANC treasurer general, T. T. Nkobi, sent me on a fund-raising tour. My host, Robert Bennett, was a remarkable lawyer who had known and worked with our comrade Jeff Radebe. After 1994 Jeff became a minister in various capacities, mining, public enterprises, justice, and constitutional development, and most recently as minister in the presidency. Robert took me to see many people, including the Coca-Cola vice president for civic responsibility. As usual, I asked for two things: corporate support for our campaign (on this occasion for voter education) and his personal contribution. I was astonished by his cold response, which excluded any personal contribution, and the assertion that Coca-Cola in South Africa would perhaps consider the matter.

In Chicago Robert took me to meet with an ex–South African, the chairman of a strongly Zionist organization. I presented our case for the group's support for a voter education campaign. I thought I was getting somewhere until a man sitting quietly in the shadows asked me my personal opinion on Israeli-Palestinian politics. The upshot was that he lectured me on the need to tailor my beliefs to those of potential donors. There was no way he would allow the group to contribute, and so we got to his membership in the Jewish Defense League (JDL), and suddenly Jane Hunter's lessons on AIPACs and right-wing organizations became relevant. We had a terrific argument about the JDL's racist role in relation to anti-apartheid campaigning. To end matters, they told me rather triumphantly, as though playing their trump card, that they had invited Mr. Mandela to a rally in Chicago and had relayed this through the consulate of apartheid South Africa in Chicago. Their arrogance really angered me. They thought that they, a local sect, so to speak, could invite the future president of South Africa to a rally before he had made even a state visit to their country or any other country. As it happens, Nelson asked me about a state visit to Israel, and my advice was that as president he might find it necessary in the interests of the Palestinian people to visit Israel, but there were so many countries that had to come before that: the African frontline States, which had sacrificed so much for the freedom of South Africa; Eastern Bloc countries that had supported us in every way, financially, diplomatically, and through material, humanitarian, and military aid; and also countries where anti-apartheid movements had been strong and whose governments had ultimately exerted pressure on the apartheid regime to change its policies, even though their motive was to protect their investments rather than the freedom of our people.

Visits to Canada

In Canada there were also groups that had problems with the armed struggle. In the mid-1980s the Canadian section of the International Defence and Aid Fund (IDAF) as a matter of policy did not support people or their families if they had been involved in the armed struggle in South Africa. IDAF was founded by the Reverend John Collins of the Anglican Church in Britain. It gained support from allied organizations in Sweden, the Netherlands, India, and Canada. Sweden channeled extremely large sums of money into IDAF. Jojo Saloojee, the ANC chief representative in Canada, wanted me to avoid the issue of armed struggle. I insisted that I tackle it head-on throughout my tour of Canada. We could not run away from it, nor could we pretend it did not exist. Since I had just been released after twenty-two years in prison for being involved in that aspect of our struggle, I could not possibly back away from it. If we tried to do that, we would lose all credibility. We had to explain why we had undertaken the armed struggle.

In a couple of places newspaper editors who interviewed me really hammered away on the ANC policy of armed struggle. They reported what I had said quite accurately, however, but also put forward their own critical views. I met postgraduate history students who said that Canada's history was totally peaceful, and they therefore would not support terrorists like me and the ANC. I had had time in prison to read about Canada's history, and I knew some aspects of it better than they did. I asked them about such things as their treatment of the Native Canadian people, the people colonialists call Redskins. And what about wars fought in Europe by Canadian soldiers? What about a small armed uprising against the British in the early nineteenth century? I asked them to read newspapers with the same critical approach that their professors demanded of them when they read about the remote past. I added that we did not want their soldiers to free our country because they might not be called home again. What we did want was their political and financial support to put an end to a racist system of government. That approach found growing understanding and support, partly because I had been in the armed struggle, and I was talking about it rationally and with no bitterness about being imprisoned for so long. My approach was that just as the Canadian people and government had gone to war to defend liberty, so had we. These are things that sometimes you have to do in the name of liberty.

My last meeting of that tour was held in the National Arts Centre in Montreal. At the end of that meeting, the director of the National Arts Centre thanked me for coming to speak, and on behalf of them all, he wanted to thank "Co . . . com . . . comrade Denis." It was probably the first time he'd ever used the word. He struggled to say it, but in effect he said that Canadians understood and accepted our policies. That was good because he was a personal friend of Prime Minister Brian Mulroney and

Foreign Minister Joe Clark, who had stated their strong opposition to apartheid. I also had a breakfast meeting with the head of the South Africa desk of the Canadian Foreign Office, and that turned out to be very fruitful.

Three weeks after the end of my Canadian tour, the international director of IDAF, Horst Kleinschmidt, came back to London from the Annual General Meeting of the Canadian Defence and Aid Fund. He told me that the group had changed its policy and would now support the legal defense of people involved in the armed struggle and support their families. The members told him that I had explained the armed struggle to them and were satisfied there were valid reasons for it. Six months later the Canadian government made one million Canadian dollars available to organizations, including the Canadian Defence and Aid Fund, for projects with the ANC and others. I know that I did not do it on my own. A lot of work had been done, before and after, but I am also sure that having been imprisoned for participating in the armed struggle, and having come out of prison able to explain it in terms that people could understand, I got a good hearing.

It is also clear that it was the intensification of the struggle inside South Africa that was most influential in shaping people's views. The continuous resistance of unarmed black men, women, and children against the soldiers and police who patrolled the townships in their armored vehicles and arrested or acted with arbitrary brutality against protesters inspired international support against apartheid racism.

What was especially pleasing was that many of the people involved in solidarity in numerous countries began to recognize racism and inequalities in their own countries. Looking at far-off South African apartheid was like holding up a mirror in which they could see similar features in their own societies. On the east coast in Newfoundland, a burly construction worker of Native Canadian and Eskimo origins came after my talk to greet me and to send greetings to the people in South Africa because, he said, "What you said about the life of the South African people is what my life is like in Canada." Those similarities help explain why Canadian anti-apartheid activists took up the cause of discrimination against the Native Canadian people. I learned from them that in the 1940s, South African and Canadian officials met to discuss how to deal with the "Native question" in their respective countries.

In Norway anti-apartheid activists took up the cause of the nomadic Lapp people, or Sami, who were being discriminated against, especially by power companies who wanted to force them off their ancestral nomadic grazing grounds to build hydropower plants. What alerted the activists was the media coverage in their own countries that mimicked South African racist talk of "lazy men who sat around drinking while women did the work" or of crime increasing when the herders returned to their winter quarters.

Our solidarity campaigning was not a one-way street in which we stood with political begging bowls.

In Sweden I was moved by a South African who grew up in Alexandra Township. He left the country, and, after qualifying as a doctor in the Soviet Union, he moved to Sweden, where he was in medical practice. He had arranged my lecture at the university that evening. He said, "Through your lecture you've helped me to understand my life under apartheid." I was touched because he accepted that I had really tried to understand at an emotional level what the life of black South Africans was like. The fight against apartheid was not just an intellectual exercise; one fought it passionately because it was an inhumane system. I found that there were too many of my comrades who would not give in to their emotions. They thought that because Marxism is a science of society that they were all scientists, and as scientists are unemotionally objective, they could ignore people's feelings.

Solidarity from Faith-based Communities

In several countries I was the guest of religious groups whose members were perceptive and tough campaigners against apartheid. For me as a South African that was quite fascinating. They were so different from churches in South Africa, which were divided by race. Most of the white church members in South Africa were indifferent to the suffering under apartheid. There were some opposition clerics, however. In 1985 an ecumenical group of forty-six South African theologians working in grassroots organizations produced the Kairos Document. "Kairos," the document explained, is a moment of crisis in which one has to reexamine one's beliefs, and that moment was at hand in South Africa. They approached the question of apartheid from the point of view of the poor and oppressed, and they came to a theologically based conclusion that apartheid is prophetically false and that the churches have to stand by the marginalized people to find a way forward in opposition to apartheid. They also came to the conclusion that there are circumstances in which it is legitimate to take up arms against a tyrannical system. When I addressed religious groups, I was careful to tell them that I am a freethinker, or rationalist, but I understood the theological arguments. Sometimes people would remark that I understood their beliefs better than they themselves did!

I gave a talk in a Unitarian theological seminary in Windsor, Ontario. I finished my talk and people were clearly very moved. The head of the institution had introduced me and now thanked me for coming to bear witness to my experience, and to the broader struggle against apartheid.

In West Germany (Federal Republic of Germany) there was a strong anti-apartheid movement of writers and dramatists and various kinds of social activists and progressive academics; religious groups were also deeply engaged. I spoke at many meetings from north to south and east to west and found really committed people at well-attended gatherings. Many acted out of conscience, following the lines of arguments found in the Kairos Document. They were often the same people who supported the worker priests in Latin American countries. I was a bit puzzled by this religious predominance until it was explained to me that in Germany the Lutheran and Catholic churches are supported by taxes, much like the concept of the biblical tithe. In exchange for this agreement with the state, the churches provide many social services; they are thus quasi state apparatuses and have an enormous social impact. That was very strange for those of us who had grown up with the idea of the separation of church and state as fundamental to democratic theory and practice. The German laity were strong in their financial support for our exile community in Tanzania, for example, and for the political work of our solidarity campaign.

It was important for us to experience the support of evangelical women, who were the main pillar of the fruit boycott, and the sharp criticism of the German government's and banks' support for apartheid. The crude approach of "anything goes provided we can make a profit" was abhorrent to progressive people. There were academics who actively propagated racist ideology in support of the apartheid regime, and they were confronted by our supporters. There was active support from the German War Resisters' Organization for young white South African war resisters who refused to undertake their military service in the occupation of the townships. These young whites had reached their personal "Kairos moments" of conscience and concluded they would defend our country against foreign invasion but would not be oppressors of our own citizens.

Of course, the intensity of the war in Angola and Mozambique, which took the lives of too many people, including young whites who were buried in the "Heroes Acres" of the white graveyards, had an influence on the development of their moral outlook. Those who remained in South Africa faced prison sentences of up to six years for refusing military service.

In Germany, as in other countries, there were people among the anti-apartheid campaigners who had problems with the armed struggle. I undertook a speaking tour that started in Munich, and, city by city, I wound my way up to Hamburg and Bremen. Quite early on I realized that I had to be very attentive to the translations my usually amateur interpreters were making. At a press conference I noticed the journalists looked a bit puzzled by what the interpreter said and listened very carefully to her. I repeated that our struggle rested on four pillars: legal politics, underground politics, the armed struggle, and international solidarity. She left out armed struggle. I repeated it and she did the same again. I asked her why she felt she could change what I was saying. She said that she was a member of Amnesty International and we could not have an armed struggle! I had just done twenty-two years in prison for just that, and she said it did not exist. I asked her to say what I said, in the same tone of voice as mine, and she started to argue with me. So I invited her to join the audience and we would ask someone else to be my interpreter. She translated properly thereafter. I had thought, after coming out of prison, that my thoughts would be free from control, but here was a supporter trying by underhanded ways to control my thoughts!

There were other forms of solidarity. The Soviet Union, German Democratic Republic, and other Eastern European countries gave us direct financial, diplomatic, material, and military assistance, without which our struggle would have been much less effective.

The Cuban example of international sacrifice and sympathy is an epic of liberation solidarity within the international struggle for freedom of oppressed peoples. It is akin to but much farther reaching than the International Brigades that fought for democracy in Spain in the 1930s. The Cuban contribution was enormous and, having assisted in the struggle for the recognition of Angolan sovereignty, Cuba had to withdraw all its forces once they had defeated the South African army at Cuito Cuanavale. The Soviet Union's contribution was enormous, too. The building of the radar network and the fighter aircraft protection, which gave Angola air superiority against South Africa, was crucial. And at a psychological level it was important in Southern Africa that white South Africans could be killed by bullets fired by black Africans and black Cubans. Being white did not make apartheid's soldiers bullet-proof.

Our ten thousand MK fighters in Angola were equally important because apartheid South Africa had to stop that force from returning as a combat formation to South Africa. Our forces could not have been sustained without the backing of the Soviet Union and Angola and Cuba. The United States wanted Cuba out of Africa and pressured apartheid South Africa to withdraw from Angola to achieve that goal.

I have to tell of a sacrifice by Mozambique in the struggle for Zimbabwe. What Mozambique gave up and what Zambia gave up for principle were enormous. Mozambique suffered massive casualties and destruction of its poorly developed infrastructure inherited from its colonial overlords. Zambia would not willingly trade through Zimbabwe on principle: that required that exports and imports go through South Africa, the shortest route through Mozambique having been closed. Zambia, with Chinese aid, built a railway line up through the north, through Tanzania to Dar es Salaam, which added enormously to the cost of transportation of imports and exports. In addition, this line could not handle the volume of traffic, which created major problems for the poor, developing country. What an enormous internationalist sacrifice that was.

Quite early on I was invited to Spain for two almost simultaneous events. The first was a six-hour television panel discussion program on Africa. The second was a visit as an ANC representative to the annual summer festival of *El Mundo Obrero* (Workers' World), a Communist Party newspaper. The TV program was interesting for me because the other panelists were diplomats and government officials who were careful not to say anything really significant other than that Africa is a corrupt continent; they had no idea who was paying the dirty money to bribe officials and governments to buy arms they did not need, for example. Clearly, they would not criticize themselves. The exception was the Angolan deputy minister of foreign affairs, Afonso van Dúnem. He and I signaled to each other below the level of the camera who would answer a particular point, especially when some of the European participants were too slanderous in their attacks on Africa; a diplomat such as he would have had difficulty in saying what had to be said. In the end, some of the Spanish officials said they did not really believe what they were saying but were just being the devil's advocate. Such a dishonest, dangerous game!

On the other hand, the television station put me up in a hotel opposite the Prado Museum. The hotel was luxurious and the carpets so thick it felt like wading through thick syrup to get to my room. The Prado had such wonderful paintings, which I had seen only as prints in books, and they glowed with life and passion. I loved the paintings of Francisco Goya for his representations of people's struggles.

The main boulevards of Madrid were very wide and flanked by buildings that looked as solid as fortresses. They were government ministry buildings, so strong that during the civil war heavy cannon could be mounted on the roofs to protect the fascist state set up by General Franco. There are, of course, also modern steel and glass buildings that look fragile in comparison. Those, I was told, are banks where money is protected, and, judging by the architecture, it would seem that protecting money is far less important than protecting the state.

My television hosts provided me with a driver and a young woman interpreter. On inquiry, it turned out that neither of them knew anything about the civil war in which the Franco fascists overthrew the elected social democratic government. They could not take me to the Ebro River or to the University City, where key battles were fought. They did take me to the *El Mundo Obrero* fête. It fascinated me that at that time such a festival would be the main summer attraction for two million people—and finance the Communist Party newspaper for a whole year. It was a burning-hot summer's day, and I stopped at the first stall to try to buy something cold to drink. My driver and interpreter introduced me as the comrade from South Africa who had spent twenty-two years in prison. "Oh, twenty-two years," remarked a man a bit older than I. That woman sitting there, he told me, she had thirty-two years, another only thirty years, and so on, until I inquired how long he had been inside, and he apologized that it had been only twenty-five years. There they were, in the new conditions after Franco's successors had been ousted, doing their bit for the internationalist revolution. Such principled, determined people have to be respected.

At a Cuban stall I was at last offered something cool and tall to drink. It was very fruity and delicious, and I downed it with relish to quench my thirst. My hosts observed me closely and offered me another, which I drank down just as quickly. Some chitchat in Spanish followed, and one asked me in English if I was okay. "Yes, sure, why should I not be okay? I was just too hot." Well, they said, "You have had two Cuba Libres." "Ah, si, Cuba Libre, does that mean Cuba is free?" No, not exactly, though it is a drink of free Cuba. Only after the third drink was half gone did I detect a slight blurring of my vision and then heard that the drink is not a straight fruit drink but one with a hefty slug of rum in it. Let me say that I had a high old time for the rest of the afternoon, and the rum seemed to have burned out the incipient runny tummy I thought was developing in the heat.

Most of the stalls were established by regional organizations of the Spanish Communist Party; each specialized in its own regional cuisine and handicrafts. I still have mementos and plates given to me by internationalist supporters of our struggle against apartheid in South Africa. Not being sure what customs officers would think, I actually scraped off the words *Parti Communist* from an earthenware plate. I did not feel I was ready yet to face interrogation. I should have realized I was not in South Africa, where such a plate could have got me ten years in prison.

Now, as I write in 2009, the Spanish government, under pressure from families and their organizations, are beginning to exhume the graves of the "disappeared," who were often buried in mass graves. The young people will, I hope, learn their history in the schools so that they can at least know what they have to avoid in the future.

The year 1987 was a turning point in Southern Africa. At Cuito Cuanavale, in eastern Angola, the final face-off took place from January to March when Cuban and Angolan military forces together confronted the South African forces and Jonas Savimbi's UNITA. It was the greatest battle on the African continent since the end of World War II. With it, the military conflict between liberation movements backed by the Eastern Bloc and NATO-backed oppressors came to an end. The South African army that had marched into Angola with the backing of the United States in 1975 had to withdraw. In 1988, one month before the end of Reagan's presidency, the three-party treaty that ensured Namibia's independence was signed in New York by Angola, Cuba, and South Africa. The treaty provided for the withdrawal of all Cuban military personnel within thirty months. The left-wing, ANC-friendly government in Angola remained in office, and our cause had won.

In the first year and a half there was so much excitement that I hardly noticed how exhausted I was. When the chance of a solidarity holiday at Yalta in the Soviet Union arose, Ez and I leapt at it. The Soviets' situation was quite desperate, as Gorbachev's attempts to reform the system to make it work foundered. Department stores had no goods to sell. Officials had special shops where they could buy goods that the general public could not buy, and there were the usual excesses by the overzealous that exacerbated the problems and did not solve them. But they certainly went out of their way to look after us. What was surprising after our return to London was that Ez was the one who told our friends that the Soviet people really were peace-loving and wanted good, friendly relations with other countries. We watched the Friendship Games in Moscow and saw how sports, athletics, and especially mass gymnastics were employed not just to demonstrate athletic prowess but also to develop the health of young people.

In 1990 the apartheid regime had to take account of the winds of change and released Nelson Mandela. During a further four difficult years of transition, when the long-envisaged negotiations between the ANC and the white minority government took place, the reactionary forces drifted close to starting a civil war. At last, in 1994, Nelson Mandela became the first black president of South Africa.

The Scottish AAM joined with the U.K. AAM in a new organization, Action for Southern Africa (ACTSA), after Nelson Mandela became president in 1994. Scottish ACTSA seemed more dynamic than the U.K. ACTSA because in Scotland the organization addressed the people, whereas in London its role became one of lobbying government, and that left little space for its members to be active. Scottish ACTSA organized two tours to South Africa and asked me to accompany them. The first, in December 1994, was especially moving. Brian Filling was the main coordinator, and John Nelson was quietly in the background organizing and recording the events for future reports. It was great for me to be a friend, companion, and a kind of host to my comrades who had contributed so much to the freedom of my country. I think the tourists gained a deeper understanding of what apartheid had done to our people and found it far worse than they had imagined.

In Cape Town we toured the Parliament buildings, and I was able to show them the porch of the Tuynhuis, the official residence cum office of the president, where Nelson Mandela, a prisoner and future president, and President P. W. Botha took tea together as they discussed the future of South Africa.

17

T-Shirts, Music, and More Solidarity

In the months after I started my incessant round of speaking engagements in 1985, I found that there was a wonderful array of T-shirts, badges and buttons, posters, and pamphlets available from the Anti-Apartheid Movement in Britain. There were many well-researched publications on economic policy, on starvation wages, and on the multiplicity of ways that race laws affected the lives of the people and published studies that showed South Africa's vulnerability to economic sanctions.

The British Anti-Apartheid Movement had also carried through O. R. Tambo's "Release Mandela" international support campaign based on Mandela's "I Am Prepared to Die" speech in the Rivonia Trial. It was a successful campaign that caught the imagination of many people. Mandela's name was better known than that of the ANC.

We in the ANC worked hard to focus on the ANC-led alliance of ANC, SACP, and trade unions rather than focusing only on a personality. Some anti-apartheid supporters in Britain and other countries felt that any and every element and faction was equally worthy of support. We were certain that all our efforts had to be concentrated in support of the ANC, not simply because it was the oldest and largest organization inside South Africa, but also because through the Freedom Charter it appealed to and offered guarantees for the place of all South Africans in the free country we envisaged.

In our Europe-wide campaign we often found ourselves in conflict with the splintered left organizations in those countries. Governments in several Western countries, using the age-old tactic of divide and rule, sought to make use of the various South African exile groups, including the Black Consciousness Movement, the Pan Africanist Congress, and especially Chief Mongosuthu Gatsha Buthelezi's Inkatha Freedom Party, originally a Zulu cultural movement, to counter the ANC. It was one thing to support those groups in Europe against the ANC, but they financed Inkatha inside South Africa, and that led to the deaths of thousands of Africans who refused to support Chief Buthelezi.

The powerful political forces of governments and corporations wanted to weaken and control us to protect their corporate holdings and political interests in their former colonies, and South Africa was the key to Southern Africa and the continent. We were caught up, like it or not, in the Cold War between the West and the Soviet bloc and had to rely on the international support of people and their organizations in Britain and the West in general, but not their governments, which opposed the ANC. Oliver Tambo during this period was brilliant in maintaining a principled position between East and West that upheld the concepts of the Freedom Charter against pressures from every side.

I set about convincing my comrades that one way to establish our presence more widely in the mass consciousness of the British people was to produce and sell our own specifically ANC materials to our supporters. In the 1980s all kinds of progressive parties and organizations, such as the peace movement, relied on slogans on T-shirts for publicity. T-shirts were fashion items among the youth, and "youth culture" was a growing opportunity to gain the support of people as human carriers of our message: support the ANC against apartheid. First we produced T-shirts promoting the ANC in general, and then the ANC Women's League and the Youth League. The T-shirts were followed by buttons, flags, badges, caps, and jewelry. Then as now, I preferred and remain committed to issue-driven politics rather than personality-driven campaigns because of the dangers to a democratic future inherent in a cult of personality.

We developed an ever-expanding range of shirts and other memorabilia that I took with me wherever I spoke in public. We were helped by a supportive group of T-shirt printers who were the adult children of Greek and Cypriot activists who had resisted British rule and then their own colonels' regime. Slowly the idea of a mail-order service we called ANCSA (ANC of South Africa) Merchandise was born. Gill Marcus of the ANC's Department of Information and Publicity designed and produced simple and effective catalogues for us. The range of goods kept growing to include sterling silver pendants of our MK Warrior, our logo on high-quality enamel badges, brooches, earrings, watches, coffee mugs, and pens until we were shipping more than £110,000 (about $250,000) in goods a year. The apparent loss each year of about £10,000 was good value for a large amount of publicity that showed in a very public way people's identification with the ANC as the leader of the struggle against apartheid. Our best sales representative in the United States was Vicki Erenstein, who declared that she was the "queen of the ANC's rag trade." That small loss also covered my subsistence as a full-time activist.

One of my more delightful moments was giving O. R. Tambo our enamel logo badge. He insisted that he must have more of them in presentation boxes, immediately, in numbers to take with him on a trip to visit heads of government in the Caribbean. Frene Ginwala, a South African journalist and full-time adviser to Tambo, was in his party on that trip, and she told me that he enjoyed giving them to prime ministers as tokens of appreciation and explaining to them the symbolism of our logo: the four-spoke wheel of the 1955 Congress of the People, each spoke representing a national group—African, Coloured, Indian, and white—bound together in a wheel representing the unity of the Congress Alliance, out of which comes a fist holding a spear together with a shield, which represent both the historic resistance against colonial conquest and *Umkhonto we Sizwe,* the shield and spear of our people; above these flies the ANC flag and its bands of black for the oppressed people, green for the fertile land, and gold for the mineral wealth beneath our soil.

Making the ANC known was important for fund-raising too. As the situation inside South Africa heated up, greater media coverage brought home to the British and the international public the need to support our movement. Sylvester Stein, a South African who had emigrated to Britain in the 1950s, approached our office to offer his services for fund-raising. I knew him well from the 1940s in Cape Town, when he was often a visitor in our home. I was asked to supervise his efforts to ensure that whatever was written and published through the unit he established outside our office did not distort our basic political policies. He and his daughter Lyndall became very effective indeed at raising funds through advertisements placed in the *Guardian* and *Observer* newspapers. There were occasional full-page advertisements in the *Observer* that listed hundreds of signatories supporting the demand for the release of Nelson Mandela. Sylvester financed the operation until it could sustain itself and guaranteed the ANC against loss should there be an inadequate response.

Sylvester found a marvelous copywriter who, through draft after draft, managed to encompass our policies in only three hundred words. The responses were so great that Anazora Tikly, daughter of Mohammed Tikly, our education secretary, was taken on to assist Lyndall. Not only did I have to ensure the political integrity of our fund-raising materials, but I also had to protect the unit from comrades in our office who, though they did not have enough time to do all the work that needed to be done, felt they had to have their say on every minor detail of the fund-raising, too. I am delighted that Anazora developed into a successful fund-raiser in her own right through the experience of working with Sylvester and Lyndall. The fund-raising unit also needed a full-time IT assistant to handle their growing database, and Sylvester found a British supporter who did a very good job of it at a time when electronic data processing was a relatively new thing.

Each advertisement gave donors a set of check boxes where they could indicate what they wanted their donation to be used for: education, welfare, medical care, or humanitarian needs. Every so often donors would write across their coupons, "Use it for armed struggle." We had to ignore that, of course, because involvement in that aspect of our struggle would have upset the U.K. government and jeopardized our stay in Britain. The London office of the ANC was the key communications center for ANC representatives in many countries throughout the world.

Secretary General Alfred Nzo was in London when our first advertisement was to appear. We wanted his signature on it. He looked at the draft copy and immediately started to add our usual harsh adjectives that would make the copy too long to fit into the space available. I explained the need for brevity. He asked if the copy was okay. I said it was and he responded by signing it.

Wolfie Kodesh raised large sums of money through prize drawings. He found donors of prizes ranging from holidays in exclusive resorts to electronic appliances and systems, music instruments, and the like. Tens of thousands of pounds poured in. That created a bookkeeping problem for us, and, because we were short-staffed, I suspect that some money was lost through pilferage.

It fascinated me that we had many exiled musicians in London. Generally, when they performed at a concert to raise funds, they would do so without charging a performance fee. There were, however, rehearsal fees and meals and transport and refreshments. Some local authorities, such as Islington and Camden, offered their halls free of charge; some even paid for the advertising. Yet we would lose money on the events, even though they were politically a great success in bringing exiles and Londoners together. On the other hand, I saw the effective fund-raising done by the Anti-Apartheid Movement Netherlands (AABN), which provided platforms for emerging bands in an era of socially relevant rock-and-roll music. They nurtured a number of bands that made it to the big time.

In Britain Artists against Apartheid held a Freedom Festival on Clapham Common in South London. It was phenomenal: 100,000 people took part in the march to the common. The audience numbered 250,000. There was such a crush of people that underground railway stations were closed to prevent people being pushed onto the tracks by the pressure of the crowds behind them. The Metropolitan Police put the number who attended at a few tens of thousands! Jerry Dammers and Dali Tambo, the founders of Artists against Apartheid, worked tirelessly to make it the success it was. The crowds came to hear the musicians express their solidarity with the people of Namibia and South Africa through their words and music. Speakers from the ANC, SWAPO (South-West African People's Organisation), and the British Anti-Apartheid Movement (AAM) addressed the crowd. Alienated black British musicians played a leading role in the event, and anti-apartheid activity served the much wider purpose of trying to overcome racism in general.

In the United States, Artists United against Apartheid was formed in 1985 by Steven Van Zandt as a protest group. They produced the song "Sun City" and the album *Sun City* that year when Danny Schechter, a journalist who was then working with ABC News' *20/20* program, suggested turning the song into "a song about change not charity, freedom not famine." These artists also vowed never to perform at Sun City, a resort in Bophuthatswana, because to do so would in their minds seem to be an acceptance of apartheid.

It was astonishing to see entertainers who so often avoid controversy that might alienate any part of their potential audiences take a strong stand against racism. Our struggle benefited as we showed the influence of the nonracial policies of the ANC-led alliance on attitudes far beyond our shores. Danny Schechter made a fresh and exciting music video of a performance of the song "Sun City" using triple split screens and cuts made on the beat.

The most famous of the concerts was the first Mandela concert at Wembley Stadium in London on 11 June 1988, mounted on behalf of the British AAM. It was a great success in every way. It had a television audience of 600 million people in more than sixty countries. I went to the stadium but was so tired I went home to watch it on television. It netted a lot of money for the Bishop Ambrose Reeves Trust, which supported the AAM—which doubled its membership in one month. Many of the artists who performed the "Sun City" rock number performed at Wembley. "Free Nelson Mandela" became a song widely known around the world.

For us in the ANC it was a strange new feeling to be part of a movement that had such popular appeal. In London I took part in a march soon after I arrived there. Marching in the front row, I felt very vulnerable. Our march was flanked by policemen who, from the exchanges I overheard, were indeed concerned about protecting us. What a strange thing to experience! I also saw the police attacking marches of striking British miners and print workers. It seems democratic rights have their limits, too.

The second Mandela concert at Wembley, on 16 April 1990, was interesting because he was by this time free and was to appear at Wembley. There was enormous excitement. The promotion company that had mounted the Free Mandela Concert were again called on. This time some ANC comrades were included in the organizing committee. Any surplus was to go to an election-education fund in South Africa to prepare our millions of people who had never been allowed to vote in an election to know what to do. I was told by an ANC comrade involved in the promotion that the concert made no surplus, and I gathered it had lost money. Some of the enthusiasm of the 1980s activist rockers had evaporated.

I was involved in a peripheral way. A group of promoters was working with me to create a line of sports and leisure shoes carrying Nelson Mandela's signature. We had, with their help, made a T-shirt that portrayed Mandela as a boxer and included his signature. We auctioned it at a launch event my promoter friends had organized. John Barnes, a Liverpool and England footballer, bought it for £1,000. Now these promoters offered to ensure that the latest Mandela concert would yield big bucks for our movement. They made an offer to deposit £1,000,000 into a trust account as an upfront payment, which indicated how big the music industry was. Any profit beyond that amount would be split, 85 percent going to us and 15 percent going to them. They were prepared to pay the existing promoter for all his expenses up to that time, keep him in the team, but take over the promotion. Such sums of money boggled my mind. They told me that erecting the stage structure at Wembley alone would cost as much as building a five-bedroom, multistory house in North London. The stage would then be decorated and artists' lounges provided for a similar sum of money. The word in the music service industry was that the "gravy train was rolling." Naturally, I wanted to know how the promoters could offer such a large guaranteed payment. They said that music companies spend fortunes to get their current top performers to headline such concerts. I refrained from asking if they were over- or under-the-table payments. I asked my ANC comrades who were involved if there was any way in which we could negotiate such a deal to guarantee the profit. They assured me everything was under control and there was nothing more I could do.

The concert was a political success. Nelson Mandela appeared to wild acclaim. His tribute to O. R. Tambo, his friend, law partner, and political comrade, was incredibly moving and well justified. Tambo had held our movement together for thirty years and achieved a successful first step on the road to democracy.

For me there was a charming moment before the concert when I met a radical Conservative MP at a reception for visiting South Africans. He said it was a pity that Mr. Mandela was not planning to see Prime Minister Thatcher during his visit to Britain. My response was that such a visit is not something like casually dropping in for afternoon tea. Important visits of that kind are prepared for long in advance. Furthermore, I said, Mr. Mandela was really coming not to Britain but to Wembley because that stadium provided a platform from which he could address the world. Wembley happened to be in Britain and was an exceptional venue for a concert, which was the realization of the goal of the earlier Free Mandela Concert at Wembley. Therefore, there was no rebuff of any kind. He was impressed and said he would inform the governing Conservative Party's central office immediately. I thought that such quick thinking qualified me for a diplomatic post! I watched the concert from home and enjoyed it very much.

In the mid-1990s, Jan Braun, a German student doing his doctorate in molecular biology at the Glasgow Caledonian University, proposed me

The inner facade of the Pretoria Local Prison.

G 371

REPUBLIEK VAN SUID-AFRIKA· REPUBLIC OF SOUTH AFRICA

DEPARTEMENT VAN GEVANGENISSE · PRISONS DEPARTMENT

VRYLATINGSERTIFIKAAT · RELEASE CERTIFICATE

BEWYS VAN VRYLATING VAN 'N GEVANGENE UIT   GEVANGENIS OP
PROOF OF RELEASE OF A PRISONER FROM ...... SECURITY PRISON ON   85·02·28

1. Naam
   Name ..... DENIS THEODORE GOLDBERG .....

2. Ras   3. Identiteitsnommer   4. Datum van vonnis
   Race ... WHITE ...   Identity number ... 330407202001   Date of sentence .. 1964-06-12

5. Hof en plek van vonnis
   Court and place of sentence: ... SUPREME COURT OF SOUTH AFRICA PRETORIA

6. Misdryf
   Crime ..... SABOTAGE ....

7. Vonnis
   Sentence ... IMPRISONMENT FOR LIFE

8. (a) *Magtiging   gevangene   is deur die Administrasieraad te
     Authority No ....   dated ....   was issued by the Administration Board at ..... verleen dat die oud-gevangene na .....   mag terugkeer.
     the ex-prisoner to return to .....

   (b) *Die oud-gevangene is gelas om na .....   wat sy tuisdistrik is, terug te keer.
      The ex-prisoner was instructed to return to ..... which is his home district.

 * Skrap wat nie van toepassing is nie/Delete whichever is not applicable.   B.O./P.T.O.

My release certificate.

G 371

9. Materiële bystand:
   Material assistance:

   (a) Gratifikasie   Maaltye   Privaat kontant
      Gratuity R .....   Meals R .....   Private cash R 1823·11

   (b) Klerasie en artikels in besit
      Clothing and articles in possession ... ONE BAG OF CLOTHING

   (c) Gereedskap
      Tools .....

   (d) Treinkaartjie na
      Train ticket to .....

   (e) Ander   AIR TRANSPORT TO TEL AVIV
      Other .....

10. Aanbeveling (t.o.v. Swart oud-gevangenes)
    Recommendation (in respect of Black ex-prisoners)

   Daar word aanbeveel dat die oud-gevangene vrygestel word van die betaling van belasting vir die tydperk wat
   It is recommended that the ex-prisoner be exempted from the payment of tax for the period he/she has been
   hy/sy in gevangesetting was .....
   incarcerated.

              1985-02 .....

Kantoorstempel   PRETORIA   Hoof van die gevangenis
Office stamp   SECURITY PRISON   Head of the prison
         HEAD OF THE PRISON

Neil, Denis, and Hillary Kuny with me at Johannesburg International Airport after my release on 28 February 1985 (Hillary [Kuny] Hamburger collection).

Hillary and me at Johannesburg International Airport, 28 February 1985, before my departure into exile (Hillary [Kuny] Hamburger collection).

I am reunited with Esmé and Hilary at Ben Gurion Airport, Tel Aviv, 28 February 1985.

Delivering my first speech after arriving at Kibbutz Mayan Baruch. Herut Lapid is next to me.

O. R. Tambo, the ANC president who received me in Lusaka at ANC Headquarters after my release (Robben Island Collection, Mayibuye Centre, University of the Western Cape).

At home with Esmé in London,
March 1985.

Hilary (Hilly) Goldberg, 1981.

With my son, David Goldberg,
in London, 1985.

With Anne Mitchell, of the Canada Defence and Aid Fund, in the Rocky Mountains.

With my grandchildren, Jane, Katie, and Jack, circa 1994.

At a lecture in Sacramento, California, I hold a model of a U.S. antipersonnel mine widely used in Angola and Mozambique against the Popular Movement for the Liberation of Angola (MPLA) and the Mozambique Liberation Front (Frelimo) (photo by Ivor Markham).

"Mayibuye Afrika" at Ostersund, Sweden, December 1985.

An antiracism conference at Ferramonti, Calabria, Italy: "Walls torn down; walls still to be torn down." I am at the far left.

With Gillian Nilsson in Lund, Sweden, at a meeting organized by the Workers' Education Association (ABF).

With Madame le Maire Janine Thomas, naming Place Nelson Mandela at Les Clayes-sous-Bois (near Paris), September 1989.

Archie Sibeko and Chris Hani in Lusaka after my release (Robben Island Collection, Mayibuye Centre, University of the Western Cape).

Ray Alexander Simons, who was always an inspiration (Robben Island Collection, Mayibuye Centre, University of the Western Cape).

T. T. Nkobi, ANC treasurer general, who was always known as Comrade T.G. (Robben Island Collection, Mayibuye Centre, University of the Western Cape).

Joe Slovo, the general secretary of SACP and cofounder of MK (Robben Island Collection, Mayibuye Centre, University of the Western Cape).

Eddie Funde in 2008, when he was the ambassador to Germany. He is now retired.

Flowers in the Altstad (old town) in Siegen, Germany.

At a protest against the manufacture of German submarines for the apartheid regime (photo by Don Etkins).

(Right) The logo of Community H.E.A.R.T.

(Below) A visit with members of the ANC at the Constituency Office, Hout Bay, circa 2009.

With the South African delegation to the Woodcraft Folk International Camp, 1995 (courtesy of Kate Lewis).

Students visiting from Osnabrück, Germany, and Belhar, Cape Town, at my home in Hout Bay, Cape Town (photo by Wolfgang Bieler-Kentsch).

Walter Sisulu with Arthur Goldreich and me shortly before Walter passed away.

Old MK comrades Alfred Willie Sippetto and Sandile Sejake return with me to the campsite at Mamre (photo by T. Krehwinkel).

Meeting up with Govan Mbeki in London, circa 1993.

With Oscar Mpetha, November 1990.

With O. R. Tambo in 1990 in Sweden
(ANC photograph).

With Mac Maharaj, who was
convicted in the Little Rivonia Trial,
in November 1990.

With Zoli Malindi, November
1990.

Arndt Hopfmann and I present a
copy of *Der Staat gegen Mandela,*
Edelgard's German translation of
Joel Joffe's book on the Rivonia
Trial, to Nelson Mandela,
December 2006.

Ronnie Kasrils and I at a memorial for Edelgard (photo by Konrad Hochhold).

With Archbishop Trevor Huddleston and Jan Hoogendyk, a longtime comrade who was terminally ill but lived to see freedom, 1994.

With Henry Makgothi, one of the accused in the 1956 Treason Trial, July 1994.

Wolfie Kodesh, my oldest comrade and dear friend (Robben Island Collection, Mayibuye Centre, University of the Western Cape).

Mandela veterans' party, Johannesburg, from left: Mandela, Hillary and Tony Hamburger, Thabo Mbeki, myself, and Edelgard (behind Mbeki).

My marriage to Edelgard at the Registry Office, 12 April 2002.

Edelgard and I with Ronnie Kasrils at the Dortmund, Germany, launch of her German translation of his book *Armed and Dangerous* [*Stechbrieflich gesucht*], 1997.

Reading biographical notes at the Zentrum für Aktion, Kultur und Kommunikation (ZAKK) in Düsseldorf with Edelgard and Lutz Reinhardt, chairman of ZAKK, 1996.

Michael Rice and Ruth Fischer-Rice (Bram Fischer's son-in-law and daughter) and me with Ahmed Kathrada, November 2008.

Rivonia Trial comrades Ahmed Kathrada, Andrew Mlangeni, Nelson Mandela, and me in 2009 (courtesy of the Nelson Mandela Foundation).

From left: Ahmed Kathrada, Richard Stengel, Arthur Chaskalson, Nelson Mandela, George Bizos, Laloo Chiba, Zweledinga Pallo Jordan, and me in 2008 (courtesy of the Nelson Mandela Foundation).

(Above left) Professor Dave Walsh nominated me for an honorary LL.D., awarded by Glasgow Caledonian University (courtesy of Glasgow Caledonia University). *(Above right)* Chancellor Dr. Ephraim Mokgokong confers on me an honorary Ph.D. from the Medical University of South Africa (courtesy of the Medical University of South Africa).

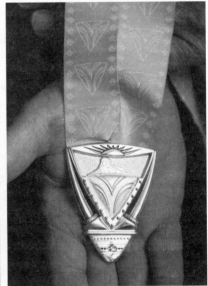

(Above left) At the University of South Africa's Special Graduation Ceremony, 21 June 2003 (courtesy of the University of South Africa). *(Above right)* The silver medal of the Order of Luthuli (photo by M. Willman).

Happy at home (photo by M. Willman).

President Kgalema Motlanthe presenting me with the Order of Luthuli (Silver), 2009 (courtesy of GCIS).

Dieter W. Haller, the German ambassador to South Africa, invests me with the Cross of the Federal Order of Merit (*Verdienstkreuz am Bande*), 2010. My granddaughters, Katie and Jane, were in attendance (courtesy of the German Embassy).

At the botanical garden, Kuala Lumpur, Malaysia.

A copy of the diary I kept of Bram Fischer's illness.

and campaigned for me to be elected as the honorary president of the GCU Students Association. I addressed the annual Burns Night Dinner to honor the great Scottish nationalist and internationalist poet Robert Burns. In true Scottish fashion, having taken sufficient whisky, I sang "Auld Lang Syne" in Zulu.[1] I also read aloud a poem, "Freedom Come All Ye" by the modern internationalist poet Hamish Henderson. He opens the poem with the statement (in a translation from the dialect) that there is a strong wind blowing throughout the great valley of the world. But it is more than a wind. It is an idea that people can live in freedom and the rich exploiters will be overcome. The lines that particularly appeal to me are the ones that say that the great vision we have shall be realized and "all the bairns of Adam, will have breid and barley bree, and paintit room" (all the children of Adam will have bread and barley stew, and painted room). He is saying that hunger will be no more, and everyone will have somewhere decent to live. Then people all over the world will no longer fear "Scotland the Brave," meaning they will no longer fear the Scottish regiments that subjugated them to British imperialism. So they can all come home in freedom.

There were some highlights of this period of my life, and I share them here as little stories on their own.

My release was followed by that of Govan Mbeki. His was followed by those of Walter Sisulu, Ahmed Kathrada, Raymond Mhlaba, Elias Motsoaledi, Andrew Mlangeni, and Wilton Mkwayi, who was sentenced in the Little Rivonia Trial in December 1964 together with David Kitson, who joined us in prison, and others who were sent to Robben Island.

Moscow Border—No Visa, No Problem (or, To the Finland Station)

I was invited to an Afro-Asian People's Solidarity Organization (AAPSO) conference in Helsinki on apartheid South Africa's relations with Israel. The invitation to me came to the ANC office, but I was invited as an independent expert to make one of the keynote speeches.

The ANC chief representative instructed me to go to the Soviet consulate to arrange for my flight to Moscow, train to Helsinki, and back again. There, after the normal queuing and waiting, I was given an Aeroflot ticket and a voucher for the train from Moscow to Helsinki. Obviously, I was to go "To the Finland Station."[2] I asked about a visa and was told that it would take too long to get one, and I should simply go to Heathrow, where Aeroflot would know about me and make no difficulties about the lack of a visa. I had also been told that somebody from the Soviet Afro-Asian Solidarity Committee would meet me to take me from Sheremetyevo Airport outside Moscow to the railway station for the trip via Leningrad to Helsinki.

Everything went according to plan! I arrived in Moscow as scheduled and went to the Passport Control. There a young officer took my passport and compared the photograph with me. I could see his eyes flick from left ear to photograph, right ear to photograph, left nostril, right nostril, strong chin, high forehead, charming smile, and so on, and then . . . the one dreaded word: "Visum." "Er—um," I responded. "Do you speak English?" One word in Russian was the reply. From the accompanying gesture it clearly meant "wait."

After a few silent minutes a youngish officer, short like me, broad like me, but in uniform with the large Russian officer's peaked cap, advanced on me with hand outstretched and a warm smile. I had heard about false teeth made of stainless steel and now saw that in an unself-conscious person the smile really could be warm. Suddenly I felt less anxious because even though my papers weren't in order and there was not much time to retrieve my baggage and get to the Leningrad Station, I was officially there and I was met with friendliness. I explained why I was there, why I was in transit, and that there should be somebody from the Afro-Asian Solidarity Committee to meet me. I explained that I did not have any names or phone numbers, and though I had previously visited the committee and spoken to a number of the top people, my mind was a blank. He said he'd find out for me. All was calm and unthreatening. I was led to a soft-chaired waiting room. An elderly American couple was there, looking glazed, dazed, and anxious; they had clearly waited a longish time. It seemed, upon inquiry, that their visas were off by one day because of time zone changes or some such reason, and this needed to be clarified. On the basis of my treatment, I felt that they should not be anxious and all would be well. They seemed relieved that an English-speaking person was so relaxed, and they relaxed too. I do hope all turned out well for them, because my lieutenant arrived very soon with a sheet of paper with names and phone numbers of the Solidarity Committee people, and he said that somebody would be there very soon to assist me. My passport was stamped, or rather an insert sheet was stamped, and off I went.

Baggage collection was not so simple. Sending bags through on every belt but the one announced from time to time seemed to be part of the security arrangements, or perhaps it was just simple, innocent muddle. In any case, Soviet Ambassador Vassily Solodovnikov, emissary to countries in Central and Southern Africa (whom the West German media called "Moscow's Fist in Africa"), was also waiting, and he kept me company. He assured me that we would get to our train station in good time. My Solidarity Committee person arrived very late because the airport is a long way outside the city, but we piled into taxis and duly got to the Leningrad Station, the main station for departures to Leningrad and Helsinki.

Now the visa problem really reared its ugly head. A young woman lieutenant stopped me from boarding the train. Ticket, passport, visa, where are they? Of course, no visa! No way would I be allowed to board. The ambassador introduced himself and vouched for me. "Nyet!" No! The Solidarity Committee representative introduced herself and vouched for me. "Nyet!" I sympathized with the lieutenant and explained again what had happened, and, after all, the border guards at the airport had been instructed to let me through. "Nyet!" I felt that I was quite naive to think I could travel without proper papers.

A thirty-something man wearing white trousers and vest and white shoes stepped down from my carriage onto the platform. He looked like the bed maker on a South African train. He wandered around the circle of people appearing quite uninterested in what was happening. My companions began to speak more loudly in the face of the obstinate and unmoving young lieutenant. Her pretty face was flushed as we badgered her. She appeared to be quite deaf to all our arguments. Then I saw the train attendant catch her eye and nod very slightly. She appeared to pause for thought, and then, with a small smile and a small wave of her hand, she indicated that I should get aboard. Immediately thereafter, the train pulled away. What a wonderful observation post for the security officer in our part of the train! Mr. "White-trousers-and-vest" was clearly somebody significant.

The Soviet ambassador came to collect me and we drank tea from a samovar in his compartment, and so the journey passed rather pleasantly for me with an interesting discussion. I was struck by the huge size of the passenger cars on the broad-gauge track and by the fact that the ride was very smooth compared with the rocking, shuddering, and shaking of our narrower-gauge trains in South Africa.

Two hours before our arrival in Helsinki, the border-crossing process started on the train. Inspections of compartments and baggage, passports, and visas took place. For me: no visa, no problem. I arrived in Helsinki in time for the conference.

Meeting Walter Sisulu

Walter Sisulu was a highly respected leader of the liberation movement from way back. To millions of South Africans he was uTata (father). To me and those close to him he was Comrade Walter.

We had last seen each other when we were sentenced in the Rivonia Trial on 12 June 1964. Now, in 1989, we would meet again. He had been in the prison on Robben Island and, like Ahmed Kathrada and four others imprisoned for life, was released as a result of the changes in Southern Africa and the upheaval in Eastern Europe. The Cold War was over, and South Africa's white regime could no longer present itself as the bulwark against communism, or the opposition African National Congress as the fifth column of world communism.

To meet Walter, I had flown to Stockholm from London to attend a dinner given in honor of Walter and others. We arrived directly from the airport, together with Archbishop Trevor Huddleston, Sipho Pityana, Horst Kleinschmidt, Billy Masetlha, Mendi Msimang, and a few others. As we walked into the large room where the dinner was being held, there was a series of embraces and handshakes. Andrew Mlangeni and Elias Motsoaledi came out from behind their tables. As we embraced there were many cries: "Is it really you, Denis?" "Is it really you, Andrew?" "Really you, Elias?" These were repeated as I met Govan Mbeki, Wilton Mkwayi, and Raymond Mhlaba. There was a welling over, an eruption, of emotion on meeting these comrades with whom I'd shared so much during our trial and afterward, even though we were separated by a thousand miles in segregated prisons for so many years. Sipho commented that he'd never before witnessed such emotion.

Eventually I made my way over to Walter Sisulu, saying, "Walter, I must touch you." Holding out his hand he replied, "And I must touch you, Denis." We held hands while he asked me, after twenty-five years, how we had been caught. That was his first question!

I replied that I thought we'd been betrayed by Bruno Mtolo, but I wanted to recall what had happened just before we had arrived at the Rivonia farm on the day of our arrest, 11 July 1963. On the way in the minibus, one of my comrades asked what we should name the new ten-acre farm that we had bought near Krugersdorp. I suggested that we should call it SHUFISA. "What's it mean?" several had responded. It sounded African but it wasn't a real word, they said. I explained that during World War II General Eisenhower name his headquarters SHAEFE—Supreme Headquarters Allied Expeditionary Forces in Europe. Ours should be Supreme Headquarters United Front in South Africa. This was greeted with gusts of laughter but, "Walter, you said that you weren't sure that it was correct to speak about a united front at that time! But I want to tell you that now, twenty-six years later, we do have a united front!" He laughed out loud and almost in wonderment asked if I could really remember what had happened on that day just before we had been arrested.

Among all the great leaders of the liberation movement, he was acknowledged by all, including Nelson Mandela, as the one who always reminded us of the concept of unity in action. He believed in and lived this principle and always found ways of drawing people together to achieve the end of racism in South Africa.

Walter's greatest attribute was his ability to transcend so much difficulty in his early life—the rejection that so many young men experience in their families, for him intensified by his white father's denial of his son, who was raised by his mother, a domestic worker, and his Gogo, or Granny—to become an adult who genuinely embraced everybody in his vision. He was a person who was at ease with himself. He did not need adulation and high office to feel that he was recognized. He knew within himself the value of his contribution as a great political architect of our new South Africa that would have a place for all who lived in it.

It was not any different when I first met him in Cape Town at a secret meeting during September 1962, when he and Nelson Mandela traveled around the country together after the stay-at-home in 1961. There we discussed the state of the campaign to end apartheid and the need to introduce armed struggle as a politically directed campaign against the white supremacist government—but not against whites as such. That view was the expression of Sisulu's understanding of unity in action and the Freedom Charter adopted in 1955 at Kliptown, which in its preamble said, "South Africa belongs to all who live in it, black and white. That now sounds like a very mild expression, but at the time it was a revolutionary concept. The Freedom Charter's epilogue states, "These freedoms we shall fight for together side by side all our lives, sparing neither strength nor courage, until we have won our liberty." That is what Walter Sisulu lived up to all his life, including the time of the trial that followed the arrests at Rivonia, the twenty-six years in prison, and the years thereafter.

In the weeks before our arrest on 11 July 1963 at Liliesleaf Farm in Rivonia, we had lived together with Govan Mbeki, Raymond Mhlaba, and Wilton Mkwayi, organizer and leader from the Eastern Cape. Walter was an undemanding companion to share a house with. He seemed always lost in thought, always analytical but always good-humored. He was not a dogmatic person. He preferred to convince you of his views by rational argument and analysis. He did not ever demand acceptance because he was the leader. Yet we knew that he should be, indeed had to be, consulted over just about every significant decision, and we did it willingly because he was always worth listening to. Walter Sisulu was worried about me, a young man of thirty living the restricted life of an underground activist. He insisted I visit safe friends, the Sepel family, who had been his host family underground, to play squash or just to visit. He of course warned me to ensure that I was not followed back to Travallyn.

During a moment of privacy in Stockholm, Walter's caring concern showed when he asked about the Sepels' children, whom he hadn't seen in nearly thirty years. He had been very fond of them, and he hoped that their connection to him through the family's protecting him all those years ago had not caused them too many problems.

During my last real conversation with Walter Sisulu, some months before he passed away in May 2003, I thanked him for teaching me the greatest lesson of all, "To draw people to us, and not to drive them away." Washing my hands with his hands, he said he was grateful that I had learned this from him.

Meeting Nelson Mandela

On the day that Nelson Mandela was released, 11 February 1990, I was invited to the ITV studio in London to comment on the live video feed from South Africa that was broadcast to hundreds of television stations around the world.

Nelson and his wife, Winnie, stopped the car in which they were traveling just inside the prison grounds and walked hand in hand into freedom. I told the story of the prison security chief who said we would never walk out of prison on our own feet, and here was the last of our group now walking out from behind the walls. It was a moment that changed my life in many ways. There was a sense of fulfillment, a sense that perhaps I need not be quite so intense about the freedom struggle. Esmé remarked to friends that I was much more open to talking about prison and all those years away from real life. I said over the airwaves that I had a deep-seated wish to return to South Africa to embrace him. I had last seen him on the day we were sentenced to life imprisonment. Thereafter we were segregated. He and the others were taken away and held on the Robben Island.

One year after meeting with Walter again, I met with Comrade Nelson Mandela in Sweden. He was on his first journey abroad to the United States, Europe, and North Africa. I must admit it was disappointing not to have been able to meet him immediately, but that was clearly not possible. He was heavily engaged in political work from the moment of his release, and I was needed in London to continue my work in the ANC mission. It was also quite disappointing not to have been able to fly to Lusaka to meet him on his first trip outside South Africa, when he went to the ANC headquarters in exile.

Now things had moved on. A group of ANC comrades drove down together from Stockholm to Arlanda International Airport, some twenty miles outside the city. Nelson and Winnie were flying in on that day together with an entourage of South African activists as guests of the Swedish government, which had carried on the policies of the late, great Social Democratic Prime Minister Olof Palme, who had been murdered in 1986. The first reception was to take place on the tarmac, with a receiving line and an enclosure for Swedish anti-apartheid supporters. The protocol and security were something to behold. The Swedish government was not only showering Nelson with great honor but also making damn sure no crazy individual or agent of apartheid fanatics would be able to harm him. All the formality and double-checking added to the tension and excitement of the thousand people on the tarmac, which vied with the excitement and hope of millions of people in Sweden who watched the proceedings on television. The plane touched down and rolled to its parking place. The door opened, steps were pushed into place, and the carefully arranged line of dignitaries, anti-apartheid movement officials, ANC members, and others lost its precision as we all pushed forward. The line was curved; I am not tall, and I could not see where he was. Then the press photographers and television crews heralded his advance down the line by backing into us and butting us aside.

Suddenly, from amid the melee, Nelson stood in front of me. We shook hands quite formally. He held both of my hands. I held both of his. Silence. This tall, older friend and comrade stood there looking tired and gaunt. Receiving lines are a bit like hell. They press in on one. "Hello, Nel," I said, "we've not met since the day we were sentenced." "That's right. You look good, boy," he replied, and embraced me. Without too much thought I took off my ANC scarf and placed it round his neck. Winnie followed him. She did not recognize me—not surprisingly, for we had not really known each other, and I had become older and a lot balder in the twenty-six years since the trial. "I'm Denis Goldberg," I said. "It's wonderful to see you." She was absolutely radiant. Holding my hands and leaning away from me as if to see me better she said, "Oh! I had forgotten that face of yours. How wonderful to see you."

The formal proceedings at the airport were over. Back into the ANC's minibus for the trip in convoy to the Haga Palace, very close to Stockholm. What a wild ride it was, with the Swedish police security teams' cars speeding along the highway to make it difficult for anyone to intrude. Our minibus was not built for, and did not look as though it should have been part of, a convoy of sleek black state limousines.

What a crush there was at the formal reception. O. R. Tambo was recovering in Sweden from a series of strokes that had resulted from his untiring efforts to lead us to freedom. He had held our movement together for thirty years in exile through his outstanding leadership. It was very moving to see O.R., as he was known to one and all, glowing with the pleasure of his first meeting with Nelson. They had not met since O.R. had left South Africa in 1960 to establish the external ANC. These two friends, comrades in the ANC, partners in the first law practice opened by black South Africans, were back together again.

They sat in adjacent armchairs as we well-wishers stopped to greet first O.R. and then Nelson. Nelson was in a relaxed mood, laughing and smiling and reveling in being with close friends. He exchanged delightful stories with Wolfie Kodesh, who had housed him and cared for him for a large part of the time that he'd been underground before his capture in September 1962.

After the initial excitement, I felt a new sense of completeness. Now all the comrades I had been sentenced with were out of prison and I had met them all.

Esmé arrived the next day. Her first meeting with Nelson and Winnie took place in another lineup when they went to lay a wreath at Olof Palme's grave.

Nelson greeted me, "You're here again, boy," and moved on to greet Esmé. He shook her hand and made the kind of stiff response you make when meeting someone you don't know. "I'm pleased to meet you," he said. "Nel," I said, "this is Esmé, my wife." "Oh!" he replied, leaning down from his great height to embrace her, and said, "You have been looking after him very well. The boy looks good." He really is warmheartedly generous.

Esmé was appalled by Nelson's appearance; though he was buoyed up by the excitement of his meetings with O.R. and so many other comrades and the visit to Sweden, he looked exhausted to her professional eye. He admitted to her that he wasn't sleeping too well and that all the flying and time zone shifts had upset his digestion. His entourage was demanding that he eat, but he was too tired, he said. Esmé persuaded him to have a reflexology treatment instead, and her magical hands relaxed him and soothed him, and he said later that it had made a great difference to his well-being.

Esmé also had the opportunity to speak with Winnie alone. Esmé told me that she had said to Winnie that she knew the pressures of being the wife of "the hero in prison" and of having to satisfy the public demand for personal loyalty, but after the release and a decent interval it was possible to publicly acknowledge being separated. The reason, of course, was that the media often suggested that Winnie was in the midst of an affair, and the gossip hurt both of them. Esmé, though not in the eye of the media as Winnie had been, had had the same conflicts. Her words to Winnie were something like this: "Now that the hero is free, you too are free to choose to openly take a new partner." It would have saved a lot of personal pain for both of them had Winnie taken her advice.

In 1992 Nelson Mandela separated from his wife, and in March 1996 they were divorced.

18

Training in Asia

Commonwealth Secretariat Study Program

After Nelson Mandela was released and the ANC and other banned organizations were legalized in February 1990, a four-year period of transition began. The Convention for a Democratic South Africa was followed by a constitutional conference in which virtually every political party negotiated the future of South Africa. During this time the ANC sent representatives throughout the world to study the political and economic systems of other countries.

In December 1991 the ANC sent me to an advanced administrative training program organized by the Commonwealth Secretariat. It was a wonderful experience. For three weeks, together with civil servants from Commonwealth countries from East and West Africa, the Caribbean, India, and Malaysia, I studied at the Administrative Staff College of India in Hyderabad and then went for a further two weeks at the Malaysian National Institute of Public Administration, INTAN, in Kuala Lumpur.

The range of attitudes, skills, and experience among my colleagues was fascinating and led to interesting discussions. Hyderabad, a city with a large group of people of Muslim belief in a very large Hindu community, seemed at peace with itself. The Grand Mosque is very beautiful, standing at the center of an open-air place of worship that accommodates three thousand people. There are also many shrines to Hindu deities. The museums and art galleries are handsome, and I spent hours enjoying their artistic and cultural treasures. Motorized rickshaws based on Vespa-like scooters provided cheap, rapid, and quite frightening travel: swarms of them buzzed down the main roads, horns blaring. There are seven universities in the city, and hundreds of bookstalls line the sidewalks along several miles of road, each stall the width of one's outstretched arms. When you asked to see a book the stall holder would fetch it and keep his hand on it to prevent theft while you looked through it. Prices for computer handbooks, for example, were less than a quarter of the price of the equivalent book in Britain or America. In part this was due to the poor quality of the paper, binding, and printing, but prices were in line with the capacity of Indian students to pay.

The participants in the course were given thirty rupees a day for personal expenses. Local cigarettes cost two rupees for a pack, whereas international brands such as those owned by Mr. Rupert's Rembrandt group cost over twenty rupees. Local whisky cost four rupees, and imported Scotch whisky, the preferred tipple of the elite, cost thirty rupees a tot. In comparison, porters and cleaners at the college hostel for visiting students were paid twenty-seven rupees a day, on which they had to maintain their families. The absurdity of pocket money for smokes and drinks that cost more than the daily wage for a head of a family shocked me. The indifference of the Indian civil servants who participated in the course was even more alarming. They said they had to ignore the wage disparity or drive themselves mad. (I imagine that in South Africa today many have sadly adopted the same attitude.)

The lecturers at the Staff College were extremely interesting academics and experienced administrators, and through the information they passed on, I saw that the Indian economy had grown enormously since independence in 1947. Heavy industry using advanced technology and agriculture that was modernizing, together with a rural population that largely fed itself, were the basis for future development. Solving the problem of abject poverty is as much the real issue now as it was then.

One of our Indian colleagues, a director of a state-owned regional bus company, owned a farm that used masses of labor to implement modern agricultural techniques and, because he was "connected," he received free seed for testing and free consulting. His workers dressed in rags and worked seven days a week.

In the city I saw construction of multistory buildings where women carried bowls of sand, cement, and everything needed up three and four stories of scaffolding built of bamboo poles. They wore a simple work sari and, while walking like an army of ants up the scaffolding, used one hand to keep the sari closed at the front and the other hand to steady the basins on their heads. Such straight-backed elegance was something to behold: they demonstrated to my critical eye that wealth is accumulated through the backbreaking efforts of low-paid workers.

The many private schools, in addition to state schools, showed a hunger for education. The private schools' signs stated their names and the qualifications of the owners, such as B.A. or M.A. degrees from prestigious universities. I assume the statements were true because there were also those who stated that they had a "B.A. (failed)." That seemed to be proof of the saying that "in the land of the blind, 'one-eye' is the king."

The crowds in the streets were enormous but unthreatening until you offered a beggar a few small coins, for then you were surrounded in seconds by hundreds of people demanding equal treatment. My Indian colleagues warned me about being overtly compassionate.

Kuala Lumpur, the Malaysian capital, contrasted sharply with Hyderabad. It is smaller and strikingly cleaner and more orderly and, at least on the surface, much richer. I loved the fast-food stalls that served dishes based on the cuisines of the three main cultural groups, Malay, Indian, and Chinese. The stalls were spotlessly clean because of strict hygiene regulations and control, and the food was cheap in relation to Malaysian incomes.

I was amused by my Hindu colleagues rushing off to find a hamburger restaurant where they could eat lots of beef, something that was boring and commonplace for me. The traditional food stalls were commonplace for them, but I enjoyed their novelty.

A visit to the first of the many state farms run on cooperative lines, which had brought the Malay (Bumiputra) people out of the forests and into direct production of rubber and palm oil as owners rather than as cheap labor on expatriate-owned plantations, showed the potential of the state in overcoming mass poverty. It was crucial that the state cleared the land and established the farms on which the families were settled. They were required to pay back the cost of establishing these farms as if they were paying off a mortgage. A special feature was that when world prices for their palm oil and rubber production fell below certain levels, they were relieved of the payments until the prices rose again to a level that enabled them to resume their payments. The payback period was lengthened to accommodate these shifts in prices. This was a clear example of state intervention in the market economy to ensure that the historically most deprived majority community did not bear the brunt of the capitalist world market's price fluctuations, which we know often result from speculative buying and selling rather than from variations in real production factors.

The production unit of land and trees was owned by the family, and it could be inherited by a member of the family, but it could not be sold to an outsider—only to the state cooperative farm itself.

One of the original farmers had come onto the farm about thirty years previously. He had expanded his original tiny one-room house, adding rooms to accommodate his seven children. He arrived at the farm on a bicycle and had progressed through a scooter, a motorbike, a small car, and then to a big 4x4. I was assured that his family's development in only one generation was the norm. The farmer looked old and dried out by his heavy work in the sun, but all seven children had gone to university. His four sons had doctorates from prestigious universities in the United States and his three daughters had master's degrees from Malaysian universities. It seems that Muslim daughters were not trusted to go alone into the outside world. It also seems that young men get doctorates and young women get master's degrees. The opportunities that the children of the first generation of state cooperative farmers had enjoyed have resulted in their unwillingness to stay on the farms. This problem is something still to be solved.

Petronas, the state oil company, was set up to challenge the major international oil companies that tried to hold the newly independent Malaysia for ransom over the prices of petroleum products. In 1974 Malaysia was able to take back ownership and control of its oilfields and stop them from being ruined by overextraction. It held down the price of petroleum and developed new technology to open up new, difficult fields. Petronas emerged during the Cold War period when Malaysia was the Southeast Asian domino that the United States would not allow to fall. Therefore, Malaysia was allowed to get the better of the oil companies. Subsequently, Petronas allowed the oil companies to have minority shares in petroleum production and distribution. Petronas is now just another international oil corporation.

At the end of our study program in December 1991, we wrote group reports and personal reports. Upon returning to the ANC office in London, I sent what I had written to ANC President Mandela and Deputy President Mbeki in Johannesburg.

So much I had seen was relevant to the new situation developing in South Africa that I urged the leadership of the African National Congress to send teams to Malaysia, after discussion with the Malaysian government, to undertake similar but longer programs. There was so much we could have learned, especially the setting up of a centralized state-run training college for all levels of civil servants. I was and am still aware that systems and processes, both political and administrative, are historically and culturally specific to each country, but visions, principles, and goals may be shared, while detailed ways of working may have to be adapted.

I wish I could have been more influential in passing on what I had learned about economic development in practice.

Some of my comments follow:

To achieve the goals of long-term economic development through their detailed five-year plans, members of the Malaysian government heavily regulated the free-market economy. The directive power resided in the office of the prime minister. The most powerful economic units were the Economic Planning Unit (EPU) and the Economic Coordination Unit (ECU). In less than thirty years state intervention had moved the economy very quickly from colonial extractive industries—rubber, palm oil, and tin—to an industrial economy. State intervention enabled the rapid accumulation of capital.

In the social sphere, the New Economic Policy was the basis for positive discrimination, or affirmative action, in favor of the Malay (Bumiputra) people, who as a group had acquired a dominant position in the civil service and the state government services. There was some alienation among the Chinese and Indian ethnic groups. The distribution of wealth was still skewed among the three main ethnic groups, but there was also widespread skewing of ownership within each ethnic group as well.

The problem of rural poverty among the Malay people had been largely overcome. Urban poverty, however, was growing among those who have neither skills nor the ability to work at the going wage rate for menial, or heavy, manual labor. The Ministry of Social Welfare appears to provide a safety net for those who have not been able to make it in the developing economy.

The New Economic Policy (1972–1991) had been replaced by the

National Development Policy (1991 onward), which signaled less affirmative action in favor of the Malay ethnic group. In part, affirmative action had a momentum of its own, and the ethnic minorities were actively seeking greater equality on social matters and a greater share in the investment opportunities that the government was opening up in the private sector.

The rapid pace of economic development brought change in social norms. Women with tertiary education were marrying later and having children later than was the custom in earlier times. Some at least were consciously having fewer children, in part because they wished to pursue their careers with no interruption (thus, later age at first pregnancy) or fewer interruptions (thus, smaller families).

Many women had discarded the head cover (except for ritual occasions). But women told me that some husbands insisted on women retaining the traditional head cover and at least a remnant of a veil.

Men assert that there is no job discrimination at work and point to the women who work in every government department and enterprise. Some women, at least, assert that there is discrimination against them. The present number in high-level posts is far fewer than the proportion of women working in various departments and enterprises. At Petronas it is said that the Human Resources Management Department is the only department in which women have a real chance of attaining high executive status. Nevertheless, one can say that there is a slow trend to accept women in high-level posts. Those who serve as cabinet ministers or general managers or higher executives in public enterprises appear to be powerful role models.

The civil service clearly reflected the commitment to increasing the participation of the Malay ethnic group in government and in public enterprises, but minority ethnic groups were strongly represented in the Petroleum Research Institute of Petronas and in the more technical government departments.

One explanation is that minority groups were granted fewer scholarships to Malaysian universities. Parents sent their children to foreign universities, where many took advanced science degrees, whereas Malay children took arts and administration degrees to become members of the managerial staffs of government and public enterprises.

I was surprised to hear overtly expressed resentment of non-Bumiputra minorities even by some very high-level officials.

What was clear is that the economic and social development of a country cannot be left to chance. A strong central authority is necessary to shake the country out of its colonial past, to coordinate efforts, and to accumulate capital and direct resources to key projects while deploying resources to deal with human problems and the maintenance of intergroup stability.

That central authority lay where it should lie, in political hands: in Malaysia, in the office of the prime minister. Historically, the commitment of the first post-independence deputy prime minister, Tun Ali Razak, to economic and social development was crucial. He carried forward these policies when he became the second prime minister, thus setting the future pattern.

As I write, in 2014, twenty years into our democracy, South Africa has now created a strong, centralized Ministry of Planning, together with a Monitoring Unit, within the office of the president. Its function is to guide the implementation of economic, infrastructure, and social development through the National Development Plan, which was established by the Planning Commission formed during President Zuma's first term of office, 2009–2014.

A determined act of political will is required to transform the economy to overcome embedded poverty. There may be a danger of overcentralization of power, but at present power is in the hands of big business, which is uncontrolled and is able to exert influence over state apparatuses. The consequence is unconstrained markets that have resulted in jobless economic expansion at a time when real unemployment is at a level of over 40 percent of the adult population. The need is for political vigilance by trade unions, political parties, and factions of the ruling party.

It was delightful to visit Kuala Lumpur. Many of the high-rise buildings are in the International Style and could be seen in any European or North American city and elsewhere in Africa or South America. There are, however, some gems. Dayabumi, the Petronas headquarters building, is striking. It is clearly influenced by Muslim art and design elements. The arches and the stone lace patterns in the arch infills, in particular, reflect this. The gleaming white tower is a delight. The materials of the wall cladding, the plastered concrete podium walls, as well as the ceramic- or cement-tiled floors, are clearly intended to require little maintenance, while being cool to the senses.

Some high-rise buildings have towers that closely mimic the minarets of modern mosques. The modern minarets are themselves superb architectural adaptations to new (that is, nontraditional) building materials and construction methods.

The central mosque in Kuala Lumpur is absolutely stunning in its adaptation of traditional elements to modern architectural possibilities. The contrasts of traditional shapes with rectangular soaring elements are striking and surprisingly harmonious.

I enjoyed strolling carefree in the botanical gardens in the heart of the city. The cool beauty and stunning tropical flora that perfume the air are a relief from the hot climate. One day I shall return to enjoy it all over again.

19

Affairs of the Heart and Community H.E.A.R.T.

Life Number 8

Nelson Mandela was sworn in as president on 10 May 1994. All over the world the ANC closed the offices of its representatives, and new ambassadors replaced those of the old regime. Our chief representative in London, Mendi Msimang, became the first ambassador of the new South Africa to Great Britain.

I too had to decide what to do. Esmé wanted to stay in London to be with Hilly and David and our grandchildren. Could I go back to South Africa and leave her again? I felt that would be very unfair to her, and I wanted to enjoy having a family. I also did not know what I would do in South Africa, although there was much to do. My old friend Wolfie Kodesh urged me to go for a visit to see where I could fit in. I think—and Wolfie insisted it was so—that if I had gone back at the time of the relaunch of the ANC and election of the new National Executive Committee, I might have been elected as a delegate from the Western Cape. That would have opened up the possibility of becoming a member of Parliament and perhaps holding high office.

The judge in the Rivonia Trial said that he thought that the idea of holding office was a driving force for revolutionaries, but it was never my motive for being politically engaged. I decided that I would stay in London and be with my family. To explain my decision I said, "Granny loves the grandchildren and is staying, and as I love Granny, I am staying too." It was true, but there was more. I had never been very good at forming alliances with people whose ideas I did not really support in order to get support for my own ideas. In the situation that was developing I knew that is what would happen, and the idea of having to play those games did not sit well with me.

My work in the ANC had been building solidarity, and I felt we should try to hold on to the support we had developed. Our focus and that of the AAM had been Mandela's release. After Nelson was released, the AAM struggled to find a reason for remaining in existence. So what now? I proposed to our ANC Office Committee that the AAM needed to become an organization that would involve its members, who had enormous expertise in developing project work in the fields of health and education, in enabling ordinary people in South Africa to take command of some aspects of their lives. Activists would make good lobbyists for British government support for the new government in South Africa, which would need time to sort out its new policies and the human resources and financial capacity to implement them. Being a "do-gooder," as we rather disparagingly called charity workers, did not appeal to me either. Therefore, we would not be handing out food parcels. That was for governments and the specialist agencies of the United Nations to do if it was needed. We would work to develop human resources through direct involvement in the work of development inside South Africa.

Our Office Committee, with Mendi's agreement, decided that we would propose that AAM use its large membership base to become a development support organization in the form of a charity. At a meeting called to finalize the proposal, Billy Masetlha, Mendi's deputy, firmly stated that this idea was dead. AAM would become a political lobbying organization. Mendi spoke with the authority of our head office on such major policy issues, and that was that. But it soon appeared the decision had not come from headquarters in Lusaka. At my next party cell meeting I was told that I was being disciplined for not discussing the idea with a higher organ of the party before presenting it. That really angered me because our policy was that we did not discuss ANC matters in party cells to avoid creating divisions in the ANC. I very firmly rejected the censure because I had presented the paper to the ANC Office Committee as a full-time activist in the ANC, and I therefore had acted in accordance with our own rules. The censure was withdrawn. When I asked what the substantive objection to my proposal was, there was no response at all. What was done was to turn AAM into ACTSA (Action for Southern Africa), an information center that would try by professional lobbying to influence the British government to support the redevelopment of South and Southern Africa in ways that would empower the historically deprived to improve the quality of their lives. This was, of course, a necessary activity, but it left out the need to engage the energies and loyalties of our supporters, who were reduced to being mere payers of their membership subscriptions. There was no further active campaigning for them to do under the new approach. How experienced comrades could give up the "mass line" is beyond me.

On a visit to Johannesburg I met with Thomas Nkobi, the ANC's treasurer general, and he agreed that establishing a development fund to maintain support for reconstruction and development programs would be a valuable activity. He obtained a letter of support from President Nelson Mandela.

I needed the backing of British people, who were strong supporters of our new country. I asked Brian Filling, Jane Coker, Robert Bruce, and Nat Perez (a fellow South African), who all agreed to be the trustees but said they did not want to be very much bothered with the details.

We launched the new organization, called Community Health Education and Reconstruction Training (Community H.E.A.R.T.), on the first anniversary of our freedom, on 26 April 1995, in South Africa House. Ambassador Mendi Msimang agreed to this because when we asked him to hold the event there, he had no funds from the Department of Foreign Affairs to hold a celebration. In the end, he had an official reception at lunchtime on that day and we provided the "big do" in the evening. It was a great occasion and brought in donations that enabled us to buy a vehicle that would serve as a mobile clinic for student doctors and nurses studying at the Medical University of Southern Africa from which they could provide health care to children in rural schools in an area northwest of Pretoria. Working under supervision, they did their practical training, seeing a wide range of illnesses and treating patients where there were no other medical facilities yet available.

UNISON trade union, a merger of three unions of local government officials, gave us enormous support. Its general secretary, Rodney Bicker-

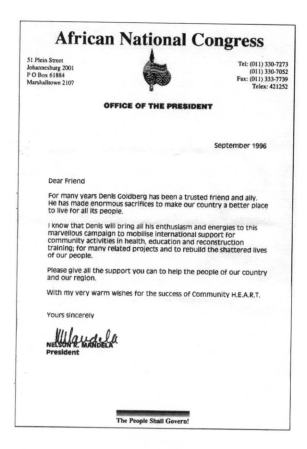

African National Congress

51 Plein Street
Johannesburg 2001
P O Box 61884
Marshalltown 2107

Tel: (011) 330-7273
(011) 330-7052
Fax: (011) 333-7739
Telex: 421252

OFFICE OF THE PRESIDENT

September 1996

Dear Friend

For many years Denis Goldberg has been a trusted friend and ally. He has made enormous sacrifices to make our country a better place to live for all its people.

I know that Denis will bring all his enthusiasm and energies to this marvellous campaign to mobilise international support for community activities in health, education and reconstruction training; for many related projects and to rebuild the shattered lives of our people.

Please give all the support you can to help the people of our country and our region.

With my very warm wishes for the success of Community H.E.A.R.T.

Yours sincerely

NELSON R. MANDELA
President

The People Shall Govern!

The letter signed by President Mandela in support of Community H.E.A.R.T.

staffe, let it be known that his publicity people could help us. They designed our logo, printed flyers and letterheads, and placed articles in their various journals, which reached the union's 1.3 million members. Building the new organization was a slow process, and Esmé financed me for two years before I could gradually recover the money we had invested as a loan to get the group going. There also seemed no point in taking a salary that could come only from money she would have lent to Community H.E.A.R.T.

Two big breakthroughs were, first, the launch of our "Book and Ten Pence" campaign to get children to donate the books they had finished, together with ten pence to cover the cost of collecting, sorting, and shipping them to South Africa. It became a very popular campaign. The second was when, through Bubbles Thorne, I was asked by Rape Crisis Cape Town to seek funding from Comic Relief, the British charity that holds Red Nose Day, which raises some 30 million pounds every two years with a twenty-four hour telethon. Steven, a wonderful Welshman whose surname I have sadly forgotten, was assigned to work with me, and his board granted us a large sum of money, including 10 percent of the total sum to cover our administration costs. That kept us going. The grants were repeated a number of times. Trade unions also contributed, and individuals who liked the approach of mass involvement made donations, too. The book campaign would have collapsed under the sheer amount of work involved in sorting and packing the books for shipment—about 50,000 filled a shipping container—if Nat Perez and his wife, Elsa, had not taken charge of that work.

At some point it struck me that our children should become computer literate. I started collecting used computers and getting friends to check them out to make sure they worked. I persuaded sea captains to take them as "captain's luggage" to South Africa. The project needed many more resources than I had, and I was greatly relieved when Tony Roberts and Sonia Sinanan asked if I would mind if they set up an organization called Computer Aid International. They too were backed by UNISON, and I was pleased to become a board member of their organization. To get them going, Community H.E.A.R.T. paid for their work in collecting, refurbishing, and shipping some two thousand computers to South Africa and Namibia. They are a very professionally run organization, and I am happy to be their patron.

The details of our work and building the organization took its toll on my health. I thought I would have time to be with Esmé and my family, but I was on a new treadmill and seemed to have even less time than before. At some point Sydney Mufumadi, a cabinet minister, on a visit to London asked me what I was doing. I explained about the millions of rand donated to Rape Crisis and the half a million books we had at that time shipped to and distributed in South Africa. He then asked what else I was doing, as if that were of little account. I said that 500,000 books were probably worth about 25 million rand. That evoked a spark of interest and the remark "That is indeed a lot of books." South Africa had 20,000 schools with no libraries at all. Simple arithmetic tells us that if each school is to have only 1,000 books each, we actually need 20 million books. (The total we have sent is now nearly 3 million books worth at least ZAR150 million, or about $15 million at that time.)

During 2002 I finally retired from Community H.E.A.R.T., and a new director, Isobel McVicar, who had been a UNISON branch secretary in Glasgow, took over. She had been on both ACTSA Scotland tours to South Africa and was inspired to help. She married the UNISON branch vice chair in Manchester, Brian Stangoe, and that led the UNISON North West Region of England to donate office space and facilities to us. Their support has been invaluable.

During 1995 a German-sounding female voice on my Community H.E.A.R.T. office telephone said the speaker was Edelgard Nkobi, the daughter-in-law of Thomas Nkobi, the ANC treasurer general. He had suggested she phone me for an explanation for an article she was writing about the ANC. Since I had worked under him when I created and ran ANCSA Merchandise and had also been a spokesman for the ANC, and he had supported the founding of Community H.E.A.R.T., I had no problem with that. That was the first of many calls, and sometimes she spoke for so long I would indicate to Giullieta Fafak, who worked with me, that she should tell me I was needed to deal with a visitor to the office. I could not be rude to the daughter-in-law of "T.G." and needed a reason to end the conversation. Late in 1985 Edelgard came to my office to interview me. I was struck by her background knowledge, and she told me she was the widow of T.G.'s eldest son, Zenzo, and had lived for many years in Bulawayo, in Zimbabwe, after that country's independence. I rather fancied what I saw and late in the afternoon drove her to where she was to meet her sister-in-law, who lived in London. It was a pity that Edelgard was not staying on her own; by then I would have liked to be invited to spend more time with her.

Her phone calls continued. She wrote articles about Community H.E.A.R.T. to promote its work in Germany. She arranged for me to be invited to a weekend workshop on international affairs for shop stewards. It was held in Wuppertal at the DGB (German Trade Union Congress) school. Edelgard met me at Düsseldorf Airport, and we traveled by train and underground train until we arrived at our destination and met our study group. I spoke about apartheid and my own experience and evoked a lot of sympathy. I wanted, of course, to raise funds for the work of Community H.E.A.R.T. The upshot was that they would help, provided that their contributions would be properly controlled, and they would trust only their German Finance Ministry to exercise the oversight. They would not contribute to a foreign (British) registered charity. Edelgard was my interpreter, as I knew just a few words of German through a beginner's course I had taken nineteen years earlier in prison.

Overnight accommodation was in the attached hostel, and when I hesitantly suggested in my few German words that she share my room, she scuttled away like a frightened rabbit. It was a good weekend, and Edelgard took me back to her flat, where I realized I would stay until leaving the next morning for London, when she would go off to work. By this time I was exhausted from the flying, train travel, coming to grips with a new audience, and trying to win their support. I lay down to rest while Edelgard prepared supper, and I thought she would prepare the couch in the living room for me. She kissed me lightly and I dozed off. In her room was an enlarged photograph of me taken when she interviewed me. She told me, but much later, that our friend and ANC chief representative in Switzerland, Ruth Mompati, upon seeing the photograph had remarked that if Esmé saw it, she would scratch Edelgard's eyes out. I was right about the meal and the relaxed chatting about our lives. The chemistry was good, but the couch was not prepared. And so started a complicated relationship that lasted for twelve years, until her death.

I knew I would not leave Esmé because we had shared too much, and I liked having such an intimate family. More and more our lives went in separate directions; we slept in separate rooms, and it seemed to me that I could live this dual life without hurting Esmé. When I came home from prison, she had said she knew I would have affairs, but I should not "bring them home," which meant she did not want to know about them. In reality, though there were many opportunities, I rarely indulged. I would go to conferences and meetings for a political purpose and felt, as I had in underground days, that I would not use politics as an excuse for indulgence. Usually there wasn't time, and when there was time I was exhausted—except for a delicious once or twice when there were no long-term consequences. Now it was different.

Edelgard set about creating a German sister organization to Community H.E.A.R.T. Through her old university friend Sabine Kebir, a noted biographer of Bertolt Brecht, or, rather, the women in his life, Edelgard got to Tina Jerman and her colleague Dodo Schulz, partners in EXILE Kulturkoordination e.V. We met in Düsseldorf and, despite the language difficulties, they agreed to provide the office resources for Community Heart e.V., the charity we registered in Germany. Their accountant, Hermann Hibbe, agreed to be on the board and to guide us through the registration process. Tina Jerman became the deputy chairperson and I was the chairman. I quickly expanded my knowledge of German to include phrases such as registered association; donations are tax deductible; a social-benefit organization; and bank transfer—all key phrases in fund-raising. To make the new outfit known, EXILE organized speaking tours for me. At first my hosts were people who had in one way or another been active in anti-apartheid work, often through religious-based groups, and I traveled to many parts of Germany by train.

Sarafina!—A Journey to Siegen, Germany

While on a lecture tour in Germany in February 1997, an additional lecture was unexpectedly added to my heavy itinerary. I stayed overnight in a motel near Much. Herr Reinhard Hillnhütte, a music teacher accompanied by a pupil, Christian Krell, at the Evangelisches Gymnasium in Siegen-Weidenau, came to take me the next morning to address pupils at the Gymnasium. They promised I would be in time to give a lecture that evening at the training establishment of the Ministry of Foreign Affairs in Bonn. I did say it was a heavy itinerary!

Herr Hillnhütte explained that they had invited me to the Gymnasium because in their music classes the pupils had been learning songs from *Sarafina!*, a South African musical about resistance to apartheid. To understand the deeper meaning of the songs, they wanted more information. They needed to understand the motives of the children of Soweto who rose up in 1976 against the apartheid regime's imposition of Afrikaans as the language of education.

Christian Krell had undertaken to get the information. Active in the Socialist Party of Germany (SPD) youth organization, he knew whom to ask for information about South Africa. What could be more natural than to write to *Liebe Genosse Rau* (Dear Comrade Rau), the *Sehr geëhrte Minister-Präsident* (the Right Honorable Prime Minister) *von Nordrhein-Westfalen*. The prime minister, of course, referred the letter to the head of his administration, Herr Staatskanzlei Brückner, to help the young people of Siegen in their cultural activities. Herr Brückner referred the matter to a frequent adviser on cultural matters to the State Government of North Rhine–Westphalia, Frau Tina Jerman, cultural expert of EXILE Kulturkoordination in Essen.

EXILE organizes my lecture tours in Germany. EXILE also provides the administration for Community Heart, which supports development projects in Southern Africa. Perhaps Staatskanzlei Brückner remembered that EXILE had introduced me to him, and I would know about South Africa. To cut a long story short, Tina Jerman told Christian Krell that his Gymnasium could invite me to speak to their school because I would shortly be on a lecture tour in Germany and would be nearby in Much.

Knowing that I was to address the young people for two hours, and knowing that young bottoms find it difficult to sit still for so long, I asked them to sing for me. Such well-trained voices singing in such harmony with a genuine South African sound and beat was startling. That they had taken *Sarafina!* as a source of musical teaching material was inspired pedagogy. It had led immediately to a wider quest for knowledge, an inquiry into politics with a small "p," an investigation of ethics, and a greater understanding of history and geography and singing in English and Zulu. But at the Evangelical Gymnasium in Siegen this was not so amazing because Herr Dr. Ockel, the director, had told me that his school consciously set out to give its pupils an awareness of the wider world by arranging for exchange students to spend a year with them in Siegen. At that time they had exchange students from more than twenty countries!

Christian Krell was my German voice, reading passages I had selected from Nelson Mandela's autobiography that showed that I had taken a few steps with the president on his long walk to freedom. In forty years of activity, including twenty-two years in prison, I had walked quite a few steps. After forty minutes of reading and explanations of what had been happening in South Africa, we took a break, and the whole group of young people sang again for me. Then we moved on to questions and discussion.

The young people wanted to know so much. What were the conditions like in South Africa, and in prison there? How could the former white South African state impose racism by law? I think they wanted to try to understand the Nazi era in Germany as well. How could it be that schoolchildren played such an important role in putting an end to the apartheid system? Why did I, a white South African, take up a struggle for the freedom of black South Africans?

And so we came to the kernel of what I wanted to talk about: even to put the question in that way is to assume that there is some fundamental difference between people who have different color surfaces! Thus, we have all been conditioned by the way in which history is written. After all, I told them, when we are born, we have no sense of color. Gradually we come to perceive the different colors of light, and then we learn words for these colors. Only much later do we learn to give social meaning to skin color.

The meanings we give are learned, often subconsciously; but usually older people impose their social definitions on us.

That led us to a discussion of the morality of the political decision to resist oppression; at what point can taking up arms against state tyranny be justified? I do not think there is one simple answer to that question. It depends on so many factors, such as the nature of the tyranny: Who makes the law? Can the laws be changed by a political process? What are just laws and what are unjust laws? They were such an intelligent and interesting group of young people that I had a wonderful morning with them.

The young people were dedicated, and their progress had been rapid, so they had decided that they would perform the musical as their summer concert at the City Hall. I was able to help the Gymnasium make arrangements with the South African poet and composer Mbongeni Ngema for the performing rights. I was invited to be at the first of their performances in the Siegen Summer Festival. I was delighted to be there, accompanied by Herr Brückner, who represented Prime Minister Rau, who had agreed to be the patron of the performance.

The performance on Sunday evening, 22 June 1997, was an unforgettable theatrical experience. Along with the audience of eight hundred people, I lived through the shifting emotions of the South African pupils who rose up against apartheid racism in Soweto in 1976. The musical tells the story of Sarafina, a girl who takes to the streets with her classmates in protest after the arrest of their activist teacher. Thousands of students protested against the imposition of Afrikaans as the language of education in their schools. Their protest ended in a hail of police bullets. By the end of that year, 1976, about a thousand young demonstrators had been killed.

For me it was a miracle that these young Germans, who lived in a country that had not experienced a climate of violence and terror for over fifty years, were able to imagine themselves in the lives of young South Africans who had not experienced a peaceful climate for fifty years and more. The cast of students and their music teachers gave an inspired performance of singing, dancing, and accompanying music, linked by an informative commentary. Cultural forms and expression truly transcended national boundaries and experiences.

These lovely, talented young people made us live through the emotional experience of that generation of schoolchildren who were indelibly marked by events that helped transform South Africa away from its apartheid racist system. I think the cast of *Sarafina!* in Siegen has been marked by their experience in coming to grips with those events and emotions. I have been marked by their performance. I laughed at the humor and wept at their portrayal of courage and determination to achieve social justice. I enjoyed their musicality, spontaneity, and joie de vivre.

I was also delighted to hear that they had decided that Community Heart would benefit from the net income from the two performances, and I gave the assurance that the money would be dedicated to the teaching of mathematics and science to the young people of South Africa who had been deprived of proper education for so long.

Since then I have visited Siegen many times as a guest of the Evangelical Church's Institute for Church and Society, whose director, Günter Hensch, has arranged for me to speak to adult groups and to school and university seminars. I have made many friends and always enjoy visiting this beautiful, ancient city and meeting my friends again. A group of them visited me in Cape Town, and it was a delight to reciprocate their hospitality.

Edelgard enjoyed being my interpreter, but it became very difficult for me to work with her. She insisted on adding explanations of what I said, making my addresses too long and too detailed. At first I simply went along with her interventions, changing sentences and paragraphs to fit what she was doing. Then I asked her to simply be my voice and stick to translating what I said because explanations could be given during question time. In the end I had to ask her not to be my interpreter. That almost led to an end to our relationship, but we endured the strife. The number of express trains I caught simply to get back to her place in Düsseldorf to spend the night with her is beyond counting.

Once again I was living in top gear, rushing from place to place and feeling young and excited again. My friendship with Tina and Dodo grew steadily, and they have become very dear friends. Tina in particular has helped me make ever more contacts among people who lead organizations, schools, and state institutions that invite me back again to speak to audiences they have contact with. Reinhard Stolle of the Action Center Third World in Osnabrück has broadened my base in Lower Saxony to include civil society organizations, universities, grammar schools, and federal NGOs. Wolfgang Ebert of Arbeit und Leben (Work and Society) in Wuppertal has been a wonderful supporter, and his wife and daughter have become good friends after the numerous times I have stayed over with them.

Esmé visited her brother in South Africa in 1996, and on the return flight her plane had to stop in Nairobi for repairs. The passengers were taken to a hotel where she ate fresh mangos at breakfast. Mangos handled by someone with dysentery are known to become hosts to an amoeba that causes acute diarrhea. She had an awful, messy trip home in the plane, and I was called by the airline to fetch her from the clinic at the airport, to which she had been taken from the plane by ambulance. They had rehydrated and stabilized her and urged her to go to a hospital for treatment. She refused to go to the Hospital for Tropical Diseases in London, where the treatment would have been excellent. After all, the British knew about tropical diseases. They had had an empire, and its colonial governors and civil servants who came home with every imaginable tropical disease had to be treated. Ez said she was too fat and the doctors would not treat her properly. I could not persuade her otherwise. It took years for her to fully recover.

Then in 1997, because she was a cricket nut, she went on a tour with British supporters to watch the English team play in the West Indies. Perhaps I should have gone with her, but I was not a cricket groupie, and such a tour was not how I would choose to spend a holiday. She became exhausted and dehydrated and fell ill. This resulted in a condition in which her heart would suddenly beat rapidly and wildly irregularly. It upset her that I did not go to fetch her home, but our daughter, Hilly, insisted on going, and we had had too many disagreements in the past for me to try to stop her. Perhaps this was a sign that there was already a growing distance between Esmé and me. She and Hilly would see each other and speak to each other four or five times a day. I felt excluded and was ripe for an affair.

I needed the intellectual stimulus that Edelgard gave me as much as the romantic loving that we enjoyed. I always feel that we tut-tut over such real-life matters, but when we see them in the movies with Ingrid Bergman or Marlene Dietrich playing the third person in the love triangle, we reach for a box of tissues and weep over the complexity of their lives. The sense of "time's winged chariot" galloping "at my back" (from a poem by the English Elizabethan poet Andrew Marvell) toward my life's end made me hungry for something new and exciting. How it would end I did not know, but this time I grabbed figuratively and literally at the life-affirming relationship that Edelgard and I developed.

I got Ronnie Kasrils's agreement to let her translate his autobiography, *Armed and Dangerous,* into German as *Stechbrieflich gesucht.*[1] I enjoyed working on the translation with her and learned a lot more German than I had previously known. It was also good to be working together on something we both believed was important. It certainly brought us closer together.

It all resolved itself when Esmé became very ill in 2000, in the depths of the coldest winter in Britain for twenty years. I was about to enter a lecture hall in Cologne when my son, David, phoned me to say Esmé had to have emergency surgery to remove a part of her bowel that had become gangrenous through lack of blood supply. The surgeon wanted my approval. He said that without the operation she would die in a few hours. He also said there was a 50 percent chance of success, and I realized that there was also a 50 percent chance of failure. He said that if the operation did not succeed, they had through experience found that the operation could not be repeated. There was no choice but to agree.

I canceled my lunchtime lecture and rushed back by train to Düsseldorf to pick up my bags from Edelgard's flat and grabbed the first plane to London. I was at Esmé's bedside before she came out of the anesthetic. She seemed to be doing well, and all her vital signs were good. But after I spent a few days watching the monitor in postoperative care, it was clear that something was not right, and indeed she was nearing the end. She had been in a semicoma for days but rallied when our younger granddaughter, Jane, came to see her. Esmé was lighthearted and fun, and Jane laid her head on her Grandma and in her simple way showed her love. I said to Esmé that it was good to have her back again, and she responded that she was back because she realized that there was so much to live for.

I was hopeful, but not too much so, having already prepared myself through days of being at her bedside once the surgeon said that, though the operation was successful, she might not survive. Her rally petered out. How she fought to hold on to life! And so ended a forty-six-year relationship of love and support, separation, and a shared life with the mother of my children. She had worked with me and supported me in a life that was in some ways obsessively driven to make our country really a home with dignity for all our people. She was once asked how she could remain married to one man for forty-six years, and with her typical sharp humor she said, "It's easy: send him to prison for twenty-two years!"

Hilly and David and I were with her when she died, trying by holding hands with each other and her to will her to live. I think David summed up what we all felt when I pulled him away saying, "We all know we have done things that hurt her in some way." He said, "No, it's not that. It is the many things I should have done for her, but did not . . ."

I asked Jo Vellerman, a very close and capable friend of Esmé's, to arrange the funeral at the Golders Green Crematorium. She said that the chapel there was too small for the number of people who would want to attend, and she arranged for television screens to be put up outside on a sheltered porch. Indeed, she was right, as over four hundred people arrived to bid her farewell. There were many South African exiled comrades, many British friends, and many physiotherapy patients she had treated in a practice spanning thirty-seven years. Young people who had stayed in her house, both before and after my return, flew in from Australia and elsewhere. Friends of Hilly and David and many of my comrades came from all over Britain.

We had married in a Registry Office in Cape Town in 1954 to avoid the religious ceremony her mother wanted, and neither of us had changed our minds about that. I asked Brian Filling, the Scottish anti-apartheid activist, to conduct a rationalist commemoration of Esmé's life. Time was left in the proceedings for people to mourn silently in their individual ways because we were tolerant of people's beliefs as long as they did not seek to impose them on us. Her simple coffin had flowers from Hilly and David and a single rose from me signifying the rose in Saint-Exupéry's *Little Prince*. The rose said that because he had cared for and protected her, the prince was bound to her for life.

Esmé had bequeathed her house to me, and I wavered between converting it into two and a half apartments or simply selling it. In the meantime, I found I had huge pent-up stores of energy and set about cleaning the house and doing repairs that Ez had put off. In her illness, she would demand that I help her run the house, but when I did she would order me to stop. She had become obsessive about money, crowding the house with paying guests to bursting point, and now the big house was empty. I asked Hilly and David and our grandchildren to take whatever they wanted of her things, and the rest went to our local hospice shop to raise funds for the care of terminally ill people.

Looking back from a distance of about thirty years, I see that I behaved from 1985 onward as I had done when I first became politically active in 1953 and 1954, when Esmé and I met and got married. There was such intensity and perhaps an obsessive need to prove that I had agreed to being released in order to fight back against the apartheid system that still had my comrades locked away, and the oppression within South Africa was becoming ever greater. I was away from home more and I could think of little else than office politics and how to rise above the pettiness. All this affected Esmé and me, too, because only to her could I rail against the personalized internal opposition not based on any political principle. After many months Esmé said she had wanted to warn me but knew I would have rejected her views because I would not have wanted to believe that they could be true. They were true and I am grateful to her for letting me find out for myself and dealing with and overcoming those obstacles.

I have loved and been loved since she passed away in 2000, but what a tumultuous life we had together and apart and together again for forty-six years. I wake up sometimes thinking about her and feeling for her, stretching out my hand and finding her place is empty, though, as I have said, there have been others since. I think I have to say each has her place in my life and each has been special, and I am a very lucky man.

Working myself to exhaustion in the house and catching up with the work I had not been able to do for many weeks at my Community H.E.A.R.T. office helped carry me through my grief. It was very lonely without her presence. I did not wish for her death, yet I have to acknowledge that her death eased the inner conflict about where my relationships with her and with Edelgard would go. After some time Edelgard came to stay with me and worked very hard to help me clean up the house, which I had decided to sell. I did not need a five-bedroom house with a large dining room and a large living room. Prices of houses in London had skyrocketed, and it seemed the right moment to benefit from that because I had no meaningful pension and no reserves of cash. You do not earn money in twenty-two years in prison and nine years of working in the ANC office for pocket money that was less than half the average national British wage and much less than that of a cleaner or street sweeper.

Edelgard took time out to go to Zimbabwe to cover the national elections in that country. She was to be away just a couple of weeks, but she did not return and it felt as though she was not coming back again. It felt like a second bereavement, but she did return after some months, when the postponed elections had finally been held.

A very nice couple agreed to buy the house at my price, but then I found I could not buy even a small flat in the area that I wanted to live in and leave myself enough to live on. I canceled the sale and started to prepare for converting the house so that I could have a small apartment and lease two apartments that would provide an income for my future. The buyers were very upset and kept the real estate agent busy trying to persuade me to go through with the sale. They wrote me personal letters explaining their need and offering a small increase in the sale price. I explained that it was not a question of just a few thousand pounds, and they seemed to accept the notion that they would not get the house. Just before I started on the alterations to the house, they offered me an extra £50,000 because they had checked me out on the Internet and discovered why I had to have greater resources. They wanted to help me because of my role in the anti-apartheid struggle. I was overwhelmed by their generosity and grateful that I would be able to live in a flat and not in a single room getting older and more dilapidated with time. I did visit the buyers after some months, and they had turned the old house, which had become grubby and messy internally, into something really very nice. As it happens, house prices in London went up by over 20 percent a year in the next couple of years, so they have done well and I am pleased for them.

That property boom did wonders for me, too. I bought a flat and did it up, plastering damaged walls and ceilings, renovating kitchen cupboards, and laying new carpeting myself, and having new windows fitted. Edelgard came to live with me, and she made it into something very special. Deliberately I had left the buying of curtains and cushions and the interior decor to her so that she would feel it was her home, too.

We equipped her study, where she worked away at her journalism and translating my articles and speeches into German for me. It was fascinating to work with her because by this time my understanding of German had grown enormously, and I could see when she had not quite grasped the meaning of an original English text. In part my language ability had grown from the numerous lectures I gave in Germany, and as I knew what I was saying, I also knew what my interpreter should be saying. When a negative was left out of the translation, for example, I could pick up the omission. But Edelgard deliberately spoke to me in German and laughed tolerantly when I told acquaintances that I had learned German out of self-defense so that when she told me off, I would know what I had done wrong. Though working with her on the translations developed my understanding of German, the best learning occurred after waking up in the early morning hours when I could not sleep. I would nudge her and she woke immediately, and we would speak in German until we fell asleep again. I dreamed in German and woke up when I could not find the way to express my thought. I once asked, "Edel, how do you say 'little white horses' that one sees on the crests of waves?" Oh, she would have to think about it because she came from the mountainous country of Thuringia. Eventually she suggested *wellenreiter* (wave rider, or surfer). Always such a request ended in a conversation on literature or economics or philosophy, and so I learned the language.

She also translated Tim Jenkin's book *Escape from Pretoria* as *Und vor uns die Freiheit*.[2] The publishers had insisted I write a longish chapter, and that is the origin of the piece I have called "The Escape—Precision Was the Key."

Edelgard had become very worried about my health. The cold, wet London winters were crippling me, and I started using a walking stick. I was breathless and had dark rings under my eyes. I could not get up on time and went to my office at odd hours with long lists of what I had to do; I then left after a short time because I could not concentrate. I had become a "burnt-out" case. Edelgard insisted that she should take me home to South Africa to see if we could make a life there; if not, we could return to Britain or to Germany. After all the years of political activity and prison, we had few resources. My struggle pension was a pitiful sum, and London was too expensive for us. We could have just about managed in her flat in Berlin, to which she had moved from Düsseldorf, but she felt I would be too isolated even though my conversational German had developed quite rapidly. On our combined resources we thought we could live in South Africa.

One day in the office I told Nat and Elsa Perez and Mmapula Tladi-Small, a South African nurse who had emigrated to Britain and worked closely with us at Community H.E.A.R.T., that I needed to stop working at Community H.E.A.R.T. because I was destroying what had taken so much work by all of us to build up. I was going to go home to South Africa. Without any surprise at all they said they had wanted to tell me that I should have stopped a year earlier because they saw that I was quite ill. They refrained, they said, because it would have hurt my feelings. Dear friends can be too dear for one's own good! It took five months to get Isobel McVicar and our board to agree to her becoming the new director and for me to actually hand over to her. Even though I knew I could not continue, it was not easy for me to hand over because Community H.E.A.R.T. had become my life.

We had to move our office and the thousands of books that awaited shipment to Manchester. Nat did sterling work in getting that task done.

Once the decisions were made, I felt as if a huge, dark cloud hanging over me had been lifted: there was a new beginning in sight. In December 2001 Ronnie Kasrils, minister of water affairs and forestry, at the launch of the Liliesleaf Trust in Johannesburg had asked me to be his special adviser. I accepted the offer. We packed up everything we had, including all of Edelgard's things that we had brought from Berlin to London, in several trips by station wagon and then a hired van packed to the last cubic inch of space. We enjoyed the ferry journey overnight to Hamburg and the drive to Berlin, finding that easier than the route from Dover to Calais, and the long drive via Essen, where we stayed overnight with Tina Jerman, and then returned to Berlin.

In Berlin we inquired at the South African Consulate about a residence permit for Edelgard and heard that we would have to put down a deposit of ZAR100,000 (at that time about $10,000) unless we got married before going or within three months of getting to South Africa. We got married in a London Registry Office for a cost the equivalent of about ZAR750 (about $75). We had many farewell parties in various places in Britain, as I was "going home" after nearly eighteen years of living in Britain. I don't know when an exile stops being one. But I felt I was leaving my home in Britain, where we had made so many friends. I longed to find out if we could make it in South Africa, but I also felt a real sense of loss of friends made during those eighteen years. Hilly was able with Esmé's help to establish a kindergarten we named Ruff 'n Tumble. She was a trained nursery nurse and had a wonderful way with children. So-called problem children would stop crying, yelling, or refusing to do whatever they found unpleasant when she picked them up, gave them a hug, or merely sat with them. She had worked in the special care baby unit at the Royal Free Hospital in London with a colleague, Barbara Stoodley, who joined her as a partner in the kindergarten. Esmé spent a lot of time with them enjoying being a kind of super granny to all the kids.

Hilly became very ill and the underlying cause was not identified. She needed to lose weight and was losing it, but without going on a diet. Eventually she had a number of small lung embolisms and also showed symptoms like those of deep vein thrombosis (DVT). She had not flown anywhere for over two years, and long-distance travel was thought to be the cause of DVT. She was in and out of hospital but was well enough to come to Edelgard and my wedding in the Tottenham Registry Office in London. Then she went back to hospital, where extensive tests were conducted. I visited her one evening, and she rather sadly remarked that she would not see her son, Jack, finish school. I tried to comfort her because the tests were only just being done and there was no diagnosis of what was wrong with her. Very tearfully she said that I had known a year earlier that she was very ill. "How so?" I asked. Because I had said that I wanted her to look after herself to live for another ten years to see Jack grow to be an independent adult. I explained that I thought she was being careless about her health and wanted her to look after herself better. Jack phoned her to ask when she was coming home because he missed her. She comforted him as best she could. She and I chatted a bit longer until she insisted I leave because I looked so tired. Twenty minutes later she had a massive heart attack and died within minutes.

Her funeral was a remarkable event: our family was there, but also the parents of the children and the children who had passed through her kindergarten, Esmé's and my friends and comrades, and Hilly's friends. She was well liked and loved and I thought more generations of young children were going to miss out on the abundant love she had for children.

Barbara, Hilly's friend and partner, kept the kindergarten going for a year or two, but her heart was not in it with Hilly gone. She was the natural foster mother for Jack, having known him literally all his life, and so his life continued in the same place and in the same way, except that his mum had died. In that year the nine-year-old little boy became the unofficial counselor for many children at his primary school who knew that Jack could help them through their emotional problems. He also did extremely well at his studies and has continued to do so.

Edelgard and I had all our plans made for our departure to South Africa, and I needed to get there to take up my post as adviser to a minister. I also knew that there was little I could offer Jack in the way of family support, especially as he was not alone. When we left Britain at the end of August 2002, we each left some resources behind in Britain and Germany in case we had to return.

20

Life Number 9, 2002–2014

It helped enormously that I had a post to go to. Ronnie Kasrils was meticulous in requiring me to provide real information showing that I could indeed handle the post of special adviser to the minister of water affairs and forestry. It is a technical ministry and I am a trained civil engineer. The minister and the Department of Water Affairs and Forestry have their offices in Pretoria, and so Edelgard and I had to live there, too.

We flew to Johannesburg and stayed in a flat in Pretoria we rented from our comrade Freddy Reddy, the ANC's psychiatrist, who lived in Norway, until we bought a house. Suddenly we had a bit of cash because the rand was very weak against the pound sterling, which enabled us to buy a house for cash, so we wouldn't have mortgage payments. We made the purchase between our arrival by air and the arrival of our goods, by sea and then by land, six weeks later. To save money we had done most of the packing ourselves. Our friend Kishor Shah, who had been such a generous shipping agent for the ANC when we were sending large amounts of stuff from the United Kingdom to our settlements in Tanzania, sent in his packers at the last minute. We were astonished that only one plate was broken, and Edelgard said she had packed it herself. Our goods filled a shipping container to such a degree that when its doors were opened at our new home in Pretoria, things began to fall out.

It was exciting being back in South Africa, even though I knew Pretoria only as the city of my imprisonment. But we both liked it. The sky was so high, unlike the one in London, where it seemed always to press down on one's head. Finding our feet there, and, for me, coming to grips with my work as Ronnie's special adviser, was not easy.

In my mind the minister and his Department of Water Affairs and Forestry were involved, on the one hand, with taps and toilets and, on the other, with trees. I found that the focus was on the need to provide clean water and safe sanitation (taps and toilets) and there was a great reluctance to get involved in the promotion of tree plantations tended by peasants for timber production. The state-owned plantations for which we were responsible were being allowed to deteriorate at an alarming rate, destroying job-creation potential. Within a month of becoming the minister's adviser, I had developed a comprehensive plan that could have transformed the rural economy of the Eastern Cape in ten years. The project extended also to KwaZulu-Natal. It saddened me to see the way officials could block development by simply passing paper around and around and spending fortunes on external consultants who had been government officials in the previous apartheid government.

For example, they took two years just to develop the terms of reference for an environmental impact assessment if trees were to be planted in a particular area of the Transkei in the Eastern Cape Province. Something similar happened in KwaZulu-Natal, but there we were able to push things along with the help of the minister in that province, Narend Singh of the Inkatha Freedom Party, who received me at the request of my minister. He was as distressed as I was that officials blocked tree planting because they said the poor should grow food for subsistence.

The prospect of participation in the real economy was of no interest to the officials. They had not asked the people concerned why they did not plant food crops. Had they done so, they would have found what I had learned: rainfall was too unpredictable, they lacked fertilizer and equipment, there was no market for their surplus product, and it was cheaper in terms of money and effort to buy what they needed from the supermarkets. In the short space of a year, maps were prepared that are a model of what rural development planning should be, identifying land usable for different purposes so that environmental impact reviews could be done in advance; detailed work for each project could be done quickly, depending on the particular application. Having retired, I am not sure what was done with this great piece of work.

I found it distressing that economic development was held back by what I believed to be a lack of political decisiveness. This left heads of government departments (directors general) to wage turf wars instead of getting on with the tasks of economic development. I believe also that some ministers were afraid of making decisions. Fearing criticism, they wanted perfect projects, but as an engineer I know that there is no such thing. There are only good projects and very bad ones. They needed to grasp a principle that all engineers learn, namely, that there is a point at which design work has to stop and the actual work has to begin. Weaknesses will, of course, be improved on and, furthermore, the implementation of major projects inevitably creates new conditions that require rethinking and adjusting what we do. Even at an ANC economic forum I was advised that raising these issues was inappropriate. If it was inappropriate to raise such fundamental matters at a closed forum of the ruling party, where else should one raise them? I was asked to prepare a paper based on my remarks, but it was not circulated for comment. I am sure it was ignored, and I should not have been surprised because the people I was criticizing were the very ministers and top officials who would not make the decisions required to implement policies endorsed by the cabinet.

There was also a culture of bonuses paid to top officials for "exceptional performance." They got these bonuses every year, and therefore the requirement of exceptional service was ignored. I believed this was utterly wrong when the annual salary of top officials was so high in relation to workers in the field. The bonuses were sometimes equal to a lower-paid worker's annual salary. Our revolutionary élan did not last very long. The bonus culture in the civil service had a negative effect. Officials were reluctant to take initiatives to find novel solutions to the massive problems of service provision that were inherited from the apartheid past. Novel ideas, if they did not work out perfectly, might lead to losing that bonus. Therefore, it was safer to do nothing!

Our ministry was directly responsible for providing water and sanitation, and it exercised tight control over the newly established municipalities that came into existence in 2000. The national government insisted that all the powers be transferred to these new municipalities at the stroke of a pen on a certain date. It was a serious error because they had neither the financial capacity nor the human resources to carry out the responsibilities given them in the constitution. It was also my opinion, after a thorough analysis of the relevant laws, that it was unconstitutional to transfer these powers at a stroke because the constitution said explicitly that the powers were to be transferred when a municipality had the capacity and resources required to carry out these functions; therefore, each municipality should have been assessed before those powers could be transferred. I wrote a very detailed paper on this and hoped it would be fully argued by government. It had little effect on minds already made up. Today we see the consequences: many local governments are unable to fulfill their development functions. Worse, the central government's frontline departments have lost the trained and experienced personnel who should have formed the expert teams guiding municipalities in the fulfillment of their tasks. In part I came across the need for tight central control and the use of expert "strike teams" from a study of development institutions in Malaysia during the training program I had been sent on by the ANC.

About a year after settling in our new home in Pretoria, Edelgard was diagnosed with ovarian cancer. Radical surgery and a long course of chemotherapy appeared to have stopped the disease, and we lived in hope that she would survive. Sadly, the cancer flared up again, which required more chemotherapy with its accompanying periods of nausea. We were having a house built in Cape Town, and her determination to see it finished seemed to give her strength to fight the disease. We moved into this house in September 2005. She furnished it and made it beautiful.

Working as an adviser gave me wonderful opportunities to visit many parts of the country as a troubleshooter, and I gained an appreciation of the magnitude of the problems our country faces. I am appalled by the widespread negativity that persists within our country and abroad in relation to how much has been achieved. Nearly 3 million homes, albeit small ones, have been provided, but there are still more people who need homes. These people say nothing has been done. Similarly, whereas millions have been provided with safe water and sanitation, a few million still need these services, and they say nothing has been done (for them). Our hospitals are overcrowded and often not well maintained because they are serving many times the number of patients they were designed for. They are failing because of their successes in providing for millions of people for whom there were previously no medical facilities; under apartheid they were not recognized as people who needed such services. I am critical of some aspects of our health-care system, especially the weaknesses of management, but I recognize that medical personnel and resources are being overwhelmed by the needs of our people.

After two years Ronnie Kasrils was given another ministry, and Buyelwa Sonjica became the new minister in the Department of Water Affairs and Forestry. I was pleased that she took me on as her special adviser for a short time to get to know me, and then for a longer period. When she was moved to another ministry two years later, in 2006, I was a little disappointed to end up being retired. We had, however, moved to Cape Town, where I had an office in the minister's suite near Parliament. I took part in conferences via an audiovisual link; sometimes I sat with my minister in Cape Town, and at other times she would be with the department managerial staff in Pretoria. Edelgard's cancer flared up and I needed to be with her. She had survived major surgery and I had nursed her back to health from a weight of under 110 pounds and throughout two rounds of chemotherapy. When the cancer flared up again in 2006, she started a third round of chemotherapy—but with no great hope of success.

During the prison years many of us in prisons around the country studied through the University of South Africa. The university initiated a process of having graduation ceremonies for students who could not attend the normal ceremonies because they were in prison or banned from attending gatherings for political reasons. I was pleased to help Professor Barney Pityana, the vice chancellor, track down former prisoners. The Special Graduation Ceremony in Pretoria was well orchestrated, and one photograph shows that I was awarded three degrees obtained during my time in prison. That led to my being invited to give a talk at the university, which I called "My Universities." Important as my formal studies were at the University of Cape Town and through the University of South Africa, I said that I also have the degree P.G.—Prison Graduate—and that was perhaps the most important one because it taught me so much about life, endurance, and trying to uphold one's principles. It was a privilege that I hoped others could avoid.

The role of art and culture became significant in my life. Through Tina Jerman in Germany I was invited to speak at conferences and seminars about murals and about art in international relations and its significance for historically deprived people. My approach was, I suppose, always from the social and political point of view rather than as an art critic, and always with the thought of the poem of Bertolt Brecht that I have cited in this book. He said that during the struggle, there was no time for art and for beauty. And I can say that we always drew on artists and folk music and, in the rock era, that socially significant style as well to draw people together in the struggle.

Over the years and many reading and lecture tours in Germany, I have been to numerous places in that country. I have crisscrossed the land using its enviable train service to reach big cities and small villages where people have wanted to hear about South Africa and how we achieved our freedom. I have returned again and again, and it was not just to enjoy the typical supper cuisine (*Abendbrot*), with its wonderful breads, cheeses, and cold meats. I went back because I was invited to return to the same cities and to the same grammar and other schools to address new cohorts of young people, who were soon to be fully fledged voting citizens; I wanted them to become believers in the idea of human dignity and in the concept that democracy is best protected by using the rights it promises to all people. One such city that I am invited to over and again is Osnabrück, where the Action Center Third World and its director, Reinhard Stolle, do such excellent work promoting the dignity of people in the less well-developed countries of the world. I have come to know the city well. I know it is one of the cities where the peace treaty that ended the Thirty Years' War was signed. It is a city that takes its heritage as a peace city seriously. It has wonderful museums, galleries, and memorials to those who survived and those who did not survive the Nazi terror. There is the Erich Maria Remarque Museum, containing the papers and mementos of that great writer's life, work, and anti-Nazi beliefs that led him to be ostracized even after the Nazis were defeated! There is the Felix Nussbaum Haus, which commemorates that famous artist, whose depictions of suffering through war and intolerance speak so eloquently of the need for peace. There are the memorials to the victims of the Holocaust: homosexuals, Jews, Sinti and Roma peoples. It is a city that keeps our awareness of the past alive so that we do not repeat the same horrors in the future. It is my kind of city. I like to return there. In 2007 I made a speech at the opening of the city's Africa Culture Festival at a gathering in the Marienkirche.

Opening Address at the Africa Culture Festival, Osnabrück,
17 June 2007

Madame Burgermeister,

[In German:] There are many invited guests from Africa here today. I intend therefore to speak in English so that your guests, Madame Burgermeister, may better understand what I am saying. I am sure that most of the Germans present here today will also be able to understand what I am saying.

As we say in English, "All protocol observed."

[In English:] Yesterday was the 16 June. That is the day we celebrate the courage of our young people who in peaceful protest against apartheid racism were shot dead. More than six hundred were killed on that day by the racist regime, and many more were wounded.

Their rejection of apartheid spread throughout the land, and we older veterans said, "Roar, young lions, roar."

We remember the famous photograph of a young boy, Hector Pieterson, who was the first to fall on that day. That thirteen-year-old whose life was snuffed out like the flame of a candle was carried by a bigger boy with Hector's sister next to him, with an agonized face and raised hands pushing away the horror of what had happened.

Today you can see the memorial to Hector Pieterson in Soweto. That photograph and the memorial (*denkmal*) are part of our cultural heritage, part of Africa's cultural heritage.

Frau Burgermeister, it is an honor to have been invited to participate in this opening ceremony of this cultural festival. I take part in the name of those who died and those who lived through our struggle for freedom, a struggle for a land where our people of many cultures are becoming a land of one nation.

Your Africa Festival is part of that dream that Africa, with its many cultures, can again become a great continent. Where it can again become a continent of many people's striving for the African renaissance that President Mbeki of South Africa has made the theme of his presidency.

Our radio and TV show and report every day on the great diversity of Africa. It is wonderful that Osnabrück has invited cultural workers from numerous parts of Africa so that you in Europe can see and enjoy our continent's diversity.

Nelson R. Mandela says in his autobiography, *The Long Walk to Freedom,* that he realized during his twenty-seven years in prison, as I also realized in my twenty-two years in prison, that freedom requires that the oppressed and the oppressor must both be set free to regain their dignity as human beings. He said: "To be free is not merely to cast off one's chains, but to live in a way that respects and enhances the freedom of others." (*Um frei zu sein genügt es nicht, nur einfach die Ketten abzuwerfen; sondern Mann muss so leben dass Mann die Freiheit des Anderen respektiert und fördert.*)

Without that respect for each other's dignity, we will fall short of creating a land, a continent, a world, of equal opportunities for all our peoples in a nonracist, nonsexist society. Please note in all this, the key word is DIGNITY. (*Bitte beobachten das Stichwort: Menschenwürde.*)

It is good that Osnabrück, a city born out of the violence of long ago, and having lived through much violence and brutality since then, should take its name, the Peace City, so seriously that we can today in this cultural festival enjoy each other's cultures. I read to you a quotation from Erich Maria Remarque, your so very famous author who said in 1946: "One must believe in the future, in a better future. The world wants peace in spite of certain politicians. And the world wants the things back in which it can believe. The problems are—as always—utterly simple: humanity, understanding, progress, willingness to help. Man is good, in spite of everything." Your city is so rich in its museums and memorials to the terror and those who acted against it.

What is truly significant about this festival is the respect shown to the diverse cultures of Africa. In respecting these cultures and bringing performers from various parts of Africa, we respect and advance their freedom to be human beings. We respect their dignity!

I hope, I do hope, that that respect is shown not only during the festival, but every day of the year, every year!

Picasso took his new art form from the old art of West Africa and changed European art forever. A century later Paul Simon took the music of Ladysmith Black Mambazo to revitalize his own music. I think of Fela Kuti of Nigeria, of the church choirs of the former Belgian Congo that created the vital liturgical music of the Missa Luba. I think of the slaves who died in the Middle Passage from Africa to America, and the pain and suffering of such indignities that led to the blues and jazz and gospel music. Please think of how African culture has shaped music around the world.

I return to my opening words about freedom. Dignity requires that people be able to feed themselves and not be so exploited that they cannot survive. Dead people have no culture, and people whose weakness due to hunger makes them excessively susceptible to diseases do not have the energy to be cultural beings.

Europe must take the lead in getting rid of agrarian subsidies that are destroying the lives of African people and depriving them of their dignity.

It is in the interests of the people of Europe to enable Africa to reclaim its dignity. For moral, social, political, and economic reasons, cultural events such as this one in the Marienkirche in the Peace City of Osnabrück must help us to move towards a world of respect for DIGNITY.

I wish you all a wonderful Africa Culture Festival.

I thank you.

Joel Joffe, at my request, had given Edelgard permission to translate his book, *Story of the Rivonia Trial*. She had completed the translation, and it was to be published by the Dietz Verlag in Berlin in 2006 as *Der Staat gegen Mandela: Ein Protokoll über den Rivonia-Prozess* (The State versus Mandela: A Report on the Rivonia Trial). That came about because Arndt Hopfmann, a fellow German Africanist, had been sent by the Rosa Luxemburg Foundation to open its office in Johannesburg. He got the foundation to fund the publication of the book, and he personally made a significant contribution to editing the German translation. Edelgard was so determined to see the book launched at the first Frankfurt–Cape Town Book Fair in 2006 that she went to Germany herself and came back with six copies of the book just in time for that event. There our roles were reversed: she read excerpts and spoke in German and I was her translator into English. Shortly afterward, Joel brought out a new edition in English of his book, using the title Edelgard had worked out, *The State versus Mandela,* and used large parts of her epilogue, which I translated into English for that edition.

Upon Edelgard's return from Germany to Cape Town, it was found that she had a newly developed breast cancer, which was surgically removed. She recovered from that operation, but the chemotherapy was not controlling the original ovarian cancer. The chemotherapy made her very ill and was not even going to prolong her life. With her cancer specialist she made the very tough decision to stop the treatment, knowing that she did not have long to live. I found her one morning a crumpled heap under her blankets, quite shriveled up from vomiting, and had to half carry her, half drag her, into the back of my car to rush her to the hospital. The nurses were magnificent, swiftly taking control and in a few minutes had a drip going to rehydrate her. She pulled through, but the cancer was wearing her down, and eventually I became her nurse at home, changing drips and meeting her needs until her condition and my utter exhaustion required that she go into hospital some weeks before the end of December 2006. On one occasion I was caught on the horns of a dilemma. The hospital phoned me to say my Edel was very weak and I should get there as soon as I could. Again I dashed the twelve miles over a winding road that was her favorite drive in Cape Town. When I got to the hospital, she was in a diabetic coma. In a short while she would have been free of all pain forever. But what if a doctor or a nurse came in and pulled her out of her coma but perhaps too late to avoid brain damage? Then she would lie there as a helpless cabbage, and she would have hated that. I called a nurse, who was not very efficient. She fumbled around until she got the drip going and Edelgard opened her eyes as though she had taken a short nap. But she deteriorated quite quickly over the next weeks, becoming ever weaker and able to speak only in whispers. We spoke of many things in her last days, and she said how sorry she was that she could not look after me until I should die. She had wanted to do that, she said, because in our time together she had enjoyed the happiest years of her life. I wept because there was nothing else I could do. When we had got together, I had hoped that we could enjoy a companionable relationship. But the happiness I felt with her was extraordinary, for it was much more than just companionship. One morning after many months of knowing her I woke up and saw that her face was free of its usual stressed look, and in the corners of her eyes laugh lines had appeared. I fell in love all over again. In the words of a poet I once read, her smile turned my desert into an oasis. There had been a great closeness and the opening up of new friendships and travel in various countries. We spoke about the weekends away in the countryside of the Gauteng, Mpumalanga, Limpopo, and KwaZulu-Natal provinces. We had driven through Botswana to Zimbabwe to visit her former home and her daughter Tina in Bulawayo.

One of the things that kept her alive so long was her wish to see the house we were building in Cape Town where we would end our days. She did get to see it and live in it for fifteen months. We did many things together, such as visiting art galleries and museums and exploring some of the beauties of the Western Cape that in the days "before prison" there had never been time for. Now I was going to be alone again. It was devastating, and my exhaustion deepened the sense of doom. Her death on top of losing Esmé and then Hilly all in the space of six years seemed just too much to bear. I felt emotionally battered as never before. I went through the motions of living, but it was hard to pull myself together to do anything useful. Paperwork lay around, and I waited for my energy levels to rise again.

Throughout her time with me, Edelgard continued to report on and analyze developments in South and Southern Africa. She kept well-organized working files and, at her request, they were bequeathed to the University of South Africa (Unisa) Archive together with her magnificent library of German literature, both classical and modern, and her cookbooks and books on numerous topics so that students of German and Germanistics could get a real feel for the language and the people. That wish of hers was like the closing of a circle because it was through her study of Africanistics that she made her connection to Zenzo Nkobi and then to me and lived in various countries on the African continent, spending the last years of her life in South Africa.

Zenzo had trained as a photographer in Leipzig and that is where they met. He wanted to return to take part in the Zimbabwe and South Africa freedom struggles. They lived in various countries and for a long time lived in Lusaka among the representatives of various liberation communities. Zenzo was for a time the personal photographer of Joshua Nkomo, the founder of the Zimbabwe African People's Union (ZAPU), and that gave him access to many African leaders such as Kenneth Kaunda, Julius Nyerere, O. R. Tambo, Alfred Nzo, Robert Mugabe, and others. He also photographed the aftermath of the brutal raids on refugee camps by the Rhodesian Air Force. When he died, he left an archive of some 10,000 negatives. Edelgard had preserved them in her deep freeze after the couple returned to free Zimbabwe. She hid them from the raiding Zimbabwe African National Union (ZANU) gangs who were after Zenzo.[1] Zenzo having died of a stroke, she took them to Germany when she returned to that country. She took them to London and, when we moved to South Africa, she brought them along. I bought equipment so that we could digitally scan them, and Edelgard worked at identifying places, occasions, and people he had photographed. Eberhard Neugebohrn came from Germany for a few weeks to scan images. Edelgard's younger daughter, Tina, did a bit of scanning as well. Then Edelgard's ovarian cancer returned, and the third round of chemotherapy made her very ill, so working on the scans and negatives became difficult for her. In the meantime she drew up a proposal for the South African History Archive (SAHA) to house them, scan and identify them, and make them available for historical research in a way that none of us could do as individuals. As the illness took hold, she lost interest in the negatives. After her death I shipped them off to SAHA so that Zenzo's work could be made available for historical research and to honor his work with his camera in the struggle for freedom. Neither Edelgard nor I had any interest in making money from the images, and SAHA would have to find considerable resources to make the archived images useful. They have been taking the project forward. The Rosa Luxemburg Foundation has provided significant financial support for the project.

We intended to go together to present a copy of her translation of Joel Joffe's book to Nelson Mandela in December 2006, but Edelgard was too weak and she was not able to take part in the handover. Arndt Hopfmann went with me.

Edelgard died on 26 December 2006 in hospital. Her breathing became weaker and her voice slighter, and she seemed to finally and slowly fade away until she stopped breathing.

Neighbors came to commiserate when Edelgard died. Among them were local ANC members, and they dragged me back into the sunlight of activity. One of the activities that has helped me enormously is to be the active chairman of a cultural organization called Sentinel Experience, which functioned in our suburb of Cape Town called Hout Bay, about fifteen miles south of the city center, along one of the most beautiful coastal roads that I have ever seen. Our suburb is surrounded by mountains and the sea and is a microcosm of the ethnic distances between communities that in the main still occupy the land in the same pattern as that imposed by the Group Areas Act. Local people who had set up the organization asked me to join them in this work.

We organized two documentary film festivals in the hope that they would help draw together elements of our community deeply divided by our legacy of apartheid separation. We slowly created a track record of helping with musical instruments for a children's brass band and also for music lessons through a music teaching project. We held an exhibition in Hout Bay of the work of the Bethesda Art Centre of New Bethesda, of which I am a patron. The project was founded by Jeni Couzyn, a South African psychotherapist whom I had met in London and whom Community H.E.A.R.T. had helped with some funding during its start-up phase. Conceived as a healing process, Bethesda Art Centre specializes in quilted artwork depicting the traditional culture and oral tradition of the Khoisan people. The project is also about social values and the Coloured women of this small village in the desolate Small Karoo learning to insist on and uphold their rights in a repressive society. It has uncovered remarkable talents among the women involved.

A friend came to comfort me after Edelgard died, and she has become a special friend who has helped put some sparkle back into my life. I think, however, that there were times when I must have been very boring. In some magical way, nevertheless, we seem to each provide something the other needs: we see each other frequently and phone and text several times a day. It is nice to have a companion to go to lectures and the movies with and not to be totally alone again. She is a developing talented artist, and I have learned a great deal about art from her and from our many visits to art galleries. As a result, I have become fascinated by the work of local artists and have a growing collection of paintings, sculptures, and ceramics that delight my senses.

Slowly my life has come together again. I still travel to Germany to undertake lecture tours on the need for committed action to transform our country in defense of democracy. I have a simple thesis that the primary way of defending democratic rights is to use them. If we do not vote in elections, we get elected politicians who have no regard for those they represent. If we do not use our rights to gather together in praise of good government and we do not use those same rights to criticize bad government, we will soon find that "they" have taken our rights away from us. In the past few years I have been speaking to Cape Town students in the eleventh and twelfth grades and to history teachers as part of a program entitled "Facing History and Ourselves," organized by Shikaya, an NGO that seeks to make the history of the struggle for liberation come alive for young people and for their teachers. My lecture tours extended to the United States in 2014, as well as a brief visit to Nigeria, and it was especially pleasing to be invited to Oxford in England to deliver the Annual Bram Fischer Memorial Lecture.

I take part sometimes in my ANC branch but find the efforts through our cultural organization more personally satisfying. I have no personal political ambitions and find the jockeying for position by those who are ambitious very tedious and a distraction from the task of rebuilding our society.

In Hout Bay, I came across a music project started by a remarkable young woman, Dwynne Griesel. She is a trained musician and multitalented. She invested the whole of her father's bequest to her in the project that she intends should use the universal language of music to bring together young people from our still ethnically divided community. I have become a patron of this Kronendal Music Academy (KMA) of Hout Bay and have helped the project grow to include 150 young musicians, and the number is rapidly increasing toward a target of 200 students. There are fifteen part-time teachers and an additional ten coworkers who provide security, help with the supervision of the young people, and provide bowls of soup and sandwiches for the youngsters when they come after school for their lessons or practice sessions. An instrument-repair workshop has been started so that three previously unemployed people can learn the special skills needed to maintain the instruments. This is funded by the government's Expanded Public Works Programme. I love dropping in at KMA to enjoy the warm, welcoming atmosphere; there are so many young people who come there, and I see so many of them blossom. I always believed that our revolution had to be about people, and it is deeply gratifying to see what can be done with and for young people, many of whom come from deeply deprived backgrounds. Our liberation has opened up opportunities for people to realize their human capacities together and overcome their difficulties. It is about dignity.

In July 2012 we were able to take the jazz band, composed of seven young people, and its director on a two-week tour of Germany. Numerous local people helped in cash and in kind, and the Goethe Institute kindly agreed to pay the airfares. Tina Jerman coordinated the whole tour, which was a huge success. All the musicians grew musically and—perhaps more important—as personalities with a whole new perspective on their lives. The band also improved mightily. Most of the musicians would not have been able to go abroad without the funds we were able to raise. The tour was made possible by the many years of my speaking tours in Germany. Reinhard Stolle in Osnabrück was important, as were Henry Schneider and Gareth Lubbe (a South African), of the Gewandhaus Orchestra in Leipzig, and friends in Siegen at the Bertha von Suttner Comprehensive School. The tour included performances at the Hochschule in Essen, the Africa Culture Festival in Osnabrück, and eight other schools; the climax was the Stelzenfestspiel bei Reuth, to which we were invited by Henry Schneider, who founded this festival in 1993.

As I have previously described, I was arrested with my comrades on 11 July 1963 on the Liliesleaf Farm in Rivonia, in Johannesburg, and ended up sentenced to life imprisonment. The farm has been bought by the Liliesleaf Trust. Its CEO, Nicholas Wolpe, the son of Harold Wolpe, has restored the buildings as they were in 1963 and, using the most modern electronic and audiovisual techniques, has created a museum that recaptures the spirit of our struggle. This museum has its place beside the museum on Robben Island, dedicated to the triumph of the human spirit; the Apartheid Museum in Johannesburg, which records the nature of apartheid and the resistance to it; the Red Location Museum in a former township of Nelson Mandela City (Port Elizabeth), which memorializes the migrant workers of the Eastern Cape Province; and the Nelson Mandela Museum in Mthatha. The Liliesleaf Museum records in the place where it happened the dedicated planning and commitment to the ending of apartheid and the spirit of selfless courage of those who were there and those elsewhere who put their lives and freedom on the line for others' freedom. There are also a museum dedicated to Stephen Bantu Biko in Ginzberg, near Grahamstown, and the magnificent Freedom Park in Pretoria, with its wall of names of those who gave their all for freedom in our country.

At the official launch of Liliesleaf I made one of the speeches, and Andrew Mlangeni, a cosurvivor of the Rivonia Trial, also spoke in the presence of ANC President Jacob Zuma, who later became president of South Africa. He, of course, was the main speaker at the inauguration. I kept changing the speech I had prepared as others spoke and what follows are excerpts from my notes for the speech at the opening of Liliesleaf Museum, 30 May 2008.

Madame programme Director. All of those here tonight are important. I shall not greet specific people, but simply say, "All protocol observed."

There is a great continuity of links to Liliesleaf. President of the ANC Chief Albert Luthuli agreed, albeit reluctantly, to the armed struggle. He said, "when thieves come to steal my people's chickens they have the right to defend what is theirs." Nelson Mandela was the first Commander in Chief of MK and he lived here for a time. The great O. R. Tambo was the President of the ANC and as such commander in chief of MK, and was a co-accused in the Rivonia Trial. Nelson Mandela on his release became President of the ANC. He was followed by our current National President Thabo Mbeki who officially launched the Liliesleaf Trust at an event held at this place. Now the current President of the ANC, comrade Jacob Zuma, is here to officially open this Museum, this heritage site. He was a warrior, a deputy head, then head of intelligence; he came back courageously to pave the way for the negotiations that led to the end of apartheid and negotiated the peace in the civil war in kwaZulu-Natal. Forgive me if I say, President of the ANC Zuma, that the former herd boy negotiated with kings and princes, traditional leaders, business people and statesmen, to achieve peace. He negotiated the peace settlements in Rwanda and Burundi. It is appropriate that he should open this museum. Liliesleaf was the headquarters of the underground people's army, *Umkhonto we Sizwe*.

We speak of heritage. What is that heritage? We need to know because [in a variation on something we often say], unless we know where we came from, how do we know where we are, and how do we decide how we should continue to shape our future?

Like other people all over the world, we tend to take for granted what we have, those who count ourselves among the "haves," and forget how we came to have it, and even more we tend to forget those who "have not." It was for the "have nots" that we made our struggle and that is what Liliesleaf is about.

Liliesleaf helps us to remember, so that we and those who come after shall not be able to say, but we did not know!

Liliesleaf is an irony of history. But for the tip-off the police[2] got from intelligence agencies of countries that said they opposed racism, Liliesleaf might have remained in obscurity. If we had been more diligent in our housekeeping, Nelson Mandela's documents might not have been found in the coal bunker. He might not have been accused number 1 . . . and he might not have made his "I am prepared to die" speech that made him and the ANC famous throughout the world. Let me say now that I am very pleased that though we were prepared to die, and indeed did not expect to live, I am pleased that we did not. It is a matter of record, as lawyers like to say, that I told my mum, who had not heard the sentence, that we had got "Life! Life is wonderful!" . . .

There are sadnesses on occasions such as this: there are comrades who are here in spirit only. One of them is Bram Fischer, who with his team of lawyers got us life sentences. As I said, life sure as hell beats death sentences.

How I regret that comrades like O. R. Tambo, Raymond, Govan, Rusty, Elias, Walter, and Bram Fischer cannot be with us tonight. . . .

Let me say that the Rivonia Trial was a marvel of dignity, of courage, of nobility, of people who "rose above themselves" in their willingness to serve. I feel very privileged to have been part of it, to have shared in the highs and the lows of that time. You might recall the judge saying that he doubted our altruism because revolutionaries expect to take power. I saw no signs of that as the driving force in my comrades.

Let me return to one of the great highs: Nelson's "I am prepared to die" speech.

What an honour it was to be sitting almost alongside him when he closed with his famous last words, that the ideal of living together in harmony was one he hoped to live to see achieved, but if needs be, it was an ideal for which he was prepared to die. In effect he challenged the judge to hang him, and the rest of us too. But there was another high: life, we laughed with relief, and joy.

My comrades were always calm during the trial. But I saw anger, and distress, when Elias Motsoaledi's wife, Caroline, was arrested; when Andrew Mlangeni's wife, Beauty, was arrested; in Walter [Sisulu] when his son Max was arrested in the courtroom. Esmé was also arrested before the trial started. I think we do not give enough honour to our wives and children who paid a very high price for the freedom of our country. Our wives took part in the struggle in their own right and supported us and brought up our children. We take the credit that is due to them! Let us honour them. Think too of the courage of Arthur Goldreich and Hazel, his wife, who fronted as the owners and occupiers of Liliesleaf Farm knowing that they were sitting on a secret that like high explosives could go off at any time, blowing away their freedom and comfort and that of their children.

My conscience has troubled me for over forty years. We said we would tell the whole truth, but I as a trained engineer was not just a consultant to the High Command on weapons manufacture. I had been a member of the Western Cape Regional Command and later of the High Command structures. The Security Police did not know that and I did not feel the need to enlighten them. I am not sure how the judge would have reacted if I had enlightened the court on this matter. I also did not say that the famous camp at Mamre was in fact the first MK training camp inside South Africa. We will never know if that would have tied the rope around my neck and those of my comrades. I also did not feel it necessary to say that whether or not Operation Mayibuye was agreed upon, we would have started to make our weapons to carry on with armed propaganda. I have to apologise to our lawyers who are here tonight, Arthur Chaskalson, George Bizos, and Joel Joffe, that I kept this information from them. It might have troubled them to know these facts! . . . Comrade President Zuma of the ANC, I have a task to lay upon you: Inspire our civil servants at all levels of government to deliver services to our people. We have seen the most awful violence in the past few weeks stirred up in the fertile ground of a belief that our government does not care about our people. So much has been achieved, but much more must be done. We have a slogan for our civil servants, servants of the people: *Batho Pele,* people first. But unless we move forward faster we, if you will excuse me for mixing up languages, shall end up with *Batho Pelile* (*batho,* the people, *pelile,* finished). The matter, Comrade President of the ANC, is urgent.

I said earlier that we decide how we shall go forward. That is the task that lies before us.

All of this is what Liliesleaf is about.

Thank you.

President Zuma was charming when he responded off the cuff to my remarks. He said: "My Western Cape Commander has spoken. I accept the task he has laid upon me."

Professor Reinhold Goerling of the Heinrich-Heine-University in Düsseldorf had seen my speech to the U.N. Special Committee for the Day of Solidarity with Political Prisoners in Southern Africa, published on the Internet by South African History Online.[3] I was invited to participate in the conference on torture that he organized at his university. I spoke of my personal experience of torture and the way it was used against some of us and the lifelong mental scars torture leaves. At least a thousand people were murdered by apartheid interrogators and the police. I pointed out that torture has been forbidden by the constitution of the new South Africa. There is a difficult problem of implementation. Education and training of the police, firm administrative control over personnel, and determination to stamp out the practices are essential. For the first time, more than forty years after my own experience, I became very emotional when discussing this topic and at times had to pause to regain control.

A journalist reported as follows: "Over and over Denis Goldberg fell silent. He spoke haltingly of some episodes of torture and brutality that appeared in his own report. Sometimes he stopped reading, his gaze directed downwards when he described particularly brutal scenes. Psychologically and physically he has not completely recovered. He asked, 'Am I normal? I don't know.'"

(My paper "South Africa, the Transition to Democracy and the Banning of Torture" and a report by the journalist Maksim Hartwig, "The Brutality Was Immense," are in appendix 1.)

On 27 March 2009, six months after Thabo Mbeki had been recalled and President Motlanthe had been sworn in, I was awarded the National Order of Luthuli (Silver) for my part in our liberation from apartheid and service to the people of South Africa. I have to say that it was a proud moment, and I wished that Esmé could have been with me. I asked her cousin Rochelle to represent her at the ceremony. After I received the medal, high-ranking ANC and government members commented or asked why it had taken so long for it to be awarded to me. My answer was simply that I did not know, but it was nice to receive it while I was still alive. I was more surprised that others who should have been honored years before received similar awards at the same ceremony, and so I guess (but it is only a guess) that personal likes and dislikes and a refusal to give up one's right to be critical of one's own government had something to do with it. I often said that though I did not agree with every detail of government policy, it was great to live in a political system where I can say that and not be imprisoned for it.

Since then the German president has awarded me the Order of Merit (*Verdienstkreuz am Bande*) for developing the relations between the peoples of our two countries. President Zuma has awarded me the Military Veterans Medal in Platinum Class II for my contribution to the armed struggle against apartheid. The Gandhi Development Trust in Durban has awarded me their Mahatma Gandhi Peace Award for my contribution to human rights in South Africa. The Glasgow City College in Scotland has granted me their World Scholar Award.

My eightieth birthday was celebrated in April 2013 by the Kronendal

Music Academy, and some 150 friends and comrades from South Africa and several other countries attended. It was a warm, friendly event and some of the students entertained us. A celebratory volume, or Festschrift, had been published by my friends in German and it came as a complete and wonderful surprise.[4] They spoke about their work with me in the period after my release from prison until the present. The project had been kept secret from me for the three years that it took to prepare. Since then the text has been translated into English, and additional pieces by South Africans who knew me before my release have been included.[5] Thirty-one authors and editors, as well as photographers, contributed, and it pleases me that many people know more about the international component of the struggle for liberation and reconstruction.

In June 2013 a friend said he read in a newspaper that I had been appointed to the Integrity Commission, set up in accordance with a resolution of the ANC National Conference held in Mangaung in December 2012. I had not been asked if I wished to be a member of the commission. I had also not been briefed about how it would carry out its work.

The media often reported on conflicts of interest of some members of the ANC, which led to self-enrichment by officials both elected and appointed at every level of government at the public expense; dereliction of responsibility; statements made in stark contradiction to the policies of the organization; and other embarrassing actions by some of its members. Corrupt money practices in the private sector, especially in relation to state infrastructure contracts, were also rife, which implied connivance by officials. It seemed to me that government and the ruling party in particular had to begin to set an example to combat these tendencies.

Despite the manner of my appointment, of not being properly informed or consulted, I felt I had to participate. The task is an immense and important one. The other commission members were, like me, veterans who no longer had a desire to seek high office. The chairman was my comrade Andrew Mlangeni, who after twenty years in Parliament had at last retired and been appointed to this post. Meetings, I discovered, were to be held every Saturday. I had to get a very early start to fly to Johannesburg and be picked up and taken to Liliesleaf, which provided space for the commission to meet. Then I would fly home the same day. It was exhausting.

There were no protocols as yet established, and we vigorously debated whether the Integrity Commission was in fact an autonomous body or a committee of the Secretariat of the ANC under the control of the secretary general. The latter instructed us to investigate and report on any accounts, including those by the media, of actions or utterances of members of whatever rank that appeared to bring the ANC into disrepute. The secretary general would from time to time instruct the commission on who and what to investigate. The commission, we were told, is a subcommittee of the Secretariat. It has no permanent staff of its own. Two very capable comrades, professional people, both of them members of the organization, voluntarily devoted spare time to perform the secretarial functions of the Integrity Commission.

If investigation is needed, we are required to ask the secretary general to carry this out. There is no sense of urgency. The commission has the authority to order any member to appear before it, provided proper notice is given of when and where a hearing is to take place and the substance of the complaint is made clear. The member so summoned is required to give an explanation of his or her conduct, and the commission reports to the secretary general, who determines what action should be taken, including the possibility of a full-scale disciplinary procedure under the constitution of the ANC.

Some of the members, including myself, could not attend every meeting. Age, tiredness, and other activities got in the way. My travels on lecture tours abroad prevented my regular attendance. I also felt that what we were doing should have been important, but there seemed to me to be an increasing tendency for us to seek to solve political problems by judicial and quasi-judicial means when determined political leadership was required to guide policies. This was especially true regarding the appointment and dismissal of officials who relied on slack administration to flout the commonsense rules and values of serving all our people, not just a small elite whose members have access to power.

In 2014 I had a very heavy schedule of lectures abroad, in Germany, Britain, and the United States, and in South Africa. In addition, I had to make time for a hip replacement operation, after which six to eight weeks would be required for me to become fully fit again. I took a leave of absence from April to September and in October decided that I could not continue to be a member of what is in fact a toothless structure, lacking administrative and investigative resources; what appeared to be tackling rampant abuses was actually not empowered to do much at all. I resigned at the end of October, stating:

If I felt that the Commission could fulfill its mandate, one could make the effort to regularly attend meetings. But as presently constituted and serviced by the Office of the Secretary General, the Commission cannot function as effectively as it should do.

The Commission depends upon the SG's office for its secretarial and investigative resources. Those resources are inadequate to the tasks of the Commission. In addition the dependence upon the SG and his Office for such services subjects the Commission to intended or unintended controls that remove the Commission's autonomy and therefore its ability to function with integrity. It cannot possibly act against any and every member if so required because of these constraints.

Without going into detail, I am convinced that the highest echelons of leadership of our organization have to be more upfront and open in their condemnation of actions by members that bring the ANC into disrepute. Instead we often see media reports of statements, utterances, comments and actions by our leading elements that are seriously embarrassing to the organization.

As one gets older, time and energy seem to become more valuable. Fund-raising for social projects and working at developing social cohesion through these projects and the lecturing I do both here and abroad are extremely satisfying and directly feed into what I have always believed we struggled for, to make the lives of our people better. Since no government can do all that is needed to overcome the deeply engraved disadvantages imposed on the vast majority of our people, I am happy to work with civil society organizations to assist in whatever way I can.

I am deeply aware that a lack of management skills, especially the ability to foresee problems before they arise, is often at the root of failures to implement well-thought-out policies in every sphere of government. After the revolutionary shake-up such as we experienced, I hoped that our comrades who were appointed to the administration would, through their enthusiasm—I mean revolutionary fervor—overcome our lack of experience in government administration. But there were too many officials who seized on the lack of experience, especially at supervisory and control levels, to deliberately abuse the system. Some twenty years after our liberation, our national minister of social development reported that of his staff of some 60,000 people, 40,000 had been or were under investigation for disciplinary offenses involving fraudulent diversion of funds to their private accounts. Problems were collusion between officials and the lack of trained accountants and auditors. Something similar occurred at a university where a catering contractor and the officers in the Accounting Department of the university colluded to fraudulently divert 9,000,000 rand (about $75,000) into their pockets. It was even more surprising that the internationally renowned external auditors failed for years to spot these activities.

21

Last Thoughts—For Now

2015

Great gains have been made since Nelson Mandela became president in 1994. The first is that the-old guard racists have in general come to realize that there is no going back to the apartheid past. Some older people find it difficult to break down the walls in their heads, and that makes it hard for them to behave with simple courtesy and tolerance toward people of other races. Young people, though there are some striking exceptions, appear to socialize in fairly normal ways. Where overt racism appears, as it did at one of the former Afrikaans universities, there are huge outcries of disgust.

Thabo Mbeki was the deputy president for the whole of the first five years of government; he created and ran the new administration—a new public service organization—and new democratic political structures for the functioning of Parliament. At the same time the need for widespread discussion to enable the democratic promise of the Freedom Charter and its realization in our new constitution makes everything government does take a very long time. Our Constitutional Court has been vigilant in upholding democratic rights of citizens and organizations against the demands of government officials and ministers, and that has been a very positive development. But within the ANC and the government, our party list system of proportional representation made it almost certain that personal likes and dislikes and some nepotism would emerge because that is the way of ruling elites everywhere.

Failures by a cluster of ministries to achieve their goals led to a committee to oversee a committee to solve its problems. And within that setup, the intellectual brilliance of President Mbeki, in addition to his constitutional powers to appoint certain officials (and therefore to get rid of those who disagreed with him), ensured an excessive centralization of power. It was a style that was perhaps necessary at the beginning, but when it became entrenched, it began to hold things back.

President Mbeki established a remarkable track record, and his efforts to ensure that South Africa and Africa as a whole are influential in world affairs through the African Renaissance, the leitmotif of his presidency, have been very successful. Having on various occasions persuaded African presidents not to change their countries' constitutions so that they could be "president for life," he accepted that limitation for himself, too. Thus, he would serve only his constitutional two terms of office as president of the Republic of South Africa. His decision to "allow himself to be nominated," as he put it, for a third five-year term as president of the ANC was inexplicable; he must have believed that only he had the answers to our problems. But his arguments against third and further terms in office for national presidents were equally relevant: that patterns of decision making, policy, and implementation become entrenched and encrusted, and the top people are unable to recognize that the very success of the policies they have implemented requires new solutions from people with fresh ideas and enthusiasm.

At the ANC National Conference in December 2007, Mbeki was defeated by Jacob Zuma, the deputy national president he had dismissed, in an unseemly political contest that he had no hope of winning, given that he had been heavily defeated at the preceding National General Council meeting of the ANC. His candidacy left the organization divided. Some members were expelled by the new leadership, and some resigned from the ANC. If Thabo Mbeki had wanted to ensure an internal opposition to his successor, he himself had to stand aside because the tensions had become so strong that the very fact of his accepting the nomination, even though it was legal in terms of the ANC's constitution, would result in a split.

What puzzled me was that not one of those who had access to him, such as members of his cabinet or National Executive Committee comrades, called on him publicly, not as president but as Comrade Thabo, not to stand for reelection. That for me was the measure of the excessive centralization of power that had developed. It was such a pity because President Mbeki, despite disagreements I have had over some of his policies and practices, was an exceptionally capable and innovative politician. In the end he was compelled by the new Executive Committee to resign as national president a few months before the end of his term of office. I found that the decision to recall Thabo Mbeki from the national presidency was more an act of revenge by some elements in the leadership of the ANC who had been previously sidelined and humiliated by him than a matter of political principle. I also admired the dignity of his speech when resigning and his statement that he would be a loyal member of the ANC.

The centralization of power in the government led to a loss of support by elements of all sections of the population that had previously been loyal supporters of the ANC. Coupled with this was the fact that too many leaders at every level appeared to use their political party as a vehicle to promote members of this or that faction to high office, where access to power provided access to opportunities for self-enrichment. That led to further factional activities that weakened the ANC's power as a party to hold its members in government to account.

A consequence of the sharp turnover of top members of the ANC after the National Elective Conference at Polokwane, Limpopo, in December 2007 was the formation of a breakaway party called the Congress of the People (COPE). Some of those who resigned said they had done so because of the indignity heaped on President Mbeki when he was recalled and resigned the presidency. My interpretation was that some of them had lost very heavily in the election of members of the ANC National Executive Committee and would not be kept on as ministers under a new president and therefore had nothing to lose by resigning. It was disappointing to see the breakaway party, but I have to admit this was a test of our democracy. Given the massive support the new party received in the mainstream media, it did less well than many had hoped in the national and provincial elections in April 2009. The party won seats in all nine provinces. Its members campaigned freely and, though there were undisciplined ANC members who resented the new party, the ANC need not have worried excessively because COPE's election campaign was based not on any clear policy differences with the ANC but on personalities and style.

It was a great pleasure to be invited by the ANC parliamentary chief whip to address a gathering in New Town Johannesburg in honor of Nelson Mandela's ninety-first birthday, when Mandela Day was inaugurated as an official day of celebration and rededication to building our nonracial, nonsexist democracy. Below is the speech I prepared. I wanted to use the occasion to make a call for morality in public life and service through principled decision making in the interests of our people and not in the interests of the decision makers, who look first to their personal interests. I had to cut the speech short because others spoke for too long, but it was published in full on the ANC website as the "Address by Denis Goldberg to Mandela Day gathering convened by Parliament 18 July 2009."

In wishing my comrade and friend Nelson a happy ninety-first birthday I spoke about his commitment (he was prepared to die for his ideals, he said). He was principled, not wavering from his ideals, and all the adulation he suffered did not lead him to deviate. He always upheld the non-racist principles of the Freedom Charter. Equally, the MK Manifesto said that a negotiated settlement was preferable to a destructive bloodletting. When the time came, he led the way to a negotiated settlement. He was critical of corruption in both the ANC and in government.

As I am writing in 2015, it is clear that achieving political democracy without striving for a more equitable sharing of the wealth of our country has left us with serious social and economic problems. The Randburg Ward 102 Branch of the ANC has renamed itself the Denis Goldberg Branch, and I was asked to make the First Denis Goldberg Annual Lecture on 6 October 2012. I called it "Close the Gap" in recognition of what we have still to do to achieve the equality we speak of in our Freedom Charter and the constitution of our new South Africa. In a certain sense my lecture summarizes my understanding of where we are in our transition from the old apartheid era to our new society.

In my speech I said, among other things:

I accepted the honor of the naming of the branch because I come from a previous generation who saw little prospect of surviving the struggle, and it is rather nice for a new generation to acknowledge that others came before them in the struggle. We are all products of the old society. We still see each other as belonging to different ethnic groups. We always spoke of the national liberation struggle, in which the sharpest contradictions were those affecting black African workers in a capitalist society. Then there were the national minorities—Coloured, Indian, and white. To have African comrades who stand up and implicitly proclaim that "South Africa belongs to all who live in it," by choosing to name their branch after a member of the most privileged of the national groups, demands that I have to respond positively. Not least because this adherence is to the principle spelled out so clearly in the Freedom Charter of 1955. This is especially important in this period of nation building, of attempting to achieve cohesion, while there are some younger leaders who espouse the opposite: a narrow national chauvinism that creates enemies of our party, the ANC, the ruling party in the national government. . . .

In the political sphere our Constitution of 1996 sets out many goals that still have to be achieved in terms of equality and the restoration of the dignity of our people, stolen from them by the history of colonial and racial oppression, coupled with economic exploitation or super exploitation. It is the Inequality Gap, the disparities in the opportunities we are able to offer our people, that we must deal with; the gap between urban people and rural, poverty stricken or well off, that we have to close with all the efforts we can muster. I must add that it is clear to me that it will take a number of generations to achieve all our goals, but that means we have to make even greater efforts if we are to remain true to the principles of our struggle led by the ANC and its allies. . . .

In October [August] 2013 [2012] mine workers went on strike at the Marikana platinum mine in Northwest province. Dreadful violence followed. The striking miners killed eight other workers and two policemen. A week later the police opened fire on the strikers and killed thirty-four and wounded many others. A Judicial Commission of Inquiry was instituted by the President to determine the immediate and deeper causes of the strike and the violence that occurred. The Commission has been sitting for two years so far.

The miners of Marikana have been the spearhead of the newly reawakened realization that we have not changed the basic relationships of low-wage cheap labor and high-waged skilled labor and even obscenely high salaries of supervisors and managers in the private and public sectors.

The emergent trade unions of the seventies and eighties of the last century established the principle that working conditions do not stop at the factory gate. Living conditions, education, and health care were all part of the conflict. Have we forgotten this? How is it that so many who came out of that period of struggle became high-ranking politicians and top civil servants and then fled the governmental scene to get rich quick? Apparently earning ten times as much as an entry-level worker or teacher was not a quick enough route to wealth. They felt that being in government and trying to sort out the mess we had inherited was too frustrating. Others stayed to enrich themselves through access to resources.

However we define our National Democratic Revolution, and the simplest definition is the extension of the democratic rights held by whites under apartheid to the historically disadvantaged national groups, together with the aspirational rights to better living conditions in the Constitution, I think that we have made enormous strides in a mere twenty years since 1994, when the formal transfer of political power was made from the white minority to the people as a whole.

We always demanded "power to the people, *Amandla ngawethu.*" I cannot go on shouting slogans, comrades. The people have the power, and the question has become how do we use that power? How do the people exercise control over their elected representatives who so often come to believe that having been elected, the power is theirs for their benefit alone. This is especially important at the local government level where service delivery must take place. Hence the title of my talk: CLOSE THE GAP. . . .

Have we made real progress in enlarging our economy? [Yes, the economy is three times greater than it was in 1994 but] there is still over 40 percent unemployment in the formal economy. To employ our people we need to double the size of the economy very quickly in order to simply stand still, so to speak. It is a formidable task. I think that so far we have simply divided up the cake to accommodate a new section of the ruling class. I am nearly eighty years old and I have lived through a lot of history. I have seen English-speaking capital and international capital rape our country and screw our people. In 1948 a new group, Afrikaans speakers, took their bite at the cherry.

And now we are repeating the process with a new group of aspirant and arrived capitalists. We can find these relations, or distribution of what we might call the wage fund, in the national convention of 1909—no political rights in order to have cheap black labor for industry, commerce, farming, and the mines. Then we had the Lands Act to force people off the land as cheap labor, and they were compelled to work as wage labor by having to pay taxes in cash. Payment in kind was no longer permitted. Hut tax, poll tax, wife tax, dog tax, etc. The 1922 strike by white miners where the ratio of how many cheap black laborers to how many high-paid white workers was the issue was a significant moment. That strike led in the 1924 general election to a coalition of Afrikaner Nationalists and the White Labor Party, with the Chamber of Mines making white workers high paid—eighteen times the pay of black workers—and as "managers to control black workers."

This was reinforced in 1946–1947 in the great African miners' strike and the subsequent Judicial Commission into mine workers' wages. The Chamber of Mines, the bosses, presented a classic cost of reproduction of the workforce argument. They said that since they give them land on which to live rent-free, they can deduct the cost of rent from their needs. Since families often grow a bag or two of maize on that land, the value of these crops can be deducted from what migrant mine workers have to be paid to survive and reproduce.

Note that the mine owners consider the land conquered by the settlers and vested in the state as land that they, the mines, gave to their workers' families! They said they provide a bunk in a barracks and they provide three meals a day and this is part of their wage too. The lack of social services, schools, clinics, etc. in the reserves meant that the cost of raising children, the next generation of workers, was very low. The learned judges of the Beaumont Mine Wages Commission perpetuated the differential wages of so-called unskilled workers and skilled artisans. These differentials were not determined by relative contributions to production and the values created. They were determined by class interests blatantly reinforced by the segregationist apartheid state. We took over these differentials and some of our great leaders allowed themselves to be willingly co-opted. We have not significantly set about changing these differentials.

I boasted that my generation of activists and leaders saw the prize as freedom, not what we would get out of being in the struggle. I have a difficult problem for us to solve. What is the role of the trade union movement in a developmental state in a period of transformation? How is it that public sector unions affiliated to the Alliance are so little concerned with transformation in practice rather than in rhetoric?

I end by saying that we as members of the ANC are collectively responsible because we allowed ourselves to be demobilized by the Mbeki ANC. The turning of Mandela into the great one who single-handedly brought us freedom implies that we should wait for a new "Saint Madiba" to come and solve our problems. It is not enough to dream of what our country must become. We must act to make the dream come true. Join me, comrades, in this exciting and enormous task.

Nevertheless, it is clear that the ANC will not be able to continue forever as a political party that still tries to preserve its unity as a cross-class liberation movement. Interests of business and workers well organized in trade unions cannot be forever managed within a single party. There will at some point be a separation along class lines. COPE, from its pronouncements, appeared to herald such a division and took its position to the political right of the ANC.

More recently, in April 2014, there have been the fifth national elections for Parliament and the provincial councils. The infighting in the ANC and symptoms of abuse of power, as well as failures to deliver services at the local government level, led to the ANC's being returned to power as the majority party but with a reduced majority. The narrow majority of 53 percent in Gauteng province, the economic powerhouse of the country, shows that there has been a serious erosion of confidence among the electorate. Similarly, the loss of support in the Nelson Mandela Bay Metro (Port Elizabeth), the main city in the Eastern Cape province, which has long been an ANC stronghold, reveals the decay within the ANC.

The official opposition in the national Parliament is still the Democratic Alliance. A new party, the Economic Freedom Fighters (EFF), was formed shortly before the elections and is the third-largest party in Parliament. It is led by Julius Malema, the former president of the ANC Youth League. He was expelled together with other members by the ANC after a long and complex disciplinary process. The EFF's main platform is the nationalization of mines and banks and all major economic activities to carry through economic reform in the interests of the historically dispossessed. My interpretation of this party's politics is that it represents a second generation of black activists, some of whom were expelled from the ANC, and younger adults who cannot find an adequate foothold in major corporations and seek their own benefit through access to resources by means of control of state-owned industries and commerce.

The EFF feeds on the inadequacy of economic policies to provide jobs in a globalized economy and to close the gap between the low income of the mass of workers and the incomes of managers and skilled professionals. Growth of the economy has not produced the formal jobs that are absolutely necessary if real and sustainable improvement in the lives of the people is to be achieved. South Africa was affected by pressures from the World Bank in the early years of the new government, which inherited a technically bankrupt state from the apartheid regime.

Building the stadiums and infrastructure for the 2010 Fédération International de Football Association (FIFA) World Cup demonstrated the need and the possibilities of state intervention in the economy to create long-term employment. This will have to be taken further. An uncontrolled market system with uncontrolled investment in extractive industries is not the way forward if the capitalist market system of production and distribution is to put our people to work. We have to cut unemployment or, rather, create jobs in the formal economy so that we can reduce the number of jobless people from well over 40 percent to, say, 15 to 20 percent in the next twenty years. I cannot see a socialist revolution in the near future, but the idea of unbridled greed and exploitation cannot be allowed to continue. I believe that our hopes for a nonracial and nonsexist society are inextricably bound up with the creation of sustainable jobs that give people not only an income but also the dignity of providing for themselves from their own labor.

I pointed out in my report on a training course in India and Malaysia that South Africa needed to develop a national economic planning unit and monitoring system to speed up development programs in sectors where they are most needed.

At last this has occurred. The National Planning Commission, established by President Zuma in his first term of office, has produced a comprehensive National Development Plan based on continued and accelerated infrastructure development, improved education, and, in particular, skills training at academic and vocational levels. The last is important as there is a dire shortage of trained artisans and technicians of all kinds. In terms of physical infrastructure, there is a critical shortage of electric power, which hampers investment in industry.

President Zuma in his State of the Nation Address, made at the start of the parliamentary session in June 2014, after the national elections, has committed his ANC government to radical implementation of the National Development Plan.

There is a tendency among some elements in the ANC to subvert the Freedom Charter and the constitution by seeking to deny the equality of all who live in South Africa. This is shown by paying lip service to "South Africa belongs to all who live in it" while using access to power to advance members' separate ethnic groups. This is accompanied by a tendency to try to divide the cake of the economy into ever smaller pieces when what is required is a bigger economy more equally distributed among all our people, and that again requires job creation and closing the gap between starting wages and the huge salaries and bonuses of management.

Bertolt Brecht in his poetry dug deep to show the humanity of our socialist thinking and the activist revolutionary lives we led in seeking to make a better life for our fellow human beings. In South Africa now, as I write, there are deep wounds engraved in our psyches. All of us find it very hard to see people. We see groups defined by race, those who were the oppressors and the oppressed, and who were the most oppressed. It is not as easy to build a nonracist society as we thought it would be. It is even more difficult to build a nonsexist society when too many men see women as meat to be taken rather than as fellow human beings, activists, thinkers, companions, mothers, daughters, friends, and the bearers of the seeds of the future who need to be respected and, in their personal relationships, loved.

Brecht's poem "To Posterity," as I have previously said, captures the harshness of the struggle for freedom and the wounds it inflicted on us, the freedom fighters.[1] But that is no excuse to say that, because we were hurt, we have no choice in the way we govern now that we have acquired power. We sometimes seem to forget that our purpose was freedom and equality. Nelson Mandela said in his autobiography that "to be free is not merely to cast off one's chains, but to live in a way that respects and enhances the freedom of others."

The carpet weavers of Kujan-Bulak, in another of Brecht's poems, live in a poverty-stricken village on the Trans-Siberian Railway, deep in Central Asia.[2] The order comes from the far-off capital that they must collect money to buy a plaster bust in honor of the great Comrade Lenin. They collect the money but a revolutionary army veteran proposes that instead of buying the plaster bust they buy oil to spread on the bog to kill the mosquitoes that carry the illness that makes them weak with fever. They follow that suggestion and, after they have destroyed the source of their illness, another veteran proposes that they put up a plaque saying what they have done so that all who pass by can see it. And in so doing they have improved their lives and honored the great leader. Brecht movingly shows that we have to turn our theory and wishes into practice because it is action that translates fine visions into reality. Empty, formalized ceremony is no substitute for actively building our new society through working together.

These themes have occupied my thoughts for a considerable time, and I want to refer again to the ANC's Integrity Commission. Defining integrity for the purposes of political discipline is not as easy as it sounds.

When I was instructed to be a member of the Integrity Commission, I looked for definitions of integrity. In essence it must mean holding true to a set of values that are embodied in rules of conduct. The question then becomes whose values? Whose rules? Basically, the rules to be obeyed are those of the society as a whole. A religious body, a club or association, and personal belief all reflect sets of values. In a constitutional democracy the values expressed through laws and judicial decisions become paramount and override the rules of lesser groups within the general society.

But again, whose rules are expressed through the constitutional provisions? Society is undoubtedly not homogeneous; otherwise, we would not struggle to find consensus on the values and rules. Throughout history the hegemonic values have been imposed by a dominant group, and as power bases rise and fall new values—at variance with the old, but informed by them—emerge.

In the capitalist era the idea of a free labor force emerged, but the dominant capitalist class imposed its values on all. Within that class there was the need for what one might call "fair play," so that one did not unfairly overwhelm another by dirty tricks. Judging by the litigation that goes on in every country over contracts, insider trading, collusion over interest rates, and foreign exchange rates, we see that rules are there to be broken. More interesting is that working people in their organizations of trade unions and political parties adopt the same values and seek to compel the dominant group to play by its own rules.

We see in South Africa today the conflicts that come about when the apparent consensus is flouted on a daily basis by the very people who through their elected representatives created the rule book, the constitution. So where does a person of integrity find the meaning of those values and what are the limits to that consensus?

It cannot be in the laws alone because laws are written in natural language and subject to interpretation. The intention of the laws is to be found in the underlying history that brought about the passage of the laws, as in the preamble to the 1996 Constitution of the Republic of South Africa.

By chance, while wrestling with these issues, I saw that Deputy Chief Justice Dikgang Moseneke delivered a keynote address—"Reflections on South African Constitutional Democracy: Transition and Transformation"—at the MISTRA-TMALI-UNISA Conference "20 Years of South African Democracy: So Where to Now?" held at the University of South Africa on 12 November 2014.[3]

I quote from this remarkable speech:

Our constitutional democracy was forged on the anvil of division, past injustice and economic inequity, but also on the hope for reconciliation, nation building and social cohesion. Notionally, our Constitution is premised on the will of the people expressed in representative and participatory processes. It does not only establish its supremacy, rule of law and fundamental rights but also recites our collective convictions. It contains our joint and minimum ideological and normative choices of what a good society should be. It enjoins the state, all its organs, to take reasonable steps without undue delay to achieve that good society. The virtuous society envisioned has a significant social democratic flavour, some reckon, and yet others take it to be a neo-liberal compromise. Aside facile tags, the Constitution provides for many progressive things. It protects and advances fair labour practices. It compels all to preserve an environment that is not harmful; for the benefit of present and future generations. It envisions restitution of land to victims of dispossession but does not permit arbitrary deprivation of property. It permits expropriation and redistribution of land for public good provided that it is against just and equitable compensation. The envisioned society sets itself firmly against poverty, ill health and ignorance. This it does by promising everyone the right to have access to adequate housing, healthcare, food, water and social security subject to available resources and progressive realisation. A child's best interests are of paramount importance in every matter concerning it. And everyone has a right to basic education including adult basic education.

The Constitution enjoins and hopes for an effective, responsive, open and accountable governance from all organs of state inclusive of parliament, the executive and the courts. Parliament must make laws, hold the executive accountable and provide a forum for the debate of matters of national importance. The executive must implement laws, make policy and spend fiscal allocations. Courts must resolve disputes in accordance with the Constitution and the law which includes African indigenous law and the common law.

It must follow from what I have said that our constitutional design is emphatically transformative. It is meant to migrate us from a murky and brutish past to an inclusive future animated by values of human decency and solidarity. It contains a binding consensus on, or a blueprint of, what a fully transformed society should look like.

Justice Moseneke deals with the conflicts that arise between various groups within our society. He says:

Our courts have developed a proud jurisprudence on justice at the work place. That is a consequence of the vital choices our founding mothers and fathers have made on worker rights, the recognition and formation of trade unions and employers organisations, the resultant collective bargaining and fair labour practices. Properly so, courts have refused to sacrifice work place justice on the back of claims or promises of economic growth that a so-called open labour market will bring to us. That may, or may not, be so. But that is not for judges to decide. Courts are bound by labour laws. Just labour laws are integral to a more equal and caring society where the dignity of all, including of working people, is well shielded.

Why then are there conflicts within the labor movement? Why are there separate federations of trade unions? Why within the biggest of them, the Congress of South African Trade Unions (COSATU), allied to the ruling party, the ANC, are there conflicts that lead one group to expel another by a small majority of votes? The arguments go back and forth, each side claiming to uphold the values enshrined in the national constitution and in the COSATU constitution. Each accuses the other of bad faith, of not upholding the values of their movement and the transformative agenda of our present political situation. So is it about strategy and tactics in the interests of the working class? There is deep-seated frustration at the inability of the state and thus the ANC government to transform the economy to create jobs, to close the gap between the incomes of masses of low-paid workers and an elite of higher-paid artisans and highly paid managers, and to curb the profits earned by shareholders (often concealed by transfer pricing and clever tax-avoidance schemes).

Other factors emerge, such as the morality of particular leaders often in relation to financial probity, but also in matters of sexual conduct and managerial style. It becomes about such things as access to government resources and possibilities of preferment and opportunities for personal enrichment.

In the end the search for integrity lies within an individual and group conscience that upholds the fundamental values that have been agreed on, as Justice Moseneke describes them. I would contend that those of us who broke the apartheid laws acted with integrity: there was no consensus possible unless we could put an end to that brutish system of denial of human rights on racial grounds, for purposes of exploitation and profit making.

The consensus seemed to hold until shortly before the general election of 2009, although there were conflicts within the ANC-led alliance with COSATU and the Communist Party in the early years of Mbeki's presidency over the policies of restructuring imposed by the International Monetary Fund (IMF). The party political break came with the formation of a new party, COPE, by former ANC members critical of the perceived cronyism in the ANC and in government. COPE drew a considerable membership across the racial spectrum. It was saddening to see that the same cronyism and lack of financial probity was carried into COPE, though it did well in the 2009 election campaign, winning seats in all nine provinces. It did not fare very well in the 2014 elections, as it lost many seats.

Unrest in municipalities has grown in frequency and violence as these governments have not been able to meet the service needs of their rapidly growing populations; poverty-stricken people have fled the countryside to find a place in the cities, towns, and villages. ANC members were challenging their elected local representatives, and this led to violent protests. In some places parents kept children out of school for nearly a whole year as a protest in support of their demand for paved access roads to their communities.

The year 2012 was the turning point during which striking mine workers in a breakaway union killed members of the recognized National Union of Mineworkers. That was followed a week later by armed police, ostensibly looking for the killers, opening fire on the striking miners, killing thirty-four of them in the process.

What is clear to me is that politicians and individuals have the responsibility to uphold the values expressed in our constitution. The president, as the head of the executive arm of government and as head of the ruling party, has in my view the ultimate responsibility to lead in matters of integrity. Equally, the secretary general of the ANC must play a leading role in his party. Leaders of provincial structures share the same responsibility. I believe that our leaders have failed to live up to these values and the ensuing duties. The patronage culture surrounding national and provincial leaders is alarming because it has become self-perpetuating.

We live in a patronage society constructed through centuries of indigenous formations that were absorbed into the structures of colonial rule and the subsequent segregation and apartheid in South Africa.

Indigenous society of chiefly authority was generally tempered by the power of a people in a tribe to democratically control the actions of their chief through their power to replace an authoritarian chief or simply to leave his tribe and join another. But with population growth, and particularly the limits placed on tribal members' options by colonial conquest and control, chiefly authority became more authoritarian.

South Africa was colonized by Great Britain, and its early twentieth-century Colonial Secretary Lord Lugard formalized the power relationships first in Nigeria as "indirect rule" by incorporating the chiefly structures into the colonial administration. The chiefly authority was backed by the political and military power of the colonizers through the district commissioners, who controlled the actions of the chiefs. Acceptance of that control gave the chiefs the patronage that they could pass on to their favored supporters. The so-called traditional powers of chiefs are thus not ultimately traditional but adapted to authoritarian colonial rule.

In South Africa the control was intensified by white settler colonial governments to ensure that the benefits of authoritarian rule over the majority would benefit the white settler society, its farmers, companies, and investors. It became a system of patronage of whites in general and English speakers in particular under British colonial rule, and from 1910 onward it was the form of legalized racial segregation in the Union of South Africa established by an act of the British House of Commons. This changed in 1948 with the election to power of white Afrikaans speakers, who through state patronage enabled this part of the white society in general and new recruits to the capitalist ruling class to become well-off through the intensification of segregation in the form of an even more strict separation of races under the policy of apartheid. Apartheid, like segregation before it, was not merely a matter of social attitude but the basis for intensified economic exploitation of the mass of black workers through administrative controls and denial of political and trade union rights.

The end of apartheid, signaled by the election of the new Parliament by all adults in 1994, brought a new group of political representatives to power in a system that clearly carried within it the systems and practices of the past. In particular, it soon became apparent that patronage through access to state resources would enrich a new stratum of people historically deprived by segregation and apartheid. They are part of a new group of capitalists willingly co-opted into the exploitative system. The private sector actively sought to co-opt representatives and leaders onto their boards and into well-paid managerial positions. Their salesmen devised many dodgy get-rich-quick schemes involving some greedy leaders whom they would pay well to sell their schemes to the people they could exploit.

One of the earliest actions of the new government was to put through Parliament a massive increase in the salaries and privileges of members of Parliament, thus negating the idea that the more egalitarian ideas contained in the Freedom Charter would be the focus of political programs. The new elite quickly accepted that the gap between the wages of workers and the incomes of managers would be perpetuated. When I protested to comrades in leading positions, I was met with statements such as "You must think that we blacks are not as good as the whites we have replaced!" That was not the point. The point was that the old system artificially paid relatively enormous incomes to privileged people, mainly white, and it should have been a priority to overcome those income relationships. There was, and still is, a distinct attitude that "now it is our turn" to benefit from the patronage system.

This was given expression through the legislation on black economic empowerment, intended to ensure that a new middle class of shareholders in the big concerns would emerge. And so a narrow elite emerged. This was followed by broad-based economic empowerment, which sought to expand the emergence of a broader black, middle-class component through insistence that both public and private sectors be required to obtain goods and services from black-owned businesses. Entrepreneurship has become the watchword for economic growth. What it has done is to create a group of politically connected people who obtain contracts through their connections in contravention of laws and regulations designed to block the machinations that lead to "tenderpreneurs" winning lucrative contracts by unfair and illegal means through patronage and backhanders.

I have previously remarked that the electoral system agreed to was proportional representation by votes for party lists. This system has become entrenched. All parties have the potential to manipulate the lists to ensure that elected representatives will be biased toward one or some particular leaders. A mutually reinforcing system of patronage is thus entrenched at the heart of the democratic system. "The ruling party is in crisis," stated President Zuma in December 2014 to the ANC Youth League national conference.

I am deeply concerned for the future of the reconstruction and transformation process we were able to start after my generation achieved our victory over apartheid. I see that the president is himself at the center of that crisis. It is a crisis that affects the future of our country as a country under the rule of law, as we see him personally lurch from one constitutional crisis to another. In our movement we believed that the individual must be protected, but the future of our movement and, since we are the ruling party, our country's future must take precedence over the individual. That ultimately is the meaning of integrity in the life of committed political activists. That is what we and the world praise in the life of Nelson Mandela and that generation of activists.

I see that though our government speaks about combating corruption, patronage is at the center of the practices of the ANC, and President Zuma is its elected leader. I see that a circle of people, political, private, and public, has gathered around the name of the president. I do not hear him emphatically cry, "Stop these practices!" His spokespersons say only that he does not authorize such behavior. He refuses to appear before Parliament until he is guaranteed respect, but respect once lost has to be earned all over again.

My comrade Jacob Zuma has given so much so courageously through-out his life, together with tens of thousands of people, to set us free and rebuild our nation on new foundations. I hope that he can be brought to honor his own achievements by recognizing that words are not enough; by his failure to act decisively against the patronage society, he is undermining our constitution, which is at the heart of our fragile democracy. An important question is: Will he step down before the end of his term of office to enable a renewal of the leadership at all levels? There are widespread rumors about his health. Deputy President Cyril Ramaphosa is daily in the news as he appears at national and international events representing the government and the country. Are we being prepared for him to be the successor to the president?

Ramaphosa often speaks about upholding the values of the late Nelson Mandela, and he seems to be riding on his coattails. But Comrade Cyril also needs to be seen to be acting against the corruption that has become endemic in the ANC and the government. This is not a matter involving just a few people.

Because of the losses the ANC suffered in the 2014 elections, there is cause for concern about the outcome of the next municipal elections, to be held in 2016. If the trend continues, the opposition parties will gain a momentum that will threaten the ANC's majority in Parliament after the national elections in 2019. There is a widespread public perception that the president is himself a threat to the ANC's electoral future. I hope he can see the need to act in the proper way. Many older members, veterans of the freedom struggle, are calling for a renewal of the leadership so that the values for which so many gave their lives and energy can be reestablished at the core of the ANC and the government.

My generation created and shaped the opportunity to make our lives better in a country where we can now "live in a way that respects and enhances the freedom of others." Nelson Mandela said when he was released from prison that "we are not yet free; we have merely achieved the freedom to be free." I say to my fellow South Africans, our future is in our hands, and, like the carpet weavers of Kujan-Bulak it is we, and only we, who can build our country.

And so I say to those born after, I say to posterity, go and build our nation because you are free to do it.

For me the work continues within my community to try to realize in practice the vision we had that our children shall not be hungry, shall be

Dominic Benhura's sculpture, *Skipping Girl* (54¾ inches high, stone carving; photo by M. Willman).

well cared for, shall go to school, shall have jobs to go to, and shall be able to laugh a little. And so let there be brass bands and music lessons for historically disadvantaged children in the hope that, being bound together by the chords of the music they make, they can enjoy that future so beautifully depicted by Dominic Benhura's skipping child, for whom life is clearly wonderful.

Torture and the Future

I presented a paper, "South Africa, the Transition to Democracy and the Banning of Torture," at a seminar titled "Torture and the Future" at Heinrich-Heine University, Düsseldorf, on 25 June 2009.

My thanks to Professor Goerling for inviting me to present this paper to the conference on torture and the future. Torture has recently been often in the news because of the revelations of the use of torture by the United States in its so-called "war on terror." Security forces say there is no future without torture! Human rights activists say that with torture there is no future worth striving for because torture by security forces destroys the very society we wish to protect. Therefore we who believe in the development of society to protect the rights of every human being have to care about putting an end to torture and the general atmosphere of social violence that goes with it.

Turning now to South Africa:

I am happy to report that South Africa has become a democracy and we have, in our Constitution, banned torture. We brought an end to the apartheid dictatorship based on racism by law and the inherent violence and use of torture to maintain the system. Our democracy was officially born in 1994 when Nelson Mandela became President. We have just celebrated our fourth free democratic elections. The election results came out and there were few complaints. Despite a few minor incidents caused by undisciplined individuals, the elections went off peacefully.

Let me go back a bit to the past. I was arrested with others in 1963 and held under our infamous 90 days law (later 180 days) that allowed police to arrest people and hold them without contact with anyone except the Security Police for the purpose of providing information to the satisfaction of the head of police. The secrecy alone made this a "licence to torture."

Was I tortured? I don't know! It depends on the definition of torture. According to the Stanford University philosophers I was not tortured, merely put under psychological pressure. According to the U.N. Declaration I was tortured even though I was not physically beaten because the use of physical and psychological abuse with the intention of extracting information constitutes torture. It later appeared that there was to be a show trial, the famous Rivonia Trial, in which Nelson Mandela, Walter Sisulu, and other great leaders and I were convicted and sentenced to life imprisonment for conspiring to overthrow the apartheid state by armed force. Therefore I had to be unmarked when shown to the world. Nevertheless 90 days of solitary confinement with the possibility of it being repeated for eternity, as the Police Minister B. J. Vorster said, provided a certain pressure. To have my interrogator sit opposite me pointing his revolver at me and playing with the trigger provided even greater pressure. That is what the Stanford University philosophers say: it was just pressure to give up my personal freedom. I can report that I thought they would kill me and this was reinforced when they told me that I could safely speak about Looksmart Ngudle because he was dead. I accused them of murdering my comrade. They denied it, of course, but said they would be happy to hand me over to the interrogators who had dealt with him. The threat was clear.

Then they threatened to arrest my wife under the 90 days law if I did not speak. (They had in fact already arrested her.) Knowing what they were capable of doing, was that pressure or torture? When they threatened her with the removal of our children and putting them in separate government institutions, was she pressured or tortured?

In my case they had made a fundamental error. They had seriously informed me that I would be charged with offences that carried the death penalty and they would ensure that I was hanged. Since I would die anyway, better to resist their torture, or was it merely pressure, and die with honour. In fact they removed me to an isolated prison where they expected me to be more vulnerable. However, I was able to engineer my escape.

Though they recaptured me almost immediately and I got a few broken ribs in the process, they gave up on the interrogations. They pretended to be hurt because they thought I was ready to cooperate and I had tricked them, they said. They implied that I was a really naughty dishonest person! They had offered me money, new identification documents and help to settle anywhere in the world that I chose, in exchange for information about every person and place I had met or used in years of resistance to apartheid. They were offended when I rejected their offer as dishonourable, silly and futile. The words I used were not as polite as that, however.

As early as 1960, during the State of Emergency called by the apartheid government after the Sharpeville massacre, when thousands of political activists were arrested, torture was used against some of the detainees including some of the comrades I worked with. Johnny M-T [Morley-Turner], already more than 60 years old, was forced to stand for days and nights on end until he was delirious. He was not allowed to use a toilet. He appeared at the doorway of the courtyard of the prison while we were on parade. He looked awful: unshaved, grey with exhaustion, and his clothes yellow with urine from above his waist downwards. But more, he looked ashamed to be seen in such a state. I suspect too that he had been compelled to say more than he intended. My response was simply to defiantly break ranks and go to him and embrace him. He needed support and comfort and above all acceptance. I took him to the shower bath and saw to it that he was cleaned up and dressed in spare clothes that I fortunately had with me. The guards knew they could not easily stop me doing what had to be done and I demanded a bucket and hot water so that I could wash his clothes. Another comrade, Bernard, who was released after being tortured, left the country. Stephanie's ankle was broken when her interrogator applied more pressure than he should have. In the end the state paid her compensation for the physical assault. These are just a few cases known to me personally.

After the commencement of our armed struggle in which I too was involved and as the resistance heightened in the 1970s and 1980s, we know that many were tortured to death. We know too that many were physically tortured and would never recover their health. We know that many were psychologically tortured and would never become fully functional again. I have already mentioned Looksmart Ngudle, the first to be murdered in 1963 under the new laws.

The killing of Steve Bantu Biko in September 1977 is notorious. Donald Woods, a white newspaper editor, broke the story and was himself hounded out of the country by violence and murder attempts on him and his children. The case was notable for the role that the police doctors played. They covered up the seriousness of Biko's condition and signed a death certificate saying that he had died of natural causes when in fact he died from brain damage inflicted by his interrogators. The doctors were eventually found guilty of professional misconduct by the statutory Medical and Dental Council and given very mild punishment. Dr. Neil Aggett, a trade union activist, was murdered during interrogation in February 1982 and that became a cause célèbre with thousands of people of all races marching in the streets of Johannesburg in protest, even though such a march was illegal.

These cases and others led to the formation of a new association of progressive doctors who opposed the use of violence and indeed opposed apartheid as the cause of the violence. One of the more famous of these doctors was Dr. Wendy Orr who as a police doctor kept detailed records of the torture suffered by the patients she saw in police custody and published the information. Her life too became endangered but she acted out of conscience and would not retract. Eventually the Detainees' Parents Support Committee emerged and much more information was recorded. The University of Cape Town carried out a study showing that some 90 percent of detainees were physically mistreated by the police. The "licence to torture" was no mere figure of speech. Over the years at least 1,000 people were tortured to death or simply killed while in police custody during the struggle against apartheid.

My comrade Issy Heyman was made to stand in 1964 for days and nights until he was so exhausted he simply and quietly betrayed the whereabouts of another comrade who was then arrested. Issy tried to commit suicide. He bore thick scars around his ankles and wrists where he had slashed the arteries, but before he could bleed to death a night guard saw what he had done and his life was saved. Issy was himself sentenced to five years' imprisonment and the comrade he had given up was sentenced to life imprisonment and in fact died in prison from cancer that was not diagnosed in time. Issy recovered and his comrade never once berated him, but Issy felt ashamed for the rest of his life. We were always gentle with him, and on one occasion I had to take him in my arms while he wept about his sense of shame for the betrayal he had been forced into.

At a book launch I participated in quite recently with my comrade

Joyce Sikakane, she described the life-long consequences for her of having been tortured into a confession that involved others. While speaking about the book, a volume in a series, *The Road to Democracy in South Africa,* she suddenly started to talk with great emotion about the use of torture and stood weeping as she spoke. Oh, the cost of freedom and democracy . . .

A good summary of relevant information appears in a paper presented to a conference in Mexico in April 2002 by Piers Pigou of the Centre for Violence and Reconciliation. [I have summarized the information taken from the Internet.]

During the apartheid era and as the struggle for freedom intensified, there was mounting police violence and torture in South Africa.

There were 21,000 submissions made to the Truth and Reconciliation Commission by victims of human rights contraventions, mainly by the apartheid security forces.

Three hundred submissions were made by members of state security forces in the course of amnesty applications.

It was clear that there was support at the highest level for the use of torture.

At least 78,000 people were detained between 1960 and 1990, when the negotiations between the apartheid government and the African National Congress began after the release of Nelson Mandela.

In 1986/87 alone, 25,000 were detained.

That long nightmare is over and it is just the families of the victims and some of the survivors who are never free of the nightmares.

In understanding our past it is necessary to know that the ANC in its exile years in its camps in Africa was faced with serious disciplinary problems and massive infiltration by the apartheid security forces. The ANC's internal security apparatus resorted to the use of violence and torture against its own members. It instituted its own inquiry and later an independent inquiry into these human rights abuses. It voluntarily submitted its findings to the Truth and Reconciliation Commission (see below).

It is fair to say that many of us were shocked by these revelations and I have to conclude that the evidence from psychotherapists that victims often become perpetrators has great validity. It is especially true where fear of betrayal by people who pose as comrades leads to a despairing attempt to use violence to maintain unity where there are not the large state resources required for dealing with such issues. Besides being wrong in principle, these methods not only failed to maintain unity, they actively caused disunity. The ANC leadership under the late O. R. Tambo and Chris Hani largely succeeded in bringing these abuses to an end.

What is clear is that torture and violence flourish in conditions of secrecy and impunity.

The Truth and Reconciliation Commission [TRC], established as part of the settlement, agreed on between the apartheid government and the ANC and its allies, fulfilled a useful function. I am not sure that all the truth was told, and I am sure that reconciliation cannot happen overnight. Only 300 perpetrators came forward to tell their "truths" and claim amnesty from prosecution by the new democratic post-apartheid state. The security forces had used the four years of negotiations before the first democratic elections in 1994 to destroy the evidence of their crimes against human rights, four years in which documents were shredded and incinerated. So much "had to be" destroyed that they used the blast furnaces of steel mills to do the work for them. They mostly felt safe enough to thumb their noses at the commission. The TRC enabled ordinary people who had suffered not merely the indignities of apartheid but specific acts of violence against persons to become a part of history.

By telling the TRC their stories, which were carried in the media, many achieved some kind of catharsis. Many achieved closure when the TRC's investigators were able to ascertain what had happened to those who had been made to "disappear." Some, however, saw the TRC as a kind of whitewashing of the perpetrators who, by appearing before the TRC, escaped prosecutions for crimes as serious as murder. This was part of the legislation enacted by the new Parliament that decided that getting at the truth was more important than formal justice and revenge by judicial punishment. This was a tricky balancing act between the apartheid perpetrators who were demanding total amnesty without evidence and the liberation movement which knew that we would not be able to hold a kind of Nuremburg Trial of the perpetrators. Ultimately the political judgement was that beginning the process of reconstruction was more important than court processes.

What was surprising was the general (anecdotal) indifference of the white population to the painful stories told. The denial of complicity in apartheid was evident. When pressed, the answer was often: "We did not know what was happening. It was all done in secret!" Who then were the perpetrators? Just some ghosts? Who elected the white regime that turned our country into an imprisoned society? That society of daily indignity, violence and torture did not just happen!

The TRC had a team of therapists at hand to provide relief for victims of the apartheid crimes against their human rights, but the treatment was only at the hearings themselves and could not be long-term therapy. As important was the need for counselling for the commissioners who day after day were exposed to the harrowing tales of brutality and sorrow revealed by the witnesses.

Could the TRC fulfil its role of reconciliation? I do not know if there is a conclusive answer. At the very least, we know from evidence led in public and subject to cross examination that our allegations of what was done to our people were true and not figments of our imagination, as alleged by the apartheid state, its supporters, that included governments of the great powers, and the media who always demanded that we produce evidence of what was done in secret! The secret has been blown wide open. It seems to this observer that reconciliation requires the victims to accept that the nightmare is over and the perpetrators get away free of punishment and have no need even to apologise. They draw their pensions and golden handshakes and get on with their lives. The victims also have to get on with their lives and the pain and grief they suffered.

In the Constitutional Court established under our new constitution there is a wonderful art collection organised mainly by Judge Albie Sachs, who was himself the victim of a booby trap bomb attached by apartheid agents to his car in Maputo. He miraculously survived. He told me that he felt that having been blown up and having lost an arm and an eye justified his existence because he had spent his time in exile writing laws for the newly liberated Republic of Mozambique while I remained and spent 22 years in prison. That, I said, was unacceptable self-abnegation. Each of us contributes what we can to liberation. A victim of torture and terrorism by the state, Albie played a leading role in drafting our democratic constitution, which bans torture as illegal.

Among the exhibits in the art collection is a glass-fronted showcase in which there hang an evening gown, an elegant trouser suit and a frock, all made of blue plastic material. They were made by an artist, Judith Mason, to honour a young woman freedom fighter whose male interrogators, unable to break her will, had stripped her naked—and we know what men can do to humiliate women. She had covered her nakedness with a panty made of a blue plastic shopping bag. One of her torturers forced her to kneel and put his revolver to the back of her head. The threat of death was supposed to make her talk. He executed her when he pulled the trigger, "by accident," he said in evidence to the TRC. He then buried her illegally on a farm.

He took the commissioners to her burial place so that she might be exhumed. All that remained of her was her skeleton. He had buried her in a tiny hole in the ground, upright, in a crouching position. Uppermost was her skull with the bullet hole left by the shot that killed her. Around her pelvis was the blue plastic bag. The artist, so moved by the story, made the clothes to restore her dignity and, I would say, the dignity of all the victims of such brutality.

The remains of others were never recovered. Some were dropped into the deep southern ocean from helicopters; some were thrown into crocodile-infested rivers to remove the evidence of the brutal illegality. Murder had become a sport for some "protectors of the state." We even heard stories of police officers celebrating a murder expedition at a barbecue organised by their superior officers.

How can one fail to be moved by the brutality used to maintain a dying system? What I do know is that to be human we have to find ways of stopping such things from happening because not only is the victim dehumanised, the perpetrators and the whole society lose our sense of the value of human life.

Since the end of apartheid and the achievement of our new democracy, things have undoubtedly changed for the better. Yet, according to Pigou, it is true to say that police violence and torture have not yet ended.

Basic police training includes study of the Bill of Rights and human rights training. An Independent Complaints Directorate has been created. It has been limited in its efforts by the way in which the police report complaints against their own members, in the sense of the categories of offences that are used.

The South African Police Service adopted a Prevention of Torture Policy in 1998/1999.

Yet there were an average of 14,000 cases a year between 1994 and 1997 and on average 1,200 officers were convicted each year of violent abuse of prisoners. Not all were torture in terms of the definition which requires the intentional use of physical and psychological abuse for the purpose of extracting information from a person. Deaths in custody range up to 700 a year. It is not clear how many are the result of police violence and how many are caused by neglect of prisoners in ill health, drunk or under the influence of other substances.

It is worth noting that in apartheid times torture was not reserved for political opponents of the regime. It was used against petty thieves and other criminal accused. Judges would allow evidence obtained through such methods, asking merely if it was "true."

Just recently, in 2009, a judge in the Supreme Court of Appeal ruled that evidence obtained by torture of a witness could not be used to convict an accused person even in cases of serious crimes, and even if the evidence is reliable and necessary for conviction. In the case in question it was not the accused but a key witness whose evidence was obtained by torture. The judge ruled that section 35(c) of the Constitution prohibits the use of torture whether by official or private agencies. He said that the use of such violence was a violation of the human rights of the individual. Indeed Chapter 2 of the Constitution is South Africa's Bill of Rights and our courts have zealously upheld those rights against the government and others.

I do not think it is possible to legislate for the limited and controlled use of violence to protect the majority, the state or whatever. We have to legislate against the use of violence and torture and terror by the state and its agencies, whether official or private. And yet I know that we can dream up scenarios of ticking bombs and suffocating victims of abduction, where we can find some kind of rationale for the security of the many against the rights of the individual. I am also sure, having lived through a few dark times, that there will be incidents where abuses occur and police officers and others will justify their actions in some way. Let our courts and an informed public decide on the merits of each individual case as we strive to overcome abuses and uphold respect for human life, freedom and dignity.

To return to my introductory remarks: it is right that we point to the misuse of violence against persons by governments such as that of the U.S.A., but what about our individual and collective acquiescence in the silence of our own governments, in Europe for example, in the face of such widespread systematic abuse?

South Africa has played a leading role in the African Renaissance, especially during the Presidency of Thabo Mbeki. The concept of human rights and the adoption of African Regional Charters on such rights have been strongly promoted. Among the developments has been the adoption on 23 October 2002 by the African Commission on Human and Peoples' Rights of the "Robben Island Guidelines" for the prevention of torture and degrading treatment of prisoners. The guidelines were decided upon in

2002 at a workshop held at the famous prison which is now a museum to the triumph of the human spirit.

Some of the elements of the Robben Island Guidelines are: The prohibition of torture; the criminalization of torture; to combat the use of torture; "necessity," "national emergency," or "public order" and "superior orders" are not to be invoked as justifications for the use of torture or degrading treatment. Torture is to be prevented by basic procedural safeguards and pre-trial procedures are specifically mentioned. Secret detention centres are not to be permitted. An independent judiciary is essential and the state must respond to the needs of victims of torture and degrading treatment.

The Robben Island Guidelines are in full accordance with other international instruments but make concrete practical proposals for putting an end to these abuses.

In all countries we have to strive to ensure a future free of such abuses. It is essential that there is openness and transparency and a committed leadership that acts against those who abuse their power and position to deprive people of their rights as human beings. A committed leadership can only come from us the masses, the electorate. We who have democratic rights must use them to make sure those rights are protected. If we elect political representatives who are either indifferent to the issue or who support the use of torture and abuse of the rights of prisoners, who are the abusers? We then are the abusers, of course. We cannot escape our responsibility.

The events I talked about in my paper happened fifty years ago, and I thought I had myself well under control. But I broke down during the course of my delivery, and I do not know why that happened on this occasion because I have described those moments many times before. However, I am taking the liberty of quoting an article by a journalist who was present at my lecture. "The Brutality Was Immense" by Maksim Hartwig, published on 2 July 2009, was published in Kontextschmiede on the Internet. I have translated it from the German original.

On 25 June 2009 at the Heinrich-Heine University in Düsseldorf a conference was held on the theme "Torture and the Future." Denis Goldberg, a longtime campaigner with Nelson Mandela, reported on his experience of inhumanity.

When I [Hartwig] entered the lecture theatre before the beginning of the presentation there was hardly anybody there. Two men in suits were in discussion at the podium. A student sat alone in a middle row of the auditorium. I greeted him and sat next to him and asked in amazement where all the people were. The guest that day had after all something to say on the theme of "Torture and the Future." For 22 years Denis Goldberg was a political prisoner in the Central Prison in Pretoria. South Africa's apartheid regime separated the white human rights activists from Nelson Mandela and other black campaigners, who were locked up in the Robben Island prison.

Apartheid was the policy of separation and systematic discrimination of citizens according to "racial" criteria. For nearly five decades they determined the life and suffering of the majority of the population who were not considered to be part of the ruling "white race," or those who were against the oppressor. Denis Goldberg personally experienced in those times what it meant to be an opponent of the unjust regime.

Respect for human rights requires that torture must be prevented.

Slowly the auditorium filled up. When the guest from South Africa entered the room he was full of humour and approachable. He made himself comfortable in front of his audience. In the course of his evidence, however, the gentleness faded away. He stared down the barrel of a revolver while his interrogator played with the trigger. He understood what they meant to do. Whatever he did, he would die.

"The brutality was immense." One woman, Goldberg recalls, after being mistreated many times over, was covered in a plastic shopping bag and shot from behind. "It is funny to dehumanize a person who is not a person in your eyes," he said, in trying to understand the motive of her tormenter. "White" farmers would drive their vehicles over their "Coloured" workers. Human rights did not extend to all.

Over and over Denis Goldberg fell silent. He spoke haltingly of some episodes of torture and brutality that appeared in his own report. Sometimes he stopped reading, his gaze directed downwards when he described particularly brutal scenes. Psychologically and physically he has not completely recovered. "Am I normal? I don't know."

He turned to the present. To respect human rights means preventing torture, Goldberg said. Torture in Guantanamo and during the Iraq war is evidence of lack of respect. The necessity for changed attitudes in our consciousness of human rights, Goldberg explained in German: "The white oppressors, because they were oppressors, were themselves not free." The change was necessary in order to set free both the oppressor and the oppressed. That became clear to the perpetrators themselves.

Goldberg quoted his friend Nelson Mandela, "Freedom has to be built. The 'whites' have to be freed from their inhumanity."

At the end of the thirty-minute report Denis Goldberg was exhausted. He asked that questions should not be asked. "It is not enough to say I don't have it in me to be a torturer." The categorical imperative is not always present in the real world. Even those who are free are not freed from violence. "We are too comfortable," he says in warning about believing that people are treated as equals.

Walking with very tired steps, he was the first to leave the hall.

Appendix 2

Time Line of South African History

(based on Birgit Morgenrath's version for the first German edition)

In precolonial times South Africa was occupied by Khoisan people in the west and Bantu-speaking people in the east.

1652: Jan van Riebeeck lands at the Cape with ninety soldiers to establish a refreshment station for the Dutch East India Company. Members of the occupation forces are settled as free farmers. They almost exterminate the Khoisan people of the Cape region and develop a slave-based agricultural economy.

1779: Bantu-speaking people and white intruders meet each other. The expansionary efforts of the white settlers result in numerous wars against the indigenous people.

1795: British troops temporarily occupy the Cape as a reaction to the French occupation of the Dutch colony at the Cape during the French Revolutionary Wars.

1805: The strategic importance of the Cape leads Britain to reoccupy the Cape to stop the French from controlling this strategic sea route during the Napoleonic Wars.

1834: Britain prohibits the possession of slaves. In the following decades there is a struggle between the British and the Boers for dominance. The Boers establish several republics.

1867: This year marks the beginning of modern racial segregation (later developed as apartheid). After the discovery of diamonds and gold, ever cheaper black labor is required in increasingly large numbers. Only whites are allowed to own diamond claims.

1893: Mahatma Gandhi comes to South Africa and until 1914 organizes protests by Indians against racial discrimination. His philosophy of nonviolence strongly influences the African National Congress (ANC) in later years.

1899–1902: The Second Anglo-Boer War for control of the gold and diamond fields is fought. Africans mostly support the British and hope to acquire the voting rights that Africans had under the British in the Cape Colony. The Boers are defeated and lose the independence of the Transvaal Republic and the Orange Free State. A peace treaty, however, is signed whereby the British give up the principle of equal electoral rights for whites and blacks.

31 May 1910: The Union of South Africa is formed by combining the Cape Colony, Natal, and the former Boer republics (Transvaal and Orange Free State).The British colonial power, through its Parliament, enacts the constitution that denies Africans voting rights, except in the Cape Colony, where Africans are allowed a limited franchise right. South Africa becomes an independent member of the Commonwealth.

1912: The African National Congress is formed.

1913: The Lands Act prohibits Africans from owning land outside the Reserves, eventually 13 percent of the land. Landless peasants can no longer legally live as sharecroppers on large farms.

1914–1918: During the First World War black South Africans are auxiliary soldiers on European battlefields.

1921: The Communist Party of South Africa (CPSA) is formed. (In 1953 it becomes the South African Communist Party [SACP].)

1923–1927: The first apartheid laws are passed. The separation of residential areas by race is introduced, the right to strike by Africans is limited, and sexual relations between white and black people outside marriage are forbidden.

1939: On 6 September South Africa declares war on Nazi Germany. The pro-British party of General Jan Smuts achieves a small majority in the all-white Parliament over the Afrikaner nationalists, who want South Africa to remain neutral in the war. Organizations loyal to the Nazis sabotage the government, assist German U-boats to land agents on the South-West African (Namibian) coast, and fight against South African troops. Many whites in South Africa are openly sympathetic to the German fascists. The ANC supports the Allied war against fascism but at the same time wants full citizenship rights for black South Africans.

1944: The ANC Youth League is founded by Nelson Mandela, Walter Sisulu, Oliver Tambo, and others, including Anton Lembede, A. P. Mda, and Robert Sobukwe. The ANC Youth League calls for and achieves an activist organization for liberation. The document "Africans' Claims in South Africa" sets out the demand for equal rights for all people, the first modern call for universal human rights.

1946–1947: Strikes by African mineworkers are crushed.

1948: Afrikaner nationalists win the parliamentary elections. Apartheid becomes official state doctrine. Many acts of Parliament establishing or strengthening apartheid are passed. Marriage between whites and all non-whites is forbidden by law.

1949: Walter Sisulu is elected ANC secretary general.

1950: At birth South Africans are classified and registered in accordance with "the race of the father." The Race Classification Board classifies people as White, Coloured, Indian (Asian), and Bantu (African); there are subcategories in some instances. Residential areas are created for each race group (Group Areas Act) and people forcibly removed to achieve the separation. Permission is required to enter the residential areas of other race groups—and this applies to whites, too. The Communist Party is declared illegal. The minister of justice "bans" people, limiting their personal freedom of expression, movement, association, and employment through prohibitions on publication, of certain occupations, on entry into factories, mines, and so on, and on attending gatherings, and through confinement to specified areas and house arrest. Between 1950 and 1970, 1,400 people are banned.

1952–: The pass laws of 1923 are repeatedly amended over the next years to tighten control over all adult male Africans and then adult African women, and the Pass Book (called the dompas—or "damn pass") is introduced. Migration of African workers from the land to the cities is more systematically controlled. Between 1948 and 1974 more than 10 million court cases are brought for contraventions of the pass laws.

1953: The so-called Petty Apartheid Laws order racial apartheid in public institutions and places from parks to cinemas and railway stations and all public transport—trains and buses. Whites meet with members of the ANC, the SACP, and the South African Indian Congress (SAIC) to form the Congress of Democrats (COD). The ANC wants to make its policies better known among white South Africans.

1955: The ANC, COD, SAIC, and Coloured People's Congress agree to coordinate their activities in the Congress Alliance, led by the ANC. They are later called the Charterists because they all accept the Freedom Charter as their goal.

25 and 26 June 1955: The Congress of the People convenes to adopt the Freedom Charter, which outlines the future democratic and free South Africa. It declares, "South Africa belongs to all who live in it." The ANC writes the Freedom Charter into its statutes as its policy objective.

December 1955: One hundred and fifty-six activists, the leaders of practically all the Congress Alliance organizations, are arrested on the grounds that the Freedom Charter is allegedly a call to violent revolution and thus constitutes high treason.

1957: Denis Goldberg joins the underground Communist Party. Prominent members of the Central Committee of the SACP include Bram

Fischer, Brian Bunting, Ivan Schermbrucker, General Secretary Moses Kotane, Joe Slovo, and later Chris Hani, Ronnie Kasrils, and Jeremy Cronin.

1958: Hendrik Frensch Verwoerd becomes prime minister. Territorial apartheid is sharpened, and the so-called homelands (Bantustans) are established for the various ethnic groups (Transkei, Ciskei, Bophuthatswana, KwaZulu, and so on). The "citizens" of these areas automatically lose their South African citizenship.

1960: Chief Albert John Mvumbi Luthuli, president general of the ANC, is awarded the Nobel Peace Prize, the first African to win any Nobel Prize.

21 March 1960: At a peaceful demonstration against the pass laws at Sharpeville, 69 people are shot dead and 189 severely wounded when the police open fire on the demonstrators. In Langa, Cape Town, 3 protesters are shot dead.

30 March 1960: A state of emergency is declared. Eighteen thousand activists are arrested. Denis Goldberg and his mother are detained.

31 May 1961: South Africa withdraws from the Commonwealth after the heads of state of the newly independent countries in Africa, India, and Malaysia issue an ultimatum that either the racial policies of apartheid be abolished or South Africa be expelled from the Commonwealth. Verwoerd evades the expulsion by withdrawing. The country now declares itself to be the Republic of South Africa. The ANC calls for a stay-at-home (strikes by African workers are illegal) to protest the racism of the new constitution.

16 December 1961: *Umkhonto we Sizwe,* or MK (Spear of the Nation), is formed as the armed wing of the liberation movement.

1962: In January Nelson Mandela goes underground after the accused are found not guilty in the Treason Trial. He is arrested in August and in November sentenced to five years' imprisonment for leaving the country illegally (he had toured Africa and Britain) and for calling a strike (the stay-at-home protest).

June 1962: The state reacts to the sabotage attacks with new laws: the Sabotage Act broadens the powers of the police and permits the arbitrary arrest of any person.

1963: The Ninety-Day Detention Law comes into effect. The police are permitted to hold suspects for ninety days at a time for the purpose of extracting answers to the satisfaction of the police. No access is allowed to family, friends, or lawyers, and the courts are denied the right to intervene. Previously, all suspects had to appear in court within forty-eight hours of being arrested. The detention period can be repeated as often as the police wish.

11 July 1963: The police raid Liliesleaf Farm in Rivonia, Johannesburg. Eighteen men and some women are arrested. Later, in October 1963, Nelson Mandela and ten others, including Denis Goldberg, are charged on two counts under the Sabotage Act, one of contravention of the Suppression of Communism Act, and one of furthering the aims of a banned organization (the ANC). The main charge is "conspiracy to overthrow the state by force of arms."

11 August 1963: Arthur Goldreich, Harold Wolpe, Mosie Moolla, and Abdulhay "Charlie" Jassat escape from police cells. Wolpe's brother-in-law, James Kantor, is arrested shortly thereafter.

12 June 1964: Judgment is delivered in the Rivonia Trial. Eight of the accused, including Denis Goldberg, are sentenced to life imprisonment.

1966: Prime Minister Verwoerd is stabbed to death in the House of Assembly (Parliament) by a white person, who is declared to be psychologically disturbed and unfit to stand trial. He is sentenced to be imprisoned at the "State President's pleasure," meaning he can be held indefinitely, as if he were sentenced to life imprisonment. The new president is the former Nazi supporter B. J. Vorster.

December 1966: The United Nations General Assembly declares apartheid to be a crime against humanity.

1970: The Citizenship Act is passed by Parliament. It removes the citizenship of all Africans and declares them to be citizens of one or the other homeland. Millions of people are effectively made stateless because no country other than South Africa recognizes the homelands as independent countries.

1973: Workers in Durban strike. Five trade unions with black members are established. This marks the beginning of the modern trade union movement in South Africa.

1975: After the revolution against the fascist dictatorship in Portugal (the "carnation revolution") Angola and Mozambique become independent states.

16 June 1976: Students protest in the streets of Soweto. The immediate cause is the introduction of Afrikaans as the language of instruction in schools for African children. In countrywide protests some six hundred young people are shot dead and two thousand wounded by the police.

1977: MK sends hundreds of fighters into South Africa. They are to strengthen underground structures and accompany mass action with "armed propaganda."

12 September 1977: Stephen Bantu Biko dies from brain damage caused by mistreatment suffered while being held in detention without trial by the police.

1978: Through an internal government scandal, the former defense minister, Pieter Willem Botha, comes to power as president.

December 1979: Tim Jenkin, Stephen Lee, and Alex Moumbaris escape from prison in Pretoria.

1980: MK changes its strategy of attacking symbolic targets to attacking important institutions and installations of the apartheid state. In the following years an oil refinery, a power station, and military installations are heavily damaged. For the first time there are civilian victims of the attacks.

1983: The United Democratic Front (UDF) is formed. It is made up of six hundred organizations with two million members in a federal-type structure.

1984: Militant youths take over power in the townships. They set fire to schools, buses, and businesses and kill alleged police collaborators. "Radio Freedom" sends out the ANC call to "make the country ungovernable." The all-powerful apartheid State Security Council takes over the executive branch and governs under state of emergency regulations.

December 1984: Archbishop Desmond Tutu is awarded the Nobel Peace Prize.

28 February 1985: Denis Goldberg is released from prison.

20 July 1985: State of emergency conditions are intensified—tens of thousands of activists are arrested. MK decides "to take the armed struggle to the white suburbs."

15 August 1985: President P. W. Botha says in his "Crossing the Rubicon" speech, broadcast live: "Today we have crossed the Rubicon and there can be no turning back." Economic sanctions are beginning to bite. Secret negotiations between Nelson Mandela and the apartheid government begin.

December 1985: The most important independent trade union federation, the Congress of South African Trade Unions (COSATU), is founded as a federal structure to coordinate union activities.

September 1986: Bomb attack by the South African secret services on the ANC office in Sweden.

1987: From 13 January to 23 March the apartheid South African forces are defeated at Cuito Cuanavale in Angola by Angolan and Cuban forces in the greatest battle on the African continent since the end of World War II.

May 1987: Two and a half million take part in a two-day stay-at-home in response to the white elections on 6 May.

7 May 1987: Apartheid secret forces bomb the COSATU headquarters building.

5 November 1987: Govan Mbeki is released from prison.

11 June 1988: Free Mandela Concert is held in Wembley Stadium in London. Six hundred million people throughout the world watch the live television broadcast.

1989: President P. W. Botha is replaced by F. W. de Klerk after a long power struggle within the ruling National Party. This opening up of the apartheid system leads to intensified secret talks with Nelson Mandela and also separately with O. R. Tambo, who is represented by Thabo Mbeki.

14 October 1989: Walter Sisulu, Ahmed Kathrada, Raymond Mhlaba, Andrew Mlangeni, Elias Motsoaledi, and Wilton Mkwayi are released from prison.

11 February 1990: Nelson Mandela is released.

March 1990: The first round of talks inside South Africa are held between the ANC and the apartheid government.

In Natal violent conflict between Inkatha and the ANC reach unprecedented levels. Repression by police and murder squads intensify. The conflict becomes a virtual civil war in the townships in and around Johannesburg. State security forces stoke the conflict through massacres and attacks on civilians to destabilize the country. The conflict is brought to an end shortly before the 1994 elections and has taken between 10,000 and 12,000 lives.

27 April 1994: The first free general election is held. The ANC wins with a large majority, and Nelson Mandela is elected president by the new Parliament. He is later installed as the first president of the free democratic South Africa.

1994: The government decides on the broadly discussed Reconstruction and Development Programme (RDP) to meet the basic needs of the people.

1995: The Truth and Reconciliation Commission (TRC) begins its work.

1996: The government pushes through, under the influence of the World Bank, a change in economic policy from RDP to the neoliberal GEAR policy (Growth, Employment, and Redistribution).

16 June 1999: In the parliamentary election the ANC increases its majority. Thabo Mbeki is elected president by Parliament.

2003: Parliament receives the report of the TRC. Twenty-two thousand victims or relatives of victims give evidence before the commission. Many facts about human rights violations under apartheid are revealed. Human rights violations numbering 37,672 are established, including 9,980 fatal human rights violations. The perpetrators are given amnesty from criminal and civil proceedings in exchange for full testimony about their actions.

2004: At parliamentary elections in April the ANC receives nearly 70 percent of the votes. Thabo Mbeki is reelected president.

9 May 2009: Jacob G. Zuma becomes the new president.

2014: The ANC is reelected to Parliament with 62 percent of the vote but loses support in Johannesburg (Gauteng) and Nelson Mandela Bay Metro (Port Elizabeth, Eastern Cape)

Denis Goldberg has received several awards and honors:

City of San Francisco Special Mayoral Greeting, 5 February 1988
Albert J. Luthuli African Peace Award, by a group of twelve U.S. organizations (American Friends Service Committee, American Red Cross, and others), April 1988
Visiting professorship and honorary LL.D., Glasgow Caledonian University, 1999
Order of Luthuli (Silver) by the president of South Africa, 2009
Honorary life membership, UNISON Trade Union, United Kingdom, 2010[1]
Honorary Ph.D., Medical University of South Africa, 2010

Cross of the Order of Merit (*Verdienstkreuz am Bande*) from the Federal Republic of Germany, 2010

Military Veterans Medal (Platinum Class II), 2012

Mahatma Gandhi Satyagraha Peace Award by Gandhi Development Trust, Durban, 2012

Randburg Ward 102 Branch of the ANC named Denis Goldberg Branch, 6 October 2012

World Scholar award by City College, Glasgow, 26 November 2012

The Freedom Charter

As adopted at the Congress of the People, Kliptown, on 26 June 1955

We, the People of South Africa, declare for all our country and the world to know:
that South Africa belongs to all who live in it, black and white, and that no government can justly claim authority unless it is based on the will of all the people;

that our people have been robbed of their birthright to land, liberty and peace by a form of government founded on injustice and inequality;

that our country will never be prosperous or free until all our people live in brotherhood, enjoying equal rights and opportunities;

that only a democratic state, based on the will of all the people, can secure to all their birthright without distinction of colour, race, sex or belief;

And therefore, we, the people of South Africa, black and white together equals, countrymen and brothers adopt this Freedom Charter;

And we pledge ourselves to strive together, sparing neither strength nor courage, until the democratic changes here set out have been won.

The People Shall Govern!
Every man and woman shall have the right to vote for and to stand as a candidate for all bodies which make laws;

All people shall be entitled to take part in the administration of the country;

The rights of the people shall be the same, regardless of race, colour or sex;

All bodies of minority rule, advisory boards, councils and authorities shall be replaced by democratic organs of self-government.

All National Groups Shall Have Equal Rights!

There shall be equal status in the bodies of state, in the courts and in the schools for all national groups and races;

All people shall have equal right to use their own languages, and to develop their own folk culture and customs;

All national groups shall be protected by law against insults to their race and national pride;

The preaching and practice of national, race or colour discrimination and contempt shall be a punishable crime;

All apartheid laws and practices shall be set aside.

The People Shall Share in the Country's Wealth!

The national wealth of our country, the heritage of South Africans, shall be restored to the people;

The mineral wealth beneath the soil, the Banks and monopoly industry shall be transferred to the ownership of the people as a whole;

All other industry and trade shall be controlled to assist the wellbeing of the people;

All people shall have equal rights to trade where they choose, to manufacture and to enter all trades, crafts and professions.

The Land Shall Be Shared Among Those Who Work It!

Restrictions of land ownership on a racial basis shall be ended, and all the land re-divided amongst those who work it to banish famine and land hunger;

The state shall help the peasants with implements, seed, tractors and dams to save the soil and assist the tillers;

Freedom of movement shall be guaranteed to all who work on the land;

All shall have the right to occupy land wherever they choose;

People shall not be robbed of their cattle, and forced labour and farm prisons shall be abolished.

All Shall Be Equal Before the Law!

No-one shall be imprisoned, deported or restricted without a fair trial;
No-one shall be condemned by the order of any Government official;

The courts shall be representative of all the people;

Imprisonment shall be only for serious crimes against the people, and shall aim at re-education, not vengeance;

The police force and army shall be open to all on an equal basis and shall be the helpers and protectors of the people;

All laws which discriminate on grounds of race, colour or belief shall be repealed.

All Shall Enjoy Equal Human Rights!

The law shall guarantee to all their right to speak, to organise, to meet together, to publish, to preach, to worship and to educate their children;

The privacy of the house from police raids shall be protected by law;

All shall be free to travel without restriction from countryside to town, from province to province, and from South Africa abroad;

Pass Laws, permits and all other laws restricting these freedoms shall be abolished.

There Shall Be Work and Security!

All who work shall be free to form trade unions, to elect their officers and to make wage agreements with their employers;

The state shall recognise the right and duty of all to work, and to draw full unemployment benefits;

Men and women of all races shall receive equal pay for equal work;

There shall be a forty-hour working week, a national minimum wage, paid annual leave, and sick leave for all workers, and maternity leave on full pay for all working mothers;

Miners, domestic workers, farm workers and civil servants shall have the same rights as all others who work;

Child labour, compound labour, the tot system and contract labour shall be abolished.

The Doors of Learning and Culture Shall Be Opened!

The government shall discover, develop and encourage national talent for the enhancement of our cultural life;

All the cultural treasures of mankind shall be open to all, by free exchange of books, ideas and contact with other lands;

The aim of education shall be to teach the youth to love their people and their culture, to honour human brotherhood, liberty and peace;

Education shall be free, compulsory, universal and equal for all children; Higher education and technical training shall be opened to all by means of state allowances and scholarships awarded on the basis of merit;

Adult illiteracy shall be ended by a mass state education plan;

Teachers shall have all the rights of other citizens;

The colour bar in cultural life, in sport and in education shall be abolished.

There Shall Be Houses, Security and Comfort!

All people shall have the right to live where they choose, be decently housed, and to bring up their families in comfort and security;

Unused housing space is to be made available to the people;

Rent and prices shall be lowered, food plentiful and no-one shall go hungry;

A preventive health scheme shall be run by the state;

Free medical care and hospitalisation shall be provided for all, with special care for mothers and young children;

Slums shall be demolished, and new suburbs built where all have transport, roads, lighting, playing fields, creches and social centres;

The aged, the orphans, the disabled and the sick shall be cared for by the state;

Rest, leisure and recreation shall be the right of all;

Fenced locations and ghettoes shall be abolished, and laws which break up families shall be repealed.

There Shall Be Peace and Friendship!

South Africa shall be a fully independent state which respects the rights and sovereignty of all nations;

South Africa shall strive to maintain world peace and the settlement of all international disputes by negotiation—not war;

Peace and friendship amongst all our people shall be secured by upholding the equal rights, opportunities and status of all;

The people of the protectorates Basutoland, Bechuanaland and Swaziland shall be free to decide for themselves their own future;

The right of all peoples of Africa to independence and self-government shall be recognised, and shall be the basis of close co-operation.

Let all people who love their people and their country now say, as we say here:

THESE FREEDOMS WE WILL FIGHT FOR, SIDE BY SIDE, THROUGHOUT OUR LIVES, UNTIL WE HAVE WON OUR LIBERTY

[From the website of the African National Congress]

Acknowledgments

Birgit Morgenrath in Germany was my primary editor and a sympathetic but very hard task master. I wrote in English and she translated my text into German so that we worked on editions in both languages simultaneously. The German edition is titled *Der Auftrag, Ein leben für der Freiheit in Südafrika* (Berlin: Association A, 2010). At the same time she forced me to structure the story. There would not have been a book without her work. I must add that Tina Jerman, who for over fifteen years had arranged my many speaking tours in Germany, had become a dear friend. She urged me to write and indeed arranged that Birgit Morgenrath, whom I had known since anti-apartheid days, would be my editor. Tina, thank you. The friendship with both has continued and become closer.

Hugh Lewin, who was a prison comrade and is a great writer, agreed to be my editor for the English-language edition and I am grateful to him for his expertise. He of course appears once or twice in my stories.

The publisher of the original text, Reedwaan Vally of STE publishers, urged me to put down my story as a contribution to our "struggle literature." The new generation of young people, and especially the "born frees," are mostly unaware of the harshness of apartheid life before freedom in 1994 and of the human cost of achieving the freedoms we take for granted. Freedom is something to win and to defend at all costs when it has been won.

Gratitude

I am grateful to the Ford Foundation for a grant for editing and producing the first edition of this book, translating it into German, and making it possible to give five thousand copies of the first edition to high schools and libraries in South Africa. The director of the foundation's South African office, Ms. Alice Brown, guided me through the grant-making process with great understanding.

The South African office of the Rosa Luxemburg Foundation made a major contribution to the replication of the DVD that accompanied the first edition.

Community Heart e.V. in Germany contributed to the costs of editing the book and the translation and printing of the German edition.

The German Evangelische Entwicklungsdienst (EED) contributed to the printing of the German edition and to the compilation of the DVD accompanying the first edition.

Other donors included Eine Welt Haus, Osnabrück; Goethe-Institut, Johannesburg; Bochumer Initiative Südliches Afrika; and private donors.

I am grateful to the University Press of Kentucky for publishing this edition, which is an edited and revised version of the book first published in 2010. Ann Twombly, my copy editor, worked hard to get me to make the book more readable and to check the facts. It was a bit of a shock to find how fallible one's memory of sequences of events can be. Steve Davis, who interviewed me many years ago for his doctoral thesis, suggested to Stephen Wrinn, the director of the University Press of Kentucky, that a North American audience should have access to my story. Steve Wrinn has encouraged me to prepare the text for this first U.S. edition. It has been wonderful to have the support of Professor Mark Kornbluh, a longtime leader in the United States of Southern African studies.

Notes

2. Respect for All

1. In later years I have had to deal with my own attitude to religious belief, and I have come to the conclusion that gods, or supreme beings, are constructs of human minds and not the other way round.

It does not seem to me to be important to know what came before the beginning of our universe. If there was something that made the universe, then there had to be something that made that something, and so on without end, or should I say beginning. In my own lifetime, scientific research has pushed back the boundaries of understanding of what was previously presumed to be unknowable. Perhaps we shall never know everything, and at this point I am quite happy to shrug and say, so what? It seems to me to be an intellectual cop-out to accept modern physical science saying that energy and matter are interchangeable and indestructible, and then say they came into existence because some preexisting primordial being, a spirit, a god, ordered the origin. What did this spirit order? How to create order out of something that did not previously exist? Or, how can an order, a command, be given to something that did not exist? I am content to say that matter and energy exist and to be concerned with the social aspects of our lives. I also see that dominant groups seek some divine justification for their dominance. Simple issues spring to mind: the divine rights of kings, replaced by a social contract that found a different explanation for inequality, for example. It is not surprising that dominant groups seek to justify keeping things as they are, with gross inequalities in our societies, especially when it comes to ownership of wealth and natural resources and control over the means of becoming and remaining wealthy. Religions seem somehow to find themselves allied to powerful economic groups, though individuals may use their beliefs to challenge those power relationships.

When it comes to morality, my understanding is that we human beings in society make rules for ourselves to regulate our behavior in our various groups. Those rules are what we call morality. We maintain them or not according to our personal commitment to them. The fear of divine punishment does not seem to make people more or less moral. Some uphold the rules and some don't. The tragedy is that so many of the custodians of the rules do not themselves uphold them. Having lived in apartheid South Africa and having found that the major religions all supported and obeyed the rules of apartheid, which were in complete opposition to the values advanced by those religions, I could not be a part of those religious structures. On the other hand, I have to say that over the years there were in later times many people who because of their religious beliefs opposed apartheid and similar discriminatory social systems. Therefore I cannot simply say I reject all people who are religious, for that would be quite absurd. My conclusion is that I have no problem with people who choose to believe and observe their religious practices in their particular ways, and I can be tolerant of them until they demand that I have to believe in their way or be rejected from society or even be killed.

2. The term *Native* is now frowned on as derogatory and racist—and people are proud of being called black.

3. University

1. After the end of the Second World War and the defeat of the Nazis, all former German colonies other than South-West Africa (SWA) were put under the control of the United Nations Trusteeship Council. South Africa refused to submit to this for SWA. It agreed only to submit annual reports on the territory to the United Nations. In 1948 the National Party Government repudiated this agreement and refused to make reports to the United Nations, and it treated SWA as a province of South Africa. SWA was never under the U.N. Trusteeship Council.

The main objectives behind the formation of the Ovamboland People's Congress, which became the Ovambo People's Organisation, were to request the United Nations to force South Africa to place SWA under the Trusteeship Council and to do away with the contract-labor system imposed on the Ovambo people. The idea of independence emerged with the formation of SWAPO at a time when all the colonies in Africa were demanding independence.

4. Political Activity, 1953–1964

1. The apartheid government enacted the Suppression of Communism Act of 1950, which included empowering the minister of justice to ban people from political activity, from attending gatherings of more than three people, and from publishing any material or working on a newspaper or magazine, for example. Anyone found taking part in any such actions would be immediately arrested. That encouraged secrecy within democratic organizations, which needed to operate openly. That made it difficult to recruit new members. They would often

have the feeling that decisions were being made behind the scenes by people other than the Executive Committee they had elected. They were not wrong. But we, on the other hand, could not simply accept the unjust and arbitrary banning measures and denial of the rights of our members by excluding our banned members.

2. See appendix 3 for the full version.

5. Last Resort

1. In 2009 I presented a paper entitled "South Africa, the Transition to Democracy and the Banning of Torture." It is presented as appendix 1 in this book, together with a journalist's report on my presentation. More than forty-five years after the events, I was hoping to remain fairly relaxed about my experiences, yet I found it impossible not to break down. It seems that even though you consciously set out to control your response to the experience, the emotional wounds remain lying in wait to leap out at you.

8. The Rivonia Trial

1. The verb *uku-funda* means to read as well as to learn; *uku-fundisa* means to teach. Mfundisi derives from the latter—like a rabbi, the priest is also the teacher.

10. Problems of Imprisonment

1. These are notes I made at the time, in prison. I hid them. They were later taken out of the prison by Baruch Hirson. They were transcribed and used in part by Stephen Clingman in his biography of Bram Fischer. The full transcript was submitted to the Truth and Reconciliation Commission hearing on the Prison Service through the intervention of Hugh Lewin, who was involved with the preparation of witnesses and evidence for the TRC hearing in 1997.

2. Now called the Pretoria Academic Hospital.

11. The Escape

1. See Raymond Suttner, *Inside Apartheid's Prison: Notes and Letters of Struggle* (Melbourne: Ocean Press, 2001).

12. More about Prison

1. The eight others were Ian David Kitson, John Matthews, Alexander Moumbaris, John Hosey, Raymond Suttner, David Rabkin, Jeremy Cronin, and Charles (Tony) Holiday.

13. A Negotiated Release, 1985

1. Bubbles says that she does not remember the discussion about the word "authentic" but that David Kitson had said to her it was time I should come out of prison.

2. In Afrikaans, *stywe pap* is a maize porridge or polenta, which in Xhosa is *putu*; *tjops* are chops, and *nyama* is meat. *Amasi* is a fermented milk much like yogurt.

14. Out of Prison

1. This refers to the time in 1970–1971 when Palestinians in the PLO fought for equal rights in Jordan against the armed forces of King Hussein. Thousands of people, mainly Palestinians, were killed and the PLO leadership expelled.

16. The World Is My Oyster

1. United Nations document A/AC.115/PV.610.

2. There is an official list (at www.dcs.gov.za/docs/landing/gallows/Gallows%20Final.pdf) of political prisoners executed in Pretoria. I could not find the name of Mawasi on the list. At the time I made this speech 118 executions had been carried out. The list now has 132 names.

3. Ebrahim Ismail Ebrahim.

4. Paul Baran and Paul M. Sweezy, *Monopoly Capital: An Essay on the American Economic and Social Order* (New York: Monthly Review Press, 1966).

17. T-Shirts, Music, and More Solidarity

1.

Auld Lang Syne
Should auld acquaintance be forgot
and ne'er brought to mind?
Should auld acquaintance be forgot
and auld lang syne?
Chorus:
And for auld lang syne, my Jo [dear],
for auld lang syne,
We'll tak' a cup o' kindness yet,
for auld lang syne.
Zulu translation by *Edith Hleziphi Yengwa*

Ukwazan'akukhunjulwe	We remember those we know
Kungakhohlakali	We do not forget
Ukwazan'akukhunjulwe	We remember those we know

Ngenxa yasendulo	For [times past] long, long ago
Chorus:	[Literal translation of the Zulu]
Ngenxa yasendulo njalo	Ever for long, long ago
Ngenxa yasendulo	For long, long ago
Sobusa ndawonye njalo	We ever drink together
Ngenxa yasendulo	For long, long ago

The Zulu is not a literal translation. It is a singable version conveying the same sentiments.

2. *To the Finland Station* is the title of a 1940 book by the American critic Edmund Wilson.

19. Affairs of the Heart and Community H.E.A.R.T.

1. Ronnie Kasrils, *Steckbrieflich gesucht undercover gegen Apartheid* (Essen: Neue-Impulse, 1997).

2. Tim Jenkin, *Und vor uns die Freiheit: Ein Bericht über Südafrikas sensationellsten Gefängnisausbruch unter der Apartheid* (Leipzig: Evangelisches Verlag, 2002).

20. Life Number 9, 2002–2014

1. Zenzo was a well-known member of Joshua Nkomo's ZAPU (Zimbabwe African People's Union). There was an alliance with the Zimbabwe African National Union (ZANU), led by Robert Mugabe, who alleged that ZAPU armed forces were plotting a coup against ZANU. ZANU was firmly based among the majority Shona-speaking people. Mugabe ordered a preemptive strike against ZAPU, essentially Ndebele people in Matabeleland, in the western part of Zimbabwe, and it is said that some 20,000 people were killed.

2. In chapter 7 I discussed more fully the unanswered questions about our arrest, including the possibility of a tip-off by a foreign intelligence service.

3. The speech is available at www.sahistory.org.za/archive/statement-dennis-goldberg-anc-meeting-special-committee-against-apartheid-observance-day-sol.

4. *Denis Goldberg: Freiheitskämpfer und Humanist* (Wuppertal: Peter Hammer Verlag, 2013).

5. *Denis Goldberg: Freedom Fighter and Humanist* (Johannesburg: Liliesleaf and Community H.E.A.R.T., 2014).

21. Last Thoughts—For Now

1. I found on the Internet a translation of "To Posterity" by H. R. Hayes; part 3 is particularly pertinent: www.poemhunter.com/poem/to-posterity/.

2. Bertolt Brecht, *Poems, 1913–1956*, trans. John Willett and Ralph Man-

heim (New York: Methuen, 1976), contains the original German and the English translation side by side; these are the best translations I have found.

3. Available at www.mistra.org.za/Library/ConferencePaper/Pages/Reflections-On-South-African-Constitutional-Democracy-Transition-And-Transformation .aspx.

Appendix 2

1. UNISON has 1.3 million members. This award has been given to Nelson Mandela, Aung San Suu Kyi, and Denis Goldberg.

Index

110; divorce of, 315; documents of, 358; elected South African president, 7–8, 299, 324, 366, 387, 407; on freedom, 383, 398; Free Mandela concert appearance of, 306; Goldberg's post-prison meeting with, 313–14; JDL invitation extended to, 290; at Liliesleaf Farm, 82; as MK cofounder, 66, 83; as MK commander-in-chief, 3, 68, 357; museum, 357; ninety-first birthday celebrations, 369; PLO and, 229; protests called by, 82–83; release from prison (1990), 7, 176, 189, 249, 299, 305, 306, 312–13, 316, 325, 383, 407; release negotiations, 208, 215, 262, 406, 407; in Rivonia Trial, 98–99, 100, 104, 105–6, 300, 359; as SACP member, 109–10; sentencing of, 111; Treason Trial (1956–1961), 48; underground activities, 102, 403; "unity in action" concept and, 311; U.S. visit of, 289; at Zion Christian Church meeting, 249

Mandela, Winnie, 312–13, 314–15
Mandela Day, 369
Mange, James, 189, 191
Marcus, Gill, 302
Marikana miner strike (2012), 370–71
Market Theatre (South Africa), 134, 135
Marney, Cardiff, 70, 71, 72
Marshall Square Police Station (South Africa), 89
Martins, Dikobe, 98
Marvell, Andrew, 335
Marxism, 109–10, 293
Masetlha, Billy, 310, 325
Mason, Judith, 393–94
Matanzima, Kaiser Daliwonga, 208
Matsepane, Alex, 270

Matthews, John, 171–72, 421n1
Matthews, Z. K., 43
Mattson, Burye, 279
Mawasi, 270, 422n2
Maxeke, Charlotte, 253
Mazimbu (Tanzania), 251–55
Mbeki, Govan, 90, 100, 359; arrest/imprisonment of, 89, 96; Goldberg's post-prison meeting with, 310; at Liliesleaf Farm, 81, 86–87, 312; Operation Mayibuye and, 83–84; as a political prisoner, 270; release from prison, 307, 310, 407; in Rivonia Trial, 104, 106; Sisulu Freedom Day speech cowritten by, 79
Mbeki, Thabo: as ANC deputy president, 320; as ANC president, 357–58, 367; Goldberg release negotiations and, 205, 206–7; Goldberg's ANC activism and, 240, 247; recalled as South African president, 361, 367–68; as South African deputy president, 366; as South African president, 367, 408
McGeoch, David, 277–78
McGeoch, Sheila, 277–78
McVicar, Isobel, 328–29, 340
Mda, A. P., 401
Medical Aid to Russia Fund, 20
Medical and Dental Council, 165
Medical Association, 171
Medical University of South Africa, 408
Mexico, 129
Mhlaba, Raymond, 359; arrest/imprisonment of, 89, 96; Goldberg's post-prison meeting with, 310; at Liliesleaf Farm, 81, 86–87, 312; Operation Mayibuye and, 83–84; as a political prisoner, 270; release from prison, 307, 310, 407; in Rivonia Trial, 104, 106–7, 110